From Interwar Pluralism to Postwar Neoclassicism

From Interwar Pluralism
to Postwar Neoclassicism

Annual Supplement to Volume 30
History of Political Economy

Edited by Mary S. Morgan
and Malcolm Rutherford

Duke University Press
Durham and London 1998

Contents

American Economics: The Character of
the Transformation   1
MARY S. MORGAN AND MALCOLM RUTHERFORD

Part 1. Contexts of Transformation

Clearing the Ground: The Demise of the Social Gospel Movement
and the Rise of Neoclassicism in American Economics   29
BRADLEY W. BATEMAN

The Patrons of Economics in a Time of Transformation   53
CRAUFURD D. GOODWIN

Part 2. To Be an Economist

The Transformation of U.S. Economics, 1920–1960,
Viewed through a Survey of Journal Articles   85
ROGER E. BACKHOUSE

Institutional Economics: A Case of Reproductive Failure?   108
JEFF BIDDLE

Entrenching Disciplinary Competence: The Role of General
Education and Graduate Study in Chicago Economics   134
ROSS B. EMMETT

Part 3. "Market Failure" or "Market Efficiency"

Hope for America: American Notions of Economic Planning
between Pluralism and Neoclassicism, 1930–1950   153
MÁRCIA L. BALISCIANO

How American Economists Came to Love the Sherman
Antitrust Act   179
ANNE MAYHEW

Wandering the Road from Pluralism to Posner: The Transformation of
Law and Economics in the Twentieth Century   202
STEVEN G. MEDEMA

Part 4. Mathematics, Formalism, and Style

From Rigor to Axiomatics: The Marginalization of
Griffith C. Evans   227
E. ROY WEINTRAUB

A Paradox of Budgets: The Postwar Stabilization of American
Neoclassical Demand Theory   260
PHILIP MIROWSKI AND D. WADE HANDS

The Money Muddle: The Transformation of American
Monetary Thought, 1920–1970   293
PERRY MEHRLING

Contributors   307

Index   309

From Interwar Pluralism to Postwar Neoclassicism

American Economics: The Character of the Transformation

Mary S. Morgan and Malcolm Rutherford

One possible interpretation of our volume title, *From Interwar Plural-ism to Postwar Neoclassicism*, is to understand interwar pluralism as a code name for the "old institutionalists," postwar neoclassicism as full-fledged general-equilibrium mathematics, and the path between them as the natural and inexorable victory of mathematics and science over bumbling historicism. It is not difficult to recognize this account for what it is: a set of straw men ready to be blown over. Pluralism con-sisted of more than just institutionalism, and there was nothing prede-termined about the waning of pluralism and the waxing of neoclassi-cism. The challenge is to provide a more convincing account. What exactly was the nature of that pluralism and of the neoclassicism that apparently replaced it? And by what set of processes did the one turn into the other? These are complex questions, and the essays in this volume provide critical components of the answers. They also place constraints on any overall account, particularly with respect to the

This introductory essay draws directly on the stimulating discussions and papers presented at the special *HOPE* conference on the subject of our volume held at Duke University in April 1997 and on the subsequent comments of conference participants in their capacity as refer-ees for the essays submitted for the volume. Unfortunately, we were unable to include all the conference papers in this volume, but we thank all the participants for their help and apolo-gize if we have unwittingly quoted them without acknowledgment. We thank the *HOPE* edi-tors for their invitation to edit this special issue and the *HOPE* office for their help and advice during the conference and in the preparation of this volume. We thank the Lynde and Harry Bradley Foundation for its generous support of the conference.

timing of the transformation. We use this essay to lay out the borders of such an account and to sketch a general picture of how these components fit together in a particular way.[1] We are all too aware that we still lack knowledge of many of the elements we need to understand the full process of transformation: our account remains speculative and incomplete.

Pluralism

The first two elements for late-twentieth-century historians to understand are the extent and dimensions of the pluralism within American economics in the interwar period. One strong indication is provided by the practical difficulty of characterizing interwar economics or economists in any convincing way. It is common to think of interwar American economics in terms of institutionalists versus neoclassicals, but when one probes more closely, the picture becomes much less clear.

Although its roots extend back to the 1880s, institutionalism became a self-identified movement only in 1918 (Rutherford 1997). In the interwar period, institutionalism made strong claims for itself as a school and succeeded in becoming the most visible, if not the dominant, group in American economics. The movement cohered not around a tight theoretical agenda but around a particular view of science and a conviction of the inadequacy of the unregulated market. It cannot be said that institutionalists such as Thorstein Veblen, Wesley C. Mitchell, Walton H. Hamilton, John R. Commons, J. M. Clark, Rexford Tugwell, and M. A. Copeland all pursued exactly the same research program or utilized the same techniques of investigation. Institutionalism included Mitchell's quantitative methods, Commons's documentary histories and interviewing, Hamilton's case studies of firms and industries, and Clark's applied theorizing. Institutionalism consisted of a number of loosely related research programs, one cluster centering on business cycles and unemployment, with a reform agenda involving some notion of overall planning, and another cluster centering on the legal dimensions of markets, with a reform agenda focusing on labor law and business regulation. Institutionalism also shaded off into more "orthodox"

1. Landreth and Colander (1997) offer another account of the transformation in their broad survey paper. Samuels (forthcoming) offers an account, as well as a survey of all the conference papers and a report of the discussion that followed the presentation of each paper.

theory. For example, J. M. Clark never rejected J. B. Clark's theoretical contribution but saw himself as attempting to continue his father's efforts to develop a dynamic theory. J. M. Clark's accelerator, Mitchell's and Simon Kuznets's work on national income accounting, and Copeland's flow of funds all became standard tools.

Institutionalism, then, was a broad movement and quite nonexclusive. Institutionalists as a group had no one method to defend and no one economic theory to peddle. What they did have was a commitment to serious scientific investigation, detailed empirical work (though with no one method), serious theory building (which eschewed simple assumptions), and a commitment to understand the importance of economic institutions in determining economic outcomes. This last point relates to the institutionalists' view that new institutions or methods of "social control" were required to overcome the economic and social problems created by the existing market system.

Similarly, it is especially difficult to define "orthodox" or "neoclassical" economics in the interwar context and to provide a grouping of individuals under these labels. The marginalism of J. B. Clark was highly influential in America, but most economists of the time, including Clark himself, felt that his static theory of competition was only a starting point for a more complete and dynamic analysis. Austrian and subjectivist ideas were also important. The more "orthodox" group in the period from the 1880s up to the First World War was highly diverse and included Arthur Hadley, Frank Taussig, J. B. Clark, Frank Fetter, H. J. Davenport, and Edwin Seligman. Most of these individuals continued to contribute during the interwar period and were joined by others, such as Frank Knight, Irving Fisher, Jacob Viner, and Allyn Young. These individuals had a greater respect for the existing body of economic theory and for the market system than the more outspoken of the institutionalists, but they did not all adopt the same theoretical or methodological positions; nor did they ignore the shortcomings of the existing theory or remain unconcerned with advancing its scientific status. Hadley studied institutions and the problems of the railroads, Davenport combined Austrian and Veblenian influences, and Young brought to his theorizing, and to that of his students, an institutionalist sensibility concerning the need for greater realism. Adopting a more "orthodox" theoretical position also did not necessarily imply a lack of commitment to reform or a rejection of advocacy. Fisher is only one of many examples of this, and it is worth noting that Fisher and Commons could profess mutual respect for each other and join forces in the Stable Money League. However, the nature of scientific economics, the nature of the reforms indicated, and the place of advocacy were all actively contested. The profession as a whole was very much in the process of defining itself and its social roles.

As we have said, pluralism is not to be understood as a code word for "institutionalism." It was a genuine pluralism, to be taken in a positive sense. Pluralism meant variety, and that variety was evident in beliefs, in ideology, in methods, and in policy advice. We are used to thinking about the institutionalists as difficult to pin down because of their varied interests and practical approaches. But variety appears to be true in general, for there are no clean lines separating schools; indeed, it is not even clear that one can specify schools. And it is no easier to provide simple, accurate labels for many other economists active in the interwar period. Economists felt at liberty to pursue their own individual combinations of ideas. Pluralism, as Warren Samuels remarked at our conference, describes not only the difference between individuals; pluralism was in each economist. Coats (1992), in a wide-ranging survey of the period, suggests that the most "influential" economist of the period was Mitchell, an institutionalist renowned for quantitative analysis, whereas the most "representative" economist was J. M. Clark, who bridged the divide between institutionalist and neoclassical thinking. Clearly, then, in the interwar period it was possible to hold a number of different economic beliefs and to do economics in many different ways without being out of place or necessarily forfeiting the respect of one's peers. The major institutionalists and noninstitutionalists alike published in the major journals, held professorships at leading universities, and became presidents of the American Economic Association (AEA).

This variety, along with a certain tolerance, was a feature not only of the interwar period, but also, as Bradley W. Bateman shows in this volume, of the period before the First World War. Admittedly, the original AEA statement of principles had excluded a number of "old school" economists, but the association dropped its statement to effect a conciliation and become a more catholic organization. It is worth noting that this was done out of a feeling of strength and that the laissez-faire economists were a small and fading minority. This was a time when a very wide range of economists, from marginalist to historical, shared a commitment to economic justice. This commitment was supported by the population at large, as evidenced by the manifesto known as the "Social Creed" that the Protestant churches adopted before the war, as we learn from Bateman's essay. An extraordinary document, the manifesto called for economic regulation and intervention, along with high wages, to ensure the economic well-being of the American population. Rather than a social creed, it was an economic creed and a call for action fully in keeping with the Progressives' program. The creed provided neither a set of theoretical economic beliefs nor methods of economics but a concrete statement of faith in economic intervention and a set of specific economic aims.

But although the collapse of the Social Gospel movement and the consequent loss of impetus behind the Social Creed undermined that faith and left a vacuum in terms of ideology and policy action, the underlying plurality of economic approaches was unaffected. Economics carried its pluralistic beliefs and methods into the interwar period. When the Great Depression brought an urgent call for economic action, that plurality blossomed into a variety of analyses of, and possible solutions to, the problems. Proposals for intervention or "planning" of many different types became the fashion of the 1930s. As economic historians have long recognized, no one set of consistent economic policies made up the New Deal; even within each agency, economic aims were often at odds with each other. This reflected the variety of "planning" approaches held by the individuals concerned, as Márcia L. Balisciano documents in this volume. Although seen as a considerable failure both at the time and in most modern accounts, the New Deal made "the economy" an important responsibility for all subsequent American governments. The associated creation of demand for economic advice from the political sphere and its continuation through the period are important parts of our story of transformation, and we shall return to them later in this essay.

The Changing Standards
of Scientific Economics

Understanding the pluralism of the interwar period in terms of the concept of variety does not necessarily give us any grip on the process of transformation. In order not to prejudge exactly what the outcome might be, let us start with a very broad characterization of the changes in American economics during the period by considering changes in what it meant to be "scientific." It seems that in the 1920s many different kinds of economists considered themselves "scientists." From our current perspective, the mantle was broad: An economist was an investigative scientist whether he or she used the methods of history, statistics, theoretical deduction, empiricism, mathematics, or whatever. There was no hegemony of method: Whatever method might be appropriate for a particular investigation, or favored by a particular economist, might be adopted. This does not mean that all these methods were equally popular, as Roger E. Backhouse reminds us in his essay in this volume, for neither statistics nor mathematics was a popular method during the period. Nor does it mean that the label "scientific" was uncontested with respect to methods. On the contrary, it was hotly contested.

Among institutionalists, the concept of science seems to have been based on a view of natural science methods as empirical and experimental. Mitchell's quantitative approach was quite explicitly modeled on what he thought of as the nearest approach to the methods of the natural scientist that it was possible to achieve in economics. But other institutionalists did not place the same emphasis on quantitative methods as did Mitchell; Tugwell talked of experimental economics, and Copeland talked of the natural science point of view. Although the specific techniques of investigation used by institutionalists varied, in all cases the goal was to investigate actual conditions and to create a theory that was based on realistic assumptions and that could address real-world issues and problems. Institutionalists contrasted these methods with what they saw as the overly abstract nature of much of the standard theory as it then existed. This is not to say that most, or even very many, of the more orthodox economists were pure theorists but to suggest that their theories of rational behavior and competitive markets were seen by institutionalists as relying on highly simplified and unrealistic assumptions that limited their applicability and usefulness in solving real-world problems.

Institutionalist claims concerning the nature of scientific investigation appropriate in economics echoed similar arguments being made in other social sciences, and such ideas impacted on the economics profession even beyond the institutionalists' own ranks. One result of this was the highly concrete and problem-oriented nature of the vast bulk of work in economics, whether conducted by institutionalists or not. It was in this period that the specialist areas of labor economics and industrial organization developed, and much of the work in these areas was of a highly empirical and concrete nature. Differentiating the institutionalist from the noninstitutionalist on the basis of the work produced in these areas is often extremely difficult. Even in the more theoretical areas of the discipline, the effect can be seen in the development of more "realistic" theories of imperfect competition, market failures, and business cycles. Of course, the institutionalist conception of a scientific economics was not simply conceded by all economists, and counterarguments were made, appearing more frequently in the late 1930s and 1940s. Individuals with more orthodox theoretical predilections, such as Knight, launched something of a counterattack, arguing that natural science methods could not simply be brought into economics without modification and that natural science was more theoretical and abstract than was being contended (Rutherford 1997). Their success was slow in coming, but particularly after the Second World War, their notions of science were reinforced by other factors impacting on the discipline, as discussed later. Ross B. Emmett's essay in this volume outlines the changes in the nature of the University of Chicago's economics curriculum from the 1930s to the 1950s, which reflected a growing emphasis on neoclassical theory and a move from problem-oriented to methods-oriented field courses that stressed the application of "core" theoretical and statistical methods.

Although interwar pluralism was characterized by arguments over what constituted the correct set of scientific methods for economics, this does not mean that there were no shared scientific standards. Indeed, economists must have held some shared standards that allowed them to argue over matters of method and yet share the same platforms and contribute to the same journals. Looking back from today, we gain a sense that several kinds of standards were operating across interwar pluralism. First, it is revealing that today's natural categories of economic science, "theoretical" and "applied," simply do not fit well in this earlier period, as Backhouse points out. The fact that economists from the late nineteenth century through the interwar period wanted to find out about the world with a scientific spirit did not mean that they used one single method of approach. But it did mean that most economics was expressed in concrete rather than abstract terms, whether the topic was one of specific or of general import.

Second, the scientific status of the work was associated more with the personal qualities and attitudes of the economist qua scientist than with any particular method used. This is consistent with several recent history-of-science accounts suggesting that, at various times and places, personal factors have been particularly important in establishing claims to scientific objectivity. Daston (1995) has described this kind of objectivity as dependent upon a "moral economy": a set of personal virtues or values of scientific inquiry (honesty, integrity, etc.). Respect for these qualities and values seems to have been shared by all economists, be they working in academia, in government (such as the Bureau of Agricultural Economics), or in the new privately funded institutes of economic research (such as the National Bureau of Economic Research [NBER]).

Third, economists' integrity and commitment to a spirit of scientific investigation did not necessarily mean they pursued a value-free or policy-free scientific agenda. Both in the period before the First World War and in the interwar period, economists could characterize themselves as being scientific in their approach to their material while holding strong values and views concerning the aims of economics via economic policy. Furner (1975), in her wonderful account of American economics during the late nineteenth and early twentieth centuries, associates objectivity with evenhandedness. It became the professional ethos of economists of the period to teach both sides of a case: both free trade and protectionism; gold standard and bimetallism; labor unions and capitalism. Professionalization demanded evenhandedness. But this very demand recognizes the existence of different analyses, with different results, resting on different beliefs and values. Evenhandedness meant acknowledging differences of opinion, but it also meant impartially rejecting sectionalism in favor of the promotion of the social interest. The social interest, of course, could be variously defined, and different economists could hold different policy positions. So evenhandedness did not necessarily imply silence or neutrality on available policy options, and many economists argued strongly for particular reform packages. The economist could be an advocate in the policy domain, but only if his or her views were buttressed by a properly objective scientific inquiry.

Economists of the early twentieth century shared a kind of scientific economics (more often concrete than abstract), a moral commitment to ensure standards of scientific inquiry, and an evenhanded objectivity combined with advocacy. Pluralism was supported, not compromised, by these standards. How do these characteristics contrast with the kinds of scientific standards and objectivity we associate with postwar neoclassicism? Modern neoclassical economics takes for granted objectivity at the level of investigation, but what is striking is that now objectivity is thought to extend to the level of beliefs and to policy advice. Two transforming processes brought about this shift.

In the first process, the notion of objectivity associated with a set of personal attributes that guaranteed the standards of scientific economics gave way to a notion of objectivity vested in a particular set of methods, namely, mathematics and statistics. These were methods that could be pronounced unambiguously scientific on the grounds that they had to be used in a technical, i.e., nonsubjective, way. The late-nineteenth-century development of statistical methods has been portrayed as ensuring the "objective" treatment of economic data (see Gigerenzer et al. 1989), while the parallel development of mathematical methods in economics carried an equivalent "objective" label for theoretical analysis. These technical treatments of both inductive and deductive arguments, and of ways of dealing with evidence, provided economists with an apparent neutrality. Economists who could rely on such technical methods no longer had to be so scrupulously evenhanded or to depend so entirely on their virtues. These technical approaches created a new kind of professional expertise that enabled economists to offer "objective" policy advice, for they could argue that the objectivity of their methods warranted the objectivity of the results of the analysis and of the associated policy advice. Porter (1995) has described, in convincing detail, the American development of cost-benefit analysis during this period of transformation to show how the turn to technical expertise (rules of calculation, mathematical formulas, and statistical data) provided economists with a defense of their analysis against attacks by those promoting political agendas or those with strong opposing values.

These "objective methods" were slow to catch on in American economics, with agricultural economics, the statistical analysis of Mitchell and the NBER, and the emerging econometrics (including the Cowles Commission) probably being the strongest areas between the wars. But the development of technical expertise, wherein scientific credibility depends on methods, was a necessary prerequisite for the application by economists of simple mathematically and statistically based problem-solving techniques in various government departments during the Second World War, as discussed in Craufurd D. Goodwin's essay in this volume.

Of course, the claim to "objective" methods works only when different economists using similar methods produce the same answers. When they don't, the economists' whole claim to scientific objectivity is doubly undercut. So disagreement over how to measure and what to count among economists working on cost-benefit analyses for different arms of the government meant, in Porter's case, that technical expertise could not force closure in the policy debate. But the very fact that technical methods are debated so vehemently speaks to their importance to modern notions of scientific economics. Disagreement over what constituted the correct set of statistical methods was one element in the famous "measurement without theory" debate between the NBER and the Cowles Commission that epitomized the divide between institutionalists' and neoclassicals' use of alternative types of statistical methods in the late 1940s.

The second and equally important transforming process was the growing faith in the "market solution" and the virtues of free competition. As we see in Bateman's and Anne Mayhew's essays in this volume, these beliefs cannot be taken for granted as part of the American tradition. Rather, such beliefs were not generally held by American economists of the late nineteenth century. They might have been precipitated by the perceived failures of economic intervention in the New Deal. But it was only in the postwar period that economists began to see and portray the free market, perfect competition, and individual economic rights as, in themselves, embodying objective, value-free truths for reasons we shall discuss later. Thus the primacy of economic efficiency as the guiding value and the possibility of separating economic values from other considerations were both postwar developments among American economists, according to Steven G. Medema's discussion in this volume in the context of the relationship of law and economics. By contrast, the old idea, dominant in the pre–First World War period and holding into the interwar period, was that there is a necessary interrelation, indeed interdetermination, of legal and economic institutions. Institutions embody economic values, and values, by definition, cannot be value-free.

It may help to stress what we are *not* arguing here. The fact that the ethical commitments of the pre–First World War period went out of fashion (because of the failure of their supporting ideology) does not mean that a "value-free" and technical neoclassical economics would necessarily fill the vacuum. Modern neoclassical economics was not the only possible response. The loosening of the ethical ideology allowed the commitment to self-interest freer rein. This could have meant a retreat to classical laissez-faire economics, also presented as value-free by its proponents but no more technical than nineteenth-century historical economics. Yet the original AEA statement of principles had been formulated exactly to exclude the old-style classical economists such as William G. Sumner. That option was ruled out. Another possible outcome of these changing standards might have been a move to statistical empirical economics, one way for our two processes implying a more technical and value-free economics to link up. Indeed, such a picture fits Mitchell and NBER economics at least up to the 1950s. Neoclassical economics was not the only viable option, and it took some time to catch on.

What does emerge from the two processes we have described is that, in the postwar era, economists increasingly adopted methods that carried the warrant of objectivity to the results of their analysis and to their policy advice. At the same time, they learned to present certain economic beliefs as value-free and therefore objective. For reasons that will become clearer, the professional ethos of economics changed. In this new ethos of economics, it became the fashion to offer consensus advice, in strong contrast to the contrary advice economists offered in the New Deal. The economist became the neutral, professional scientist, offering expert, value-free advice in a language the public could understand. At the same time, internal professional disputes began to be expressed in a separate technical language.

Economists and the Economy

Since it is widely thought that the mathematical method and neoclassical beliefs are inseparable, it might be taken as natural that changes toward quantitative tools and neoclassical beliefs occurred together. These two changes may have been concurrent, and possibly they were driven by the same causal factors, but the essays in this volume suggest that the causal factors operated in different ways.

One factor we have already discussed is the economic historical context. The Great Depression, the key event of the period from 1920 to 1960, demanded that economists take up the challenge of diagnosing and treating the illness in the economy. It is difficult to imagine an economy in which output fell by 25–30 percent and in which unemployment reached a level of 25 percent and did not return to its 1929 level until 1942 (despite the demand stimulus from wartime allies). Even the most laissez-faire economists would have doubts about the efficacy of the market solution. But this was not the only depression of the interwar period. A very sudden and severe depression occurred in 1921–22. And during the war years, most economists were convinced that after the war ended, the economy would return to the 1930s depression or else would fall into a sudden slump, as after the First World War. In wartime itself, of course, the economy required considerable planning. In these circumstances, it comes as less of a surprise to find that, on the whole, economists remained pro-interventionist into the 1940s.

These historical problems in the economy not only turned economists toward intervention but also created the demand for their services to make concrete plans and suggestions for which the new technical tools of simple mathematical models and statistical techniques were well adapted. It was not that the old tools could not provide answers or that they were not technical tools. Economists were accustomed to providing specific answers to concrete questions. Railroad regulation had long depended on economic analysis of rates, and agricultural economists were used to measuring and manipulating the agricultural sector. It was not even that the Great Depression was immediately regarded as something different, requiring new solutions. The problem was seen as massive but not new. It was only in the New Deal that the demand for economic solutions widened: Every aspect of the economy became open to economic attack. American economists of every stripe responded. Charles Roos, one of the active econometricians in the early years of the Cowles Commission, became chief research economist at the National Recovery Administration (NRA), building mathematical and statistical models of industrial competition. Mordecai Ezekiel, agricultural econometrician, and Tugwell, institutionalist, both became involved in general planning. But by and large, economists did not find the New Deal a successful experience; it did not improve their reputations. And to the extent that institutional economists were involved in these schemes, they, along with the other economists, shared in the failure.

Only in the war years, and only after the United States entered the war, did the economy regain its old strength. The war, as Goodwin's essay discusses, was a watershed in several ways. Economists not only found their technical expertise useful in making decisions about how to deal with economic shortages (rather than oversupply as in the Great Depression) but also turned their techniques to any number of wartime questions, using simple mathematical optimizing models, linear programming techniques, and statistical measurement devices. Economists were brought in to fight the war directly, planning the optimum bombing-raid design and statistically analyzing firing patterns. Economists found that by using tool-kit economics and the developing neoclassical technical expertise they could answer questions in very different fields. Economics emerged from the war covered in glory, perhaps launching the "economic imperialism" in social sciences over the last half century.

In the postwar world, as Goodwin shows, the nascent neoclassical technologies continued to prove useful, but note that this was tool-kit neoclassical economics, formulated to answer clearly specified, well-defined questions, not grand general-equilibrium theorizing. Advice remained at the level of basic microeconomics, both during and after the war, and may not have been very different from the earlier advice offered by economists at the Bureau of Agricultural Economics or in the New Deal administrations. This was the economics of Hadley (the American Marshall) rather than the sophisticated neoclassicism of Paul Samuelson. Thus, although for this new generation the concrete kinds of questions investigated and answered might have been no different from those investigated by earlier economists, the methods had become more technically oriented and the role of the economist had changed. He (mostly) offered answers but without the accompanying advocacy of the earlier period. These answers were naturally "correct" because they were the result of "objective" methods and because by that stage economists were beginning to spurn intervention and to turn to their new love: the belief of neoclassical economics in the market, in competition, and in the primacy of the self-interested individual.

The timing of this change is something of a puzzle. Why did economists fall fully in love with the market and out of love with control and intervention just as they became successful at practicing the latter in response to the events of economic and political history? It might be a question of selection: The new sort of economics expertise provided by neoclassical tool-kit methods of analysis was best adapted to the demands created by this set of events. According to such an argument, it is because of the success of their tools that economists came to

believe in the ideas behind them. This is certainly an interesting rever-
sal of the normal internalist history of economics that portrays ideas
("thought") as the leading light in any account. This reversed argument
is also consistent with the claim usually made for Britain that the success of Keynesian tools and concepts used in running the war economy
encouraged economists', and politicians', belief in that system of ideas
and led to its popularity in the postwar period. The wartime experience
of active tool-based intervention is an important causal factor in the
transformation, but it is only part of the story.

Economists, War, and Society

It might seem perfectly reasonable that a society tired of war and
depression and delighted with the postwar boom should react by
embracing the goals of free markets and healthy competition. These
views might well take time to emerge, given the still vivid memories of
the Great Depression, and might take equally long to become fixed in
the minds of economists. A more cogent claim, and one which surfaces
in a number of the papers, relates to the cold war, a war, Goodwin
reminds us, of economic ideologies. This explanatory factor has the
virtue of fitting our timing puzzle, for at just the right point, American
society moved solidly in favor of the virtues of free markets and open
competition. In so doing, it reinforced, at a critical point just after the
war, the neoclassical belief system. We find this argument more cogent
because in this case the "reasonable" argument of reaction implies that
European societies, more borne down by wartime economic controls,
would embrace the free market more enthusiastically than the United
States, but they did not. In addition, the cold war was not nearly as
frozen in Europe, where reconstruction planning and welfare statism
evolved into the mixed economy and the effect on social scientists'
ideas was less dramatic.

The moment at which society's values line up with those of economists is a point to watch. Just before the First World War, the Social
Creed was accepted by the mainstream Protestant churches, society
lined up behind the economics of the AEA founding generation, and its
program seemed ready to be put into practice. As Bateman tells us, the
Social Gospel movement provided economists with a language and an
opportunity to talk to the wider community and supported a pluralism
of economics under the ethical umbrella. The moment was temporar-

ily lost because of the nationalist turn taken by the churches in response to the First World War. Not until the New Deal did economists again have an opportunity to talk with conviction, and a similar plurality occurred then because the ideas and approaches were those of the pre-1920 period, brought forward partly by a new generation. It is one of the ironies of our tale that just as something close to the Social Creed of the churches became politically well supported and official economic policy at the end of the Second World War, a new form of nationalism appeared. (A comparison of the episodes revealed in Bateman's and Balisciano's essays is instructive.) At this second moment, the nationalism of the cold war pushed society's commitment to economic freedom well ahead of that of the main body of American economists. In the climate of those times economists found it safer to conform, and the developing neoclassical economics, which incorporated similar values, was given a big boost.

The effects of McCarthyism surely cannot be ignored in any account of the transformation of American economics. Although we have records of émigré economists who arrived in America to escape fascism in the 1930s (see Hagemann and Krohn 1991, Craver 1986), we have little more than anecdotes of economists who left America to avoid anticommunist persecution. Some of these, of course, held views that might be communist, or prosocialist, but even Keynesianism was a suspect heterodoxy, and those who had espoused planning for the postwar economy a few years before, let alone staunch New Dealers, might well have found themselves outcasts. Some of these economists returned, others did not, but their absence was certainly one of the factors that made for a narrowing from the earlier pluralism of American economics in the postwar period.

The result of these pressures on those who remained was both to narrow the range of beliefs and to restrict the acceptable ways of expressing them. Goodwin's essay suggests that this narrowing was achieved partly through a turn toward greater technicality and toward the apparently "neutral" languages of mathematics. As we have noted, this post–Second World War technical defense by itself does not necessarily imply neoclassical economics. Although Keynesianism might have been thought dangerously close to Marxism, an IS/LM diagram probably looked innocuous to an outsider, and statistical numbers such as those of Mitchell had long held their own neutral status as "data." Economics expressed in geometry, algebra, or numbers could be a good self-defense in the cold war days and pass muster in the classroom as well as in the government. Indeed, in our more general framework, this move to technical methods was precisely the move that Porter (1995) suggests made economics defensible against democratic power, whoever wielded it on whichever side. The cold war enforced, if it did not create, the trend toward economists offering professionally neutral, objective expertise, which contrasted strongly with the ethical, and strongly held, advocacy of the late-nineteenth-century professional economist. Even in their "evenhanded" mode, public statements of the late nineteenth century offered considerable political ammunition compared to the expert jargon and tool-kit style of postwar economics, which could be used to disguise theoretical content and ideology to the outside world.

Although this move to mathematics was partly a self-imposed defense undertaken by individuals (see Johnson 1977), it was also encouraged by academic institutions seeking "safe" teachers and research institutes seeking "acceptable" researchers. As Goodwin's essay suggests, patrons of economic research exacted an obligation of political correctness in line with the cold war that had the effect of narrowing the views that could be expressed and count within the mainstreams of economics, be they academic or governmental. There is some suggestion that patrons and economists colluded in hiding radical ideas from the public, for institutions, as much as individuals, sought safety in the climate of political repression. Elsewhere there was open warfare. One of the few case studies of the academic effects of the cold war, by Solberg and Tomilson (1997), describes events in the Economics Department at the University of Illinois. There, "academic McCarthyism" drove out both nascent Keynesians and those advocating modern tool-based economics, a combination that included Margaret Reid, Leonid Hurwicz, Dorothy Brady, Robert Eisner, Don Patinkin, and finally Franco Modigliani. Regardless of the process, the effect was the same: Both open persecution and closet correctness led to the narrowing of permissible economic opinion.

The retreat was not total, for although being a follower of Keynes was a dubious label for American economists in the 1950s, Keynesianism could be made compatible with market economics in the American environment. This was accomplished both by persuading businesspeople that they could do better under a government that took the macroeconomy seriously (as Balisciano suggests) and by translating Keynesianism into the same technical form as neoclassical economics, the first step to the American "neoclassical-Keynesian synthesis." In a similar way, old-fashioned institutionalist monetarism was made compatible with American academic neoclassicism, as Perry Mehrling recounts in this volume. Economists could safely argue about the same old things, but their debate had become an insiders' technical argument, not one open to the public gaze. The public debates of the 1930s became internal technical disputes in the 1950s and 1960s.

It is clearly difficult, without a lot more research, to assess the impact of McCarthyism on the transformation of American economics. Yet the counterfactual question "What would have been the history of American economics without the cold war?" indicates the potential answers to our puzzles about timing and about the degree of belief in the efficacy of the market. Remember, the puzzle is that although the institutionalists were strongly evident as a grouping within the general pluralism of the 1930s (but failed to strike the advantage offered by this position to coalesce around a single program), the neoclassical grouping did not really become evident until the 1950s (see Rutherford 1997). The relatively sudden shift from the institutionalist (indeed general) belief in government intervention to the more neoclassical belief in the free market can be explained when we consider seriously American society's views in the cold war. The reinforcement of the technical turn in economics (and not just in neoclassical economics) emerges as an important, although clearly unintended, consequence of the same causal factor, namely, the political climate.

Thus a transformation to a tool-kit version of economics in general, and to the beliefs of neoclassical economics in particular (which was only one of many strands in the interwar period), was reinforced and given impetus by the social values of the time, so that by 1960 American neoclassicism was well established. The extent to which these moves are evident in the journals gives us some backing for our account. Backhouse's essay suggests that formally expressed economics was on the increase beginning in the 1930s, but the real change came after 1945. Empirical econometrics developed a little later, with the real change occurring after 1950. Thus once again, the war was a watershed: After this time we see both modern style and modern research categories beginning to emerge in considerable strength, concurrent with the move by economists to a self-defensive technocratic approach.

The New Style and Its Implications

Those who find modern neoclassical economics unconnected to the real-world economy are apt to blame increasing formalism in some form or other for this state of affairs and to blame the profession for this move. But instead, as we have argued, formalism should first be seen as the outcome of various external contingencies, not the cause of internal ones. We have already discussed how the demand for economists to solve policy problems led to the increasing use of technical tools both in the Great Depression and, more particularly, in the war. We described this as tool-kit economics rather than neoclassical economics, for it is important to remember that not all tools were associated with neoclassical economics; not all econometricians were neoclassical economists; and planning of whatever type demanded numbers and statistical work on a large scale. We have also discussed the way in which this technical turn was strongly reinforced by economists' and patrons' need for self-defense during the cold war. Here it was not so much what the technical tools would do for you but rather that the language of mathematics and statistics appeared to be more neutral and objective, and more difficult for the layperson and politician, leaving the economists less open to outside attacks about matters of belief. Formalism therefore offered economists both tools for practical usage and neutral language for expression and for safe professional argument.

But there are second-round and more subtle effects of these changes which are perhaps best understood through the case study that Mehrling gives us, and this is why formalism does indeed bear some of the blame for the waning of pluralism. In his account of disputes within monetary economics, Mehrling argues that the joint adoption of neoclassical beliefs and mathematical expression created a kind of monetary Walrasianism within which monetary arguments became no longer matters of belief, or even of empirical evidence, but technical matters of modeling. We can understand from this example just how the changes in language and the form in which economics was expressed narrowed down what could be said and flattened what could be questioned. The real underlying arguments about money might remain, but they could no longer be expressed fully and explicitly within the new sort of formalized economics. This process worked by integrating awkward empirical findings or theories from the other types of economics into the formal framework of neoclassical explanations. This is one way to interpret the fate of Gardiner Means's administered-pricing thesis, discussed by Lee (1997), and the developments in cost theory discussed by Naples and Aslanbeigui (1997). In all these examples, the transformation into formal economics involved changes in language, form, and tools. This new style became a set of mores that reduced in itself the possibility of pluralism within economics.

Another connected contextual factor needs to be brought in: the role of mathematics in economics. In providing the intellectual context for the work of the early mathematical economist G. C. Evans, E. Roy Weintraub's essay in this volume discusses the changing relationship between mathematics and science. This early proponent of mathematical economics, along with many of those committed to the econometrics movement in the interwar period, believed that successfully using mathematics meant hooking it onto the economic world, a view current in the sciences in the late nineteenth century. By the mid–twentieth century, economists were more likely to be enthralled by a turn in mathematics itself that viewed mathematics as a way of writing down consistent theories. Mathematics became the language for the expression of abstract and general theory rather than a tool for uncovering and writing down true descriptions of the economic world. Thus at around the time the main body of American economists began to prefer the language of mathematics on defensive ground, the scientific role of mathematics was itself coming free of its connections to the scientific (economic) world.

If early mathematical economists in general shared Evans's views, then the shift in the perceptions about mathematics in science helps explain both the formation and the collapse of the econometric movement, conceived in the interwar period as the integration of mathematics and statistics into economics. If mathematical descriptions must hook onto the world, they need to link the observable or measurable to the hypothetical. Around 1950 this dream of the econometric tradition that mathematical economic theory had to match something observable (even if not actual statistical data) collapsed, and econometrics split into mathematical economics and econometrics as we now know it. It is pertinent that another element of the late 1940s "measurement without theory" debate between institutionalists and neoclassicals focused on the correct role of mathematics in economics. Under the older commitment to a mathematics that hooks rigorously onto the world, it would not have been so easy for the neoclassicals to use mathematics to consolidate their position against the institutionalists, for as Mehrling suggested (during discussions of Weintraub's essay), American institutionalism shared some of the methodological prejudices of the nineteenth-century math. The more recent tradition of twentieth-century mathematics fits better with the prejudices of neoclassical theory, and so the shift in the role of mathematics in relation to economics tended to support the emergent neoclassical hegemony. The waning of institutionalism and the rise of neoclassical economics were shaped by the evolution of mathematics in relation to the sciences.

We have used the term "style" to describe the differences implied in American economics as it emerged through the cold war world of the 1950s and 1960s. Our term style involves, first of all, a language, one that narrowed what could be said, a language not so closely connected to the world or easily accessible except to professional economists and their students. The term could be extended to the idea of a "laboratory economics" (at Bateman's suggestion) in which the tools of mathematical modeling and statistical econometrics, though no longer fully integrated, could be rejoined in an alliance more tenuously connected to the world. (Here we should note that the term "lab" was also used as a label for the professional-level "applied-theory" training that the University of Chicago developed at this time.) These changes are epitomized in the development of consumer theory, described in this volume by Philip Mirowski and D. Wade Hands. Here we have something like the archetypical neoclassical American economics, concerned with formal puzzles created by the use of mathematical representations, using mathematics to express worries and venturing, but not too far, into statistical data. Within this, technical disagreement was expressed in professional-level debate: the pluralism of neoclassical economics. Yet nothing hangs directly on the argument—no income subsidy will be granted or abolished, although maybe someone will get a grant to do further research!

But the notion of style involves more than language and forms, for the laboratory ideal was also a practical one with practical tools. Indeed, the institutionalist tradition lives on in American applied economics, which has a reputation for care and thoroughness in its empirical inquiries. Weintraub's notions of the two roles of mathematics might also, he suggests, be seen as underlying our modern labels of theoretical versus applied economics, categories that become cogent in Backhouse's survey only in the postwar period. Thus in sorting out style from blanket descriptions of neoclassicism versus pluralism, we would do well to remind ourselves once again that this is not a history of thought but a history of a discipline, with people and institutions offering services and other people and institutions demanding those services. Patrons wanted economists to be able to solve real problems (not mathematical puzzles, high theory, or historical themes) in a professional (i.e., expert) style. They wanted usable economic science, not something esoteric, whether it was called neoclassicism or Keynesianism. This makes the outcome something more than a change of language and the adoption of certain forms and tools, something more akin to a change of approach or style.

The economics that emerged was one in which economists learned to cut up the problem into something small enough that it could be solved but still realistic enough that people could relate to it. The style change involved no great new methodological or theoretical commitment, yet it was an important part of the changing face of American economics during the period. And although such a change in approach did not necessarily require any initial changes in beliefs, it did have implications for beliefs in the long run. As Mehrling describes, an initial continuity of ideas may, through a change in methods of expression, gradually bring about changes in content and beliefs.

The Waning of Institutionalism

Our concentration on the importance of the contexts of economic, political, and scientific history has mostly focused on why formal and neoclassical economics found themselves strengthened by the course of events, but much of what has been said also touches on the relative decline of institutionalism. It is worth pulling together some of the strands of this story as it applies to institutionalism, particularly as a number of the essays in this collection provide insight into the detail of the processes involved.

As Goodwin shows, the decline of institutionalism was not rapid, and even as late as 1948 economics was still pluralistic, offering abstract theory, high empiricism, and institutional studies. Nevertheless, in general terms, the same factors that gradually strengthened neoclassicism had an opposite effect on institutionalism, so that institutional economics, so important in the interwar period, began to wane as neoclassical economics strengthened. This, however, is very much an overall view, and we should remind ourselves of the diversity within institutionalism. Different parts of the movement were impacted in different ways and at different times.

The changing concepts of science and of scientific objectivity are cases in point. In the interwar period, the NBER showed a nice combination of the two notions of objectivity discussed previously. Objectivity as evenhandedness and as recognition of differences of opinion can be seen in the NBER's appointing directors who represented different points of view and different constituencies. Objectivity as technique is embodied in the quantitative methods designed to establish facts impartially and in Mitchell's determination to keep a clear separation between scientific fact-finding and the use of facts in policy advocacy. Mitchell's desire to separate science from advocacy was not shared by other institutionalists, and the difference between Mitchell and other institutionalists on this matter may explain the ability of Mitchell's program at the NBER to sustain its relatively high standing for as long as it did. By way of contrast, Hamilton suffered attacks for his proposals for the coal industry, which may have affected his standing at the Brookings Graduate School (Ross 1991, 417), and throughout his career, Commons was at the center of political controversy. Such a professional stance was exactly what Goodwin suggests would have been at odds with the new scientific style increasingly demanded by funding agencies and other consumers of economic analysis in the postwar period.

Other aspects of the fate of the Wisconsin school of institutionalism and of the "old" style of law and economics are examined in this volume by Jeff Biddle and by Medema. Biddle examines the hypothesis that University of Wisconsin graduates went into government in larger numbers than the graduates of more orthodox schools, so that Wisconsin-style institutionalism failed to reproduce itself within the academic world. This might have been a reflection of the ideological slant and particular training provided by Commons and others at Wisconsin. Biddle finds only limited support for his hypothesis, but it is certainly true that Commons's students did little to advance his conceptual scheme involving the legal and economic system and were more attracted to his work on labor economics and to some of his specific reform efforts. Commons's students replicated his more concrete and problem-oriented kind of work, a type of work that gradually lost ground to toolkit economics. In this respect, imagine how hard Commons's type of institutionalism in all its complexity was to teach and to learn. It did not look technical (it wasn't quantitative), but it relied on detailed study, knowledge of law as well as of economics, an understanding of personalities and situations, experience in mediation, and personal integrity—a skill set that contrasts rather sharply with that imparted by the applied-theory workshops developed at the University of Chicago and described by Emmett.

The Commons-Hamilton type of law and economics, pictured by Medema as multifaceted, pluralistic with respect to methods, interdisciplinary, and based on a concept of the law and the economy as mutually determined and determining, was at odds with the changing temper, so that the old type of law and economics was in serious decline even before the development of the new type of law and economics at Chicago. The new type of law and economics, with its very different views on competition, antitrust, and other policy issues, both reflected and helped advance the ideological move of the profession away from the reform agenda of institutionalists.

Other sections of the institutionalist movement were damaged by the experiences of the Great Depression and the New Deal. This is particularly the case among institutionalists such as Tugwell and Means who advanced the "structuralist" or proplanning view during the early phase of the New Deal. As Mayhew and Balisciano make clear, the outcome of the New Deal experience was not only a move away from structural planning and to a Keynesian style of macroeconomic policy but also a move away from a regulatory approach to industry and to a more procompetitive stance involving the enforcement of the Sherman and Clayton acts.

These developments, involving a turn away from planning and regulation and toward the market and competition as instruments of control, could only be reinforced by the ideological impact of the cold war.

Conclusion

Implicit in this account of the transformation of American economics is that the decline of pluralism in American economics was neither a simple nor an obvious result of the development of neoclassical economics and vice versa. No logical relation says that this must have been so, nor does the evidence support such a direct causal story. We have also tried to avoid basing our account of the transformation on two other polar positions.

One is the Whiggish progress account. It is not clear that the evidence can support a history that neoclassicism won out because it offered better theory and better explanations. To argue that such an outcome was inevitable, that neoclassical economics offered "better science," clashes with our claim that the changing notions of science and scientific objectivity were part of the transformatory process. As we have argued, neoclassical economics grew in dominance as the notion of science changed and the two developments were connected. This being the case, there were no stable internal criteria on which to offer a historical judgment about "progress."

The other account we have eschewed is the conspiracy theory, in which neoclassical economists in positions of power ganged up on the heterodox. Since this view assumes that heterodox science might have won the battle but for the social power of neoclassical economists, the account similarly implies that one group has historically measurable claims to be a "better science." This is as problematic as before.

Furthermore, both of these polar positions are premised on some recognizable duality of institutionalist (or heterodox) and neoclassical groups that we believe cannot be identified in the interwar period. This is not to deny that one can point out individual institutionalist and neoclassical economists or that they had differences of opinion but to suggest that it is difficult to make either the progress or the conspiracy theory work, because the pluralism of the interwar period cuts across individual beliefs. The war was a watershed in which the transformation process suddenly resolved itself, so that after that time we can sensibly begin to talk in terms of such groups.

Nor do we wish to deny either that there were individual battles or that institutional power mattered to the outcomes. But such power plays took place within structures involving patrons and hierarchies operating within the context of a political and economic society that supported calls for economic intervention in the interwar period and for free markets in the postwar period. These wider economic and political beliefs are never just backgrounds against which individuals (and institutions) fight science wars; they provide content for the debate and are integral elements in any power struggle.

In seeking to provide a general account of the transformation in American economics, we have concentrated on explanatory factors within which the individual substories could be placed. Our primary aim has been to provide an account of the transformation consistent with the timing and character of changes suggested in the individual essays in this volume: They each have their own history to tell, with separate contingent circumstances. In making one account into which they all fit with ease, we have concentrated on the contingencies of the world outside: scientific, political, and economic. These have formed the basis of our explanations. It was this world that created the circumstances to which American economists adapted and within which their economics was transformed.

The story of the transformation is far from closed. Many holes must be filled, and many parts of our account remain speculative, requiring substantial historical research to turn them into documented history. Whatever historical strength lies in our account is drawn from the essays in this volume; the speculations and errors remain our own.

References

Coats, A. W. 1992. Economics in the United States, 1920–70. In *On the History of Economic Thought: British and American Economic Essays*. Edited by A. W. Coats. Vol. 1. London: Routledge.

Craver, E. 1986. The Emigration of the Austrian Economists. *HOPE* 18.1:1–32.

Daston, L. J. 1995. The Moral Economy of Science. *Osiris* 10:3–24.

Furner, M. O. 1975. *Advocacy and Objectivity: A Crisis in the Professionalization of American Social Science, 1865–1905*. Lexington: University Press of Kentucky.

Gigerenzer, G., et al. 1989. *The Empire of Chance: How Probability Changed Science and Everyday Life*. Cambridge: Cambridge University Press.

Hagemann, H., and C. D. Krohn, eds. 1991. *Die Emigration deutschsprachiger Wirtschaftswissenschaftler nach 1933*. Stuttgart: Universität Hohenheim.

Johnson, H. G. 1977. The American Tradition in Economics. *Nebraska Journal of Economics and Business* 16:17–26.

Landreth, H., and D. Colander. 1997. The Formalist Revolution in American Economics. Paper presented at *HOPE* Annual Conference.

Lee, F. S. 1997. Administered Price Hypothesis and the Dominance of Neoclassical Price Theory: The Case of the *Industrial Prices* Dispute. Paper presented at *HOPE* Annual Conference.

Naples, M. I., and N. Aslanbeigui. 1997. The Cost Controversy: Interplay between History and Ideas, 1920s–1950s. *HOPE* conference paper.

Porter, T. H. 1995. *Trust in Numbers: The Pursuit of Objectivity in Science and Public Life*. Princeton, N.J.: Princeton University Press.

Ross, D. 1991. *The Origins of American Social Science*. Cambridge: Cambridge University Press.

Rutherford, M. 1997. American Institutionalism and the History of Economics. *Journal of the History of Economic Thought* 19.2:178–95.

Samuels, W. Forthcoming. The Transformation of American Economics: From Interwar Pluralism to Postwar Neoclassicism: An Interpretive Review of a Conference. *Research in the History of Economic Thought and Methodology.*

Solberg, W. U., and R. W. Tomilson. 1997. Academic McCarthyism and Keynesian Economics: The Bowen Controversy at the University of Illinois. *HOPE* 29.1:55–81.

Part 1

Contexts of Transformation

Clearing the Ground: The Demise of the Social Gospel Movement and the Rise of Neoclassicism in American Economics

Bradley W. Bateman

How did the pluralism that characterized interwar American economics disappear so quickly by the end of the Second World War? How did a diverse and apparently yeasty mix of giants such as Richard T. Ely, John R. Commons, and Wesley Clair Mitchell give way to the world of Paul Samuelson, Robert Solow, and Kenneth Arrow? The usual suspects in the story would be a closely connected triumvirate: mathematics, formalism, and physics envy. These different dimensions of the process, which we still observe to be transforming economics at the end of the century, were already in force when Samuelson published *The Foundations of Economic Analysis* in 1947.

No one knows this better than historians of economic thought. Indeed, it is almost impossible to attend a gathering of North American historians of economic thought without getting the uncomfortable feeling that many are there to grieve over the corpse. Many come to lament a time when economics was different, when it was better, and when it had not been perverted by formalism and higher mathematics. Many grieve for John Maynard Keynes and Commons, for Friedrich Hayek and Mitchell and Ludwig von Mises.

But despite our great fondness for these dead economists and their work, we have not very often thought about the *historical currents* that carried them away from the center of the profession. The most common way we have studied the figures from the first half of the century is to focus intensively on their theoretical work. To the extent that many historians of economic thought are motivated by a desire for a different kind of economics and a different kind of economic theory, they have treated the careful exegesis of the ideas of heterodox economics as a means of preserving alternative ways of being an economist. This has produced some excellent scholarship in the close reading of texts, but it has largely kept our focus off the context in which those theories thrived or disappeared.

Or has it? Consider the list of economists mentioned previously: Keynes, Commons, Hayek, von Mises, and Mitchell. It is an international list, and yet to a large extent all were swept off the stage at the same time and by what looks like the same forces: consolidation of the highly mathematized neoclassical economics that came to the fore after the Second World War. In this sense, formalism and mathematization were certainly part of the context for decline. Mathematized neoclassical economics was the outcome despite different national contexts, but what was the particular context in which the American transformation took place?

How Was America Different?

Although neoclassicism might have triumphed in any case, this triumph was undoubtedly the result of many complex and contingent forces. In order to get a fuller picture of the changing nature of American economics in the interwar period, it is worth considering one of the major forces that helped undergird the pluralism that characterized early-twentieth-century economics and was itself swept off the historical stage just as that pluralism was about to give way: the Social Gospel movement. But for better or worse, this fact is not likely to elicit much response from contemporary economists.[1] Few people today even know of the Social Gospel movement, and still fewer know of its complex history. There is considerable irony in this fact, for the Social Gospel was an integral part of the Protestant impulse that shaped the nation and was one of two major forces within the Progressive movement before 1920. Thus, unlike many historians of economic thought

---

1. Nelson's (1993) essay in the volume celebrating the first hundred years of economics at the University of Wisconsin is a nice example. Nelson is interested in the fact that Ely was a Social Gospeler, but she does not quite know what to make of it. The exception that proves the rule is Gonce's (1996) excellent essay on Commons.

who have been forced to uncover the *tacit* dimensions of earlier times in order to make sense of past intellectual debates, we are dealing with a significant well-developed and *explicit* dimension of public life. The forces that swept the Social Gospel off the historical stage, however, were themselves a part of the increasing secularization of American life and of a significantly altered vision within the Protestant community after the Second World War. Thus, from our perspective today, we cannot easily see what was important then; what was obvious has become nearly invisible.

But although we are dealing with an important and easily identifiable part of American history, it was a complex phenomenon with its own complicated trajectory.[2] Thus, just as E. Roy Weintraub argues in this volume that one must consider the *changing* nature of mathematics and mathematical economics to fully understand the evolution of economics, one must also consider the changing ground of American Protestantism to fully understand the story of early-twentieth-century economics.

Because of its complicated trajectory, the Social Gospel has been subject to changing interpretations over time. Recently Luker (1991) has looked at the Reconstruction period and argued that the roots of the movement are more obviously found early in the nineteenth century in the Second Great Awakening than is sometimes understood and that it was a much more regionally driven phenomenon than was allowed by earlier church historians who wanted to see it as a movement centered in New England and the East. Thus, for instance, one can focus on the Social Gospelers who were concerned with race relations and find explicit links with the abolitionist ferment that arose from the Second Great Awakening. Looking at the later years of the movement, Gorrell (1988) has found that in the first two decades of the twentieth century it achieved a sudden and unexpected victory when the mainline Protestant churches institutionalized its agenda in the Social Creed of the Churches, a document focused on industrial relations that committed the churches to an activist agenda.[3]

The changes and continuities in the life of the Social Gospel are both important to our story not just because they are uniquely American but also because they help explain the force and ambiguous legacy of the

2. Perhaps the best recent attempt at a historiography of the Social Gospel is Luker 1991, 1–6, 419–32. For more standard histories, see Ahlstrom 1975, May 1949, and Schlesinger 1932. Marty 1984 and 1986 provide a richer, more contemporary picture.

3. I make more of Gorrell's (1988) argument later.

idea in early-twentieth-century American economics.[4] Likewise, study-ing the movement's vicissitudes should help us understand why there is more to our story than just the rise of mathematics and formalism.

The Kingdom of God on This Earth

One easy way to see the changes and continuities in the movement is to look at it in the mid-1890s. In retrospect, the Social Gospel movement is often said to have run roughly from 1865 to 1920, but those who par-ticipated in it did not even use that name regularly until the twentieth century. In the mid-1890s the most prominent manifestation of what we now call the Social Gospel movement was the Kingdom movement.[5]

The Kingdom movement is best known for its gyring prophet, George D. Herron, but it owed its existence to the organizational genius of George A. Gates and much of its national recognition and prestige to Josiah Strong. Gates was the president of Iowa College and had mas-terminded the purchase of the *Northwestern Congregationalist* and its transformation into the movement's national organ, *The Kingdom*, which he edited.[6] Strong was the early proponent of social Christian-ity whose *Our Country: Its Possible Future and Its Present Crisis* (1885) was the best-selling book in America in the fifty years after the publication of Harriet Beecher Stowe's *Uncle Tom's Cabin* (1852).[7]

The name of the Kingdom movement came from the one theme that remained central to the Social Gospel message from Washington Glad-

4. The Social Gospel and Christian socialism also had important careers in England, but they reached their prime earlier there. And the economists who defined late-nineteenth-century British economics are distinguished from their American counterparts by having lost their religious faith before becoming economists.

5. The best history of the Kingdom movement is Handy (1950).

6. Gates, who would later serve as president of both Pomona and Fisk Colleges, is poorly served by historians. The best source is still Isabel Smith Gates's 1915 biography.

7. See Marty 1984 for a nice history of Strong in the Social Gospel movement. After read-ing an earlier draft of this essay, a non-American questioned the significance of comparing Strong's book to Stowe's. This is a good question, although not one that would likely occur to an American reader. *Uncle Tom's Cabin* was the nation's greatest commercial publishing suc-cess at midcentury and is often credited with inciting American Protestants (in the North) against slavery. Stowe was the daughter of one of the most famous early-nineteenth-century Protestant ministers and was married to a well-known minister. The success of Strong's book both indicates the magnitude of his influence and points to the fact that by the end of the cen-tury the country's fundamentally Protestant makeup was still strong enough to determine the success of a best-selling book. Strong used his fame to revitalize the interdenominational (Protestant) movement called the Evangelical Alliance.

den in the 1880s to Walter Rauschenbusch in the first decades of the twentieth century: the realization of the Kingdom of God on this earth. The idea of the Kingdom of God had been central to American thought since the arrival of the Puritans and Pilgrims in the seventeenth century, but by the late nineteenth century it had gone through three distinct phases. Initially, the idea had referred to the "sovereignty of God" over the individual conscience and only indirectly to the church and polity created by individuals who accepted God's sovereignty in their lives. During the Revivalist period of the First Great Awakening, the Kingdom was understood in an intensely internal sense and focused more narrowly on the salvation of individual souls. In the Second Great Awakening, early in the nineteenth century, the internal "reign of Christ" was expanded through an argument about God's love to include social reforms such as temperance and abolition.

The movement of evangelical Christians toward social reform in the antebellum period marked a clear turning point in American Christianity, but the Social Gospel had still not been fully born. Its arrival would require two related changes in American society.

The first great change was the transformation of America's economy after the Civil War. As the full effects of the industrial revolution hit the nation—increased productivity, immigration, concentration of economic power, labor unrest, and urban poverty—America's traditional self-image as a rural society of pious individuals quickly faded away. In response to these economic changes came a second change: many theologians began to argue that the Kingdom of God referred not only to the need for the salvation of individual souls but also to the need to build new and more just social institutions. These institutions would be the basis for the new earthly Kingdom. Whereas their predecessors had been premillennialists, believing that Christ's thousand-year reign would come at some unspecified time in the future, this new breed of Christians looked at the human suffering around them and declared that the millennium had already arrived. Thus, the new Christians were called postmillennialists, and their task was to begin building the Kingdom then and there.[8]

Gates, Herron, and Strong were postmillennialist evangelical Christians who wanted to redeem the institutions of the new industrial

8. This account of the idea of the Kingdom of God in America draws heavily on Niebuhr's 1937 classic.

America. Fogel (1996) has referred to this movement as the Third Great Awakening. One of the group's many vehicles for evangelizing the country was the American Institute of Christian Sociology, a summer program held at Iowa College. The institute operated as a Chautauqua, with hundreds of academics and ministers traveling to Iowa to hear Strong lecture and Herron prophesy.

Among the organizers of the institute with Gates, Herron, and Strong was one of the two great Social Gospel leaders in the 1880s, Richard T. Ely. Ely and Washington Gladden, a Congregational minister in Columbus, Ohio, were the most recognized names in the social Christianity movement by 1890, although in the wake of the Haymarket riots in 1886, there had been a lessening of fervor and Ely had been investigated by the authorities at Johns Hopkins University because of his alleged support for socialism. The Kingdom movement was attractive to Ely and to his former student John R. Commons, however, exactly because of the explicit interest of Herron and Gates in continuing to explore socialism as the earthly manifestation of God's Kingdom.

The 1890s were a turbulent time in American society—labor strife (1892–94), financial panic (1893), depression (1893–96), and drought (1894)—and the "new" religion was still much on the minds of these two evangelical economists. Although Ely had toned his message down somewhat in the wake of Haymarket, he had not given up his dream. And Commons, because he was younger and had not finished graduate school, had not been forced to modify his views at all. Thus, Gates and Ely's good friend Jesse Macy, the professor of constitutional history at Iowa College, had little difficulty drawing Ely and Commons into the inner circle of the Kingdom movement.[9]

Herron's increasingly radical message was too much for either of the evangelical economists, however. Herron had risen to national prominence in 1890 with a sermon titled "The Message of Jesus for Men of Wealth" (in Herron 1894). The sermon is a postmillennialist message that Herron delivered across the country with a premillennialist's fervor. He had mastered the techniques of his rivals, but instead of calling individual sinners down to the "nervous bench," Herron called down an

9. For more about Macy, see his autobiographical writings posthumously edited by Noyes (1933). Commons and Macy shared common Quaker roots; both men's families had migrated from North Carolina to Indiana at the same time to get out of slave territory. Commons (1894a, 1894b, 1894c, 1894d, 1895a, 1895b, 1896, 1898) best demonstrate the explicitly evangelical nature of his early work.

entire group: the owners of capital. And like Billy Sunday, his most prominent premillennialist adversary, he then proceeded to lay out their sins slowly and carefully before calling for their repentance and offering them salvation. In his sermon "The Christian Revival of the Nation," Herron (1895, 179) stated: "We have failed. We have betrayed our trust, and forsaken our mission. God is disappointed in this nation. We are a fallen nation, an apostate people." After his arrival at Iowa College in 1893, Herron moved beyond his simple biblical exhortations, however. On the one hand, he edged closer and closer to an outright call for socialist revolution, and on the other, he called for a redefinition of Christian sociology along nonempirical, purely evangelical lines:

> We are in the beginnings of a revolution that will strain all existing religious and political institutions, and test the wisdom and heroism of the earth's bravest souls; a revolution that will regenerate society with the judgments of infinite love. ("The Social Revolution," in Herron 1893, 14)

> What I have here to say treats of work, wages, and wealth; of the rights and duties of capital and labor. And I approach the social problem, not from the standpoint of the political economist, but of the Christian apostle; Christ did not save the world by a scientific study of the economic conditions of society. Nor shall I make use of statistics, the value of which is largely fictitious; it is a fallacy that statistics cannot lie.[10] (11)

Any, or all, of this might have been too much for Ely. Other prominent academics, such as Albion Small, warned him to dissociate himself from Herron and the American Institute of Christian Sociology (Furner 1975, 151; Ross 1991, 126–27). And although Ely was almost certainly comfortable with a call to reexamine the relationship between capital and labor, he may not have been so keen on Herron's increasing use of the word "revolution." Nor would he have been likely to feel comfortable with Herron's preaching style. Ely had escaped his Methodist background early on to find a home in the Episcopal Church, so Herron's revivalist intensity may have been unappealing. At any rate, Ely moved away from the institute after 1894, first trying unsuccessfully to

---

10. The best statement of Herron's (1894) version of Christian sociology is in his sermon "The Scientific Ground of a Christian Sociology."

move the summer institute to New York in 1895 and then abandoning it altogether.

Commons was put off by Herron almost immediately. Although Commons was recruited by Ely to serve as the secretary for the institute, he heard Herron preach in Chicago in 1893 and was instantly wary of his message. In fact, he claims in his autobiography that after hearing Herron, he determined to change the focus of his research.

> At Bloomington I made my first venture in activities outside the academic field. The American Institute of Christian Sociology was organized, in 1893, to support an American version of what had been known in Europe as Christian Socialism. The aim was to present Christ as the living Master and King and Christian law as the ultimate rule for human society, to be realized on earth. I was made Secretary of the Institute. An eminent minister of the Gospel was made our lecturer. I became upset as to the meaning of Christian Socialism and Christian Sociology. On one night of his series our lecturer identified Christianity with pure Anarchism; on the next night he identified it with Communism. He identified each with the love of God. But I now became mystified on the meaning of Love itself. I could not make out whether Christian Socialism meant Love of Man or Love of Woman. On this issue our Institute of Christian Sociology split and disappeared.
>
> I became suspicious of Love as the basis of social reform. I visited the Amana community of Christian Communists in Iowa. They distinguished rigidly between love of man and love of woman. I studied Mazzini, the great Italian leader of Christian Socialism fifty years before. He founded Christian Socialism on the Duties of Man, including duties to wife and family. Eventually, after many years, in working out my institutional economics, I made Duty and Debt, instead of Liberty and Love, the foundations of institutional economics. (Commons 1934, 51–52)[11]

In the summer of 1893, Commons did not attend the institute because of family illness, and in 1894 he again failed to attend. But he was happy to publish in *The Kingdom*, and he worked out some of his best early ideas there between 1894 and 1898.

---

11. Commons's recollection here is not completely accurate. The questions of "free-love" and the sanctity of marriage did not become central to Herron's career for another four to five years. Commons is conflating several years of Herron's life into one year.

The combination of Herron's ability to redefine the Kingdom of God in the public mind as revolutionary socialism and the defeat of William Jennings Bryan and the Populists in 1896 took a clear toll on both Ely and Commons. Both moved toward the center in their public stances and their professional work after they were forced in academic trials in the 1890s to determine their fitness to teach.[12] They continued to champion the rights of labor, and both stayed very much at the liberal end of the economics profession, but the climate was changing and so were they. They could remain "ethical economists"—the term Ely had coined in the 1880s for his new socially concerned, activist vision of professional economists—but increasingly the focus of their work would change.

An Unexpected Turn

The tone and feel of American economics in the next two decades almost certainly could not have been predicted in 1900. The profession was now the home of several prominent former advocates of Christian socialism, all of whom had made their own compromises with their former position.

The most prominent, of course, was John Bates Clark. After leading the call for Christian socialism in the 1870s and 1880s, Clark was now the foremost marginalist in the American profession and the "scientific defender" of American capitalism.[13] Ely was the giant of ethical economics, and his *Outlines of Economics* (1893) remained the best-selling economics textbook in the country until the Second World War.[14] Commons came back from exile in the private sector and began building his distinguished career as the founder of American labor economics and the leader of institutional economics (Commons 1934).

The story, however, involves much more than just the ways each man changed and adapted his message, although this point is important. Although each of the three would go a different way in his professional

12. Ely's trial at the University of Wisconsin took place in 1894. The trustees of Syracuse University voted in March 1899 to discontinue Commons's chair. For the best account of these and other academic trials, see Furner 1975.

13. For quite different accounts of the trajectory of Clark's career, see Everett 1946 and Morgan 1994, on the one hand, and Henry 1995, on the other. The term "scientific defender," applied to Clark's defense of capitalism, is Henry's.

14. In its revised editions, *Outlines of Economics* sold 350,000 copies between the First and Second World Wars. See Rader 1966, 160–61.

work, together they demonstrate the tension that was central to the pluralism that existed up to the Second World War. Clark, who moved away from Christian socialism a decade before Ely and Commons, was the leading American figure in both marginalist and theoretical economics, but his work was nonetheless suffused with a strong moral tone (Morgan 1994). Indeed, one might argue that the moral tone was even more important after 1900, as Clark was finished by then with true theoretical innovation. And as long as Ely's textbook served as the standard-bearer of the profession and as the first text of most students, marginalism would stay in the protective wrapping of an ethical message much less conservative than Clark's. Ely's text introduced the student to marginalism but made it very clear that utility maximization and profit maximization were not the only, or the most important, behaviors of the people economists studied.[15] Commons was actually carrying out the hard work of building the historical, institutional economics that Ely championed in his text. Even a prominent economist with absolutely no background in the Social Gospel movement like E. R. A. Seligman (1902, 1905) was engaged in working out the same pattern of concerns and tensions that Clark, Commons, and Ely had helped bring to the center of American economics (Ross 1991, 188–95).

The particular historical contingencies that had brought the evangelical economists to the fore during the Gilded Age crisis had thus largely defined the ways American economics was done after the turn of the century. Marginalism and historical analysis were the two theoretical poles in the American profession, each informed by a strong desire for social amelioration. Thus, even as marginalism progressed, it was never separated from provisos that allowed for the importance of larger social concerns and for an explicit acceptance that not all behavior was self-centered and maximizing. The Social Gospel message was compatible with several types of economic analysis, as long as the focus of the analysis was clearly ethical in nature; both Clark's concern with the fairness of marginal productivity pricing and Commons's analysis of the nature and fairness of market transactions could fall within the acceptable realm of the dominant Protestant sensibility. Thus, during the first two decades of the twentieth century, the Social Gospel mes-

---

15. Although Ely was already the author of *An Introduction to Political Economy* (1889), he wrote *Outlines* expressly for the purposes of making a more analytically rigorous textbook and introducing marginal utility analysis, albeit wrapped in a tight ethical jacket.

sage served the function of sanctioning plural approaches within the economics profession. It defined a mood and temper among a large part of the profession that were stronger than any one school of thought.

American society continued to change as it entered the new century, and this change helped determine the acceptance of the newly evolved American economics and the economists themselves. The most obvious change was the Progressive movement.[16] In the first decade of the century, much of the fear, dislocation, and desire of the Gilded Age was channeled into a broad-based political movement. This movement had many fronts and varied agendas, but it was exactly the environment in which the reform message of people like Ely and Commons found an interested audience. And Clark turned away from new theoretical development to address broader questions of the legitimacy of labor unions and world peace. Institutionalists and marginalists could coexist, despite different methods, as long as the issue was reform rather than revolution and as long as ethical concerns informed their work.

The Social Gospel had itself taken a significant turn in the first decade of the century. By 1900 the movement had reached a terrible nadir.[17] Many church leaders had been suspicious of the movement in the 1880s and early 1890s, but as the Kingdom movement had grown and as Herron had become better known, they felt no compunction in shunning it altogether. Then Herron scandalized the nation in 1901 when, after being forced to resign his chair of applied Christianity at Iowa College the year before because of his mounting radicalism, he divorced his wife and married Carrie Rand, the young daughter of the philanthropist who had originally endowed his chair. He had also become a major force in the new American Socialist Party, personally helping unite the Morris Hillquit and Eugene Debs factions of American socialism. All of this was too much for the mainline Protestants to whom the Social Gospel leaders had to make their appeals. Herron's politics made him an outcast in almost all Protestant circles, but his divorce and remarriage made him a pariah. When he lost his ordination in Iowa because of his divorce, it made headlines across the country

16. I am using "progressivism" as this movement's name even though an older, rich secondary literature disputes whether "progressivism" or "reform" should be used to label the political activity these terms describe. "Reform" was the more common term at the time, although "progressivism" is the term most often used now.

17. The sense of the collapse of the movement at the end of the 1890s, including Herron's scandal, and its unexpected rebirth are captured nicely in Hopkins 1940.

and undercut his effectiveness as a Socialist leader. Because his new wife's family had paid his ex-wife sixty thousand dollars as part of the divorce settlement, the popular press termed his new relationship "the buying and selling of wives." Virtually every time his name appeared in the press in regard to his Socialist activities, the "buying and selling" comments were repeated. This ultimately led to Herron's self-imposed exile in Italy (Hillquit 1934, 62–64).

Herron's fall from grace was hard on the Social Gospel movement, but the conditions the movement addressed were not disappearing. In fact, activists like Jacob Riis and the muckrakers were finally beginning to make people aware of the abject poverty in America's cities, and the relevance of the Christian message to these conditions was obvious to churchgoing Americans. New leaders began to rise. Walter Rauschenbusch, the first great American theologian in a century, was becoming better known after 1900. He later stated: "All whose recollection runs back to 1900 will remember that as a time for lonesomeness. We were few and we shouted in the wilderness" (Rauschenbusch 1912, 9). As Gorrell (1988) has nicely argued, the defining moment of the movement's resurgence came in 1908 when the mainline churches finally gave up their historical reticence and signed the Social Creed of the Churches. The creed consisted of eleven principles that formed a manifesto for action as well as a statement of faith:

- For equal rights and complete justice for all men in all stations of life.
- For the principle of conciliation and arbitration in industrial dissensions.
- For the protection of the worker from dangerous machinery, occupational diseases, injuries and mortality.
- For the abolition of child labor.
- For such regulation of the conditions of labor for women as shall safeguard the physical and moral health of the community.
- For the suppression of the "sweating system."
- For the gradual and reasonable reduction of the hours of labor to the lowest practical point, with work for all; and for that degree of leisure for all which is the condition of the highest human life.
- For a release from employment one day in seven.
- For a living wage in every industry.
- For the highest wage that each industry can afford, and for the

most equitable division of the products of industry that can ultimately be devised.

- For the recognition of the Golden Rule and the mind of Christ as the supreme law of society and the sure remedy for all social ills. (Hopkins 1940, 291)

The Social Creed was formally accepted by virtually every mainline Protestant denomination in America through the guise of the Federal Council of Churches.[18] By 1912, the creed was being introduced to men around the country by the Men and Religion Forward movement, which was at that time "the most comprehensive evangelical effort ever undertaken in the United States" (Hopkins 1940, 296). Traveling teams of experts made nine thousand addresses nationwide to more than 1.5 million people in one nine-month period.

In this new world, Ely and Commons were in their element. Ely was widely acknowledged for his many reform efforts of the 1880s and 1890s and used his prestige to undertake two new efforts: the founding of land economics and the writing of his most important institutionalist text, *Property and Contract in Their Relations to the Distribution of Wealth* (1914). Commons evolved in this period into a leading force not only in labor economics but also in the design and implementation of social insurance schemes. The public profiles of Ely and Commons were no longer seen as threats to their academic credibility, and in this way the last phase of the Social Gospel period may be seen as one of the forces that contributed to the continued acceptance of diverse views within the profession. It was not just that Commons and Ely had moved toward the center; the Protestant population, coming from the other direction, was now standing behind them in the center as well. And the conservative Clark was by this time being dragged to the center, for instance, in his reexamination of unions and his acknowledgment of their value.

Not all American economists in 1920 would have happily identified themselves with the whole range of Ely's and Commons's work, and certainly not all American economists then were liberal Protestants, but in the glow of the Social Gospel's golden years, historical and institutional approaches were accepted and respected. Simon Nelson Patten and Arthur Hadley could fit comfortably in this world, as could follow-

18. The council amended the creed in 1912 to include the provisions demanding one day in seven as a day of rest, acceptance of a "minimum living wage" in every industry, and an effort to pay "maximum possible wages" in any case.

ers of Henry George and anyone else with religious roots and a progressive agenda. Even old Social Gospelers like Clark were swept along by this tide; in fact, Ely's text made the presence of marginalism perfectly welcome in the mainstream by qualifying and cosseting it in the language of higher ethical aims.

Another Unexpected Turn

Someone reading about the Social Gospel movement for the first time might well wonder why this movement, if it was so central to American culture, is virtually unknown to us today. How did it disappear so completely from sight if it was such a large force in American culture?

One answer would be that its influence, if not its name, is familiar to virtually all of us in the guise of Martin Luther King Jr.'s work in the Civil Rights movement. King learned the theology of the Social Gospel at Boston University. Personalism, one of the concepts that animated the Social Gospel in both the late nineteenth and the early twentieth centuries, was at the heart of the message King preached.

But although the message has been able to move America in the late twentieth century, its name is still unknown because of its ironic and tragic success in the second decade of the century. After the Social Creed of the Churches, the movement became so much a part of mainline churches and of the majority Protestant viewpoint that it was transformed into a variant of its early ancestors in the seventeenth and eighteenth centuries: it became a form of nationalist ideology in the hands of those who still conceived of America as the special land prepared for the Kingdom that was to follow the Protestant Reformation. Many Protestant ministers with a minimal commitment to social reform happily embraced the return to a nationalist theology and made this nationalism the center of their Social Gospel message.

Woodrow Wilson was an active proponent of the Social Gospel, and among his core constituencies in 1912 were reforming Protestants (Marty 1984, 361–64). Unfortunately, when the country entered the First World War, many of the nationalistic preachers used their pulpits to promote the war and excoriate the Germans. Social Gospel giants like Rauschenbusch and Edward O. Steiner were sickened by the war (Marty 1984; Jordan 1983). But amid the anti-German war propaganda, their voices were drowned out. In his somewhat biased but nonetheless chilling account of this period, Abrams (1969) documents the awful truth of the nationalistic preachers' conduct. A common refrain in sermons in 1917 was, "If Christ were alive today, he'd put the bayonet all the way in . . . and turn it" (Abrams 1969, 67–70).

Not surprisingly, in the shattered postwar world these ministers lost their moral authority. No longer was the public interested in their nationalistic idea of the Kingdom of God. The few true leaders who had refused to allow themselves to be sucked into the war mentality were shattered by the experience. Rauschenbusch died heartbroken in 1918 four months before the armistice. Steiner slowly overcame his bitterness after the war, but in the new despairing, cynical mood of the Lost Generation, he was increasingly seen as an outdated figure. Then, with the Great Crash and the Great Depression, the country slid from religious indifference to a "religious depression" marked by large decreases in church attendance, mission giving, and public discussion of explicitly religious ideas (Handy 1960; Marty 1986, 227–36).[19] The one giant of American theology in the 1930s, Reinhold Niebuhr (1932), explicitly refused to identify himself with the Social Gospel theology. He saw its dream of a Kingdom on this earth as naive and ill conceived in the face of the awesome reality of the First World War. Although he was a strong advocate of organized labor and preached often about poverty, he identified himself as a neoconservative theologian because of his deep belief in people's fundamental sinfulness. This unblinking focus on the fallen nature of humankind earned him the label of "realist."

The Changing Climate of Creativity

Although it is not surprising that Protestant theologians became more "realistic" at the same time that neoclassical economics was consolidating around a new, sharper, and unfettered model of individual optimization, it would undoubtedly be wrong to attribute any direct influence to Niebuhr or his followers. Theologians like Niebuhr saw the same reality in human selfishness as the economists did, but these were independent discoveries of old truths; the economists were no longer taking their lead from theologians. After the First World War, the ground on which American economics was being built had been cleared

---

19. In retrospect, it seems clear that the idea of a "religious depression" during the 1920s and 1930s was largely descriptive of the mainline Protestant experience. Church history was, even at midcentury, largely about the Protestant churches.

of Protestant influence.[20] The movement that had spurred the early work of many great turn-of-the-century economists and had later helped sustain some of the diversity in American economics was now a spent force in the larger culture and in the discipline of economics.

But although there was no direct connection between Niebuhr's theology and the newly evolving neoclassicism of the interwar years, it is not difficult to see their common relation to the period's new intellectual climate. Crunden (1982, ix) has described progressivism as a "climate of creativity" in which a generation of Americans attempted to create a "spiritual reformation to fulfill God's plan for democracy in the New World." Using this framework, Crunden connects the work of people in many different fields: Jane Addams, the cofounder of Hull House; Herron; John Dewey, the philosopher and educational reformer; Ely; Commons; Frank Lloyd Wright, the architect; Charles Ives, the composer; the muckrakers; Edgar Lee Masters, the poet; and Upton Sinclair, the novelist. Indeed, it is easy to see the common links in these individuals' Protestant background, their concern for social redemption, and the central place of ethical behavior in their thinking. Likewise, it is easy to see the common focus on selfish behavior in Niebuhr's work and in the newly evolving neoclassicism of an economist like Frank Knight as a reflection of the "realism" that characterized the "creative climate" of the interwar period. As Americans let go of the old world of progressivism, with its sense of hope and its ethical earnestness, they embraced the starker, more "realistic" vision of Ernest Hemingway's novels and Edward Hopper's paintings.

Initially, however, the new intellectual climate did not give a clear field to neoclassicism. Progressivism is typically described as having had two branches: the Social Gospel movement, or Christian Progressives, and the scientific Progressives such as Frederick W. Taylor, the industrial efficiency expert, and Herbert Croly, the editor of the *New Republic*. In the aftermath of the First World War, the scientific Progressives, who had come to prominence only after 1910, were much less affected than the Christian Progressives.[21] Efficiency became a

20. Another related current in American society at this time was the secularization of the universities. This was a complex process in which trustees were often anxious to point to religious life on campus while, in fact, religious tests and affiliations were being formally eliminated. See Marsden 1994.

21. Both Thompson (1987) and Danbom (1987) discuss the impact of the First World War on Christian Progressives and scientific Progressives.

hallmark of the interwar era for political and cultural reasons. Although Warren Harding had promised to return the country to "normalcy" in the 1920 presidential race, by which he clearly meant that he would move away from Wilson's preachy moralizing, he was nonetheless motivated to ameliorate friction between labor and capital. "Efficiency" served his purpose perfectly because of its explicit promise to increase both wages and profits through increased productivity and output. But in addition to providing a rhetoric that was seen as more "realistic" than Wilson's old calls for a higher, more ethical public conduct, it also helped assuage the unease and uncertainty spawned by the new culture of mass production and consumerism. Between 1916 and 1920, the number of registered automobiles jumped from one million to eight million; between 1920 and 1929, it increased from eight million to twenty-three million. In this new world of assembly-line production and the changing nature of work, the idea of efficiency was not just about making the old system more productive and fair but also about making sure that the newly evolving system would work well and in everyone's favor.

In this new "realistic" world of efficiency and scientific management, the institutionalists made a much bigger initial impact than the neo-classicists. Drawing from Thorstein Veblen's ideas about the importance of engineers to the new industrial system and Ely's and Commons's legacy of collecting data to interpret the evolving nature of economic activity, institutionalists set out after the First World War to build a science of controlling the economy. Wesley Clair Mitchell is the epitome of this movement in the history of American economic thought. When he set up the National Bureau of Economic Research (NBER) in 1920, he represented both the impulse toward a "scientific" understanding of the economy and the institutionalists' central place in that enterprise. But, of course, he was not alone; John Maurice Clark, Sumner Slichter, Walton Hamilton, and Rexford Tugwell were some of the leading names in American economics in the 1920s, and each was an institutionalist. The titles of their articles in the post–World War I period reveal their interests: "An Example of Municipal Research," "Overhead Costs in Modern Industry," "Economical Theory in an Era of Social Readjustment," "Industrial Morale," "Economic and Social Aspects of Increased Productivity," "Lines of Action, Adaptation, and Control," "Law and Economics," "The Institutional Approach to Economic Theory," "The Economic Basis of Business Regulation," "The Principle of

Planning and the Institution of Laissez-Faire." The places in which these articles were published also indicate their prominence: the *American Economic Review*, the *Journal of Political Economy*, and the *Quarterly Journal of Economics*. (See Roger E. Backhouse's essay in this volume for a study of how publishing in the top journals changed in subsequent decades.)

The institutionalists' efforts to examine, explain, and control industrial activity were very much a part of the climate of creativity that Márcia L. Balisciano describes in her essay on planning in this volume. Although the adherents of efficiency and planning were themselves often strikingly naive in their assumptions about the disinterestedness of engineers and the appeal of their ideas to laborers, they had, in their own minds, replaced the moral earnestness of the Christian Progressives with a scientific program that was vital and widely respected.

Then What Happened?

In the 1920s, it looked as though American economics would continue to be plural. Institutionalism was clearly the dominant school of thought, but its position was not monolithic. John Bates Clark's marginalist legacy was still alive and beginning to flourish in the hands of theorists like Jacob Viner and Frank Knight. Irving Fisher published regularly on index numbers, the value of the dollar, and business cycles. Allyn Young was a rising star. American economics was diverse and looked as if it would stay that way. So what happened?

One thing that happened was the Great Depression, of course. The depression might have been expected to positively affect the status of the institutionalists most among all the schools then in existence. They were, after all, the economists in 1929 most centrally involved in shaping and controlling economic performance, and so their services would have been most in demand. Laissez-faire was not a popular idea as the 1930s unfolded (see Anne Mayhew's essay in this volume). The expectation of their expertise may not have helped the institutionalists in the long run, however, for ultimately they were unable to provide a set of policy recommendations that were seen as successful against the depression. Tugwell's central place in the First New Deal and the spectacular failure of his recovery plan, the National Industrial Recovery

Act, between 1933 and 1935 must have taken some of the sheen off institutionalism's star.

More was involved, however, than just a run of bad luck. Already by the beginning of the 1930s marginalists were busy attacking institutionalism; the tolerance and pluralism of the first two decades of the century were breaking down. Knight's vicious attack on Slichter's new textbook in 1932 is emblematic of the changing environment. Knight's review ran over forty pages and elicited a long reply from Slichter (1932b). Likewise, the attack on "Measurement without Theory" by Tjalling Koopmans in 1947 was a new kind of direct confrontation in which the older spirit of pluralism was eviscerated. Koopmans's attack was especially devastating because a large part of the vitality of institutionalism in the 1920s had depended on its self-concept as "scientific." Because institutionalists collected data and examined them to establish tentative theories and hypotheses, they had seen themselves as more scientific than marginalists, who depended on a priori assumptions about human behavior and insisted on focusing on equilibrium outcomes. Koopmans's attack, however, put the very definition of science in dispute. If economic science could be redefined so that it required strong a priori theoretical assumptions, the validity of the entire enterprise set up by Mitchell at the NBER would be in question, at least in the way he had envisioned it.

In addition to attacks from marginalists and statisticians, institutionalism also faced a threat from the new Keynesian consensus that formed at the end of the interwar period. Here the problem was not unfriendly attack, however, but the attraction of Keynesianism to institutionalists, especially those in government.[22] As Keynesianism supplanted the many other kinds of planning that had been available in the late 1920s and early 1930s and became the dominant framework for economic policy and for the amelioration of capitalist dysfunction, older institutionalist research into industry structure and business cycles fell out of fashion. For some institutionalists, the functional forms and geometry of the Keynesian model must have seemed a welcome apparatus in the face of growing charges that institutionalists were nontheoretical. But this was a chimera, of course, for the neo-

22. Collins (1990) discusses how the institutionalist Leon Keyserling established the Council of Economic Advisers as a government stronghold for institutional economists who had become Keynesians.

classical synthesis of John Hicks, Roy Harrod, and Samuelson would soon make Keynesian macroeconomics into a healthy branch of utility-maximizing neoclassicism.[23]

So what happened after the 1920s is a complex story in which an aggressive, self-confident group of neoclassical economists, through luck and hard work, pushed their most vital competitor out of the picture.

Cleared Ground

At this point, we are back to the triumvirate of mathematics, formalism, and physics envy, the primary characteristics of the neoclassicism that pushed institutionalism off the stage and came to dominate American economics. But the success of the particular brand of marginalist analysis that triumphed in this story was not foreordained; it came about through a series of sometimes unlikely twists and turns.

When John Bates Clark developed his marginalist ideas at the end of the nineteenth century, his work was highly mathematical. But despite his renown, his work did not become predominant. On the contrary, it became one type of a larger American economics that focused on "ethical" solutions to social problems. Ely's and Commons's work in a more historical, less theoretical mode was equally valued as a part of this "ethical economics."

But after the First World War, the ground shifted. The old Protestant influence of the Social Gospel was swept away after 1918, and a new sensibility began to define American economics. Now, instead of an ethical economics that sought to reform the nation, America had a scientific economics that sought to make the nation more efficient and to control its economy. At first this new environment continued to support plural approaches to economics, but eventually pluralism gave way. Whereas institutional economics seemed perfectly "scientific" in 1922, by 1947, it was no longer unquestionably regarded as such.

Institutionalism had suffered other setbacks and unfortunate turns, particularly its identification with the First New Deal and the rise of

---

23. The charge that institutionalists were nontheoretical or antitheoretical was false, of course. It is more accurate to say that they were multitheoretical. Institutionalists openly debated many theoretical points of view but could not agree on any one theory. Institutionalists in the first half of the twentieth century certainly could not agree that simple utility and profit maximization sufficiently defined economic theory.

Keynesianism, but the usurpation of the label "scientific" by neoclassicists was the worst upset. By supplanting a definition of science that was akin to evolutionary biology (collect, examine, and then hypothesize) with a sense that more closely approximated physics (theorize, then use data for confirmation), neoclassicists effectively pushed institutionalism off the stage. In a world defined by "realism" and "science," it was impossible for a research program to thrive if it was not "scientific."

There is, perhaps, some irony in this end, for although the Social Gospel had undoubtedly helped sustain a more pluralistic American economics, its demise is usually seen as the beginning of a more pluralistic American society. The Protestantism that had served as a national ideology for over two centuries had helped keep Catholics, Jews, women, blacks, and Asians from effective political representation, but that would slowly begin to change after 1918 as modern interest-group liberalism began to emerge.[24] As that pluralism in the larger society began to become a reality, the more modest pluralism of American economics began to disappear. After the demise of the Social Gospel, neither American society nor American economics would ever be the same.

References

Abrams, Ray H. 1969. *Preachers Present Arms*. Scottsdale, Pa.: Herald Press.

Ahlstrom, Sydney E. 1975. *A Religious History of the American People*. New York: Doubleday.

Clark, John Maurice. 1919. Economic Theory in an Era of Social Readjustment. *American Economic Review* 9 (March): 280–90.

———. 1921. An Example of Municipal Research. *Journal of Political Economy* 19 (March): 241–49.

———. 1923. Some Social Aspects of Overhead Costs. *American Economic Review* 13 (March): 50–59.

Collins, Robert M. 1990. The Emergence of Economic Growthmanship in the United States: Federal Policy and Economic Knowledge in the Truman Years. In *The State and Economic Knowledge*. Edited by Mary O. Furner and Barry Supple. Cambridge: Cambridge University Press.

Commons, John R. 1894a. Christianity and Wages. *The Kingdom*, 2 November.

---

24. Graham (1967) shows that only a small number of Progressives from 1900 to 1920 backed the New Deal. One of the most common reasons for their disapproval of Franklin Roosevelt's programs was that they openly appealed to people as members of groups (e.g., ethnic or socioeconomic groups) rather than as citizens of one nation.

————. 1894b. Christian Sociology. *The Kingdom*, 20 April.

————. 1894c. Democracy vs. Paternalism. *The Kingdom*, 27 July.

————. 1894d. "Natural" and "Artificial" Selection. *The Kingdom*, 22 June.

————. 1895a. The Eight-Hour Day. *The Kingdom*, 12 April.

————. 1895b. The Monetary Problem. *The Kingdom*, 5 April.

————. 1896. Political Economy and Law. *The Kingdom*, 24 January.

————. 1898. Social Economics and City Evangelization: Part 1. *The Kingdom*, 24 November.

————. 1934. *Myself.* New York: Macmillan.

Crunden, Robert M. 1982. *Ministers of Reform: The Progressives' Achievement in American Civilization, 1889–1920.* New York: Basic Books.

Danbom, David. 1987. *The World of Hope: Progressives and the Struggle for an Ethical Public Life.* Philadelphia: Temple University Press.

Ely, Richard T. 1889. *An Introduction to Political Economy.* New York: Macmillan.

————. 1893. *Outlines of Economics.* New York: Flood and Vincent.

————. 1914. *Property and Contract in Their Relations to the Distribution of Wealth.* New York: Macmillan.

Everett, John R. 1946. *Religion in Economics: A Study of John Bates Clark, Richard T. Ely, and Simon Patten.* New York: King's Crown Press.

Fogel, Robert W. 1996. The Fourth Great Awakening. *Wall Street Journal*, 9 January.

Furner, Mary O. 1975. *Advocacy and Objectivity: A Crisis in the Professionalization of American Social Science, 1865–1905.* Lexington: University Press of Kentucky.

Gates, Isabel Smith. 1915. *The Life of George Augustus Gates.* Boston: Pilgrim Press.

Gonce, R. A. 1996. The Social Gospel, Ely, and Commons's Initial Stage of Thought. *Journal of Economic Issues* 30.3 (September): 641–65.

Gorrell, Donald K. 1988. *The Age of Social Responsibility: The Social Gospel in the Progressive Era, 1900–1920.* Macon, Ga.: Mercer University Press.

Graham, Otis L., Jr. 1967. *An Encore for Reform: The Old Progressives and the New Deal.* New York: Oxford University Press.

Hadley, Arthur Twining. 1906. *Standards of Public Morality.* John S. Kennedy Lectures. New York: Macmillan.

Hamilton, Walton H. 1919. The Institutional Approach to Economic Theory. *American Economic Review* 9 (March): 309–18.

————. 1929. Law and Economics (roundtable discussion). *American Economic Review* 19 (March): 56–60.

Handy, Robert T. 1950. George D. Herron and the Kingdom Movement. *Church History* 19 (June): 97–115.

————. 1960. The American Religious Depression, 1925–35. *Church History* 29 (March): 3–16.

Henry, John F. 1995. *John Bates Clark: The Making of a Neoclassical Economist.* London: Macmillan.

Herron, George D. 1893. *The New Redemption: A Call to the Church to Reconstruct Society according to the Gospel of Christ.* Boston: Thomas Y. Crowell.

———. 1894. *The Christian Society.* New York: Fleming H. Revell.

———. 1895. *The Christian State: A Political Vision of Christ.* Boston: Thomas Y. Crowell.

Hillquit, Morris. 1934. *Loose Leaves from a Busy Life.* New York: Macmillan.

Hopkins, Charles H. 1940. *The Rise of the Social Gospel in American Protestantism, 1865–1915.* New Haven: Yale University Press.

Jordan, David W. 1983. Edward A. Steiner and the Struggle for Toleration during World War I. *Annals of Iowa* 42 (winter): 523–42.

Knight, Frank H. 1932. The Newer Economics and the Control of Economic Activity. *Journal of Political Economy* 40 (August): 433–76.

Koopmans, Tjalling C. 1947. Measurement without Theory. *Review of Economics and Statistics* 29 (August): 161–72.

Luker, Ralph E. 1991. *The Social Gospel in Black and White: American Racial Reform, 1885–1912.* Chapel Hill: University of North Carolina Press.

Marsden, George M. 1994. *The Soul of the American University: From Protestant Establishment to Established Nonbelief.* New York: Oxford University Press.

Marty, Martin E. 1984. *Pilgrims in Their Own Land: Five Hundred Years of Religion in America.* Boston: Little, Brown.

———. 1986. *Protestantism in the United States: Righteous Empire.* 2d ed. New York: Scribner's.

May, Henry F. 1949. *Protestant Churches and Industrial America.* New York: Harper Torchbooks.

Morgan, Mary S. 1994. Marketplace Morals and the American Economists: The Case of John Bates Clark. In *Higgling: Transactors and Their Markets in the History of Economics.* HOPE 26 supplement. Edited by Neil De Marchi and Mary S. Morgan. Durham, N.C.: Duke University Press.

Nelson, Julie. 1993. Ely and Christian Social Reform. In *Economists at Wisconsin, 1892–1992.* Edited by Robert J. Lampman. Madison: University of Wisconsin System Board of Regents.

Niebuhr, Reinhold. 1932. *Moral Man and Immoral Society.* New York: Scribner's.

Niebuhr, Richard. 1937. *The Kingdom of God in America.* New York: Harper and Row.

Noyes, Katherine M. 1933. *Jesse Macy: An Autobiography.* Baltimore: C. C. Thomas.

Rader, Benjamin G. 1966. *The Academic Mind and Reform: The Influence of Richard T. Ely in American Life.* Lexington: University Press of Kentucky.

Rauschenbusch, Walter. 1912. *Christianizing the Social Order.* New York: Macmillan.

Ross, Dorothy. 1991. *The Origins of American Social Science.* Cambridge: Cambridge University Press.

Samuelson, Paul A. 1947. *Foundations of Economic Analysis.* Cambridge, Mass.: Harvard University Press.

Schlesinger, Arthur M. 1932. A Critical Period in American Religion, 1875–1900. *Massachusetts Historical Society Proceedings* 64:523–47.

Seligman, E. R. A. 1902. *The Economic Interpretation of History*. New York: Macmillan.

———. 1905. *Principles of Economics*. New York: Longmans, Green.

Slichter, Sumner H. 1920. Industrial Morale. *Quarterly Journal of Economics* 35 (November): 36–60.

———. 1928. Economic and Social Aspects of Increased Productive Efficiency: Discussion. *American Economic Review* 18 (March): 166–70.

———. 1932a. Lines of Action, Adaptation, and Control. *American Economic Review* 22 (March): 41–54.

———. 1932b. Modern Economic Society Further Considered: Comments on Mr. Knight's Review. *Journal of Political Economy* 40 (December): 814–20.

Strong, Josiah R. 1885. *Our Country: Its Possible Future and Its Present Crisis*. New York: Baker and Taylor.

Thompson, John A. 1987. *Reformers and War: American Progressive Publicists and the First World War*. Cambridge: Cambridge University Press.

Tugwell, Rexford G. 1921. The Economic Basis for Business Regulation. *American Economic Review* 11 (December): 643–58.

———. 1932. The Principle of Planning and the Institution of Laissez-Faire. *American Economic Review* 22 (March): 75–92.

The Patrons of Economics in a Time of Transformation

Craufurd D. Goodwin

It is customary for historians of economics to approach the topic of what happened to the discipline from the 1930s to the 1960s primarily from within the community of economists. Familiar questions include the following: What puzzles sparked the inquiry? What motivated the leaders? What drove the followers? What new models and other tools of analysis enriched the capacity of economists to explain? What seminal contributions to theory and empirical testing led economists to take one fork in the road rather than another? I concede that most of the answers to these questions may, indeed, cast light on our subject. Nevertheless, I propose to take another approach. I will examine some features of the sources of financial support of economics from the 1930s to the 1960s. My first questions are, What form did this support take? Did it involve a market transaction? Did someone purchase economics? I think not. Was it perhaps a process of "sponsorship," which may be defined as the intervention of one party on behalf of another without request? Again, that does not seem to capture the phenomenon. The best term I can find to describe the financing of economics is "patronage," a word with medieval roots meaning "defense, protection, advocacy of a benefice by a patron." The benefice in the Middle Ages, corresponding to economics in this case, was usually an ecclesiastical post or office to which property or a revenue was attached. This feudal notion especially referred to the relationship between the aristocracy and the church involving a two-way sense of right and responsibility.

During the twentieth century, there have been primarily four patrons of economics: higher education, the government, the business community, and charitable foundations. These were the sources from which economists drew their salaries and through which they conducted their research. In this essay, I will reflect on the attitudes of each of these four patrons toward economics to see whether changes in their views help explain changes in the behavior of their benefice.

Higher Education

It is difficult for the present-day academic economist, accustomed to teaching mainly the children of contented and politically conservative middle-class parents the wonders of the free market system, to appreciate that not long ago this discipline was widely feared as the seat of radicalism and the means to corruption of the young. Economics came to American higher education in the nineteenth century as a watered-down version of British classical political economy and was perceived then as a relatively minor facet of moral philosophy. Rules for good behavior in the economy were taught, often by clerics or college presidents in their spare time (Barber 1988). When American students went abroad for graduate study in continental Europe after the Civil War, stronger juices began to flow and a distinctive American economics emerged, characterized by an openness to other disciplines and a search for answers to innumerable social and economic questions that faced the new nation. Not only were the methods of these Young Turks novel; their policy prescriptions were highly creative as well. Of course, there had been radical innovators before them in American economic thought. Edward Bellamy, Henry Carey, Henry George, and Friedrich List all gained international reputations, but they remained outside the college classroom and curriculum. If these early radicals wanted to corrupt youths during their education, they had to do it from afar. By the end of the nineteenth century, this situation changed.

Hofstadter and Metzger (1955, 423) in their history of academic freedom in the United States report that "the decade of the nineties—so curiously and inappropriately called 'gay'—had seen the rise of a new kind of heresy defined as economic non-conformity." The targets of the nonconformists were many: the monetary standard, landownership, trade unions, public utilities, public finance, and others. The young academic economists of the new style were not monolithic in their views on these topics. But they were frequently vocal, iconoclastic, and publicity seeking. Inevitably they came to be seen by many college and university authorities as troublemakers, disrespectful of the status quo and of traditional social, political, and economic values.

Persecution of radical economists came to characterize the era. Some of those persecuted, such as Richard T. Ely of the University of Wisconsin, emerged from the experience largely unscathed. Others, such as Edward W. Bemis, who was fired from the University of Chicago in 1895 and from Kansas State University in 1899, were driven permanently from the profession. Ely's alleged sin had been to show sympathy for trade unions, that of Bemis to criticize the railway companies. In fact the real sin of these young economists was to offend powerful patrons of higher education: legislators who supported public institutions and donors who financed private ones. They bit the hands that fed them. Some cases were egregious. Edward A. Ross, who was both professor at Stanford University and secretary of the American Economic Association, took it upon himself to attack many of the economic institutions through which Stanford's founder had made his wealth: unorganized labor, unrestricted immigration, and unregulated free enterprise. The founder's widow, Mrs. Leland Stanford, accused Ross of being "slangey and scurrilous" and of using his privileged academic position for political electioneering. Ross was dismissed by Stanford president David Starr Jordan. Seven other professors then resigned in protest, including the economists Frank Fetter and Morton A. Aldrich. The American Economic Association established a committee of inquiry now remembered as the predecessor of Committee A of the American Association of University Professors, the guardian of academic freedom for all disciplines (Hofstadter and Metzger 1955, 425–45).

The controversiality of economists within academe rose and fell with the attention paid to the questions they addressed. But throughout most of the first half of the twentieth century, it seemed that whenever there was a crisis of academic freedom, an economist was likely to be at the heart of it. In 1915, as the nation looked with unease toward the conflict in Europe and toward social tensions at home, the economist Scott Nearing was dismissed from the University of Pennsylvania for unspecified causes, widely perceived to be his radical ideas (Metzger et al. 1969, 12). The editors of the *New York Times* approved of this action on the ground that the wealthy donors to a university should not have to see their gifts used for "the dissemination of the dogmas of Socialism or in the teaching of ingenuous youth how to live without work" (13). It was evident that the reciprocal responsibilities of patronage were appreciated outside as well as inside the university.

The 1930s were the next decade in which economists raised hackles high within academe, especially economists who became associated with Franklin Roosevelt's New Deal. Once again, the economists' views probably caused less trouble for administrators than how they expressed them. The economists were active far from the ivory tower; they were at the center of acrimonious debates in which they seemed certain to offend powerful interests important to the institutions where they were employed. Sensitivity to the political involvement of economists varied widely. In an extreme case, a regent of the University of Texas proposed the dismissal of Clarence Ayres and three other economists apparently on the ground that they had considered serving as consultants on the New Deal (Breit and Culbertson 1976, 16).

The first decade after World War II was most like the 1890s in the intensity of the attacks on academic economists. Several developments help explain this new outbreak. First, the economics discipline had become steadily more prominent in the public mind, in part because economists had played such visible and successful roles in the war effort and in part because economists of various stripes now claimed to be able to prevent a return of the Great Depression, the social nemesis many blamed even for the war itself. Second, the postwar years saw remarkable growth in higher education to accommodate returning veterans, a burgeoning population, and an increasing proportion of citizens who saw higher education as the ticket to economic success. Leaders of colleges and universities faced a continuing need to appeal to legislators and private donors not just for their customary indulgence but also for large additional capital sums for constructing buildings and expanding programs. Conversely, these patrons claimed a responsibility to make sure that the benefices deserved the added resources.

Finally, many of the issues with which economists dealt now took on new significance against the background of the cold war. For the United States, this conflict was intensified by the world role that had been thrust on it by the collapse of the European Allies and the decisive defeat of the Axis powers. The cold war bore striking similarities to a holy war such as the Crusades. One of the primary challenges it presented was how to resist the further spread of communism, the rival ideology to capitalism, and convert the infidel. But in the cold war, unlike the Crusades, the rival doctrines were not theological but economic. The dangerous heretic was not one who believed in Allah or the Antichrist but one who preached class war, the contradictions of capitalism, and public ownership of the means of production. In the cold war atmosphere, eccentric economic ideas could be more than mere apostasy; they could be treachery and even treason. Whereas a visit of inspection to the Soviet Union by the Columbia economist–turned–Brains Truster Rexford Tugwell in the 1930s led to his banishment to Puerto Rico, in the 1940s or 1950s it would have landed him before the House Un-American Activities Committee or in jail.

The attacks on radical economists in the 1940s and 1950s were motivated in part by reasoned fear of "planning" by those who were scheduled to be planned and in part by unreasoned public paranoia about conspiracies of various kinds. In some cases, the attacks were continuations of campaigns from the 1930s. After Ayres opposed the requirement of a loyalty oath at the University of Texas in 1951, his nemesis, the Texas legislature, by a vote of 130 to 1, resolved that he could no longer contribute to the "culture and progress of the state" and should be both dismissed from the university and deported from the country. Neither recommendation was carried out, but Ayres was branded an "educational termite" by the sponsor of the resolution (Breit and Culbertson 1976, 16).

Increasingly in the 1940s and 1950s, John Maynard Keynes and his American disciples, led by Alvin Hansen, became the favorite targets of cold war witch-hunters. This was partly because Keynesian macroeconomic theory seemed to provide a persuasive rationale for a strong state. Wasn't this, after all, the Marxist prescription? But in addition, the name "Keynes" was a convenient personification of economic heresy. It is easier to hate or fear a person, or at least an image of a person, than a vague set of ideas. There were no longer enough home-grown Marxists to make the name "Marx" a credible threat on the home front, and Earl Browder, the head of the American Communist Party, was more a figure of amusement than a figure of dread. But Keynes was a different matter. He was seriously and successfully evangelical. Increasing numbers of young Americans openly avowed his faith, and, most frightening of all, some of them were now in government. Moreover, Keynes was a foreigner, and an Englishman to boot, with a one-syllable name like the name "Marx." The *Chicago Tribune* called him the Englishman who ruled America. Even though Keynes's and Marx's ideas were as different as night and day, they were lumped together in this period by many a demagogue.

The attacks on economists in academe in the 1950s were wide-ranging, coming from legislators, trustees, alumni, the media, and senior administrators. John Kenneth Galbraith, who could wear both Institutionalist and Keynesian labels, was nearly dismissed for his convictions by the Harvard Corporation and was targeted by an alumni group called the Veritas Foundation. A conservative watchdog group, the Foundation for Economic Education, was set up to provide a counterweight to radical economic opinion on policy issues on American campuses. It observed that President Harry Truman's Point Four Program, the predecessor of the Agency for International Development, "strikingly resembles the proposals of the official head of the communists in this country in 1944." Similar charges were made against the National Labor Relations Act, Social Security, the Tennessee Valley Authority, and the Marshall Plan (MacIver 1955, 127). Paul Samuelson's successful new introductory economics textbook was widely vilified for the dangerous Keynesian ideas it contained. A commentator in the right-wing *Educational Reviewer* asked: "Now if (1) Marx is communistic, (2) Keynes is partly Marxian, and (3) Samuelson is Keynesian, what does that make Samuelson and others like him? The answer is clear: Samuelson and the others are mostly part Marxian socialist or communist in their theories" (quoted in MacIver 1955, 128).

The most celebrated persecution of economists occurred at the University of Illinois, where Howard Bowen, later president of Grinnell College and the University of Iowa, had been brought in as dean to reinvigorate the College of Commerce and Business Administration. He attracted to the economics department a group of promising young scholars, many of whom would later become prominent in the profession, including Franco Modigliani, Everett E. Hagen, and Robert Eisner. But the dreaded heresy of "Keynesianism" was detected by the local news media and business community (assisted by some disaffected old-guard economics faculty members), and the "scandal" was widely discussed across the state. The crisis ended when Bowen and Hagen, the chair of economics, were forced to resign, followed by seven other faculty members (MacIver 1955, 132–35; Solberg and Tomilson 1997).

Probably the most widely read tract attacking economics in higher education during the 1950s was William F. Buckley Jr.'s *God and Man at Yale: The Superstitions of "Academic Freedom"* ([1951] 1986). Buckley's theme was that traditional religious and economic values (note the coupling)—values that had made the nation great—had been banished from the training grounds of the elite. In their place had been inserted secularism and collectivism. In the case of economic virtue, "If the recent Yale graduate, who exposed himself to Yale economics during his undergraduate years, exhibits enterprise, self-reliance, and independence, it is only because he has turned his back upon his teachers and texts. It is because he has not hearkened to those who assiduously disparage the individual, glorify the government, enshrine security, and discourage self-reliance" (45–46). Buckley painted a dark picture of what was happening in American higher education. In effect, he claimed, a Marxist takeover was in progress through an insidious capture of the minds of the young, using not the rhetoric of class warfare but Keynesian arguments for a welfare state:

> Marx himself, in the course of his lifetime, envisaged two broad lines of action that could be adopted to destroy the bourgeoisie; one was violent revolution; the other, a slow increase of state power, through extended social services, taxation, and regulation, to a point where a smooth transition could be effected from an individualist to a collectivist society. The communists have come to scorn the latter method, but it is nevertheless evident that the prescience of their most systematic and inspiring philosopher has not been thereby vitiated. It is a revolution of the second type, one that advocates a slow but relentless transfer of power from the individual to the state, that has roots in the Department of Economics at Yale, and unquestionably in similar departments in many colleges throughout the country. (46–47)

Buckley examined all the introductory economics textbooks used at Yale since 1946: Mary Jean Bowman and George Leland Bach's, Lorie Tarshis's, Theodore Morgan's, and, of course, Paul Samuelson's. He reported what these books said about income distribution taxation, property rights, the role of the state, and regulation of business. He did not like what he found. The replacement of "profitability" with "social good" as the criterion determining the allocation of resources was destroying the motivating force that had made America great. Buckley's mood was not improved by a review of the members of the Yale Economics Department, a majority of whom were "collectivists," just like the student newspaper, the student union, and other parts of extracurricular life. He suspected that the provost, economist Edgar S. Furniss, played a nefarious role in poisoning the minds of students across campus against self-reliance. He concluded, "Individualism is dying at Yale, and without a fight" (113).

It would be nice to presume that this drumbeat of criticism of economics in colleges and universities from the 1930s to the 1960s had no impact on the discipline, that neither the administrators nor the economists came to behave differently as a result of these external pressures. But surely this would be naive! We cannot know precisely how the discipline was influenced by these external reactions to it, but we can presume that there was some effect in the direction that the discipline actually moved. How was the impact achieved? Mainly, I suggest, through the actions of educational administrators.

Leaders of higher education during these years can perhaps be pardoned for having hesitated to appoint or promote an economist likely to bring down on the institution the wrath of several vital external constituencies: members of the governing body, legislators, donors, or alumni. So how were the administrators likely to respond? Eliminating the subject from the curriculum was not an option; the economy was too central to the American ethos for that, and the student demand was too strong. Even Buckley ([1951] 1986, 47) conceded that about one-third of the entering class at Yale in 1946 had enrolled for introductory economics. The only administrative option was to appoint economists of a different kind. But what kind? What behavioral characteristics were to be avoided? Why did certain economists so enrage the patron community? The reason was, in part, Buckley said, that so many of the offending economists seemed to reflect a collectivist ideology at variance with the individualist mainstream of America. But it was also that they chose to make professional judgments not only on controversial national issues such as compensatory fiscal policy, tariff protection, regulation of industry, and the currency but also on highly contentious local issues such as the desirability of discount stores, public housing, and the effects of advertising on the independence of the media (Lazarsfeld and Thielens 1958, 63–64). It was particularly offensive that these dissenting economists chose to express their views not just to scientific colleagues in codes that only the initiated could comprehend but also to external audiences that ran the gamut from the local Rotary Club to the U.S. Congress. It was mainly because Ayres contributed to the *New Republic*, Galbraith wrote best-selling books (and became head of the American Civil Liberties Union), and Tugwell figured prominently in the New Deal that their ideas became so troublesome to patrons of higher education. If these economists had said the same things only in the classroom or in their departmental common rooms, or had expressed them in matrix algebra, nobody would have cared. As it was, they were a burden to overstretched administrators. Yet there was another kind of economist who did speak in tongues mainly in the cloister. This neoclassical economist had all the virtues many of his "plural" brethren lacked. Therefore, when hard-pressed administrators were faced with a choice between these two types of economist, can we doubt where their better judgment would have led? The University of Illinois was only an extreme example of the doctrinal and method-ological cleansing that must have occurred rather widely across Amer-ica during this period.

Although it is not difficult to speculate with some confidence about the direction of actions taken by administrators to change the style of economics, it is more difficult to assess the impact of the patrons' dis-pleasure on the economists themselves. With this question in mind, sociologists Paul Lazarsfeld and Wagner Thielens Jr. conducted a sur-vey in 1955 designed to reveal the impact of threats to academic free-dom on scholarly activity. They discovered many instances of "harsh pressures" on social scientists, consisting of firings, the failure to pro-mote or grant tenure, interference with curriculum, and unusually close monitoring of teaching and research. They also found "gentle pres-sures" that included polite requests from administrators that econo-mists modify their behavior. "In a typical instance, a Midwestern econ-omist, to illustrate a general discussion of social class, cited fraternities and sororities as examples of social distinction. The story was carried to an official of the university, who phoned the teacher simply to 'remind' him of it, going on to say that of course the professor had the right to say whatever he wanted" (Lazarsfeld and Thielens 1958, 254).

Assessing the effects of administrative repression on the profes-sional behavior of scholars, Lazarsfeld and Thielens (1958, 257) not surprisingly found that "a teacher who had himself been the target of an incident was especially likely to be apprehensive." But how about the others? The result was not very different. Lazarsfeld and Thielens pro-duced an "index of apprehension" that shows a clear increase in appre-hension with increasing "numbers of corroborated incidents reported," even among those not directly affected (259). "Conservative" individuals were, not unexpectedly, less apprehensive than "permissive" ones, but the frequency of repressive incidents influenced apprehension all around. Happily, faculty members found that their apprehension could be relieved by administrators' "protective performance" (251–65). Lazarsfeld and Thielens did not ask the next obvious question: How might professors be expected to change their own behavior to relieve their apprehension? My speculation is that they would have forsworn interwar pluralism for postwar neoclassicism.

Government

The second most significant patron of economics during the period under review was the government. It made use of economics for at least three purposes: advice on high policy, implementation of low policy, and the generation of social externalities that warranted public subsidy. For the first two purposes, demonstrated usefulness to government agencies was the main criterion for government patronage of economics. For the third, the long-term benefits of the discipline were at issue.

The 1930s, 1940s, and 1950s witnessed brave experiments in the application of economics to high social policy. After all, three of the greatest challenges to face the nation in the twentieth century occurred in these decades: the Great Depression and two world wars—one hot and one cold. The earliest attempts to involve economists in the consideration of high policy, such as the National Resources Planning Board and Roosevelt's Brains Trust, were not successful for at least two reasons: because specific clients for advice were not identified beforehand and because too often economists were placed front and center in the policy debate, so they took the brunt of attacks from critics and the blame if things went wrong. When public anger arose against such policy innovations as the National Recovery Administration, it was easy to blame those intellectuals who never met a payroll. The lesson that staff economists should not be given a political mantle had not been completely absorbed by World War II, when Galbraith took much of the heat for price control.

A new style in the application of economics to high policy was reflected in the Council of Economic Advisers (CEA), created under the Employment Act of 1946. The successful strategy the CEA discovered in its early years was to do whatever its client, the president of the United States, wanted. The functions appreciated most by President

Truman were prosaic ones like economic forecasting, comment on proposals for new legislation, and assistance in speech writing—not activities that would have warmed the hearts of many "plural" economists in the interwar years. With the exception of Leon Keyserling, who was in many respects a throwback to the style of the 1930s, the council members from the start kept their heads down and remembered their positions as staff aides. The style perfected by the CEA of providing flexible assistance to high-policy makers also was mastered soon by economists in the Treasury, Budget Bureau, Federal Reserve, and other places where high policy was discussed. As the sophistication of communication on economic matters among these parts of government increased, it became necessary for all correspondents to have considerable technical expertise. Just as it had once been said that lawyers talked only to lawyers, now it could be said that economists talked only to economists.

Thus, by the 1950s economists had convinced many in high places in government that their discipline could be useful. But in so doing, they made a commitment to behave as respectable professionals who took their responsibilities seriously and repressed predilections for grandstanding and, in particular, temptations to address audiences other than their clients. It can be argued, as George Schultz (1974) did some years later, that the main contributions of CEA economists required no more than the level of economic literacy that could be gained from an introductory course. Nevertheless, the utility of economics had been demonstrated. The advice that was brought to high policy in this way was certainly not advanced neoclassical economics; it was simple market analysis of the Marshallian kind, with a pinch of commercial Keynesianism thrown in. But it was also not the "plural" economics of the interwar years that had enlivened the New Deal.

The usefulness of economics in the formulation and implementation of low policy and tactics was demonstrated especially forcefully during World War II. Economists in those years were faced with a variety of problems entirely new to them, and they were thrilled to discover that they could use their skills to good effect in finding solutions. Macroeconomists in the Treasury, the Budget Bureau, and the Federal Reserve concentrated on war finance and control of inflation. Full employment, temporarily at least, took care of itself. Microeconomists dealt with all aspects of war mobilization, including resource allocation, price control, incentives, and the conversion from one productive activity to another. War provided an opportunity for microeconomists to show their stuff. The utility function had become simple; the sole objective was to win the war. Optimization problems abounded, from how to maximize the production of high-octane fuel with a given feed stock to where best to locate machine guns in a bunker. Kindleberger (1991) and Galbraith (1981) both have written eloquently about the exhilaration of applying their analytic tools to the questions of where and when to drop bombs on the enemy. The conspicuous success of microeconomics in answering such questions, almost in the manner of a dentist drilling teeth as envisaged by Keynes, assured the profession a respected place in the lower reaches of government, as well as at high levels, at war's end.

The usefulness of applied microeconomics to relatively low-level policy analysis was confirmed after the war by the work of the RAND Corporation. Established in 1945, RAND was charged with continuing the contributions that the sciences, including the social sciences, had made to the government during wartime. At first the focus was exclusively on defense, but in time it was extended to health, urban affairs, and other areas. RAND made extensive contributions to the new disciplines of operations research and systems analysis, the latter of which extended the logic of neoclassical market theory to problems involving multiple variables and objectives. It was applied first to strategic bombing questions and the selection and use of air bases (Fisher and Walker, 2). From these investigations emerged contributions to game theory, dynamic programming, and sensitivity analysis to deal with uncertainty. This application of microeconomics to problems of low policy demonstrated that interaction with the government could have positive effects on the discipline. Economists who played leading roles in this research included Martin Shubik, Oskar Morgenstern, and Stephen Enke. In 1960 many RAND contributions in the security field were reported in the landmark volume by Charles J. Hitch and Roland N. McKean, *The Economics of Defense in the Nuclear Age*. It was evident that at least this patron of economics within the federal government, the defense establishment, was very pleased with its new benefice.

The final area in which patronage of economics by the government became an issue in the years after World War II was in the debate over whether the state had an obligation to support the sciences in general. Two questions were involved in the discussion. First, was economics truly a science? Second, was there persuasive evidence that economics yielded sufficient social benefits, not captured in market transactions, to justify public subsidy?

The case for the social benefits of the social sciences was based on their wartime contributions to combat performance, productive efficiency, price control, and overall mobilization (Larsen 1992, 7, 13). The question of the status of economics as a science was raised in the debate over the establishment of the National Science Foundation (NSF), proposed most eloquently by the distinguished scientific statesman Vannevar Bush in his 1945 report to President Truman, *Science, the Endless Frontier*. In the congressional hearings on Bush's report, tough questions were raised about the possibility of the inclusion of the social sciences in any new program of support (Larsen 1992, 8–9). Legislators questioned whether the social sciences were yet "mature," whether they employed the true scientific method, whether they were organized into coherent disciplines, whether they were capable of conducting both basic and applied research, whether their research topics were too controversial and "political," and whether it was possible to conceive of a coherent research program for each discipline.

The NSF was created in 1950, but the social sciences, including economics, were not included until 1956, and then against the better judgment of some natural and physical scientists. The history of the vicissitudes of the economics program at the NSF is not significant here. It is important to note, however, that the struggle for position was carried out amid a continuous barrage of questions. In a sense, the issue of whether economics should be covered by the NSF put economics on trial for over a decade; the outcome of the trial seemed to rest on the question of whether economics was really "a science." During congressional hearings in 1945, Wesley Mitchell, sensing the skepticism, responded by avoiding the question and listing the contributions of economics to national security (Klausner and Lidz 1986, 10). But it was clear that this was beside the point. Harold Hotelling suggested very shrewdly that the doubts about the legitimacy of economics were rooted less in principle than in the fears of other scientists that economics could be "a possible incubus" as these "hard" scientists sought to secure their own funding (11). The natural confusion among legislators between the terms "social science" and "socialism" complicated the matter.

A document that helps illuminate the pressures for transformation felt by economists from their governmental patron in the immediate postwar years is a report commissioned by the Social Science Research Council in 1946 and completed in 1948 by Talcott Parsons of Harvard University, a distinguished sociologist with considerable training and contacts in economics. The Parsons report was intended to do for the social sciences what Bush had done for the rest. In any event, the first draft of the Parsons document attracted so much criticism from social scientists that he was unwilling to revise it, and it was not published until 1986, after his death. Our interest in the Parsons report lies in the observations it contained about characteristics of economics that were expected to be appealing and unappealing to Congress—a new and potentially bountiful patron of economics.

Parsons did not deal in depth with any of the individual social sciences. Rather, he employed the notion of an all-inclusive social science in the style of the Department of Social Relations he had created at Harvard. Klausner and Lidz (1986, 27) report that Parsons had grave doubts about the conceptual framework used in economics; he regretted that the subject "had not freed itself of what he termed radical rationalistic positivism."

Like other lobbyists for the social sciences, Parsons reviewed the contributions the fields had made to the war effort. In the case of economics, these included participation in the creation of new agencies such as the Office of Strategic Services and the Foreign Economic Administration, as well as the strengthening of distinguished older agencies such as the Bureau of Agricultural Economics and the Treasury. But the most impressive contribution of economists to public welfare, Parsons concluded, was the application of the Keynesian theory of income determination, primarily by Simon Kuznets, to achieve wartime full employment without inflation (Klausner and Lidz 1986, 100).

Despite the fact that the purpose of his study was to persuade the federal government to become a patron of academic economic research, Parsons could not help washing some disciplinary dirty linen in public, perhaps because he presumed that it was already laid out for all to see and a good offense was the best defense. He insisted that "impressive advances on the technical scientific level" had been made in economics. But at the same time

there have been serious difficulties . . . in the integration of the several types of work that make up economic science. Perhaps three major types may be distinguished. First is economic theory itself, which has become increasingly comprehensive, refined, and technical. Yet, there has been much controversy over various problems of the mode and exactness of its empirical applicability. Second, there has been a steady growth in empirical knowledge of a quantitative statistical sort—often without direct relevance to technical theoretical problems. The monumental statistical studies of the business cycle by Wesley Mitchell and his associates are outstanding examples. Third, there have been many "institutional" studies, generally having to do with the social setting of economic processes. Most work in the field of economic history is of this character, as are a good many contemporary studies. (Klausner and Lidz 1986, 56)

It was perhaps this reminder of the interwar plurality of economics by Parsons, in something between a confession and an apology, that so exercised the economist readers of his draft. They may have agreed with Parsons that the apparent condition of scientific confusion could be a barrier to the inclusion of economics among the benefices of the new NSF, but they concluded that true confessions were not the best public relations bridge over which to pass into the promised land of public largesse. This campaign to gain identity as a "national science" was another occasion for the leaders of the discipline to recognize that they would pay a heavy price for the appearance, let alone the reality, of pluralism.

Business

The American business community in the twentieth century has paid attention to the economics discipline for three main reasons: because economics could have a substantial impact on public policies that affected it, for good or ill; because the economist's way of thinking came to play a large role in postsecondary education for business; and because applied economics was found to make a direct contribution to the actual conduct of business affairs, especially the analysis of input and output markets.

Business leaders during the early years of the twentieth century were especially attracted by the application to public policy of simple principles of microeconomics, notably cost-benefit analysis and tools of public finance. They were alarmed by the growth of a government that they perceived was ill equipped to raise revenues in the least costly fashion and plan expenditures in a coherent manner. Robert Brookings, the steel magnate, wrote to Walton Hamilton on 25 November 1927 (Brookings Institution Archives) that the objective of his philanthropy was to restore "economy and efficiency" in government, the lack of which "had assumed the proportions of an international scandal." Sound economics was understood by Brookings at that time to be essentially systematized common sense. He favored the establishment of a budget bureau that would implement principles of "economy" throughout government and ultimately help "keep our infant ship of state off the rocks." The analogy that undoubtedly guided Brookings and other early business advocates of the use of economics for public policy was the application of the physical and biological sciences to practical problems through independent institutes and schools of engineering and medicine. In their business lives, they had benefited from resort to the "hard" sciences. The 1920s saw the growth of industrial research laboratories from three hundred in 1920 to a thousand in 1927 (Tobey 1971, 7). It was only reasonable to suppose that similar good results would flow from the social sciences in the public sphere. Moreover, the same scientific method presumably should be employed in the social sciences as in other sciences. Relationships between variables should be discovered through careful collection and rigorous analysis of data. The social sciences, like the other sciences, would yield a kit of tools to be applied to social problems. Scientific rigor and detachment from the subject of study would lead to sound advice on the social problems that faced humanity. The Carnegie Institution in Washington, D.C., which Bush later came to head, was seen as a model of the kind of independent research body needed at the national level. There the hard sciences were applied to public issues in a manner analogous to the industrial laboratory at the level of the individual business firm.

The Brookings Institution was created by Robert Brookings in 1927 to perform this function with the social sciences. The first board of trustees of Brookings, setting forth instructions to the staff in "Application to the Carnegie Corporation from the Brookings Institution, December 1, 1928," regretted "the apparently inevitable tendency in academic circles to confine investigations to narrowly specialized questions, usually historical and theoretical in character" (Carnegie Corporation Archives). Evidently, for policy research, theory (meaning mere speculation) and history (meaning unstructured immersion in the details of a particular case) were perceived by the Brookings board of businesspeople to act as a siren song to the applied social scientist charged with discovering empirically based policy rules. In the 1930s many in the business community must have concluded that the depression had given the economics discipline unlimited license to follow this speculative siren's song. For the most part, the Brookings Institution held a respectable course, focused especially on individual markets and maintaining a highly critical position on many policy innovations proposed by its academic brethren. But for the business community as a whole, the economics profession at large was widely troublesome; reforms suggested to end the depression were all disagreeable. The economists called for atomized competition, some form of central planning, or some kind of redistributive mechanism, all of which seemed disrespectful of the reality of the American market economy.

Hansen's "stagnationist" version of Keynesian doctrine was a particular anathema to the business community. It implied the need not only for governmental intervention in the trough of the business cycle but also for steadily increasing public expenditures over the long run because of the closing of the economic frontier. A proposal Hansen made to the National Resources Planning Board before its demise in 1943 was portrayed as the blueprint for the dreaded American welfare state (Collins 1981, 2, 10, 13, 97). The brief business flirtation with the New Deal through participation in the National Recovery Administration did not lead to growing respect for Roosevelt's Brains Trust or other academic economists the Democrats brought into government (30, 41). After the optimism about the use of applied microeconomics in government during the 1920s, the "plural" macroeconomics of the 1930s was an unalloyed downer for the business community.

But toward the end of the decade, some members of the business elite began to recall that "other" economists were still out there, and efforts were made to develop new connections with them. Leaders in this movement were all associated with the University of Chicago: William Benton, who had retired from the advertising firm of Benton and Bowles to become vice president of the university; Beardsley Ruml, a Chicago graduate who had moved from academe to the Rockefeller philanthropies and then to the presidency of R. H. Macy in 1934; and Paul Hoffman, president of the Studebaker Corporation and a Chicago trustee. They were all anxious to bring to the attention of businesspeople the ideas of such Chicago luminaries as Frank Knight,

Henry Simons, and Paul Douglas as a corrective to the ideas of more radical economists who, it seemed, had come to speak for the profession. This ferment in Chicago contributed to the creation in 1942 of the "progressive" business group, the Committee for Economic Development (CED), which promised a respectful hearing for all ideas that were "responsible" and consistent with the free enterprise system. The Chicago connection to the CED remained close. Hoffman became the first chairman, Benton the first vice chairman, and Theodore Yntema the research director. Neil Jacoby and Theodore Schultz served on the Research Advisory Board.

The CED was determined not to be doctrinaire in responding to the questions it addressed. It declared that it recognized the value of an objective, open-minded, scientific approach to public policy. In their optimism that, if given a chance, right thinking would emerge in economics as elsewhere, its members sounded rather like the tycoons of the 1920s. Collins (1981, 85–86) writes:

> The pursuit of responsible objectivity led the Committee to embrace expertise with a fervor still new to the majority of their peers in the business world. Businessmen, the CED announced, stood "in need of the economist and social scientist, just as much as . . . the engineer and the chemist." . . . the CED would now utilize the knowledge of experts to seek ends which were acceptable to the friends of modern capitalism.

The U.S. Chamber of Commerce, the venerable representative of the business community, followed the lead of the CED in the 1940s, avowing openness to change and calling for a "new capitalism" in which a constructive role for government would be worked out. In its search for this role, the chamber, like the CED, discovered that conservative economists, such as George Terborgh, could defend the business community effectively against the likes of Hansen and against dangerous popularizers like Stuart Chase. Terborgh joined the chamber's Committee on Economic Policy in 1946 (Collins 1981, 119).

Despite their newfound openness to fresh ideas, members of the business elite were slow to come to terms with Keynes. Until well into the 1940s, this name was often linked to that of Hansen and to the specter of unconstrained deficit spending (Collins 1981, 116–23). But increasingly economists who gained the confidence of business leaders explained patiently that a "compensated economy" could in fact be very good for business and certainly much better than a depression. Terborgh told the CED that "the day has passed when government can deal with depressions simply by whistling or wringing its hands" (119). Conservatives remained skeptical, but at least now their objections were muted.

The CED moved ahead of the U.S. Chamber of Commerce in developing a version of "commercial" Keynesianism with which it could feel comfortable—one that spoke of balancing the budget over the cycle and saw more of the countercyclical adjustment on the revenue side than on the expenditure side (Collins 1981, 123, 138, 143, 144). When the Republicans took the White House in 1953, they found that they could bring into government a number of respected professional economists with whom the business community could also feel comfortable. These economists had none of the disturbing characteristics of the "plural" profession at large. Arthur Burns and Gabriel Hauge were examples (153, 154). Thus this business patron of economics also had come to see that, with respect to public policy advice, there were "good" economists as well as "bad."

Higher education for business began after World War I as a set of practical courses in business affairs. Between the wars it had low prestige and little appeal to students or business leaders, and its prognosis was poor. There seemed, however, to be a parallel to professional education for other fields, especially engineering and medicine. In both of these other areas, rigor and dignity were given to professional training by basing the curriculum on science—physical in the first case and biological in the second. Much of the reform of professional education in all fields was stimulated by Abraham Flexner's 1910 report on medical education.

Enlightened professional practice, Flexner insisted, must emerge from broad general principles thoroughly tested in the laboratory. This lesson was not lost on business educators (Schlossman et al. 1994, 16). But the question remained: What was the science upon which business should be based? Was it economics? For some time, the answer seemed to be an emphatic no. Courses taught by economics departments for the young business schools made few concessions to the new clientele and were poorly integrated with classes in business practice. Certainly, for a long time economic reasoning was not privileged above other approaches to business studies, especially at Harvard, where the case method encouraged diversity (19, 23, 52, 62). Dean Hotchkiss of Stanford said in 1926: "Taking the situation as we find it . . . however much we may call economics the science of business . . . there is in American universities no science of economics which can be regarded as basic for business in the sense in which doubtless biology and chemistry are basic for medicine" (quoted in Schlossman et al. 1994, 68). Stanford, like Harvard, retained a varied and eclectic curriculum right up to World War II.

The question of whether business education would follow much of the rest of professional education in seeking grounding in "science" was not answered until after World War II, when many social science faculty members returned from wartime service exhilarated by the discovery that their disciplines really did have practical utility (Schlossman et al. 1994, 9). A powerful force in the reform of business education that ensued was the Ford Foundation, which granted a total of $28 million to a set of elite schools committed to change. Ford saw itself as doing for training in business administration what Carnegie had done for training in medicine — introducing scientific rigor. A core science of business was sought, and microeconomics, the science of product and input markets, seemed a good place to begin. Whereas before the war the business community had been largely indifferent to specialized education for business, and to economics in particular, after the war a new "enlightened" business elite emerged with an awareness of major technical challenges and global opportunities ahead. They joined with the universities in planning "scientific" business education, especially at the graduate level. In part, a cold war rationale lay behind this new movement: "Varied environmental factors led postwar business and government leaders to view the reform of business education as a matter of national preparedness. Americans needed a new type of business executive — one who was literate in the everyday details of conducting business, to be sure, but who was also trained to manage individual firms (and the economy as a whole) with minimal disruption and instability through a period of rapid and unpredictable change" (92). The emphasis in the new business education was to be on problem solving and mastery of analytic technique rather than on exposure to fact and experience. Initially, at least, there was little confidence that a simple transfer of the economist's tools would accomplish this objective: "At the level of economic generalization, existing theories (both neoclassical and Keynesian) seemed inadequate for the deducing of professionally useful knowledge by a new breed of business manager. To modernize, business educators would have to generate more robust theory and more up-to-date codification of practice, integrating both into the training of future managers" (93). This being the case, there seemed few alternatives to pressing for a richer and more realistic applied neoclassical microeconomics. These modern business leaders would likely find little appeal in the "plural" economics literature of the time, much of it heavily institutional with normative (critical) qualities that were not welcome in the new business education.

The extent to which applied microeconomics quickly changed business education varied widely among the major business schools. Progress was probably slowest at Harvard, where the case method constrained generalization. It was perhaps fastest at Carnegie Mellon University, where the Economics Department chair, George Leland Bach, cooperated closely with the business educators (Schlossman et al. 1994, 114–15). Bach explained in 1951 the contributions the economist could make to the businessperson's tool kit:

> Management today is in many respects where engineering was a century ago—a field of many intelligent practitioners operating largely by tradition and cumulative experience, but with little clear-cut structure or principles. Many fine bridges and machines were constructed a century ago, yet the enormous advantages from modern basic science and highly skilled engineering are obvious. The parallel may be suggestive. (quoted in Schlossman et al. 1994, 121)

Two social scientists, William W. Cooper and Herbert Simon, became the dominant intellectual leaders of the Carnegie Mellon Graduate School of Industrial Administration. Simon reflected on the experience in his autobiography:

> We were social scientists who had discovered in one way or another that organizational and business environments provide a fertile source of basic research ideas, and who therefore did not regard "basic" and "applied" in antithetical terms. Accurately or not, we perceived American business education at that time as a wasteland of vocationalism that needed to be transformed into science-based professionalism, as medicine and engineering had been transformed a generation or two earlier. . . . The postwar flowering of management science and of the behavioral approach to organization theory provided the substance of applied science we needed. (quoted in Schlossman et al. 1994, 118–19)

The American business community could only be grateful to Simon and others like him in business schools who grounded their training in serious "market science" and thereby gave the business community a new dignity and repute among the professions.

Foundations

Attitudes toward economics within American foundations have reflected all the attitudes observed in the other three communities we have examined thus far, because people with authority in foundations typically had deep roots in higher education, government, business, or some combination of these. A distinctive feature of the foundation attitudes, however, is that they were often more self-conscious. In foundations, it was necessary to address directly the question of what economics was all about, because economists were asking for support. Foundations have seldom offered funds to economics or to any other discipline because of the discipline's inherent worth. Economics has to be seen as useful for the achievement of some larger social purpose, like the alleviation of poverty, maintenance of full employment, or protection of the environment. When an appropriate program goal has been identified, it must be demonstrated that economics can be useful; only then can questions of style be addressed. How should funds be provided, and how should the economist recipients be expected to comport themselves (Grossman 1982; Sutton 1985)?

In the years between the wars, few large foundations had been established, and among them only four provided substantial support for economics: the Carnegie philanthropies, the Rockefeller philanthropies, the Sloan Foundation, and the Russell Sage Foundation. The earliest foundation support for economics came through the appointment of economics researchers directly to foundation staffs. The potentially controversial nature of economic research was discovered quickly by the Rockefeller Foundation in 1914, when it appointed William Lyon Mackenzie King, the Canadian minister of labor and future prime minister, to conduct a study of industrial relations at a time when the Rockefeller interests were themselves engaged in intense labor strife (Grossman 1982, 69). At about the same time, the Carnegie Endowment for International Peace appointed John Bates Clark to become head of one of its divisions charged with finding ways to achieve world peace through economic research. World War I put a stop to this effort, and again a foundation was embarrassed by too close an involvement with its grantee.

A more satisfactory method of dispensing foundation patronage to economics was developed during the 1920s by the Laura Spelman Rockefeller Memorial Foundation, named after John D. Rockefeller Sr.'s deceased wife and later absorbed into the Rockefeller Foundation. Beardsley Ruml, with a Ph.D. in psychology from the University of Chicago, was appointed director in 1922 and began an ambitious program of grants to such corporate entities as the Brookings Institution, the Social Science Research Council, and the National Bureau of Economic Research. In this way, Ruml distanced himself nicely from his grantees. Ruml favored an imaginative interdisciplinary approach to large social problems. For this he was criticized regularly by Abraham Flexner, then the powerful secretary of another Rockefeller philanthropy, the General Education Board. In a 26 January 1924 letter to Ruml (Laura Spelman Rockefeller Memorial Foundation, Series 3, Box 49, Rockefeller Foundation Archives) commenting on grants by Ruml to predecessor bodies of the Brookings Institution, Flexner said he far preferred the "objective basis" of one of these bodies to "the more disputaceous [sic] approach of the other." One can hear echoes of Flexner's earlier reports on medical education in his recommendations for support of the social sciences. He wanted applied social scientists to be, as it were, physicians to the bodies social, economic, and politic. They should receive sound training in the appropriate sciences and then interpret these sciences fairly for the patient's ills. Applied scientists must act as detached and dignified liaisons between patient and pure scientist. They must not be protagonists for particular approaches or schools, nor should they engage in unseemly public controversy. He suggested that the Brookings Institution become a veritable medical center for the nation, with specialized services to which government and the wider public might turn for advice and therapy. The Brookings staff, just like medical researchers, must gather the facts and arrive at a recommended therapy through open-minded application of the best scientific theory to those facts. Flexner feared that any prior commitment of social scientists to doctrines or policies might affect their selection of facts and their application of theory. Flexner clearly subscribed to the Progressive doctrine of the time that science promised salvation for society, the economy, and democracy (Tobey 1971, 169–75). But it must, he insisted, be real science, not pseudoscience. He seems to have agreed with Robert Millikan, a leader in natural science and a founder of the California Institute of Technology, that the social sciences were still in a relatively primitive state. Millikan favored use of a scientific jury system in economics to enforce agreement on theory (195, 196).

Ruml responded to Flexner that too much scientific detachment could be a barrier to understanding in the social sciences. "He advocated practical, first-hand experience, as a necessary part of the study of the social sciences" (Bulmer and Bulmer 1981, 356). It seems clear that Ruml, unlike Flexner, conceived of the social sciences as fundamentally different from the natural and physical sciences. He saw involvement of social scientists in the policy process, and indeed commitment to a policy agenda or even a vision of needed social change, as natural to the social sciences and as essential to their advancement as well as to their usefulness. Perhaps he also recognized that continuing financial support may well come to a crusader but not to the dispenser of dispassionate advice. This fundamental difference in the conception of the social sciences between Flexner and Ruml would be reflected in foundation attitudes toward funding of economics from then on. Ruml left the philanthropic world in 1929, and the views that prevailed thereafter were much closer to those of Flexner.

As with the other patrons of economics, we must ask whether foundations translated these evolving views toward the discipline into actions designed to change economists' behavior. In this case it seems certain that they were. Since the patronage was specific, the device to effect influence was simple: Projects that involved the participation of "good" economists were supported, those with "bad" economists were declined. One example may illustrate the point. In 1950 Redvers Opie, a British academic on the staff of the International Studies Group of the Brookings Institution, addressed a New York City audience concerning a Brookings plan for a study of European recovery. He suggested that, considering the success of European rehabilitation, additional generous assistance from the United States to less developed nations might be in order. Indeed, Brookings should now explore the opportunity. Despite the seeming innocence of this comment, his recommendation caused a great flutter among the businesspeople present and prompted a complaint to Harold Moulton, the president of Brookings, by John Pratt of Standard Oil. In addition, Alfred P. Sloan Jr., a longtime patron of the institution through his foundation, wrote to Moulton on 3 August 1950 (Moulton Papers, Brookings Institution Archives): "One wonders whether the United States can continue indefinitely to support the world and hand out its productivity, in one form or another, all over the place, and in constantly increasing amounts." Moulton suggested in his reply to Sloan on 7 August 1950 that the reactions to Opie's remarks had made him rethink the proposed study: "As I told John Pratt, I do however have some doubt about the possible usefulness of this study in view of rapidly changing conditions. . . . My thought at the moment is that we perhaps ought to make no decision prior to the outcome of the Korean affair." The study was not carried out, and Opie left Brookings soon thereafter.

The most generous patronage of economics by any foundation was provided by the Ford Foundation soon after World War II (Leonard 1991). Between 1953 and 1968, the foundation granted a total of $95 million to individuals and institutions associated with the discipline. Infused with vast new wealth from the estates of Henry and Edsel Ford, the foundation was looking for new problems to conquer, and economics offered opportunities. The report of the Study Committee on Policy and Program in 1949 charted the course for the enlarged foundation and speculated on how improvements in the American economy might help "advance human welfare," the foundation's stated objective. Much of the terminology in the report seemed borrowed from recent government documents, such as the Employment Act of 1946, the various reports of the Temporary National Economic Committee, and the charge to the soon-to-be-appointed President's Materials Policy Commission (the Paley Commission). The Study Committee shared the optimism of governmental patrons of economics at the time that wise policies by competent economists could strengthen "the private enterprise system" and increase "economic stability," "growth in output," employment, and conservation of resources. The committee was concerned about and directed the attention of economists to industrial concentrations, excessive governmental regulation, and "labor-management strife" (quoted in Leonard 1991, 85). The report also seemed to reflect the views of the advocates of the social sciences in the debates over the creation of the National Science Foundation. Economists, it insisted, must unfailingly employ the true scientific method and must give the subject a new discipline. They must reexamine "basic theories" and "subject them to the acid test of verification." They must reject "convenient but unrealistic abstractions." They called, in effect, for the rejection of eclectic pluralism in favor of a consensual neoclassical mainstream. Clearly, political values as well as methodological judgments lay behind the Ford Foundation's enthusiasm for economics. Rowan Gaither, author of the Study Committee report, in a memorandum to the first president of the expanded foundation, Paul Hoffman, explained that one of the main reasons the foundation should concentrate on economics was the unfolding cold war, in which the "fundamental elements of the ideological appeal and international propaganda attack of communism are economic" (quoted in Leonard 1991, 87). In a propaganda war, it was especially important that the weapons in the arsenal of noncommunist nations not fail because of confusion or complexity.

The most distinctive feature of the Ford Foundation's Economic Development and Administration program, as it came to be called, was its dependence on respected mainline figures in the discipline to design and implement the activities. Close advisers to the foundation included Robert Calkins, president of the Brookings Institution; Bach of Carnegie Mellon University; and Lloyd Reynolds of Yale. In 1955 Reynolds took leave from Yale to become program director; two years later he was succeeded by Neil Chamberlain. The economist advisers to the foundation took the position that there were economic problems aplenty in the land; economists were demonstrated problem solvers; and, therefore, if resources were bestowed on them, solutions to the problems could confidently be expected. That those outside the mainstream of the discipline were unlikely to be given access to the cornucopia of largesse was evident in the remarks of Galbraith, who, when asked to review the plans, said that he was "far from impressed" and thought there might be "a serious waste of money" (quoted in Leonard 1991, 96).

Conclusion

What are we to make of this account of the attitudes of the four principal patrons of economics over the three decades that witnessed the transformation from interwar pluralism to postwar neoclassicism? It is clear that all the patrons saw value in economics, but they also perceived problems. Moreover, they all saw "good guys" who generated the benefits of economics and "bad guys" who created the problems. For those with authority in higher education, the paradox of economics was especially poignant. On the positive side, the discipline sought to explain the market economy at the center of the American value system. Moreover, economics filled a large demand for instruction from insistent students and their parents. On the negative side, economics seemed to be the home of many troublemakers who were lightning rods for attacks on the institutions of higher education by powerful external constituencies.

Government, the second patron, began its association with economics in the 1930s on a distinctly unpromising note. Economists seemed unable or unwilling to deliver the services required of them in a suitably modest and respectful manner. World War II more than anything else taught economists how to be useful in government by advising high-policy makers and assisting middle-level policy implementers. By the 1950s economics had gained a secure position throughout the federal bureaucracy and had even managed to slip its nose under the luxurious tent of the new National Science Foundation.

Business leaders were profoundly alarmed by many of the plural economists' activities in the 1930s, especially those associated with the New Deal and the "American Keynesianism" of Hansen. But like government, business discovered during and after World War II that sober mainstream economists could be effective allies in securing sensible public policies that would respect and strengthen the free enterprise system. Moreover, "sound" economics offered hope for a strong professional business education increasingly perceived as necessary for those who would direct America's developing role on the world stage.

Finally, foundations, after a brief flirtation with the eclectic social science led by Ruml of the Laura Spelman Rockefeller Memorial Foundation, accepted the injunction of Flexner to support only rigorous economic science (as opposed to institutional studies or mere speculation) in the expectation that applications to important social problems would follow.

How, then, can we connect these attitudes of the patrons of economics to movement within the discipline? One way may be through Toulmin's (1972) evolutionary model of scientific progress, in which intellectual disciplines evolve through two processes. Conceptual variation, the process that most attracts the attention of historians of economics, occurs when new ideas are generated by scientific innovators. But then a second process, intellectual selection, occurs when some of the variations survive but others do not. It is in the latter process that the patrons of economics play a part. Although we have not established a tight causal connection between the actions of patrons and the responses of their benefice, we have demonstrated that the environment in the United States over these three decades was much more congenial to the selection of postwar neoclassicism than to the selection of interwar pluralism. And it was the selection of the former that actually took place.

References

Barber, William J., ed. 1988. *Breaking the Academic Mould: Economists and American Higher Learning in the Nineteenth Century*. Middletown, Conn.: Wesleyan University Press.

Breit, William, and William Patton Culbertson Jr. 1976. *Science and Ceremony: The Institutional Economics of C. E. Ayres*. Austin: University of Texas Press.

Brookings Institution Archives, Washington, D.C.

Buckley, William F., Jr. [1951] 1986. *God and Man at Yale: The Superstitions of "Academic Freedom."* Washington, D.C.: Regnery Gateway.

Bulmer, Martin, and Joan Bulmer. 1981. Philanthropy and Social Science in the 1920's: Beardsley Ruml and the Laura Spelman Rockefeller Memorial, 1922–29. *Minerva* 14.3:347–407.

Carnegie Corporation Archives, New York, N.Y.

Collins, Robert M. 1981. *The Business Response to Keynes, 1929–1964*. New York: Columbia University Press.

Fisher, Gene H. and Warren E. Walker. 1994. *Operations Research and the RAND Corporation*. Santa Monica, Calif.: RAND.

Flexner, Abraham. 1910. *Medical Education in the United States and Canada: A Report to the Carnegie Foundation for the Advancement of Teaching*. New York: Carnegie Foundation for the Advancement of Teaching.

Galbraith, John Kenneth. 1981. *A Life in Our Times: Memoirs*. Boston: Houghton Mifflin.

Grossman, David M. 1982. American Foundations and the Support of Economic Research, 1913–1929. *Minerva* 20.1–2:59–82.

Hofstadter, Richard, and Walter P. Metzger. 1955. *The Development of Academic Freedom in the United States*. New York: Columbia University Press.

Kindleberger, Charles P. 1991. *The Life of an Economist*. Cambridge, Mass.: Basil Blackwell.

Klausner, Samuel Z., and Victor M. Lidz. 1986. *The Nationalization of the Social Sciences*. Philadelphia: University of Pennsylvania Press.

Larsen, Otto N. 1992. *Milestones and Millstones: Social Science at the National Science Foundation, 1945–1991*. New Brunswick, N.J.: Transaction.

Lazarsfeld, Paul F., and Wagner Thielens Jr. 1958. *The Academic Mind: Social Scientists in a Time of Crisis*. Glencoe, Ill.: Free Press.

Leonard, Robert. 1991. To Advance Human Welfare!: Economics and the Ford

Foundation, 1950–1968. In Essays in the History of Economic Thought: Theory and Institutions in the Mid–Twentieth Century. Ph.D. diss., Duke University.

MacIver, Robert M. 1955. *Academic Freedom in Our Time.* New York: Columbia University Press.

Metzger, Walter P., et al. 1969. *Dimensions of Academic Freedom.* Urbana: University of Illinois Press.

Rockefeller Foundation Archives, Pocantico Hills, N.Y.

Schlossman, Steven, et al. 1994. *The Beginnings of Graduate Management Education in the United States.* Santa Monica, Calif.: Graduate Management Admission Council.

Schultz, George P. 1974. Reflections on Political Economy. *Challenge* (March–April): 6–11.

Solberg, Winton U., and Robert W. Tomilson. 1997. Academic McCarthyism and Keynesian Economics: The Bowen Controversy at the University of Illinois. *HOPE* 29.1:55–81.

Sutton, Francis. 1985. American Foundations and the Social Sciences. *Items* 34.4:57–64.

Tobey, Ronald C. 1971. *The American Ideology of National Science, 1919–1930.* Pittsburgh: University of Pittsburgh Press.

Toulmin, Stephen. 1972. *Human Understanding.* Princeton, N.J.: Princeton University Press.

Part 2

To Be an Economist

The Transformation of U.S. Economics, 1920–1960, Viewed through a Survey of Journal Articles

Roger E. Backhouse

The Transformation of U.S. Economics

In the 1920s and 1930s, U.S. economics was pluralistic in the sense that no one approach dominated the profession. Classical economists (Frank Taussig at Harvard) and institutionalists (John Commons at Wisconsin and Wesley Clair Mitchell and John Maurice Clark at Columbia) flourished alongside neoclassical economists (Irving Fisher at Yale) and Marshallians (Edward Chamberlin at Harvard). Some individuals defied classification (Frank Knight at Iowa and then at Chicago). By 1960, all this had changed, and neoclassical economics, or at least the neoclassical synthesis of Paul Samuelson's textbook, was unquestionably dominant. Heterodox approaches still existed, but they were clearly in a subordinate position. This transition involves several stories:

1. the rise of econometrics (understood in its original sense of encompassing mathematical economics as well as the use of statistical techniques) after the establishment of the Econometric Society in 1930, followed by what has been described as the mathematization or formalization of the subject
2. the Keynesian revolution and the generational shift involved (see Moggridge 1995)

I owe much to participants in the 1997 *HOPE* conference and to others whose comments have been an enormous help in this essay. In particular, I wish to thank Nahid Aslanbeigui, Jeff Biddle, Mary Morgan, and Denis O'Brien.

3. the demise of institutionalism (see Biddle, this volume)
4. the impact of immigrants from Eastern Europe, especially from Austria (Joseph Schumpeter and Jacob Marschak) (see Mongiovi 1997)

Telling such stories, important as they are, always involves the danger of focusing only on a small number of individuals thought to have been the key figures. The problem with this approach is that by choosing to examine only those individuals known to be important, we bias the evidence. To avoid this danger, such detailed stories need to be supplemented by a broader, more comprehensive picture of U.S. economics.

Such a picture is provided in this essay through an analysis of articles published in the major general journals in the United States from 1920 to 1960. The construction and content of the article database are described in the next section, after which conclusions are drawn concerning the content of the journal articles, the range of contributors, and the role of different institutions. The result is a statistical portrait of U.S. economics that provides evidence concerning some of the stories about the discipline's transformation during this period.

The Database

Given the practical impossibility of constructing a database of all economists active in the United States during this period, it was necessary to analyze a sample. The method followed in this essay was to construct a sample of economists who published in three leading journals from 1920 to 1960: the *American Economic Review* (*AER*), the *Journal of Political Economy* (*JPE*), and the *Quarterly Journal of Economics* (*QJE*). What the economists published, who they were, and where they came from were analyzed. These three journals were selected because they were the major general journals published throughout the period. The *AER* was the official journal of the American Economic Association (AEA), and the *JPE* and the *QJE* emanated from the economics departments at Chicago and Harvard, respectively.

Although these were arguably the leading U.S. journals throughout the period, it is important to note that their place in the profession has changed substantially in a number of ways. First, journal articles, especially articles in these journals, now have much greater prestige compared with other types of publication than during the period being studied. They play a greater, more formal role in academics' promotion procedures than they played in 1920. Thus in the 1920s, the editor of the *AER* sometimes worried about having sufficient high-quality material, a situation inconceivable today. Second, there has been a major change in the journals competing with these general journals. In the 1920s, economists frequently published in journals such as the *Annals of the American Academy* that did not confine their attention to economics. In the 1930s, specialized outlets for more technical (but not necessarily mathematical) economics appeared, such as the *Review of Economic Studies* (1933) and *Econometrica* (1933), and much statistical and mathematical economics was published in the *Review of Economics and Statistics* (1919). After 1960, in contrast, there was a proliferation of specialist journals that focused on specific areas of economics. Economists expected to find important contributions to the subject in economics journals, not in general journals or in books.

A database of articles in these three journals was constructed and analyzed statistically. Because of time constraints, two samples were used: every fifth volume of all three journals and every volume of the *AER*. The latter sample served as a check on possible sampling error in the former and provided a larger sample when the *JPE* and *QJE* could not be used because of their close links to their respective departments. For each volume in the sample, the following information was collected.

1. All articles published were listed, excluding those labeled as notes, memoranda, or AEA proceedings. AEA supplements were also excluded. For each article, the database contains author(s), affiliation(s), and title.[1]
2. Articles were classified according to type: empirical, theory, theory-empirical, economic history, or other.[2]
3. Articles were classified according to the mathematical techniques used: algebra, diagrams, calculus, tables of statistics, or regression analysis (including some diagnostic statistics). All these involved a simple yes/no classification.

1. Information in the database that is not analyzed in this essay, such as page numbers, is not listed.

2. Other includes history of economic thought, obituaries, methodology, and articles that defied classification, such as AEA presidential addresses reflecting on the state of the discipline.

4. For each author, information was collected, when possible, on date and country of birth and on date and institution of first degree, master's degree, and doctorate. The main source of information was AEA membership directories (1938, 1942, 1948, 1964), but not all contributors were listed in these. In addition, the 1938 and 1942 directories contain no information on date and country of birth, so this information is incomplete for the beginning of the sample period. The AEA directories were supplemented with information from other sources such as Blaug 1986 and the *Dictionary of National Biography*.[3]

Content of Journal Articles

Theoretical and Applied Economics

The balance between theory and applied work in economics journals has been discussed extensively (e.g., Leontief [1971] 1977, 1982; Figlio 1993), often in the context of arguing that insufficient attention is paid to applied work. Referring to the *AER* around the beginning of the period, Coats ([1969] 1993, 268) wrote that many of the volumes now seem "dull and heavy," for "many of the articles were concerned with current problems and descriptive materials now of interest only to historians of the period." Titles typical of articles in 1920 include "The Past Decade of Foreign Commerce of the United States," "The Regulation of Rentals during the War Period," and "Railroad Valuation by the Interstate Commerce Commission." By 1960, applied economics of this nature did not find its way into these journals. Thus the main feature of the transformation of economics during this period was not so much that there had been a shift from applied economics to theory but that the nature of the applied work had changed dramatically.

Little attention, however, has been paid to the conceptual problem of how to distinguish theory and applied articles.[4] The main reason no

---

3. Information on German émigrés is taken from Hagemann and Krohn 1991. No analysis of articles by émigrés from German-speaking countries is provided because the numbers are too small. When the database includes all articles, and not just a five-year sample, analysis of such articles may be possible. No attempt has been made to analyze émigrés from other parts of Europe because of the lack of information about economists' origins. Place of birth was not included in several of the AEA directories, and there is no equivalent of the Hagemann and Krohn study for other regions.

4. A partial exception is Leontief (1982), who classifies applied articles according to the type of data they use.

doubt is that in examining recent articles, it is not a very difficult problem: Both theoretical and applied studies are conducted using formal
techniques that can readily be identified. This, however, was emphatically not the case in the 1920s and 1930s, when most theorizing was
very informal and applied work was predominantly nonquantitative.

Setting aside articles in the (largely self-explanatory) categories of
history of economic thought, economic history, obituaries, and so on,
articles in the sample were classified as theory, empirical, or theory-
empirical.[5]

1. *Theory* articles deal with general principles or generalizations.
   Thus an article on the behavior of firms under conditions of
   monopolistic competition would be classified as theory.
2. *Empirical* articles deal with specific cases. An article on the hog
   market in Chicago in the 1930s would be classified as empirical
   (unless it fell into the following category).
3. In *theory-empirical* articles, theory is developed independently of
   the empirical work in the article. The article might be divided into
   separate sections for theory and empirical work. Alternatively, it
   might involve the development of a formal theoretical model,
   clearly based on abstract assumptions, prior to the consideration
   of specific cases. Thus an article that derives a theory of monopolistic competition, based on general assumptions about market
   structure, and then applies it to a specific sector of U.S. industry
   would be classified as theory-empirical.

Today such distinctions seem clear-cut, but they proved very difficult
to apply to many articles in the sample, especially those from the 1920s
and 1930s. The most obvious reason for this difficulty is that economists simply do not confine their arguments to either theory or empirical work but mix the two. Empirical work clearly presumes theory,
and empirical articles frequently contain material, such as definitions of
concepts or summaries of theoretical arguments, that is clearly theory.

---

5. Categories such as survey or review were used when articles did not fit into one of the
other categories (though in some graphs these are aggregated as Other). If surveys or reviews
involved material that was identifiable as theory or empirical, they were classified accordingly. The distinction between applied economics and economic history is in principle
blurred, but classification posed few problems in practice. Articles on more recent topics (such
as the articles whose titles were mentioned previously) were classified as applied economics,
while articles such as "The London Corn Market at the Beginning of the Nineteenth Century"
were classified as economic history.

Similarly, theoretical work is often illustrated with examples that should be classified as empirical. However, although it is hard to provide a mechanical rule to distinguish an illustration from an application of a theory, these problems are not fundamental. Clues were found in titles and elsewhere in the text, and in most cases the answer was fairly clear. The mixing of theoretical and empirical content was not the major problem.

A much deeper reason for the difficulty in making these distinctions is that they are derived from contemporary economics and are being applied to a period in which economic inquiries were conducted very differently from the way inquiries are conducted today. Modern economics (at least as represented in the journals here) has a highly structured view of how economic research should be undertaken. Theory starts with highly abstract, general assumptions about behavior (typically individual optimizing behavior) and constraints (technology, market structure, strategic interaction) and uses formal mathematical techniques to derive conclusions. These conclusions are then confronted with empirical evidence (frequently statistical), often using formal econometric techniques. The distinction between theory and evidence is very clear-cut. In the 1920s and 1930s, on the other hand, economists were not working within such a structured methodological framework. The categories of theory and empirical are hard to apply because they simply do not fit.

The use of the theory-empirical category illustrates a further methodological point: Articles are classified differently for different purposes. If the aim is to assess the claim that economists are doing too much abstract theorizing without paying sufficient attention to applied problems, theory-empirical articles should be classified as empirical. Indeed, in modern economics, these two categories are to a great extent indistinguishable, for it is standard practice to approach an applied problem by formulating a model and then testing it against statistical data. However, if the aim is to trace the rise of formal techniques, theory-empirical articles should either be considered separately or be grouped with theory articles.

The main trends, based on the sample of all three journals, are shown in figure 1. There has been a progressive decline in the proportion of atheoretical empirical articles (including economic history), from over 50 percent in 1920 to under 30 percent in 1960. There has

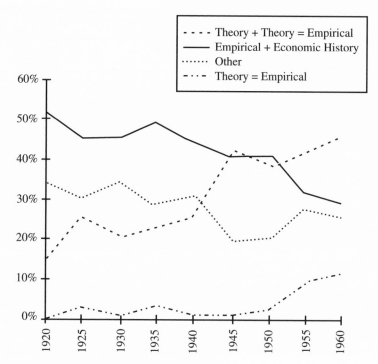

Figure 1 Theory and Empirical Articles

been a corresponding rise in the proportion of articles that either are theoretical or employ formal theory, from around 15 percent in 1920 to around 45 percent in 1960. Formal theory has, as one would expect, become more important. Equally important, however, is a substantial change, which is not quantified, in the style of writing economics articles. An economist writing in the 1920s typically constructed logical arguments that were thought to correspond closely to specific circumstances. Although these arguments were in a sense theoretical, they were not separated from empirical discussions. Thus the changes shown in figure 1 should not be interpreted to mean that theory displaced pure empirical work but should be seen as reflecting the rise of a different style of argumentation in which theoretical work can be distinguished from empirical work. The categories of modern economics, difficult to apply in the 1920s, became progressively more applicable.

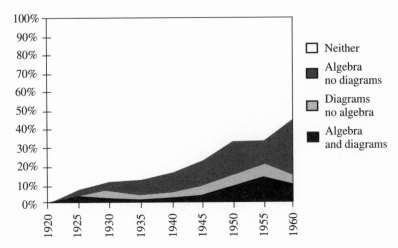

Figure 2 Use of Mathematics

The Use of Mathematics

An important aspect of this process was the increasing use of mathematics in economics, as shown in figure 2. Although mathematics is, in principle, difficult to define, the categories used here were unambiguous. The number of articles using some type of mathematics rose from zero in 1920 to 40 percent in 1960. Figure 2, however, understates the rise in the use of mathematics in an important sense, for the main use of mathematics during this period is in developing theoretical arguments. Mathematics, other than statistical analysis, is rarely used in empirical work. As figure 3 shows, the proportion of theoretical articles that used algebra rose much more rapidly, reaching nearly 80 percent by 1960. Figure 3 also confirms the commonly held view that in the 1920s and early 1930s, the *AER* was noticeably less mathematical than the *QJE* or the *JPE*. Whereas mathematics became established in the *QJE* and the *JPE* in the 1920s, it was not until the 1930s that this happened with the *AER*. There was a clear convergence by the mid-1950s, however, when a very similar proportion of theoretical articles in all three journals used algebra.[6]

6. Although it may be caused by a sampling error, it is interesting to note that the proportion of articles using diagrams reached a peak in 1955 and then declined. Between 1955 and 1960, the proportion of articles using algebra but no diagrams rose dramatically from 12 percent to 32 percent.

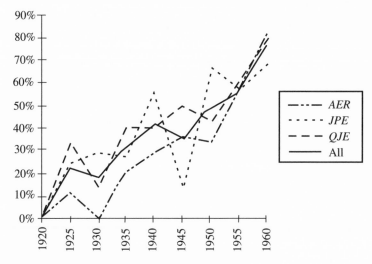

Figure 3 Use of Algebra in Theory Articles

Empirical Techniques

Econometrics is commonly viewed as beginning in the 1920s and 1930s with the work of Henry Schultz and Holbrook Working. The survey reveals, however, that these individuals contributed a large proportion of the work from 1920 to 1960 that could be classified as econometric. Table 1 shows the total number of articles using regression analysis (defined as involving diagnostic statistics) or descriptive statistics that went beyond sums, averages, differences, and the like (e.g., standard deviations, analysis of variance). The numbers are very low indeed.

An indication that this sample may understate the appearance of econometrics as the term is now understood is provided in figure 4, which shows the proportion of empirical articles in the *AER* that used regression analysis. The years in the sample of all journals happen to be years in which the AEA published unusually few articles using regression analysis. Figure 4, however, confirms the overall picture that regression analysis began to become established as a tool for empirical research in the 1950s. Far more common was the use of tables of statistics or graphs. The proportion of articles that used graphs or tables

Table 1 Articles Using Econometrics, 1920–60

Year	AER	JPE	QJE
1920			
1925		1	1
1930	1	2	
1935		1	
1940		1	1
1945	1		2
1950			
1955	1	2	
1960	2	4	

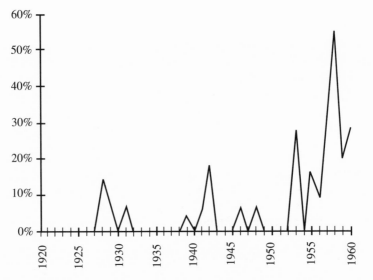

Figure 4 Use of Regression Analysis in Empirical Articles in the *AER*

Note: Empirical is defined as including economic history.

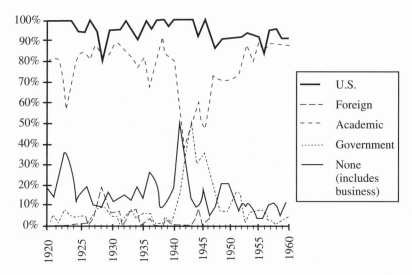

Figure 5 Classification of *AER* Authors by Type of Affiliation

rose from around 50 percent in the 1920s to over 60 percent in 1955–60.

Authors of Journal Articles

Nationality and Affiliation

Information on the authors of the articles in the study is limited but nonetheless revealing. Figure 5 classifies *AER* authors by type of affiliation.[7] Affiliations given in the journal are classified by country and by type of institution. The most important categories are academic (universities and research institutes) and government.[8] The category labeled "none" includes articles for which no affiliation was given and a very small number that gave the name of a business. The figure shows that articles in the *AER* were overwhelmingly written by economists based in academic institutions in the United States. The contrast with the two leading British journals examined in Backhouse 1997, which

7. The *AER* alone is used in order to have an annual sample. This is important in order to capture the effects of wartime, which are missed in the five-year sample.

8. International organizations, such as the International Monetary Fund, are here classified as government.

contained significant numbers of articles by economists based outside Britain, is marked. There was a very brief increase in the number of foreign-based contributors to the *AER* in the late 1920s and another increase to around 10 percent in the late 1940s and 1950s. Equally significant is the declining trend in the number of contributors for whom no affiliation was provided (most of whom were presumably nonacademic or retired).

The main event underlying figure 5 is clearly the Second World War. Large numbers of academic economists entered government service during the 1940s, then returned to academia after the war was over. Although there were exceptions, such as an article in 1943 on the kinked oligopoly demand curve by Clarence Efroymson at the War Production Board, virtually all articles were on applied topics relevant to the institution where the economist worked. Thus economists at the Office of Price Administration wrote on price controls and the inflationary gap, and economists at the Treasury, the Bureau of the Budget, and the Federal Reserve System wrote on taxation, government debt, and monetary policy. One of the theoretical contributions was Evesey Domar's " 'Burden of the Debt' and the National Income" (1944), published while Domar was at the Federal Reserve System. In 1944–45 some articles attempted to forecast postwar national income.

Although virtually all contributors were based in U.S. institutions, a large proportion were born abroad. Figure 6 classifies *AER* authors not by country of affiliation but by country of birth.[9] This figure shows a remarkably clear pattern. A wave of immigration in the 1920s was reversed by the early 1930s, followed by a dramatic decline in the proportion of U.S.-born contributors to around 50 percent by the end of the 1940s. By the 1950s the proportion had stabilized at around 70 percent.[10] This supports the conventional view that the 1920s saw an influx of émigrés from Russia and Eastern Europe, and the 1930s saw migration in response to the rise of Adolf Hitler in Germany. Although this influx is well known, figure 6 shows that it has a very significant impact on the flow of articles being published that was not confined to a small number of prominent individuals but extended much more widely.

9. Because of limited data, this is a smaller sample.

10. Because of the small number of contributors whose nationality is known (partly because there were fewer articles) at the beginning of the period, care must be taken in attaching significance to data for individual years. Thus the 50 percent figure for 1920 should be ignored because it is probably the result of inadequate data.

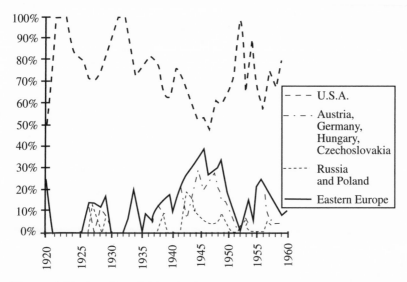

Figure 6 Nationality of *AER* Authors

Note: Eastern Europe is defined as including Russia, Poland, Austria, Germany, Hungary, and Czechoslovakia.

Age

It has been argued, notably by Samuelson, that the transformation of economics that took place in the 1930s and 1940s involved a generational change. The young took up mathematical economics and Keynesian economics in a way that older economists did not. If this is correct, we should find a change in the age distribution of contributors to these journals, especially among the authors of articles using mathematics and articles on macroeconomics. Figure 7 shows the average ages of contributors, and figure 8 shows the distribution of ages in the five-year sample.[11] The average age was around 40, rising slightly over the period.[12] There were, however, noticeable variations in the age distri-

11. These figures can be compared with those in Moggridge 1995.

12. The five-year sample shows that contributors to the *JPE* and the *QJE* were on average younger. For the entire period (in the five-year sample), the figures are 40.7 years for the *AER*, 39.4 years for the *QJE*, and 37.8 years for the *JPE*. To test the hypothesis that the differences arise because Chicago and Harvard use their journals to further the careers of their Ph.D. students, calculations were made of the time from Ph.D. to publication in the *JPE* and the *QJE*. In 1950–60, 57 percent of articles by Chicago Ph.D.'s in the *JPE* were published within four years of graduation, whereas for non-Chicago Ph.D.'s, the equivalent figure was

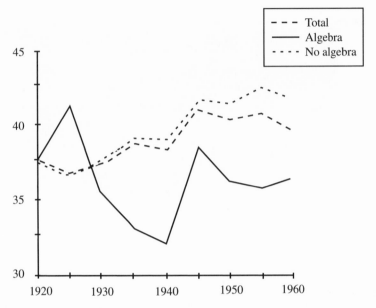

Figure 7 Average Ages of Authors

Note: This figure is based on a combined sample of annual data on the *AER* and five-year data on the *JPE* and the *QJE*. For example, 1920 includes all journals for 1920 plus *AER* for 1921–24, and 1960 includes all journals for 1960. This is to reduce the problem of small numbers of articles using algebra early in the period.

bution. There was no trend in the proportion of economists under 40, but from 1945 onward, there was a fall in the proportion of economists under 35, and, even more dramatically, those under 30 contributing to these journals. It could be argued that this reflects the growing professionalization of the discipline and the increasing technical demands of the subject. These journals were coming to be regarded as prestigious, and articles in them increasingly used mathematics, which gave an advantage to economists in their late thirties. There was certainly no evidence of an influx of young economists into these journals in the 1930s.[13]

only 25 percent. In 1920–40, the equivalent figures were 56 percent and 39 percent, respectively. In contrast, 51 percent of articles by non-Harvard Ph.D.'s in the *QJE* in 1950–60 were published within four years of graduation, compared with only 35 percent of articles by Harvard Ph.D.'s. Before the war, there was no difference, the equivalent figures being 40 percent and 39 percent, respectively. This suggests that the hypothesis may be correct for the *JPE* but not for the *QJE*.

13. This is possibly because they were publishing elsewhere. *Econometrica* and the *Review of Economic Studies*, known as "the children's magazine," date from the early 1930s.

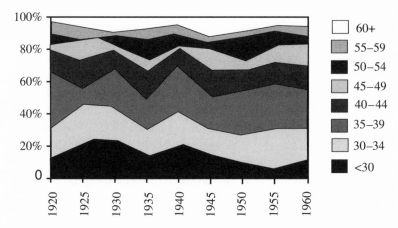

Figure 8 Age Distribution of Authors

Of much more interest is the age pattern of authors of articles using algebra. There is no evidence that mathematical economists in the 1920s and the first half of the 1930s were any younger than the average (although it must be remembered that the sample is small), but during the mid- to late 1930s a large gap emerged: in 1940–44 the mathematical economists were on average thirty-two years old, seven years younger than the authors of articles that did not use algebra. During the late 1940s, this gap closed sharply, with the average age of mathematical economists rising to thirty-eight. From 1950 onward the gap stabilized at around five years. This is consistent with the theory that mathematical economics was introduced by a new generation entering the profession in the late 1930s.[14] The rise in the age of mathematical economists in the late 1940s supports this theory, for in this period entrants to the profession would typically have been older, having spent several years in the armed forces. The rise in the average age of users of algebra in the 1950s compared with the average age in the late 1930s and early 1940s can be explained by the growing technical demands of the subject and the fact that such techniques were becoming much more widely accepted.

14. No evidence was found of any age difference between macroeconomists and microeconomists. If Samuelson's view of the Keynesian revolution is correct, this may be because macroeconomics involves more than simply Keynesian economics. It would be possible to classify articles according to their attitude to Keynes, but this has not been done.

Institutions

Analysis of the institutional affiliations of authors can throw light on two phenomena: the dominance of a small number of institutions and changes in the leading institutions as the subject was transformed. Insofar as institutions are associated with particular approaches to economics (Wisconsin with institutionalism, the Massachusetts Institute of Technology [MIT] with neoclassical economics), this may help us document the transformation of the subject. Many institutions, however, cannot be associated with particular schools of thought. From 1925/26 to 1950/51, the leading producers of Ph.D.'s in economics were Harvard (600), Columbia (394), Wisconsin (282), Cornell (244), Chicago (243), and Illinois (218) (Bowen 1953, cited in Moggridge 1995).[15] Of these, Columbia had a strong institutionalist presence (Clark and Mitchell), but Harold Hotelling was also there doing mathematical economics, although Arrow (1990, 46) claims that as late as 1940, when he was a student, the Economics Department's emphasis "was almost entirely on empirical and institutional analyses."[16] Thorstein Veblen was at Chicago at the beginning of the period, and Knight was there at its end. Harvard also cannot easily be associated with a single school: Taussig, Chamberlin, and Schumpeter were clearly not institutionalists, but they were also not neoclassical. In addition to Samuelson, Harvard produced John Kenneth Galbraith.

Institutions can be analyzed either by considering the institutions at which authors were based when their articles were published or by linking authors to the institutions from which they graduated, defined here as the institution from which a Ph.D. was obtained.[17] The data are shown in

15. See Froman 1942 for figures going back to 1904. During 1904–40, the figures were Columbia, 1,171; Chicago, 754; Wisconsin, 522; and Harvard, 490.

16. Moggridge (1995, 228–29) cites further evidence of the nontheoretical nature of the teaching at Columbia, Wisconsin, and the University of California at Los Angeles, in the 1930s.

17. This causes few problems for U.S. economists, virtually all of whom had Ph.D.'s. There are, however, problems with foreign economists. In this period, British economists, for example, typically did not have doctorates and thus would be excluded from such data. Given the preponderance of U.S.-trained economists in the sample, however, for whom Ph.D. institution was arguably more important than the institution where the first degree was obtained, this procedure seems justifiable. Moggridge (1995) classified authors by the university from which their highest degree had been obtained and found that, in the debate over Keynes's *General Theory* from 1936–48, Harvard (26 authors) was followed by Cambridge (17), the London School of Economics (16), Chicago (12), and Columbia (9). Although Moggridge's topic may have biased the result in favor of British economists, it serves as a warning that the methods adopted here seriously understate the role of British-trained economists.

tables 2 and 3. The *AER* sample was chosen to avoid the bias toward Chicago and Harvard that would result from using the *JPE* and the *QJE*.[18]

Table 2 shows little change in the degree of concentration of affiliation. In all decades except the 1940s, the top three institutions accounted for around 15 percent of articles, the top ten for around 38 percent, and the top fifteen for around 45 percent. The 1940s saw a reduction in concentration, perhaps because a disproportionate number of publishing economists from leading institutions were drawn into war work. Whatever the reason, the prewar concentration ratios were reestablished by the 1950s.[19]

The story as regards Ph.D. institutions is more mixed, although what stands out is the far greater degree of concentration. The top three Ph.D. institutions accounted for nearly 50 percent of the articles, the top ten for around 75 percent, and the top fifteen for over 80 percent. If Ph.D. training is important in determining the direction of the subject, it is necessary to consider only a very small number of institutions.

Although the system was highly concentrated, there were noticeable changes in the dominant institutions, as shown in both tables. In the first three decades of the period, economists based at Princeton, Columbia, and Harvard dominated the *AER*, while in the 1950s the leading institutions were Berkeley, MIT, and Stanford. Also noteworthy is the steady rise of Chicago to fourth place by the 1950s. In view of the decline of institutionalism, often dated to the 1930s, it is significant that Wisconsin slipped from around seventh place in the 1920s to eleventh in the 1950s.[20] The decline in the share of *AER* articles by Wisconsin Ph.D.'s is, however, more marked, from 12 percent in the 1920s and 10 percent in the 1930s to only 5 percent in the 1950s. In the 1940s and 1950s, the *AER* was dominated by economists trained at Harvard, who wrote as many articles as economists from the next two institutions, Columbia and Chicago, combined. In the 1920s and 1930s, Harvard and Columbia Ph.D.'s published *AER* articles in equal numbers.[21]

18. It could, of course, be argued that this results in an opposite bias. Because of the opportunities to publish in their own departments' journals, Chicago and Harvard economists may have been less likely to publish in the *AER*.

19. The exact figures, respectively, are 1920–29, 16, 37, and 45 percent; 1930–39, 16, 39, and 48 percent; 1940–49, 14, 30, and 37 percent; and 1950–59, 16, 36, and 46 percent.

20. During the 1940s, only two articles were written by Wisconsin-based economists, placing it in twenty-fourth place. Perhaps this is because Wisconsin economists were more likely to move into government during the war.

21. These figures are similar to those produced by Moggridge (1995, table 2). Moggridge's sample covers a wider range of journals but a smaller subset of economics.

Table 2 Leading Contributors to the *AER* by Affiliation, 1920–59

	1920s			1930s			1940s			1950s	
Institution	No.	%	Institution	No.	%	Institution	No.	%	Institution	No.	%
Total	216		Total	286		Total	290		Total	276	
Princeton	12	5.6	Columbia	17	5.9	Harvard	19	6.6	Berkeley	14	5.1
Columbia	11	5.1	Harvard	16	5.6	Columbia	11	3.8	Stanford	14	5.1
Harvard	11	5.1	Ohio State	12	4.2	Princeton	10	3.4	MIT	13	4.7
Minnesota	8	3.7	Princeton	12	4.2	FRBNY	9	3.1	Chicago	10	3.6
Yale	8	3.7	Illinois	11	3.8	OPA	9	3.1	Michigan	9	3.3
Pennsylvania	7	3.2	Cornell	10	3.5	Berkeley	8	2.8	Yale	9	3.3
Mt. Holyoke	6	2.8	Minnesota	10	3.5	Chicago	7	2.4	Johns Hopkins	8	2.9
New York	6	2.8	Wisconsin	9	3.1	FRS	5	1.7	Harvard	7	2.5
Wisconsin	6	2.8	Michigan	8	2.8	Minnesota	5	1.7	Illinois	7	2.5
Cornell	5	2.3	Chicago	6	2.1	Yale	5	1.7	UCLA	7	2.5
Ohio State	5	2.3	New York	6	2.1	Buffalo	4	1.4	California	6	2.2
Washington	4	1.9	Yale	6	2.1	California	4	1.4	Northwestern	6	2.2
Chicago	3	1.4	Buffalo	5	1.7	Johns Hopkins	4	1.4	Princeton	6	2.2
Illinois	3	1.4	Stanford	5	1.7	Michigan	4	1.4	Wisconsin	6	2.2
Iowa	3	1.4	California	4	1.4	MIT	4	1.4	FRS	5	1.8
Kansas	3	1.4	Mt. Holyoke	4	1.4	NBER	4	1.4	Pennsylvania	5	1.8
Oberlin	3	1.4	Albion	3	1.0	Virginia	4	1.4	Brown	4	1.4
Stanford	3	1.4	Lehigh	3	1.0	WPB	4	1.4	Carnegie	4	1.4
Texas	3	1.4	Pennsylvania	3	1.0	Carnegie	3	1.0	Columbia	4	1.4
Wesleyan	3	1.4	Washington	3	1.0	Iowa State	3	1.0	IMF	4	1.4

Table 2 Continued

1920s			1930s			1940s			1950s		
Institution	No.	%	Institution	No.	%	Institution	No.	%	Institution	No.	%
						Pennsylvania	3	1.0	Indiana	4	1.4
						Stanford	3	1.0	Oxford	4	1.4
						Washington	3	1.0	Rand	4	1.4
									Vanderbilt	4	1.4
									Washington	4	1.4
									Dartmouth	3	1.1
									LSE	3	1.1
									Michigan State	3	1.1
									Toronto	3	1.1
									Union	3	1.1
									Virginia	3	1.1

Note: Totals and percentages include articles for which no affiliation was given. The table includes all institutions that accounted for 1% or more of articles.

FRBNY = Federal Reserve Bank of New York
FRS = Federal Reserve System
IMF = International Monetary Fund
LSE = London School of Economics
MIT = Massachusetts Institute of Technology
NBER = National Bureau of Economic Research
OPA = Office of Price Administration
UCLA = University of California at Los Angeles
WPB = Wartime Production Board

Table 3 Leading Contributors to the *AER* by Ph.D. Institution, 1920–59

1920s			1930s			1940s			1950s		
Institution	No.	%	Institution	No.	%	Institution	No.	%	Institution	No.	%
Total	114			193			217			208	
Columbia	19	16.7	Harvard	27	14.0	Harvard	55	25.3	Harvard	47	22.6
Harvard	18	15.8	Columbia	26	13.5	Columbia	30	13.8	Chicago	28	13.5
Chicago	16	14.0	Wisconsin	19	9.8	Chicago	26	12.0	Columbia	21	10.1
Wisconsin	13	11.4	Chicago	17	8.8	Wisconsin	13	6.0	Cornell	12	5.8
Princeton	9	7.9	Princeton	11	5.7	Cornell	10	4.6	Wisconsin	11	5.3
Yale	8	7.0	Cornell	10	5.2	Vienna	9	4.1	Berkeley	9	4.3
Cornell	5	4.4	Michigan	9	4.7	Brookings	6	2.8	Michigan	8	3.8
Pennsylvania	5	4.4	Yale	8	4.1	Ohio State	6	2.8	California	7	3.4
Halle-Wittenberg	4	3.5	Ohio State	6	3.1	Yale	6	2.8	MIT	7	3.4
Johns Hopkins	3	2.6	Pennsylvania	6	3.1	California	5	2.3	Stanford	7	3.4
			California	4	2.1	Princeton	5	2.3	Yale	7	3.4
			Iowa	4	2.1				Johns Hopkins	5	2.4

Note: The totals are not the same as in table 2 because articles for which information on the author's Ph.D. institution is unavailable are excluded (this includes articles by authors who did not have a Ph.D.). The reason for calculating totals in this table differently from in table 2 is that when no Ph.D. information is available, the institution is typically unknown, but when no affiliation was given, there was none. The table includes all institutions that accounted for 2% or more of articles.

Conclusion

The analysis of U.S. economics confirms many of the stories we tell about the transformation of economics between 1920 and 1960. Immigrants from Europe had a significant quantitative impact, extending beyond the influence of a small number of prominent individuals. Evidence supports the idea that the 1930s was a crucial period in the mathematization of the subject, associated with the influx of a younger generation of economists. Econometrics as the term is now understood, however, did not take off until the 1950s. Although the evidence is far from conclusive, it is possible to see patterns that are consistent with the decline of institutionalism beginning in the 1930s: the declining share of *AER* articles produced from Wisconsin and by Wisconsin Ph.D.'s; the sudden emergence of Stanford, MIT, and Berkeley in the 1950s; and possibly the displacement of Columbia by Harvard. This is what most people would have expected.

The analysis also suggests some features of the transformation of U.S. economics that might otherwise have been forgotten. The massive impact of the war on the profession is the most obvious one. At a crucial time, large numbers of economists left academia to work in government or the military. Equally important, the mathematization of the subject, although it had proceeded a long way, was far from complete by 1960. If the dominant orthodoxy is seen as involving the use of formal optimizing models that are tested using econometric techniques, the subject still had a long way to go. For example, as late as 1960, 71 percent of empirical articles did *not* use regression analysis. The dramatic rise from 1955 to 1960 in the proportion of articles that used algebra but no diagrams suggests that a substantial change was taking place just as the period ended. This is a feature of the transformation of U.S. economics that accounts of key figures, such as Arrow, Samuelson, or Friedman, may easily overlook.

One of the most significant conclusions, however, emerges not from the statistical analysis but from the classification of the articles. The fact that it was difficult to classify many articles from the first half of the period as theoretical or empirical but less difficult toward the end of the period is evidence that a significant change took place in U.S. economics during this period. Although the change was undoubtedly associated with the transformation of U.S. economics from prewar pluralism to postwar neoclassicism—for the division between theoretical and empirical is a feature of the type of economics that has increasingly dominated the subject in the postwar period—it is not synonymous with it. Academic economics was expanding, along with the whole system of higher eduction, and the subject was increasingly able to support a range of journals, such as those discussed here, dealing with issues that were primarily of concern only to academic economists. Economics was becoming, along with many other disciplines, more inward looking.[22] Both theoretical and empirical techniques have become more formal, enabling them to be distinguished from each other in a way that was not possible in the 1920s.[23]

References

Arrow, Kenneth J. 1990. *Lives of the Laureates: Ten Nobel Economists.* 2d ed. Edited by William Breit and Roger W. Spencer. Cambridge, Mass.: MIT Press.

Backhouse, Roger E. 1997. The Changing Character of British Economics. In *The Post-1945 Internationalization of Economics.* Edited by A. W. Coats. *HOPE* 28 Supplement. Durham, N.C.: Duke University Press.

Bender, Thomas. 1997. Politics, Intellect, and the American University, 1945–1995. *Daedalus* 126:1–38.

Blaug, Mark, ed. 1986. *Who's Who in Economics: A Biographical Dictionary of Major Economists 1700–1986.* 2d ed. Brighton, England: Harvester Wheatsheaf.

Bowen, Howard R. 1953. Graduate Education in Economics. *American Economic Review* 43 supplement.

Coats, A.W. [1969] 1993. The American Economic Association's Publications: An Historical Perspective. *Journal of Economic Literature* 7:57–68. Reprinted in Coats 1993.

———. [1971] 1993. The Role of Scholarly Journals in the History of Economics. *Journal of Economic Literature* 9:29–44. Reprinted in Coats 1993.

———. [1991] 1993. The Learned Journals in the Development of Economics and the Economics Profession: The British Case. *Economic Notes* 20:89–116. Reprinted in Coats 1993.

———. 1993. *The Sociology and Professionalization of Economics: British and American Economic Essays.* Vol. 2. London: Routledge.

Dudley-Evans, Tony, and Willie Henderson. 1993. Changes in the Economics Article. *Finlance: A Finnish Journal of Applied Linguistics* 12:159–80.

22. Bender (1997) contrasts the development of universities after 1945 with their development in the prewar period.

23. Such arguments could be reinforced by linguistic analysis, which would show the emergence of a style more like that of the "scientific paper." See Coats [1971] 1993, [1991] 1993; Dudley-Evans and Henderson 1993; McCloskey 1991.

Figlio, David. 1993. Trends in the Publication of Empirical Economics. *Journal of Economic Perspectives* 8:179–87.

Froman, Lewis A. 1942. Graduate Students in Economics, 1904–40. *American Economic Review* 32:817–26.

Hagemann, Harald, and Claus-Dieter Krohn, eds. 1991. *Die Emigration deutchsprachiger Wirtschaftswissenschaftler nach 1933*. Stuttgart: Universität Hohenheim.

Leontief, Wassily A. [1971] 1977. Theoretical Assumptions and Nonobserved Facts. *American Economic Review* 61:1–7. Reprinted in *Essays in Economics: Theories, Facts, and Policies*. Oxford: Basil Blackwell.

———. 1982. Academic Economics. *Science* 217 (July): 104–7.

McCloskey, D. N. 1991. Mere Style in Economics Journals, 1920 to the Present. *Economic Notes* 20:135–58.

Moggridge, D. E. 1995. The Diffusion of the Keynesian Revolution: The Young and the Graduate Schools. In *New Perspectives on Keynes*. Edited by Allin E. Cottrill and Michael S. Lawlor. *HOPE* 27 supplement. Durham, N.C.: Duke University Press.

Mongiovi, Gary. 1997. Emigré Economists and the New School, 1933–1945. In *Zur deutschsprachiger wirtschaftswissenschaftlichen Emigration nach 1933*. Edited by Harald Hagemann. Marburg: Metropolis Verlag.

Institutional Economics: A Case of Reproductive Failure?

Jeff Biddle

Both historians and economists have speculated concerning the reasons for the decline in institutionalism in the second half of the twentieth century.[1] Prominent noninstitutionalists, for example, have argued that institutionalists lacked a coherent theory (Coase 1984, 196; Buchanan 1979, 147), while Ayres (1944, 12) chided second-generation institutionalists for turning away from the theoretical structures that early institutionalists had offered. Brinkley (1995, 46–47, 412) links the decline of institutionalism to the failure of the institutionalist-inspired reforms of the early New Deal and the subsequent emergence of Keynesianism as a body of economic thought that reform-oriented economists found more promising. Speigel (1991, 639) also argues that institutionalism might have been crowded out by Keynesianism.

In this essay I lay out yet another hypothesis concerning the decline of institutionalism or at least the variety of institutionalism traditionally associated with the University of Wisconsin. I also attempt to test

I would like to acknowledge the helpful comments of the participants in the 1997 *HOPE* conference, particularly Roger Backhouse, Warren Samuels, and Malcolm Rutherford.

1. Some may dispute what this essay takes as a fact to be explained: that American institutionalism (that is, the research programs described by Rutherford [1994, 1] as the "old institutional economics") has experienced a decline in importance and influence since the early part of the twentieth century. Other assertions and/or descriptions of the decline of institutionalism in America can be found in Landreth and Colander 1989, 398–99, and Speigel 1991, 638–40.

it empirically. The hypothesis is focused less on the content of institutionalism than on the institutional structure of the American economics profession within which Wisconsin institutionalism declined. It is based on the idea that for a school of economic thought to survive, each generation of adherents must, through some means of persuasion, convince bright and able members of the next generation to identify with and advance the ideas and the research program of the school. To speak metaphorically, in order to survive, a school of economics must successfully reproduce.

In the twentieth-century United States, this crucial process of persuasion/reproduction has come to take place primarily within the institutional structures of academe. By the second decade of the century, most of the people who considered themselves and were accepted by society as bona fide economists were found in colleges and universities. It was there that most of the research aimed at advancing and elaborating the ideas of the various schools of economics took place, and much of the general public's knowledge of such ideas was gained in college or university classrooms.[2] Since that time, a school of economic thought has needed to be well represented in academe in order to thrive.

From an academic base, the follower of a particular approach to economics can, through his or her research, contribute to the spread and reproduction of that approach; impressive research accomplishments might win converts from other schools of economic thought or attract favorable attention (and perhaps resources) from segments of society previously uncommitted to a particular school of economic thought. But arguably it is college and university teaching, especially the teaching of those who themselves will become teachers of economics, that represents the most important process through which a school of economics reproduces itself and assures its survival through several generations.

In the early part of the twentieth century, institutionalism had a strong base at the University of Wisconsin, where economists such as John R. Commons, Edwin Witte, and Selig Perlman conducted research and trained graduate students who went on to teach and do research in economics. It is the hypothesis of this essay, however, that because of

---

2. For a forceful statement of the extent to which the American economics profession came to be dominated by its academic segment by the first decade of the century, see Furner 1975, 258.

the way Wisconsin institutionalists defined the scope and method of economics and because of their vision of the role of the economist in society, they were less effective at reproducing than the adherents of other schools of thought. This "differential fertility" between Wisconsin institutionalists and more orthodox economists was ultimately an important factor in the long-term decline in the fortunes of the Wisconsin institutionalist research program.[3]

In the next section, I spell out this hypothesis in more detail. Then I offer a simple mathematical model designed to explore the extent to which the differential fertility of two schools of economic thought could lead to differences in the historical fortunes of the schools. I next present data on the careers of people who received Ph.D.'s in economics from six universities between 1920 and 1946. Considering those receiving Ph.D.'s at the University of Wisconsin as the "Wisconsin institutionalists" and those receiving degrees from other institutions as the more orthodox economists, I look for differences between the two groups with respect to type of employment (academic, government, etc.).[4] A final section reports some conclusions.

The Hypothesis Elaborated

My hypothesis combines two conjectures: first, that by the early twentieth century the placement of young followers (i.e., newly minted Ph.D.'s) in academic jobs, particularly in economics departments with graduate programs, had become critical to the reproduction of schools of economic thought and, second, that something about Wisconsin institutionalism made its young initiates less likely than neoclassically trained economists to pursue careers in academe.

Regarding the first conjecture, I do not wish to imply that no other

---

3. This hypothesis, which I have offered to students for some years, has been part of an oral tradition among historians of institutionalism for some time. I had not seen it committed to paper by another author, however, until I read Landreth and Colander's (1997) contribution to the *HOPE* conference for which this essay was originally prepared.

4. Stigler and Friedland (1975, 477–78) explored whether the "major centers of graduate instruction" were "'schools' in the sense of leaving a distinctive imprint on their graduates" by comparing the citation patterns of Ph.D.'s trained in different economics departments between 1950 and 1955. They concluded that the differences between graduates of the various departments were small compared to what they shared concerning macroeconomic and value theory. This conclusion, however, was based on comparisons of graduates of departments that would all be considered mainstream or orthodox.

means exist to spread and perpetuate the ideas of a school of economic thought than the training of graduate students who themselves teach at the graduate level. Possible alternatives include writing influential books or conducting successful research. But I would argue that over time these activities have become less effective, by themselves, as a means of perpetuating a school of thought. Since the beginning of the century, the literature of economics has become less accessible to the layperson, and those who wish to understand the literature increasingly have needed guides to teach them how to read it. As the literature has become larger and more scattered (more of it in journals, less in books), identification for the uninitiated of what is worth reading also has become an essential part of the guide's role; this screening function at least tacitly involves the teaching of criteria for determining what sorts of economic research are worthy of attention. And as this process of guiding, screening, and evaluating has become more important, it has come to be formalized in the curricula of colleges and universities. To put the point another way, although an active research program is probably a necessary condition for the health of a school of economic thought, it is not sufficient. For good research to be effective in perpetuating a school of economic thought, it must have advocates in academe. Even the proposition that an active research program is necessary to the health of a school of economic thought, however, points to the need for a school of economic thought to have representatives in academe, because that is where most of the resources that support economic research are found.

Teaching undergraduates is a way of spreading the ideas of a school of economics, but, to return to the metaphor of reproduction, the economist who teaches only undergraduates is in a sense producing infertile offspring. They may believe and act on the ideas of their teachers but will probably do little to effectively transmit those ideas to others or to otherwise shape the subsequent development of economics. Graduate students are potentially fertile, although some are more fertile than others. The new Ph.D. who works for a private firm has few opportunities to spread his or her mentors' ideas in the subsequent generation. The economist who goes into government may be able to imprint on policies or entire governmental institutions the ideas of his or her mentors. But although these policies and institutions may affect the lives of millions, they are not likely to transfer into the minds of those they affect the economic ideas they embody.

I do not wish to overstate my case. The school of economic thought whose adherents teach armies of undergraduates might have its ideas transferred, albeit in diluted form, from parent to child throughout the electorate and into institutions that influence the flow of resources to academic researchers. A government program or agency that embodies the ideas of a particular school of economics may itself become an object of study, perpetuating interest in those ideas, or it may come to represent a source of employment and resources for economists who think in terms of those ideas. It seems to me, however, that such avenues for the perpetuation of a particular approach to economics have not proven as effective and dependable as the direct transmission of ideas and research methods, in their most sophisticated form, from the economics Ph.D.'s of one generation to those of the next.

The second conjecture underlying my hypothesis is that Wisconsin institutionalists may have been less likely than young neoclassical economists to become teachers of future economists. It arises from what I see as important differences between Wisconsin institutionalists and more orthodox economists concerning the nature of the economy and the role of the economist, differences that made the young Wisconsin institutionalist more likely than his or her orthodox counterpart to see government service as an attractive alternative to an academic career.

At the risk of oversimplifying, I suggest that in the neoclassical orthodoxy of the twentieth century, the economist is seen mainly as a scientist whose job is to discover the timeless laws that govern economic behavior. Although knowledge of these laws can aid in the design of public policy, there is an important difference between the world of science, where objective, unbiased investigation is the rule, and the world of policy making, where normative values, rhetoric, and self-interested motives influence the uses to which the discoveries of science are put. The activity of scientific research—the discovery of potentially valuable knowledge—is held in high esteem, and the preferred form of public policy involvement is the disinterested communication of such knowledge to those in power from enough distance to avoid the potentially corrupting processes through which knowledge is applied to the design of actual policy.

In addition to the dichotomy between science and policy making, the twentieth-century orthodoxy has tended to see a dichotomy between economy and government and to believe that the economy is characterized by certain institutions (markets) that by and large operate in ways that promote the general welfare. Markets have their roots in human nature; they do not need much help from the government to function. The activities of government can, however, injure the general welfare by hindering the operation of markets; indeed, historically this has been the rule. This view tends to devalue the activities of making and administering economic policy. At best, economists in government might spend frustrating careers working against the seemingly natural tendency of those who govern to want to "do something" about economic problems that are best solved by letting market forces operate. At worst, they might lose their scientific objectivity, becoming hired guns for one partisan faction or another.[5]

The holistic, evolutionary mind-set of the Wisconsin institutionalists led to a different conceptualization of the government, the economy, and the role of the economist. The Wisconsin view was that economic institutions evolved along with other social institutions, including law and government. Economy and government could not be separated for the purposes of analysis because the economic institutions of a society were the product of past decisions of those with governmental authority and economic institutions in turn influenced the governmental decisions that affected the nature of future economic institutions. In such a setting, one did not seek timeless laws of economic behavior or expect to find a "natural" set of economic institutions that maximized welfare. Economic institutions that served society's interests at one time could become dysfunctional as they, other social institutions, or social values changed. This was the case with many of the economic institutions traditionally associated with market capitalism.

A prevailing view among the leaders of Wisconsin institutionalism was that the institutions of capitalism had come to promote the interests of a minority at the expense of the majority. It was necessary to alter and improve these institutions, and government action was an effective means of doing so. An important task of economic research was to determine which institutional alterations would be most effective in improving economic outcomes, and this could in part be done inductively by studying the effects of policy innovations introduced by government. To the young Wisconsin institutionalist then, a position in government likely seemed more exciting and important than it would

5. A sense of the frustrations felt by mainstream economists in government service in the 1960s and 1970s is conveyed by Allen (1977).

have seemed to a graduate student trained in a more orthodox program.[6] Through government service, one could promote the welfare of disadvantaged classes by participating in the important and necessary activity of institutional reform, while at the same time both applying and contributing to scientific knowledge by helping to design and monitor new policy "experiments."

In addition to ideological and methodological considerations, the examples set by the leaders of the Wisconsin school might have drawn their students toward careers in government as they saw or heard about the activities of men like Commons or Witte in designing, promoting, and participating in the implementation of new institutional reforms. Finally, the association of Wisconsin institutionalists with the governmental initiatives of the Progressive Era and the New Deal might have, through the simple operation of old-boy networks, increased the likelihood that Wisconsin graduate students would find employment with government agencies.

My hypothesis requires not only that graduate students trained in the Wisconsin tradition were more likely than the average Ph.D. economist to take jobs in government but that they were therefore less likely to take academic jobs, especially those that involved teaching in a graduate program.[7] Also, my argument for why Wisconsin institutionalists were less likely to go into academic jobs is essentially a supply-side argument, hinging on the preferences and voluntary choices of the young Wisconsin institutionalists. A perhaps equally plausible explanation for any underrepresentation of Wisconsin institutionalists in academic jobs would hinge on demand-side considerations: Given that the institutionalist approach to economics never dominated the profession, Wisconsin institutionalists seeking employment in academe might have been discriminated against by senior faculty and administrators who preferred more orthodox approaches to economics, whereas government employers of the time were either sympathetic to the institutionalist approach or unconcerned with the methodological distinctions taken so seriously by the academic economists.[8]

6. Barber (1981, 515–16) touches on the ambivalent attitude of orthodox economists of the 1920s and 1930s toward government service and its impact on the nature of the economic advisers employed by the New Deal.

7. The one does not necessarily imply the other, as Ph.D. economists have other career opportunities, including those in the private sector.

8. See Craufurd D. Goodwin's essay in this volume for a discussion of reasons employers might have preferred orthodox economists to institutionalists.

A Model

I have emphasized the importance to a school of thought of training followers who take academic positions in which they in turn are able to train future Ph.D.'s. But how big a difference in the tendency of adherents of different schools of thought to fill such positions is necessary to create a noticeable difference in the historic fortunes of those schools? This section describes a simple model intended to shed some light on this question. The model focuses only on graduate training as a process for transmitting the ideas of a school, abstracting away from all other methods of communication and persuasion while relying on a number of severe assumptions about the length of academic careers, the distribution of students across teachers, the age distribution of the population of economists, and so on. This is done in hopes of keeping things simple without making the model irrelevant, although it is clear that a number of steps could be taken to relax assumptions and to account for excluded factors in some way without making the model intractable.

The model describes a population of economists that remains constant in size as time passes. To become an economist, one must be taught by a member of a subset of the current population of economists I call trainers. There is a constant number (N) of trainers in the population. Each trainer produces r new economists per year, and all economists, including trainers, have careers of T years. Calling all economists who started their careers in the same year a cohort, I assume that each cohort is the same size and that the number of trainers in each cohort is the same. So each year, rN new economists enter the profession, while rN retire, having completed their T-year careers. The total size of the population or profession is rNT. New vacancies for trainers are created only by the retirement of the N/T trainers in the cohort just completing its career. It is further assumed that the vacancies for trainers opening up in a year are all filled from among the rN economists starting their careers that year. The probability that a newly trained economist takes a job as a trainer is thus $1/rT$.

Next, I assume that there are two types of economists, type P and type Q, and that all economists trained by trainers of a certain type become that type themselves. I can then make assumptions about the proportion of type P economists among trainers and in the profession as a whole and analyze how that share will change over time both among trainers and in the entire population of economists if, for example, some trainers suddenly change type or if, as this essay hypothesizes, the students of one type of economist are more likely than those of the other type to fill training spots.

For example, let p be the proportion of trainers that are type P. If the probability of getting a training spot is the same for an individual economist of either type, the model has a steady state in which each year, prN new type P economists are produced, pN/T of them become trainers, pN/T type P trainers retire, and prN type P economists retire. The proportion p remains constant, as does $q = 1 - p$, the proportion of type Q trainers and economists. However, one can relax the assumption that new trainees of both types have the same likelihood of becoming trainers themselves or, in terms of this essay's hypothesis, assume that young followers of one school are less likely than those of the other to take jobs in economics departments with Ph.D. programs. Suppose that the model begins in a steady state, with p at a stable level $p(s)$ both among trainers and in the profession. Then assume that the probability of becoming a new trainer conditional on being a type P trainee falls from $1/rT$ to α/rT.[9] In general, this will cause p to decline over time among the trainers and the profession as a whole. The rate and extent of the decline depend on assumptions about the values of $p(s)$ and α.

Table 1 summarizes four cases, with the simulations run over ninety years. In the first line of table 1 $\alpha = .8$ and $p(s)$ is .2, so that a type Q economist has about a 31 percent greater chance than a type P economist of becoming a trainer.[10] By year thirty, $p(t)$ is .14 among the trainers and .18 in the profession; after sixty years, the representation of type P economists among trainers has fallen by more than half; after ninety years, type P economists make up only 6 percent of the trainers and 8 percent of all economists. In line 2 of table 1, the starting proportion $p(s)$ is doubled to 40 percent, while α remains at .8. This leads to a doubling of $p(t)$ at every point in the simulation (not exactly reflected in the table due to rounding). Lines 3 and 4 return $p(s)$ to .2 and vary α instead, with results in the direction one would expect.

In the next section I present evidence on how the careers of Wisconsin institutionalists differed from those of other economists, including information on the tendency to take academic versus government jobs

9. This implies that after the change each type Q trainee has a probability of becoming a trainer of β/rT, where $\beta = (1 - \alpha p)/(1 - p) > 1$.

10. By assumption, the probability of becoming a trainer conditional on being type P is $.8/rT$; by the equation in n. 9, the probability of taking a training job conditional on being type Q is $1.05/rT$ and $1.05/.8 = 1.31$.

Table 1 Simulations: Time Paths of the Share of Type P Trainers and Economists, When Type P Economists Are Less Likely to Take Training Jobs

Assumed Values for Key Parameters	Difference in Conditional Probabilities of Taking Training Job ($[\beta/\alpha] - 1$)	Value of $p(t)$ for Trainers (for All Economists) after 30 Years	Value of $p(t)$ for Trainers (for All Economists) after 60 Years	Value of $p(t)$ for Trainers (for All Economists) after 90 Years
1. $\alpha = .8, p(s) = .2$	31%	.14 (.18)	.09 (.12)	.06 (.08)
2. $\alpha = .8, p(s) = .4$	42%	.25 (.35)	.19 (.24)	.12 (.16)
3. $\alpha = .75, p(s) = .2$	42%	.13 (.17)	.08 (.10)	.05 (.06)
4. $\alpha = .9, p(s) = .2$	14%	.17 (.19)	.14 (.15)	.11 (.13)

and jobs in economics departments with Ph.D. programs versus other academic jobs. Any differences between Wisconsin types and others can then be assessed in light of the model to get a sense of whether they were large enough to make a significant difference in the historical fortunes of Wisconsin institutionalism. The case reported in line 4 of table 1, for example, suggests that a 14 percent difference in the propensity to take training jobs is not large enough to be meaningful. Even after ninety years, which is roughly the length of time that the study of economics has been professionalized within the academy in the United States, the share of type P economists is still at over half its original size.

The model abstracts away from all but one of the processes by which schools of economic thought are perpetuated and treats that one in a very stylized fashion. One could imagine additions to the model that would magnify or diminish the importance of any difference between schools in the tendency to produce trainers. One extension that would be in the spirit of my hypothesis as earlier elaborated and would magnify the importance of the α/β ratio would allow for greater "professional activity," that is, the conduct of research and communication of it to other economists to aid in the spread of a school and make the possibility of "conversion" from one type to another in midcareer endogenous. One could, for example, specify three rather than two possible careers: academic trainers, academic nontrainers, and others; stipulate that the school of economics with the larger academic contingent has the larger research output; then make the probability that a school of economics gains a convert a function of the size of its academic contingent.

Evidence on the Careers of Economists
Receiving Ph.D.'s between 1920 and 1946

I have compiled a list of people who received Ph.D.'s in economics from six economics departments between 1920 and 1946. Details on the sources and methods used to compile these lists can be found in the appendix. The six departments are those at the University of Chicago, the University of Michigan, the University of Minnesota, Northwestern University, the University of Wisconsin, and Yale University. My choice of time period, 1920–46, is somewhat arbitrary but made with the theme of "from interwar pluralism to postwar neoclassicism" in mind.

The economists trained from 1920 to 1946 would become the backbone of the profession in the decades after the war, with the 1920 graduates well established in their careers in the late 1940s and the 1946 graduates having careers that would develop over the three postwar decades. If economics was "transformed" in the postwar decades, the 1920–46 Ph.D. classes necessarily played a major role in that transformation.

The choice of departments to include in the sample reflects a mix of logic and convenience. The University of Wisconsin was a necessary choice because my hypothesis involves a comparison between Wisconsin institutionalists and more orthodox economists. Because there is no consistently applicable and reliable way of identifying a Ph.D. recipient as having institutionalist or orthodox leanings, I took the route of identifying all graduates of the University of Wisconsin as the "Wisconsin institutionalists" in my sample and all other graduates as the "more orthodox" types. This is clearly problematic, as nothing ensures that all graduates of the Wisconsin department were institutionalists or that a graduate of another program would not have institutionalist or other heterodox leanings.[11] I can only hope that the split between Wisconsin Ph.D.'s and non-Wisconsin Ph.D.'s approximates the split between Wisconsin institutionalists and other (mainly orthodox) economists closely enough to be informative.

The University of Chicago was included in the sample because of its reputation, at least by the end of the period, as a graduate program that emphasized a particularly pure form of neoclassicism. Also, all but one of the departments in the sample were in midwestern universities, which provided a "control" for Wisconsin in case the proximity of a school to Washington, D.C., might play a role in the propensity of the graduates to have careers in government.[12] Another matter considered in choosing schools was departmental prestige. A key factor determining the placement of the products of a Ph.D. program is the program's reputation, which may be a function of the school of economic thought the program is perceived to be associated with but is certainly a func-

11. For example, Morris Copeland received his Ph.D. in 1921 from Chicago, wrote the dissertation "Some Phases of Institutional Value Theory," and is generally considered to have been an institutionalist throughout his career. Emmett, in this volume, provides a good account of the heterogeneity in the Chicago economics department of the interwar period.

12. Stigler and Friedland (1975, 482–83) show evidence of a relationship between the location of the university granting a doctorate and the doctoral recipient's place of employment many years later for those receiving degrees between 1950 and 1955.

Table 2 Characteristics of Graduate Programs Included in the Sample

Graduate Program	Ph.D.'s Granted, 1920–46	Ph.D.'s Granted, 1920–33	Ph.D.'s Granted, 1934–46	Program Rank, 1925[a]	Program Rank, 1957[b]
Chicago	117	64	53	3	2
Michigan	54	32	22	7	9
Minnesota	41	8	33	13	10
Northwestern	28	13	15	14	11
Wisconsin	167	81	86	4	13
Yale	59	30	29	5	3
Total	466	228	238	—	—

a. Hughes study (Cartter 1966, 34).
b. Keniston study (Cartter 1966, 34).

tion of other things as well. In the 1925 Hughes study, based on the opinions of a small "panel of experts," Wisconsin's graduate economics program was ranked fourth in the country. In the 1957 Keniston study, also based on a survey of experts, the Wisconsin department was ranked thirteenth (Cartter 1966). Harvard topped both rankings. A finding that graduates of Harvard were more likely than those from Wisconsin to take teaching jobs in departments with graduate programs might simply reflect this difference in prestige and be unassociated with matters of methodology or ideology. For this reason, I have attempted to include programs from throughout the rankings in both 1925 and 1957. Table 2 provides some basic information on the Ph.D. programs included in the sample. Wisconsin was the largest of the programs in both halves of the period and, based on Bowen 1953, was the third largest program in the country over the period 1925–35.[13]

I attempted to find enough biographical information to determine what types of job sample members held throughout their careers (academic, business, government, etc.), as well as whether they were employed by academic economics departments that awarded Ph.D.'s in economics. In doing this, I relied on a number of sources, most notably the various handbooks and directories published by the American Economic Association and the biographical publications of Marquis's

13. The Ph.D. counts given in Bowen 1953 for the sample schools are larger than mine because they include all dissertations on economics topics, not just those granted by economics departments.

Who's Who. I constructed a sixfold job-type classification: academic in economics; academic in another field (usually a business field, such as finance, accounting, or marketing); government (including the Federal Reserve System and international agencies such as the United Nations or the World Bank); private sector (work for firms or employers' associations, private consulting or mediation practices, etc.); nonprofits (a small category including research institutes and foundations); and other, for economists who had died, retired, or were otherwise out of the labor force during the relevant time period. An "unknown" category was used for cases in which not enough information could be found to make a job-type classification.

Two job-type variables were assigned to each sample member, corresponding to two career phases: the "early career" was defined as the first fifteen years after earning the Ph.D., while years after that were defined as the "late career." If a sample member held two types of job during one career phase, the type held during the majority of years in that phase was chosen; in the rare cases in which an economist held three types of jobs during a career phase with none covering the majority of years, I chose the job type that occupied the plurality of years.

The biographical sources I consulted often listed two jobs or assignments at the same time for an economist, and if a primary position was not specified, some judgment on my part was necessary. As a rule I tried to determine which job provided the majority of the person's income at the time. For example, many economists would report, concurrently with long-term academic appointments, shorter terms of service on governmental boards or commissions. In these cases, the academic job was chosen as primary. On the other hand, an economist taking a two-year leave to serve on the Council of Economic Advisers would be considered to have spent two years in government. An employee of the Bureau of Agricultural Economics who was also listed as a faculty member of George Washington University would be considered to have a government job.

To divide academics into those in economics and those in other fields, I relied on the academic title (e.g., associate professor of economics) and/or the departmental affiliation. In ambiguous cases, academics were assumed to be in economics. Many academics held administrative positions at some time in their careers. I did not create a separate classification for this but relied on the concurrent job title. For example, an individual listing his or her position as professor of economics and dean of the School of Business Administration would be classed as an academic economist. I did this mainly because it is relatively difficult to obtain information on administrative appointments held by individuals at their academic institutions, but the decision is defensible under the assumption that many academic administrators in this period continued in their teaching positions and as administrators continued to be involved in activities (such as hiring) that might influence the nature of the profession. The few sample members who became college presidents, however, were classified as academics not in economics. Finally, people dying or retiring within seven years of receiving a Ph.D. were assigned "other" as an early-career type.

A record of death or retirement was the best way to determine the length of the second phase of the career, although if death or retirement occurred before the twenty-sixth year of the career (a late-career phase of less than ten years), the late-career job type was classified as other. Otherwise, the career type was assigned using the rules described previously for the early career. Determining the length, and thus the primary job type, of the second phase of the career was sometimes problematic, however, as biographical sources did not always extend up to a person's death or retirement. If I was able to track the career more than twenty years beyond the end of the first phase (more than thirty-five years after the Ph.D.), I considered the time span for which I had information to be the late-career phase. If I could not track the career to the thirty-fifth year but could track it to a point that was both more than ten years beyond the end of the first phase and beyond the person's sixty-fourth year of life, the time span for which information was available was considered the second phase of the career.

A person was considered to be involved with a Ph.D. program during a phase of his or her career if the career type during that phase was academic in economics and if during that phase of the career he or she spent five or more years with a department that granted economics Ph.D.'s.[14] I defined an institution as having an economics Ph.D. program when it was granting an average of one or more economics Ph.D.'s per year, based on information from Bowen 1953, table 41; Cartter 1964, 1273–76; and American Economic Association 1969, 1977.

---

14. Also included are economists affiliated with the Brookings Institution in the years that it granted Ph.D. degrees.

Tables 3 and 4 show the sample distribution of job types for the early- and late-career phases, both for the whole sample and for the six departments separately.[15] A comparison of Wisconsin to the sample as a whole with respect to early-career job types (columns 1 and 2 of table 3) provides support for some elements of the hypothesis. Wisconsin graduates were more likely than non-Wisconsin graduates to have early careers dominated by government service. Wisconsin graduates were also less likely than the rest to spend their early careers in academic jobs, in departments of economics, or in economics departments with Ph.D. programs. With the possible exception of the tendencies toward government service, however, the differences are not large. Calculating the empirical analogue of $\beta/\alpha - 1$ from table 1, 16.8 percent of Wisconsin Ph.D.'s have an early-career association with a Ph.D. program, compared with 19.7 percent of the non-Wisconsin Ph.D.'s, for a 16 percent difference.[16]

Among the separate departments, only the Michigan Ph.D.'s were more likely than the Wisconsin Ph.D.'s to spend early-career years in government or less likely to be associated with economics departments, while graduates of both Northwestern and Michigan were less likely to be associated with Ph.D. programs. The evidence in table 4 on late-

15. The job-type statistics in my sample correspond closely to those from two fairly comparable samples described in Bowen 1953, 10. The first includes economists who received Ph.D.'s from a number of departments, 1930–40. In 1940 (in what I would refer to as the early-career phase), 62 percent of these were in academic jobs, 23 percent in the public sector, 8 percent in the private or nonprofit sector, and 7 percent unemployed or unknown. The second includes economists who received Ph.D.'s in 1939–40. Of those with known employment status in 1952 (again the early-career phase), 67 percent were in academic jobs, 22 percent in government, and 11 percent in the private or nonprofit sector. In my sample, the tabulation of early-career types is 63 percent academic, 19 percent government, 7 percent private or nonprofit, and 9 percent unemployed or unknown. With unemployed and unknown excluded, the proportions are 71 percent academic, 21 percent government, and 8 percent private or nonprofit.

16. I do not discuss statistical significance or report associated measures because I do not conceive this project as one involving the use of samples to make inferences about larger populations. My sample includes all economics Ph.D. recipients from Wisconsin, 1920–46, and in making statements about the behavior of this group, I am not generalizing to some larger population of Wisconsin graduates. One could consider the graduates from the other departments, taken together, as a sample from the population of all who received Ph.D.'s during the period, allowing inferences about differences between Wisconsin graduates and all others, but since my choice of departments has probably not led to a random sample of non-Wisconsin Ph.D. recipients, the applicability of the classical theory of inference to this task is questionable. My model is meant to provide an alternative approach to assessing the significance of differences between the departments.

Table 3 Early-Career Job Types, by Department Granting Degree

Job Type	(1) Full Sample	(2) Wisconsin	(3) Chicago	(4) Michigan	(5) Minnesota	(6) Northwestern	(7) Yale
Total	466	167	117	54	41	28	59
Academic	62.8%	55.1%	68.3%	64.8%	82.9%	53.6%	62.7%
Economics	52.1	49.7	57.2	40.7	63.4	53.6	50.8
Other	10.7	5.4	11.1	24.1	19.5	0.0	11.9
Ph.D. program	18.7	16.8	20.5	11.1	36.6	10.7	18.6
Government	19.1	23.4	18.0	24.1	9.8	14.3	13.6
Private/nonprofit	7.1	6.0	7.7	3.7	0.0	14.3	13.6
Other	2.2	3.0	1.7	1.9	2.4	0.0	1.7
Unknown	8.8	12.6	4.3	5.6	4.9	17.9	8.5

Table 4 Late-Career Job Types, by Department Granting Degree

Job Type	(1) Full Sample	(2) Wisconsin	(3) Chicago	(4) Michigan	(5) Minnesota	(6) Northwestern	(7) Yale
Total	466	167	117	54	41	28	59
Academic	51.9%	48.5%	52.2%	51.9%	68.3%	42.8%	50.8%
Economics	40.8	41.3	42.6	31.5	51.2	32.1	40.7
Other	11.2	7.2	9.6	24.0	17.1	10.7	10.2
Ph.D. program	25.5	25.2	24.8	16.7	39.0	17.9	30.5
Government	13.7	16.2	14.5	16.7	9.8	3.6	10.2
Private/nonprofit	9.2	6.6	11.3	11.1	2.4	7.1	16.9
Other	11.8	10.2	12.2	9.2	9.8	28.6	10.2
Unknown	13.3	18.6	10.4	5.6	9.8	17.9	11.9

career job types provides almost no support for my hypothesis, as the Wisconsin graduates have about the same probability as the others to be in departments of economics and to be associated with Ph.D. programs. The greater than average tendency of Wisconsin graduates to be in government, however, extends into the later career.

The reliability of interdepartment comparisons based on tables 3 and 4 is compromised somewhat by the nontrivial size of the unknown category and the fact that its share differs across departments. Assume as a baseline case that unknown status is uncorrelated with job type. Then the true proportions for a column of table 3 or 4 would be the proportions in the table multiplied by $1/(1-u)$, where u is the column's unknown proportion. Since Wisconsin has a higher share of unknowns than the sample as a whole, this baseline adjustment would increase the gap between Wisconsin and the sample as a whole in the government category but decrease it in categories such as academics, in which Wisconsin's proportion is close to but still lower than that of the full sample.

However, my search methods and the biographical data on which I have relied make it likely that academic economists are a smaller share of the unknowns than the knowns, while government and especially private-sector economists make up a larger share. Academic economists are more likely to be listed in the directories of the American Economic Association, for example (see Stigler and Friedland 1975, 481–82), and of the thirty graduates with unknown early-career types on whom I have some information, thirteen were in government positions or at Washington, D.C., addresses for at least one of their early-career years, while six were in private or nonprofit jobs. Finally, I would be very surprised if more than one or two economists at Ph.D.-granting universities ended up classified as unknown. As a result, the baseline adjustment described previously would still leave too small a difference between Wisconsin and the whole sample in the government category, while in the academic categories, the truth would be somewhere between what is now in the tables and what would result from the baseline adjustment. In the important Ph.D. program category, however, the table 3 and 4 numbers are probably reliable.

It seems reasonable to believe that changes on the demand side of the market for economists over the period might have affected the types of jobs taken by Ph.D. economists. If the distribution of Ph.D.'s granted by years differs across various departments in the sample, differences between departments in the job types taken by graduates might be due in part to these demand-side changes rather than to differences in experiences of graduate students of those departments. I attempted to control for this possibility using probit models. A series of dependent variables was constructed, each equaling 1 if a particular job type was chosen, 0 otherwise. Time of graduation was controlled for by a set of dummy variables dividing the period into five segments: 1920–25, 1926–30, 1931–35, 1936–40, and 1941–46. A Wisconsin dummy variable was also included. Only the probits involving the early-career phase showed anything markedly different from what can be discerned in tables 3 and 4, indicating wider differences in behavior between Wisconsin graduates and others in the likelihood of being in government or in academics.[17]

On the important matter of a Ph.D. economist's likelihood of teaching in a department with a graduate program, neither the tables nor the probit models show much difference between those trained at Wisconsin and those trained in the other programs in the sample. However, there may be differences in the types of Ph.D. programs that employed members of the two groups; such differences have implications for the relative fertility of Wisconsin institutionalism. In particular, graduates who end up teaching at larger and/or more prestigious departments may be more fertile, as the former reach more students and the latter reach students more likely to go on to graduate-level teaching. Perhaps the large and prestigious graduate programs tended to avoid hiring Wisconsin graduates, thus limiting the ability of Wisconsin institutionalism to spread.

Table 5 provides a more detailed look at the experiences of the sample members who worked in departments with Ph.D. programs. The first two columns cover the period from 1920 to 1945 and compare the graduates of Wisconsin to the graduates of all other programs. The stock of graduates row displays the number of graduates who held Ph.D.'s for five years during the period.[18] Subsequent rows show how many of those graduates spent five or more post-Ph.D. years during the

17. Probits were run with and without unknowns included. Under the assumption that unknowns were less likely than knowns to be academics and more likely to work in government, the probits indicated a gap of around 10 percentage points between Wisconsin graduates and others in the government and academic categories.

18. The stock for the 1920–45 period excludes those receiving doctorates after 1940 and those known to have died within five years of receiving the Ph.D. The stock for the postwar period excludes those known to have died or retired before 1952.

Table 5 Characteristics of Ph.D. Programs Employing Graduates

	1920–45		After 1945	
Type of Program	Wisconsin	Others	Wisconsin	Others
Stock of graduates	126	229	159	284
With any Ph.D. program	17	40	41	81
	(13.5%)	(17.5%)	(25.8%)	(28.5%)
With top Ph.D. program	9	11	2	14
	(7.1%)	(4.8%)	(1.3%)	(4.9%)
With large Ph.D. program	9	7	11	14
	(7.1%)	(3.1%)	(6.9%)	(4.9%)
With Ph.D. granting program	9	20	9	17
	(7.1%)	(8.7%)	(5.7%)	(6.0%)

period employed by an economics department with a Ph.D. program, by a department with a top-ranked Ph.D. program, by a department with a large Ph.D. program, and by the Ph.D. program that granted their degree. The final two columns report the same information for the post–World War II years. The top-ranked programs in the prewar period are the top five in the Hughes ratings of 1925: Harvard, Columbia, Chicago, Wisconsin, and Yale. After 1945, ratings compiled in 1957, 1964, and 1975 were used to identify the top-ranked programs (Lampman 1993, 251), with the result that California replaces Wisconsin starting in 1946 and the Massachusetts Institute of Technology (MIT) replaces Columbia after 1960. My identification of the five large programs is based on Bowen 1953, table 41; Cartter 1964, 1273–76; and American Economic Association 1969, 1977.[19]

Tables 3 and 4 report comparisons of graduates of different programs in the same phases of their careers, regardless of when the graduates received their degrees. The comparisons in table 5, however, refer to particular historical periods and lump together new graduates with older-vintage Ph.D.'s. Based on this different method of comparison, the second line of table 5 shows Wisconsin below the other programs for both periods in the share of graduates spending five or more years

19. Before 1945, the programs classified as large are Harvard, Columbia, Wisconsin, Cornell, and Illinois. In 1940–50, Chicago replaces Illinois; in 1951–65, California replaces Cornell; and after 1965, MIT replaces Chicago.

in departments with Ph.D. programs.[20] The next three lines of the table are best considered together, as they turn out to be related. Considering the last line first, the tendency for programs to hire their own graduates was strong in both the early and the postwar period. In the 1920–45 period, about half the sample graduates employed by Ph.D.-granting departments were employed for five or more years by their home departments; in the postwar period, the figure was slightly less than one-fourth.[21] This fact must be kept in mind while examining the information on affiliation with top-ranked programs and large programs because some of the sample departments fall into one or both of these categories at one time or another. For example, table 5 indicates that Wisconsin graduates were more likely than those of the other departments to be at large programs and at top-ranked programs in the earlier period and that the only important change in the postwar period was a considerable fall in the share of Wisconsin graduates at top-ranked programs. However, this drop is due entirely to the fact that Wisconsin dropped out of my list of top-ranked programs after 1945. All nine Wisconsin graduates in the top program cell (and in the large program cell) for the early period were at Wisconsin, and all but two of the graduates of other departments in the top program cell for the early period were at their granting departments. In the postwar period, on the other hand, only six of the fourteen graduates in the top program cell from departments other than Wisconsin were employed by the departments that granted their doctorates.

Overall, then, table 5 provides mixed evidence on the differential fertility hypothesis. Both before and after the war, Wisconsin Ph.D.'s were less likely than others to be employed by Ph.D.-granting departments but more likely to be employed by the largest programs. The Wisconsin graduates were seldom hired by top departments other than Wisconsin, and if one accepts the judgment of the available departmental rankings, this means less of a Wisconsin influence after the war in the top graduate programs in economics.

20. The 4-percentage-point difference in the prewar period translates into about a 25 percent difference, while the 2.7-percentage-point difference in the postwar period is about a 10 percent difference.

21. In analyzing a group that received doctorates in economics in 1950–55, Stigler and Friedland (1975, 482) also report "a marked penchant of . . . schools to hire their own doctorates."

Conclusion

The evidence I have presented provides mixed support for the differential fertility hypothesis. It seems that Wisconsin graduates were indeed more likely than other economists to take government jobs. It is less clear whether this divergence in behavior between Wisconsin graduates and others translated into a meaningful difference between the proportion of Wisconsin graduates associated with a Ph.D. program and the proportion of all Ph.D. economists so associated. The strongest evidence that it did is the 25 percent gap between Wisconsin and the other schools in the proportion of graduates teaching in Ph.D. programs between 1920 and 1945. However, this gap shrank to 10 percent after the war, a gap my model suggests is probably too small to matter. Also, there seems to have been a decline in the tendency of Wisconsin graduates to be associated with top Ph.D. programs, but this may be an artifact of the method used to rank Ph.D. programs. Finally, there is evidence that Wisconsin graduates were less likely to work in academe, but they took jobs in economics departments at about the same rate as graduates of other programs. One must conclude, then, that "differential fertility" as defined in this essay at most played a small part in the decline of Wisconsin institutionalism; it was one of many factors in what was bound to have been a complex process or perhaps one manifestation of some of those factors.[22]

However, this essay has operationalized the idea of the reproduction of a school of economic thought in a rather coarse manner: Doctoral students are assumed to develop into replicas of their teachers, with orthodox graduate programs producing orthodox students and institutionalist graduate programs producing institutionalist students. This is of course an abstraction, but perhaps it was even less true for students of Wisconsin institutionalists than for students of other traditions. Wisconsin students, although trained and supervised by institutionalists, may not in general have acquired the characteristics of their teachers that made the latter distinctly institutionalist.

A number of commentators, noting the difficulty of the prose with which Commons expressed his theoretical ideas, have wondered whether his students had a good understanding of his concept of institutionalism. Ramstad (1987) argues that it was not only the way Com-

---

22. Likewise, the data indicate that discrimination against Wisconsin-trained economists was probably not a key factor in the decline of institutionalism.

mons described his institutionalism but also its very nature that kept students from fully embracing it—it was "existentialist" in that it offered no promises of objective certainty and placed a heavy burden of personal responsibility on the individual economist. Both these factors may explain Speigel's (1991, 638) observation that Commons's students responded less to his "far-flung conceptual scheme of institutional economics" than to "his activities as a reformer and initiator of the study of applied fields," an observation supported by an examination of the dissertations produced by Wisconsin graduates. For example, the dissertations supervised by Commons tended to deal with labor history or case studies of particular labor unions but seldom appear to have involved the institutional theoretical framework Commons was developing.[23] All this suggests that an analysis of the reproduction of schools of economic thought through the training of graduate students based on the identity of the Ph.D.-granting institution could be fruitfully supplemented by a closer look at the individual relationships between graduate students and their advisers and the content of the early research the students produced.

Appendix: Sources and Methods Used in Compiling Lists of Ph.D. Recipients

The list of Wisconsin Ph.D. recipients was taken from Lampman 1993, table A6. The Chicago list was compiled from the Regenstein Library's collection of commencement programs, which list recipients of the Ph.D. degree along with the dissertation title and granting department. Up to 1926, recipients of degrees from the Department of Political Economy were included if political economy was listed as the first or only field; afterward those receiving degrees from the Department of Economics were included. The Michigan list was compiled from similar information found in University of Michigan commencement programs, housed in the Bentley Library. The sources for the Minnesota list were University of Minnesota 1939–1968. Names under the heading "General Economics" were included. Degree recipients listed under the heading "Economics" in Northwestern University 1935, 1935–46, constitute the Northwestern list. The Yale list came from Yale University 1961. Prior to 1931, a combined department of sociology, political

---

23. I thank Malcolm Rutherford for pointing this out to me.

science, and economics granted degrees. For those years, I separated out the economics degrees using dissertation titles and subject classifications obtained from *Dissertation Abstracts*. From 1931 on, only recipients of degrees from the separate Department of Economics were included.

References

Allen, William R. 1997. Economics, Economists, and Economic Policy: Modern American Experiences. *HOPE* 9.1:48–88.

American Economic Association. 1969. *Guide to Graduate Study in Economics*. Evanston, Ill.: American Economic Association.

———. 1977. *Guide to Graduate Study in Economics and Agricultural Economics*. 4th ed. Boulder, Colo.: Economics Institute.

Ayres, Clarence. 1944. *The Theory of Economic Progress*. Chapel Hill: University of North Carolina Press.

Barber, William. 1981. The United States: Economists in a Pluralistic Polity. *HOPE* 13.3:513–47.

Bowen, Howard R. 1953. Graduate Education in Economics. *American Economic Review* 43 supplement.

Brinkley, Alan. 1995. *The End of Reform: New Deal Liberalism in Recession and War*. New York: Alfred A. Knopf.

Buchanan, James. 1979. *What Should Economists Do?* Indianapolis, Ind.: Liberty Press.

Cartter, Allan M. 1964. *American Universities and Colleges*. 9th ed. Washington, D.C.: American Council on Education.

———. 1966. *An Assessment of Quality in Graduate Education*. Washington, D.C.: American Council on Education.

Coase, Ronald. 1984. The New Institutional Economics. *Journal of Institutional and Theoretical Economics* 140 (March): 229–31.

Furner, Mary O. 1975. *Advocacy and Objectivity: A Crisis in the Professionalization of American Social Science, 1865–1905*. Lexington: University Press of Kentucky.

Lampman, Robert J., ed. 1993. *Economists at Wisconsin*. Madison: Board of Regents, University of Wisconsin.

Landreth, Harry, and David C. Colander. 1989. *History of Economic Theory*. 2d ed. Boston: Houghton Mifflin.

———. 1997. The Formalist Revolution in American Economics. Unpublished manuscript.

Northwestern University. 1935. *A List of Doctoral Dissertations Submitted at Northwestern University, 1896–1934*. Chicago: Northwestern University.

———. 1935–46. *Summaries of Doctoral Dissertations*. Vols. 3–14. Chicago: Northwestern University.

Ramstad, Yngve. 1987. Institutional Existentialism: More on Why John R. Commons Has So Few Followers. *Journal of Economic Issues* 21.2:661–71.

Rutherford, Malcolm. 1994. *Institutions in Economics*. Cambridge: Cambridge University Press.

Speigel, Henry William. 1991. *The Growth of Economic Thought*. 3d ed. Durham, N.C.: Duke University Press.

Stigler, George J., and Claire Friedland. 1975. The Citation Practices of Doctorates in Economics. *Journal of Political Economy* 83.3:477–507.

University of Minnesota. 1939–1968. *The Register of Ph.D. Degrees*. 2 vols. Minneapolis: University of Minnesota.

Yale University. 1961. *Yale University Doctors of Philosophy, 1861–1960*. New Haven, Conn.: Yale University.

Entrenching Disciplinary Competence: The Role of General Education and Graduate Study in Chicago Economics

Ross B. Emmett

Central to the lore surrounding the University of Chicago's economics department is the story of its transition in the 1930s and 1940s from a "mixed bag" of proto–Chicago school types, institutionalists, and quantitative economists (Reder 1982, 361–62) to the unified research program we call the "Chicago school." The story of this transition is sufficiently entrenched in the historical sensibilities of economists that most contemporary treatments simply equate Chicago economics with the school (Stein 1994) and therefore focus attention only on the ideological commitments, scientific theories, and policy/legal advice that form its unique approach to economics (Miller 1962; Bronfenbrenner 1962; Stigler 1962; Friedman 1974; Samuels 1976; Reder 1982, 1987; Schmidt and Rittaler 1989).

But other perspectives may reveal aspects of the story of Chicago economics that are obscured by the standard account. Suppose that instead of focusing attention on what is unique in the department's

An encapsulated version of material prepared for presentation at the 1997 *HOPE* conference, this essay also serves as a brief introduction to an argument regarding the history of Chicago economics that I will be pursuing over the next several years. I wish to thank Malcolm Rutherford, Mary Morgan, and Roy Weintraub for helpful comments, and the University of Chicago Archives for permission to quote from unpublished materials in the Department of Economics Records. My research was supported by the Social Sciences and Humanities Research Council of Canada and Augustana University College.

activities, we sought to focus attention on what is common. For example, what would we discover if we chose to examine the department's activities from the perspective of its curricular responsibilities? How might that perspective alter our usual account of Chicago economics during the period from the 1930s to the 1950s? And what would the altered account contribute to our understanding of the process by which American economics was transformed?

The results of my initial research on these questions are outlined in the next two sections. Two conclusions emerge. First, when Chicago economics is viewed from the perspective of its curricular responsibilities, the department's distinguishing characteristic over the period from the 1930s to the 1950s becomes the institutionalization of a *disciplinary self-critique*. Through its degree requirements, course material, comprehensive and preliminary examinations, research seminars, and the model of its faculty, Chicago economics enshrined the notion that a central feature of the work of a modern scientific economist was the use of the discipline's own methods to critique the work of other economists (including the "greats" of the past). Although this disciplinary self-critique has given Chicago economics its reputation for sharp criticism and narrowness of vision, its purpose was the single-minded pursuit of identifying and defining the proper zone of the discipline's competence. As the modern art critic Clement Greenberg (quoted in Klamer 1993, 241–42) has said: "The characteristic methods of a discipline [are employed] to criticize the discipline itself—not in order to subvert it, but to entrench it more firmly in its area of competence."

The second conclusion emerges from the first. Identifying the distinguishing characteristic of Chicago economics as the institutionalization of a disciplinary self-critique suggests that Chicago economics shared in the transformation described in the other essays in this volume. Rather than adopting an interpretive position that begins with the assumption that Chicago economics is unique and separate from the mainstream of American economics (e.g., through a focus on its monetary and industrial organization theorists), the interpretive position taken here allows us to view Chicago economics as part of a transformation that narrowed the boundaries of "legitimate" economics in the attempt to entrench it in its area of scientific competence.

The Legacy of Progressive-Pragmatist
Education

To those familiar with the history of American higher education in the twentieth century, the decision to use the curricular responsibilities of a University of Chicago department as the lens through which to focus attention on its activities is obviously not accidental. The raging debates over educational reform that characterized the university during this period reflected ambiguities and uncertainties within American society with regard to how traditional values could best be recast in the context of a modern liberal democracy and what role higher education was to play in that reformulation. Furthermore, the pedagogical debates throughout the university were often intertwined with debates within (and sometimes between) disciplines regarding the scientific legitimacy of competing knowledge claims, the proper scope of the discipline's attention, and the relation between the discipline's knowledge and social discussion about policy issues.

Ostensibly, educational reform at the University of Chicago began in the early 1930s, after the installation of Robert Hutchins as the university's fifth president in 1929. In 1931, the New Plan for the College of the University of Chicago removed responsibility for general education from the divisions. From 1931 to 1942, the college provided a general education for all first- and second-year students, followed by two years of university education in a discipline supervised by a division. From 1942 to 1953, Chicago granted B.A.'s on completion of the college (which was redesigned to admit students earlier, hence creating three to four years of general education). From 1942 on, then, all students entering economics were pursuing an advanced degree—the education of a specialist.

The reforms of the 1930s and 1940s, however, were predicated on a growing uneasiness regarding the appropriateness of the educational objectives inherited from the Progressive and Pragmatist movements at the turn of the century. Disturbed by the social impotence of individualism and traditional American Protestantism in an industrial capitalist society, Progressives had sought to restore order in the context of a free society. Lacking confidence in the all-encompassing certainties that traditionally undergirded American values, Progressives typically employed divide-and-conquer strategies that created boundaries between areas of human activity (work and home, science and art, urban and rural, civilization and wilderness, professional and amateur, biology and society) in order to develop mechanisms of control appropriate to each.

One of the divisions Progressives pursued was the separation of disciplines within the academy. Traditional American higher education had emphasized the unity of knowledge undergirded by moral philosophy. Progressive education emphasized widening the circle of informed citizenry in order to eradicate ignorance. The task of spreading intelligence in a particular area of knowledge was increasingly entrusted to the "professionals"—academics who had studied the area intensively. Hence, the separation of disciplines was closely related to the professionalization of the academy. Economic problems required the attention of a professional economist—someone who had taken the time to study the issues in depth. But we need to be careful here; studying a problem in depth does not necessarily depend on the acquisition of specialized knowledge or methods of inquiry. In the early twentieth century, professionalization created a new organizational context in which the search for economic knowledge took place, but the resulting separation of the disciplines took some time to generate knowledge claims based on the application of specialized methods (Geiger 1986, 27).

Distinguishing professionalization from specialized knowledge proves useful when examining educational reform in the Progressive Era. The central educational distinction for Progressives was between intelligence and ignorance. Although experts, such as professional economists, appeared during this period, their role emerged from their professional engagement in the task of creating informed citizens and overcoming the pressing problems of the day. Graduate education, therefore, was an extension of general education. If anything distinguished the two, it was the extra time graduate education allowed for extensive examination of a particular problem. Looking back at graduate education during the Progressive Era from his vantage point in the mid- to late 1920s, the chair of the Chicago Economics Department, Leon C. Marshall, described it as a "continuation of senior college [work] . . . with little advance in method save for the thesis." Progressive Era senior college work was identified by Marshall as consisting of "miscellaneous offerings in varying 'fields' or 'problems'" in economics (Marshall n.d.).

The Progressive Era came to an end with the horrors of World War I, the frustrations of President Woodrow Wilson's foreign policy endeavors, and the recognition of the impassable void between public opinion and intelligence. The death of progressivism intensified the problem of uncertainty by demolishing any lingering hopes that the divide-and-conquer strategy might eventually lead to some form of social order. But rather than developing an alternative strategy, social scientists directed their energy toward transforming the strategy in order to continue its domination, even without its millenarian hopes.

Among social scientists, the intensification of the divide-and-conquer strategy had several aspects. First, there was a gradual turn inward: Attention was directed away from the social questions and problems that had so preoccupied the Progressive Era and toward questions circumscribed by the boundaries of the discipline. For example, in the collection of essays Rexford Tugwell edited in 1924, called *The Trend of Economics*, contemporary economic issues are often identified as "larger problems" that lie outside (or above) the purview of the economist. More frequently, attention is focused on intradiscipline controversies over appropriate methodologies.

Hand in glove with the inward turn was the practice of accepting criticism only from within the circle of those schooled in the discipline's methods. Although the lines between sociology, economics, political science, and history were still not secured in the 1920s, economists were less likely to take criticisms of their work by sociologists as seriously as they took criticisms from economists. And as methodological debate among American economists intensified during the 1920s, the circle of legitimate critics slowly shrank; legitimate criticisms became only those from within one's own methodological circle.

The interwar intensification of the divide-and-conquer strategy among social scientists also had an impact that histories of economic thought often overlook: It radically redefined social science education. Central to that revolution was the rapid demarcation of graduate education for disciplinary specialists from the demands of general education for an informed citizenry. Untethered from its stake in addressing present-day concerns, the education of the specialist gradually became focused on training in new methods and a self-referential disciplinary critique that would enable new Ph.D.'s to be better social scientists than their predecessors.

Marshall's previously mentioned memo chronicles a portion of this transformation as it occurred at the University of Chicago. By the mid-1920s, the principles of economics course had been moved to the first year, and second- and third-year students took introductory courses in various fields of economics, which Marshall identified as courses examining the various "functions" of economics rather than mere economic "problems." "Competent" senior students were admitted to "advanced work," in which the newest research methods were introduced. Graduate students continued this advanced study in their course work, although Marshall admitted that graduate education was still limited in terms of training students intensively in new methods and generating creative research. However, Marshall pointed the way toward what modernist education in economics was to become during the 1930s. What the Chicago department was working toward, he said, was a situation in which graduate students engage in only "creative" work using the newest methods. The new methods themselves were taught in university (as opposed to college) courses, which were available to competent senior undergraduate students who were considering graduate study. In his vision of graduate education at Chicago, then, Marshall encapsulated the radical transformation of social scientific education: a broadening of the economics education offered to develop informed citizens, coupled with a narrowing of the economics education offered in advanced and graduate work, the latter characterized by the acquisition and creative use of new methods (Marshall Papers, University of Chicago Archives).

Chicago Economics and the "Great Debate" over General Education

Chicago economics underwent a transformation during the period from 1930 to the mid-1950s that reflected its emerging focus on disciplinary self-critique. Integral to that transformation was the relation between Chicago's increasingly specialized research and its changing conception of economic education. In this section, we will examine the relation between Chicago economics and the changing conception of general education at the University of Chicago. The next section will examine the transformation of senior undergraduate and graduate education in the department.

The reform of general education at the University of Chicago had immediate impacts on the economics faculty. After 1931, and especially after 1942, departmental faculty had no responsibility for general education. Beginning in 1931, the college hired its own staff, who were assumed to be free from the research requirements of departmental staff in order to focus on general education: "The College is not an institution for research," its purpose rather is "to insure proper adjustment to [the] complex and changing environment" of modernity (E. H. Wilkins, quoted in Orlinsky 1992, 42).

But what type of education best ensured "proper adjustment" to modernity? That question gave rise to the "great debate," actually a set of debates over specific proposals for educational reform spread over a period of approximately twenty years.[1] President Hutchins (following Mortimer Adler) advocated a "great books" approach, but most faculty (in the college and in the divisions) advocated a continuation of the university's tradition of a Progressive-Pragmatist educational program that focused on showing how ignorance had been eradicated by the progress of science. The curricular reform emerging from these debates occupied the attention of many faculty members throughout the 1930s and 1940s and directly affected Chicago economics in three ways.

First, the development of the General Course in the Social Sciences reflected this debate and involved economists in both the college and the department. Harry Gideonese was hired in 1931 to help coordinate the new social science survey course, along with Louis Wirth (sociology) and Jerome Kerwith (political science). Under their guidance, the new course took a definite turn toward the "eradication of ignorance through the progress of science" direction. All the texts chosen were "classics" in the social sciences, but not the classics that Hutchins and Adler promoted in their "great books" course. Rather, the readings chosen were classics because they were *new* and represented the forefront of social scientific knowledge. In many cases, the new classics used the methods of a social scientific discipline to challenge conventional thinking; among the authors whose readings were included in the course syllabus in the 1930s were Max Weber, Bronisław Malinowski, and Frank Knight (portions of *The Economic Organization*). Subsequent revisions of the syllabus during the 1940s and 1950s incorporated newer classics, frequently written by Chicago social scientists.

The students' background in the social science survey courses allowed the Economics Department to assume that incoming students were both well read in the classics of social science and familiar with Knight's introduction to economics prior to taking elementary economics. Departmental courses, even at the senior undergraduate level, could therefore

---

1. Histories of the Chicago curricular debates can be found in Dzuback 1991; McNeill 1991; and Orlinsky 1992.

focus on educating specialists. Students who had accepted the survey course's message regarding the eradication of ignorance through the progress of science were ready to move to the forefront of the scientific discipline.

Second, faculty members participated directly in the "great debate." With the exception of John Nef, the economics faculty stood against the Hutchins-Adler reform proposals. Knight's 1934 (21) missive against Adler's neomedievalism is indicative of the economists' response. Asking the question "Is modern thought anti-intellectual?" Knight answered in the negative and chastened his opponents for using education as the opportunity for advocacy rather than for the search for truth:

> Any education looking toward truth must place literally all possible emphasis on the criticism and testing of individual ideas. . . . It is simply a patent and unescapable fact that the immediate product of thinking is nearly always wrong and usually foolish. . . . Yet so great is credulity that we see great numbers of persons open to influence by propaganda which, under the guise of human betterment, palpably looks toward making the promoters the rulers of society. This does not apply merely to any single small group. It is the nature of practically all social reform propaganda. . . . Neither society nor any group or class in it can be an intellectual community unless we begin with an overwhelming presumption against the soundness of any teaching whose promoters cannot place themselves above suspicion of motivation by other interests than love of truth and right. Between advocating and truth-seeking, meaning the quest of right answers to problems, there is a nearly *impassable* gulf.

Gideonese and his colleagues in the college immediately incorporated Knight's essay into the reading package for the General Course in the Social Sciences, where it remained until the syllabus was redesigned in the early 1940s. Knight and Henry Simons frequently commented on the campus debates in their classes, and Simons sometimes joined Gideonese for the weekly roundtable talks on the campus radio (hosted by Gideonese's college colleague Kerwith). Gideonese's running battle during the 1934–35 academic year with the Adlerite editor of the campus newspaper, the *Daily Maroon*, also won the support of Chicago economists. When the editor refused to print Gideonese's responses to his editorials, Gideonese posted the responses outside his office door, where they found a ready audience of faculty and students.

Gideonese's campaign against Hutchins reached its high point in 1937 when he published *The Higher Learning in a Democracy: A Reply to President Hutchins' Critique of the American University* at the same time that he pursued the deanship of the college: "'Books . . . put in place of things.' This is . . . perhaps the final comment upon an educational proposal to substitute the classics of the Western world for scientific training in our modern society. To have it come from the University of Chicago—which has always stressed the method of science since its birth—adds to the confusion of the higher learning in America" (4, 23–24). Needless to say, Gideonese did not become dean, and two years later Hutchins denied him tenure despite enthusiastic support from college and departmental faculty for his appointment (Dzuback 1991, 126–27, 181–82).[2]

Finally, the background of senior undergraduate and graduate students in general education produced a tension between disciplinary specialization and interdisciplinarity. One of the results of that tension was the creation of the Committee on Social Thought (CST) in the early 1940s. Two economists on opposite sides of the "great debate" were actively involved in the establishment of the CST—Nef and Knight—and the CST hosted Friedrich von Hayek during his stay at Chicago. The CST provided a graduate education option for those who did not want a specialist education and provided faculty who resisted specialization with a means of participating in graduate education. The CST option therefore had two unintended consequences: the creation of a cadre of specialists in interdisciplinarity who were well suited to teaching in the emerging general education programs of universities and liberal arts colleges and increased specialization in the disciplines because graduate students and faculty who resisted specialization could always be redirected into the CST.

Graduate Economics Education:
Entrenching Disciplinary Competence

Over the period from 1930 to the mid-1950s, the structure of graduate education remained relatively stable, comprised of a sequence of inter-

2. The split between the college and the departments did emerge in Gideonese's time at Chicago, however. Despite their support for his tenure, the departmental faculty did not support Gideonese's appointment as a full professor on the grounds that he had done insufficient research for a Chicago professor (McNeill 1991, 84).

mediate courses in theory and what Marshall had described as "introductions to the graduate study of . . . ," followed by subfield survey courses and then research seminars. The new face of Chicago economics is seen, however, in the changing requirements, the altered focus of the various courses in the program, the changing role of the comprehensive and preliminary examinations, and the eventual appearance of workshops and research groups, the laboratories of modernist social science.[3]

The early 1930s continued the pattern described in Marshall's memo: building on the breadth of a general education to train specialists who were equipped to address fields of study that, although perhaps originally conceived as "problem areas," were emerging as "functional" areas or applied fields. Students faced relatively few specific requirements in their advanced-degree programs, reflecting the Progressive Era's legacy of assuming that general education prepared intelligent people to tackle the problems of society. However, from the mid-1930s to the mid-1940s, the structure of graduate education was gradually tightened through the introduction of a more regulated degree program. By 1945, there was little mention of the breadth of a student's general educational background, and the focus was on the structure of course work required in the department. Doctoral students, for example, were required to complete an intermediate or subfield survey course in at least ten different fields of economics (required fields were economic theory, accounting, statistics, economic history, and money and banking; elective fields were corporate finance, labor and personnel administration, monopoly and public utilities, agricultural economics, government finance, and international economics) or related areas (only two of the ten could be outside economics and were usually international relations, human development, or social thought); to select two of those fields, along with economic theory, as specializations; to write preliminary examinations in the fields of specialization (this usually required an additional three to five courses in each area of specialization); and to complete a thesis.[4]

3. These changes were accompanied by several other changes that reflect the same movement but will not be described here: the separation of the Business School from economics; the arrival of the Cowles Commission in 1939; the simultaneous decline in the number of women students in economics and increase in the number of women students in the Schools of Social Service Administration and Home Economics; and the rise of collaborative research.

4. Information regarding degree requirements comes from the yearly *Announcements* of the University of Chicago.

The movement from flexible to structured advanced-degree programs was accompanied by an altered focus within economics courses. During the early 1930s, the focus of most economics courses, apart from economic theory, was still largely problem oriented. This changed dramatically during the 1930s, however, as the courses underwent two simultaneous changes: the subfield survey courses became method oriented rather than problem oriented, and price theory came to play a dominant role in almost every subfield. The overarching presence of Knight, Jacob Viner, and Oskar Lange—the triumvirate who taught the core theory courses—certainly had something to do with the transformation, but equally important was the extension of a focus on methods into courses in public finance, monetary theory, agricultural economics, and statistics. Patinkin's (1981, 4) comments on his experience in Simons's infamous senior undergraduate course in price theory are relevant to much of Chicago economics by the 1940s: "I learned the hard way . . . that full understanding of the principles of economic analysis could be achieved only after sweating through their application to specific problems." Thus, by the 1940s, Chicago economics courses focused on the application and extension of methods gained in the core areas of economic theory and statistics.

Two fields that are often thought to counteract the alteration in the focus of economics courses are economic history and history of economic thought. However, during this period at Chicago, this was not the case. History of economic thought was part of the economic theory core that all doctoral students had to take and was taught by Knight. From available accounts of the course and the lecture notes in Knight's papers in the University of Chicago Archives, it is clear that Knight's approach to the course is reasonably represented by his famous 1935 article "The Ricardian Theory of Production and Distribution," which begins, "On the assumption that the primary interest in the 'ancients' in such a field as economics is to learn from their mistakes, the principal theme of this discussion will be the contrast between the 'classical' system and 'correct' views" (3). By constructing a "classical" system of thought that could be separated from and contrasted with "correct" contemporary systems, Knightian history of economic thought trained students to critique economics from within in order to strengthen their hold on its contemporary competencies.[5]

---

5. Stigler 1941 is the most famous product of Knight's history of thought training and well represents the role of the history of economic thought in developing a disciplinary self-critique.

Much the same can be said for economic history, although the story is a bit more complicated in that field. Under Nef, who was sympathetic to the neo-Thomism of Hutchins and Adler, economic history became the study of an economy set in a civilization separate from the unsettling problems of modernity. (See Cantor 1991 for an examination of how medievalists constructed an account of a unified society, which could be contrasted with the perceived fragmentation of modernity.) During the 1940s, Nef twice made an attempt to bring both Harold Innis and Earl Hamilton to Chicago, in part because Nef was gradually moving out of teaching economics in order to give more attention to his interdisciplinary responsibilities. Hamilton did join the faculty in 1947 and brought a different orientation to economic history than Nef's. Hamilton's attempt to construct a price history for Spain and Europe during the period of the influx of American treasure required the application of price theory. Unfortunately for Hamilton, Chicago economists in the 1950s were well versed in disciplinary self-critique, and several were quick to show that his well-intentioned point was not supported by a correct application of price theory (Kessel and Alchian 1960). Nevertheless, the controversy over Hamilton's work opened economic history to the application of economic theory, leading soon after to the initiation of quantitative history.

The revised structure of degree programs and the altered focus of course work in economics were reflected in the changed role of the department's comprehensive and preliminary examinations. Largely under the influence of Knight and Viner, with the participation of Simons, Lloyd Mints, and new department members such as Lange, examinations underwent significant change during the 1930s. Prior to the 1930s, examinations were primarily opportunities for students to exhibit what they had learned about a specific field. Although the questions on the examinations remained basically the same during the 1930s and 1940s, acceptable answers focused more on the candidate's ability to apply price theory.[6]

The changes in the degree structure, the alteration in the focus of courses, and the changes in legitimate examination answers reflect a fundamental shift from the 1930s to the late 1940s in Chicago economics. From the Progressive Era, during which the University of Chicago

6. Copies of examinations from the 1930s to the 1950s can be found in the Department of Economics Records in the University of Chicago Archives. Evidence of the changed focus of examination is best found in stories told by former Chicago students.

was launched, through the early 1930s, a Chicago economist was an intelligent person dedicated to studying a particular set of problems and exercising a public responsibility to widen the realm of intelligence through teaching and researching. By the late 1940s, a Chicago economist was a person who possessed specialized methods for the acquisition of knowledge and the ability to discern between truth (knowledge that in principle was in accordance with the discipline's methods) and error. The Chicago economist's public responsibility now lay in acquiring new knowledge, training graduate students in the discipline's methods, and assisting the public in understanding the boundaries of the discipline's competence.

The most significant educational reform in the department after the initiation of more restrictive requirements for graduate degrees in the early 1940s was the introduction of workshops and research groups in the late 1940s and early 1950s. Collaborative research was a common feature of Chicago economics during the 1940s, and the notion that research groups could be the loci of collaborative research and the supervision of graduate students who were utilizing new research methods in their area of specialization was strengthened by the example of the Cowles Commission, which had moved to the University of Chicago in 1939 (Cowles Commission 1952; Hildreth 1986). During the late 1940s, several other research groups emerged, and in the early 1950s, the workshop model was explicitly adopted as the standard method for training Ph.D. students.

The educational rationale for the workshop model was provided in a memo to the department from H. Gregg Lewis (undated but probably from the late 1940s or early 1950s). Lewis, one of the departmental advisers of students, had been "discomforted for some time by the belief that graduate faculties of economics generally are neglecting their responsibilities for making economics an effective science and for training their students as scientific craftsmen" (Lewis n.d.). Citing Knight as a "shining example" of the economist as moral philosopher, Lewis chided his colleagues for thinking that they and most students had "the stuff that makes for good moral philosophers." While department members expend their energies primarily in that direction, "economics as a science languishes." Although no one solution would revive economics as a science, Lewis proposed a reorganization of graduate study in economics that would bring it closer to the model of scientific training in the natural sciences. Quoting Arthur Burns, who had first suggested the idea of laboratories in the social sciences, Lewis recommended that the Chicago department set up a system where

> each professor—whether of money and banking, business cycles, public finance, or what not—will have his own laboratory. He will have one or two assistants who would share responsibility for the laboratory, and other assistants as needed. The students (doctoral candidates) in a certain subject will get their training in the laboratory, by working on some project. The individual assignments will be of limited scope, but it will be the function of the professor in charge to see that they fit together. The projects will grow out of the research program of the laboratory and will be supervised closely.

The workshop model of Chicago economics began during the late 1940s when several permanent research seminars were established in fields in which students could specialize as part of their doctoral programs: agricultural economics, labor, econometrics, and government finance. The Cowles Commission had been running seminars for several years before this, and they were integrated into the departmental offerings at this same time. Perhaps the most famous of the first Chicago workshops was the one in money and banking that Milton Friedman organized in 1952. Shortly after its inception, it teamed up with the newly formed research group in economic development to create a social laboratory in Chile. Researchers-in-training were sent there to conduct experiments in monetary policy rules and the measurement of economic activity under the supervision of the department's senior researchers (Valdés 1995). In 1952–53, the Chicago department formally integrated graduate student participation in workshops and research groups into the doctoral program. By the mid-1950s, the department's research center sponsored workshops and research groups in money and banking (Phillip Cagan, Friedman); agricultural economics (Robert Gustafson, Dale Johnson, T. W. Schultz, George Tolley); public finance (Martin J. Bailey, Arnold Harberger); economic development (Hamilton, Harberger, Bert Hoselitz, Simon Rottenberg, Schultz); labor economics and industrial relations (H. Gregg Lewis, Albert Rees, Rottenberg); and the economics of consumption (Margaret Reid).

When Burns originally suggested this model, he probably thought of the laboratories as extensions into graduate departments of the National Bureau of Economic Research model developed by Wesley Mitchell.

At Chicago, however, theory and measurement existed in creative tension, and workshop discussions almost always focused on how well the analysis built on price theory (e.g., see Patinkin 1981, 15). The tension between theory and measurement in the workshops also strengthened the Chicago economics program's inculcation of disciplinary self-critique. The opportunity for graduate students and faculty to critique current research on an equal footing created an environment that, at its best, allowed for brilliant theoretical insights informing empirical studies and incisive critical exercises employing the discipline's basic principles and methods. Many of the classic articles of Chicago economics from the 1950s on emerged from and were refined by discussion in its workshops.

Conclusion

Within an institutional context that facilitated the radical demarcation of the education of the disciplinary specialist from the education of informed citizens, Chicago economics refined a disciplinary self-critique that entrenched a particular set of competencies, both theoretical and empirical, in its researchers and researchers-in-training (graduate students). If anything may be said to characterize Chicago economics, it is the intensity with which this disciplinary self-critique was carried out in a collaborative fashion. From the late 1930s to the 1950s, Chicago economics came to equate "good" economics with the construction of new "classics"—concise, clear, and elegant models that pushed the boundaries of form without abandoning the theoretical content of the discipline's mainstream.

References

Bronfenbrenner, M. 1962. Observations on the "Chicago School." *Journal of Political Economy* 70 (February): 72–75.

Cantor, N. F. 1991. *Inventing the Middle Ages: The Lives, Works, and Ideas of the Great Medievalists of the Twentieth Century*. New York: Morrow.

Cowles Commission. 1952. *Economic Theory and Measurement*. Chicago: Cowles Commission for Research in Economics.

Dzuback, M. A. 1991. *Robert M. Hutchins: Portrait of an Educator*. Chicago: University of Chicago Press.

Friedman, M. 1974. Schools at Chicago. *University of Chicago Magazine*, August, 11–16.

Geiger, R. L. 1986. *To Advance Knowledge: The Growth of American Research Universities, 1900–1940.* New York: Oxford University Press.

Gideonese, H. 1937. *The Higher Learning in a Democracy: A Reply to President Hutchins' Critique of the American University.* New York: Farrar and Rinehart.

Hildreth, C. 1986. *The Cowles Commission in Chicago, 1939–1955.* Edited by M. Beckman and W. Krelle. Lecture Notes in Economics and Mathematical Systems, vol. 271. New York: Springer-Verlag.

Kessel, R. A., and A. A. Alchian. 1960. The Meaning and Validity of the Inflation-Induced Lag of Wages behind Prices. *American Economic Review* 50 (March): 43–66.

Klamer, A. 1993. Modernism in Economics: An Interpretation beyond Physics. In *Non-Natural Social Science: Reflecting on the Enterprise of More Heat than Light.* Edited by N. de Marchi. Durham, N.C.: Duke University Press.

Knight, F. H. 1934. Modern Thought: Is It Anti-Intellectual? *University of Chicago Magazine*, November, 20–21, 23.

———. 1935. The Ricardian Theory of Production and Distribution. *Canadian Journal of Economic and Political Science* 1 (February, May): 3–25, 171–96.

Lewis, H. Gregg. n.d. Memorandum. Box 41, Folder 1, Department of Economic Records, University of Chicago Archives, Chicago, Ill.

Marshall, Leon C. n.d. Situations of Chicago. Memorandum. Box 5, Folder 17, Department of Economics Records, University of Chicago Archives, Chicago, Ill.

McNeill, William H. 1991. *Hutchins' University: A Memoir of the University of Chicago, 1929–1950.* Chicago: University of Chicago Press.

Miller, H. L., Jr. 1962. On the "Chicago School of Economics." *Journal of Political Economy* 70 (February): 64–69.

Orlinsky, D. E. 1992. Not Very Simple, but Overflowing: A Historical Perspective on General Education at the University of Chicago. In *General Education in the Social Sciences: Centennial Reflections on the College of the University of Chicago.* Edited by J. J. MacAloon. Chicago: University of Chicago Press.

Patinkin, D. 1981. Introduction: Reminiscences of Chicago, 1941–47. In *Essays on and in the Chicago Tradition.* Durham, N.C.: Duke University Press.

Reder, M. W. 1982. Chicago Economics: Permanence and Change. *Journal of Economic Literature* 20 (March): 1–38.

———. 1987. Chicago School. In *The New Palgrave Dictionary of Economics.* Edited by J. Eatwell, M. Milgate, and P. Newman. New York: Stockton Press.

Samuels, W. J., ed. 1976. *The Chicago School of Political Economy.* East Lansing: Association for Evolutionary Economics and Division of Research, Graduate School of Business Administration, Michigan State University.

Schmidt, I. L. O., and J. B. Rittaler. 1989. *A Critical Evaluation of the Chicago School of Antitrust Analysis.* Studies in Industrial Organization. Boston: Kluwer.

Stein, H. 1994. Chicago Economics. In *The Blackwell Dictionary of Twentieth-Century Social Thought.* Edited by W. Outhwaite and T. Bottomore. London: Blackwell.

Stigler, G. J. 1941. *Production and Distribution Theories*. New York: Macmillan.
————. 1962. Comment. *Journal of Political Economy* 70 (February): 70–71.
University of Chicago Archives, Chicago, Ill. Department of Economics Records.
Valdés, J. G. 1995. *Pinochet's Economists: The Chicago School in Chile*. Modern
    Economics in Historical Perspective. Cambridge: Cambridge University Press.

Part 3

"Market Failure" or "Market Efficiency"

Hope for America: American Notions of Economic Planning between Pluralism and Neoclassicism, 1930–1950

Márcia L. Balisciano

> National Planning is an essential to the future prosperity, happiness, and
> the very existence of the American people. (Franklin Roosevelt,
> quoted in Beard [1932] 1969, 340)

In 1932, at the depths of the depression, one U.S. economist noted:
"'Economic planning' recently has become the epigrammatic program
of practically every economic interest group in our Nation. From the
radicalism of the extreme left to the conservatism of the extreme right,
from the Communists to the United States Chamber of Commerce, economic planning has come to be the accepted way out of our economic
plight" (Loucks 1932, 114).[1] Indeed, pluralism was a fundamental characteristic of the ideologies of economic planning in the interwar period.

I thank all the participants of the 1997 *HOPE* conference for their helpful comments during
the initial presentation of this paper. In particular, I am grateful for the time and insight of
Malcolm Rutherford, Mary Morgan, Craufurd Goodwin, Bob Coats, and Fred Lee, all of
whom commented on the written draft. I accept full responsibility, however, for the final product. Correspondence may be addressed to me at the Department of Economic History, London School of Economics, Houghton Street, London WC2 2AE.

    1. Notions of planning in the United States between 1930 and 1950 were prevalent on
many fronts, including local (e.g., city planning efforts from Boston to Los Angeles), state
(e.g., through the proliferation of state planning boards; by 1935 all but two states, Louisiana
and Delaware, had a planning agency), regional (e.g., the Tennessee Valley Authority), and
international (e.g., debate over U.S. tariff policy). Likewise, planning was frequently suggested as a tool at these various levels for the efficient utilization of natural resources, for
redressing physical infrastructure problems, or for reshaping legal or political frameworks.

Although inquiries into the way free market processes might be augmented, especially in the wake of some economic or social problem, are a long-standing American tradition, economic planning represented a conceptual departure. Unlike previous economic policy ideals such as progressive reform (the economy needed "help" through new public and private initiatives) and regulationism (the economy needed legislation to curb economic "sinning"), planning was predicated on the assumption that intervention—either through direct or indirect methods—was necessary for a well-functioning, dynamic economy.[2]

Among events and circumstances that helped foster "planning" in the years between the two world wars was the World War I mobilization experience, which highlighted the potential of government control and government-business cooperation (Crowell and Wilson 1921; Graham 1976, 6–8); the 1920–21 recession, which hastened the search for new ways to offset destabilizing economic fluctuations (Barber 1985); and, in an age of technological advance, a growing faith in "science," which promised to deliver efficiency in both government and business. Yet by far the most pivotal event that led to the enunciation of economic planning as a national tool was the Great Depression. In the wake of the October 1929 stock market crash, economic chaos mounted. Whereas only 3.2 percent of the labor force was unemployed in 1929, by 1933 that figure climbed to 21–25 percent of the working population. In the same period, real output fell by 29 percent (Atack and Passell 1994, 584). National product shrank in nominal terms from $103 billion in 1929 to $56 billion by 1933 (*Historical Statistics* 1975, 224).

In this climate, planning developed as a flexible and fluid concept. Forward actions of all kinds were proposed beneath the banner of planning in order, it was hoped, to define, shape, and ultimately improve economic outcomes. A "planner" came to be seen as one who discussed and debated economic problems. Discussion and debate became "planning." Proposed solutions became "plans." For example, to see Amer-

---

This study, however, is principally concerned with ideologies of economic planning at the national level during the period.

2. Reform (progressive taxation, resource conservation) and regulation (laws, regulatory agencies) were responses to sweeping economic and social change wrought by rapid industrialization and urbanization in late-nineteenth- and early-twentieth-century America. In the case of regulation and the Sherman Antitrust Act, as Anne Mayhew has shown in this volume, economists were not early supporters; in a choice between large industrial combination and atomistic competition, many preferred the latter.

ica's economic problem as too much regulation and to call for greater liberty for industry became business planning. Or to see the problem as a lack of liquidity in financial markets and to call for an infusion of currency into the economy became monetary planning. Because of its many hues, planning became the "epigrammatic program of . . . every economic interest group." Planning was a mirror for the pluralism of American society in the 1930s and thus defied precise definition. As such, it was also a mirror for the pluralism of American economics and American economists during those years.

Four distinct though frequently overlapping ideologies of economic planning at the national level came to light in the depression, the strands of which affected the immediate shape of the New Deal, the tenor of the wartime economy, and, finally, plans and aspirations for the postwar era. By 1950, however, enthusiasm for planning was fading and, with it, much of the heterodoxy of American economics. Of the four approaches, only one, macroeconomic planning, appeared to survive the tests of economic success and political feasibility and, as such, held considerable sway over economic thought and policy in subsequent decades. Although the popularity of planning in general waned as the fortunes of neoclassical theory rose, a planning *ideal* (the common thread among the four) remained, leaving a definitive imprint on American political economy.

The Four Approaches and Their Influence on the New Deal

An examination of the statements of a diverse group of planners before the New Deal reveals a planning ideal rooted in common perceptions (see Haan 1931). Among these was the notion that "old economics," the "economics of original sin," had failed (Foster 1932, 52). There was further agreement on the need to identify national objectives in order to halt socioeconomic drift. Recurring national objectives included the balancing of production with consumption, more equitable income distribution, and conservation of national resources. The ultimate aim was economic democracy, a new American "right," united with an older right, political democracy. The intertwining of the two formed the essence of the planning ideal as it emerged in the depression. Planners believed the two were not mutually exclusive; they could coexist. A job for all Americans who could and wanted to work, decent housing and wages, and help through social legislation for those in need were the practical concerns of economic democracy. Yet another binding tie among an otherwise disparate group of planners was general optimism that through planning, these aims could be achieved. There was a resolute faith in America's resources, technological capability, collective intelligence, and cooperative spirit—in sum, the forces that would allow American planners to "get the job done."

Whereas representatives of Joseph Stalin at the World Social Economic Congress, held in Amsterdam in 1931, believed American planning to be a Russian import (Obolensky-Ossinsky 1932), U.S. planners countered that in fact the Russians had expropriated planning from America.[3] Planning, they maintained, was a politically neutral concept. Herein lay its principal justification. Planning could and must be separated from its execution. One could not cast aspersions on the planning idea just because it had been used in a totalitarian fashion by one nation. In its pursuit of economic democracy, Russia was willing to forgo political democracy; that is, the ends of Russian planning justified totalitarian means. In contrast, American planning, they argued, would pursue and achieve economic and political democracy simultaneously.

Although planners held the ideal in common, agreement on objectives proved easier than agreement on how to achieve them. One commentator noted, "The problem confronting us is not the simple issue of planning or no planning." The real challenge was "how much planning, by whom, [and] under whose auspices" (Beard [1932] 1969, 403). Responses to this dilemma were conditioned by planners' perceptions of economic problems, which determined the solutions or plans they put forth. Their views were based on a set of interrelated variables—

---

3. Influential economic writer and planning "popularizer" Stuart Chase (1931, 568) argued, "With highest respect these Slavs seem to think that they discovered national planning; that unless one knows Papa Marx backward he cannot locate an industry near its source of raw material or untangle a problem of cross-hauling." Yet President Herbert Hoover declared, "I presume the 'plan' idea is an infection from the slogan of the 'five year plan' through which Russia is struggling to redeem herself from . . . ten years of starvation and misery." Nonetheless he was not dissuaded from proposing his own "American plan" on the occasion (Beard [1932] 1969, 396). Hoover had actually been instrumental in fostering limited advisory planning in the 1920s at both the national level (through his sponsorship of studies into ways of mitigating the business cycle) and the state and local level (through his support for numerous local planning measures, including the Standard City Planning Enabling Act of 1927).

the planning mix—comprising their personal background, conception of history, objectives, and so forth. The planning mix was the ideological baggage planners brought to their analysis of economic issues. And from their planning mix, planners frequently pulled forth "metaphors," existing or prior economic or other experiences around which they built their plans.

In fact, the plans proposed during the early years of the depression frequently dealt with a wide spectrum of issues that resists narrow classification. However, in looking at the economic problems and solutions suggested before the New Deal, four different ideologies can be identified: social management planning, technical-industrial planning, business economy planning, and macroeconomic planning (see table 1).[4] It is important to note, however, that economic planners often straddled ideological boundaries, given the common elements in their planning mix (e.g., the influence of shared teachers and texts). None of the aspirants to economic planning, for example, sought to overturn the capitalist system; they sought only to improve it. Furthermore, their views often changed over time, making planners interesting and complex examples of the economic pluralism of the age.

Social Management Planning

Two prominent social management planners in the 1930s were Columbia University economists Rexford Tugwell and J. M. Clark. Their thinking on planning reflected the writings of both John Dewey (1920)

---

4. Indeed, these are my categories, not those of the economists I have attempted to fit within them, but I believe they are generally descriptive of the type of planning that was proposed. Noticeably absent from the taxonomy is a category for liberal planners (in the traditional economic sense), best exemplified by members of the Chicago school in those years. This group believed that it was government's responsibility to take "positive" steps in order to foster free and competitive markets (see Director 1933 and Tippetts 1933). By far the most well-known expositor of this position was Henry Calvert Simons. In *A Positive Program for Laissez Faire*, Simons (1934, iii) laid out his "'Chicago' or '100 Per Cent Reserve' plan," which called for, among other measures, government action to limit wasteful selling and advertising practices; to eliminate monopoly; to establish definitive monetary rules (including the end of universal banking); to revamp the tax system with an eye toward redistributing wealth and income; and to institute the gradual withdrawal of subsidies and tariffs. Simons believed his program was "drastic enough to satisfy the most ardent reformers" and offered "abundant opportunity for real economic planning" (36). However Simons and others are not included in this discussion because they were not considered by contemporaries as planners; in Simons's words, "The real enemies of liberty in this country are the naive advocates of managed economy or national planning" (2).

Table 1 Four Ideologies of American Economic Planning at the National Level in the 1930s

	Social Management Planning	Technical-Industrial Planning	Business Economy Planning	Macroeconomic Planning
View of economic problem	Economic collapse results from an undirected, uncoordinated, and unbalanced economic system focused on the profit motive	Industry is prone to structural imbalance; lack of rational industrial control from the center leads to economic chaos	Individual businesses, suffering from lack of information, overproduce, causing a cycle of deflation and unemployment	Savings (profits) accumulate faster than "productive" investment, creating imbalances that lead to speculation and depression
View of economic solution; planning metaphor	Collective action guided by planning board to ensure continued growth and development of the industrial economy; World War I War Industries Board	Revamp industrial structure; scientific management	Industrial combination and price contracts; trade association movement of late nineteenth century	Countercyclical expenditure and advisory planning; 1920s idea of public works as a way to offset the business cycle
Who takes the lead in planning	Government in collaboration with all economic actors	Government and technical experts	Business	Government-business partnership
Objective	Institutional restructuring of economic (and social) life to achieve full utilization of national resources	Improvement of underlying industrial structure and hence market processes	Enlightened business self-management through cartelization	Manipulation of macrovariables to achieve a stable, high-performing economy

and Thorstein Veblen (1921).[5] Dewey's theme of knowledge as a vehicle for change is found in Clark's (1936, 61) pronouncement that "economics should contribute to the solution of [societal] problems." Moreover, the lag Veblen found between changing social and economic conditions and prevailing laws and institutions provided the underpinning for their pursuit of planning (see Gruchy 1939). As Tugwell (1932, 88) prescribed, "The first series of changes will have to do with statutes, with constitutions, and with government. The intention of eighteenth and nineteenth century law was to install and protect the principle of conflict; this . . . we shall be changing once and for all, and it will require the laying of rough, unholy hands on many a sacred precedent." It was here that other economists, like Wesley Mitchell, who prized the ideal of social management planning, parted company with the stronger rhetoric—the implied compulsion—in the planning statements of those like Tugwell. Mitchell felt it was far better to concentrate on research in order to dispense valuable information to business, which could then institute its own "intelligent planning."[6]

Tugwell and Clark, like other social management planners, surveyed the debris of the depression and concluded that America's economic problem was an undirected and uncoordinated economic system focused on the profit motive rather than production based on social need (see Soule 1932 and Hinrichs 1934). Pursuit of profit for profit's sake had resulted in structural imbalance between sectors and hence price inflexibility. Although efficiencies had reduced production costs, benefits in the form of higher wages for workers and lower prices for consumers had not been forthcoming. The long-term remedy for underconsumption was a restructuring of economic and social life—with government at the helm in cooperation with other economic partners—to ensure complete utilization of national resources for the greater good (Clark 1932, 245). The interim step was the creation of planning associations by industry to oversee production and pricing, with overall coordination by a national planning board (Tugwell 1933, 211–12). Concurrent measures would redistribute income (Clark 1939, 455).

Social management planners, including economic writers Stuart Chase and George Soule, disseminated these ideas to the public at large

5. Tugwell noted Veblen's impact on his thinking in *Books That Changed Our Minds* (Cowley 1939), while he remarked of Dewey, "I feel myself deeply in his debt" (1982, 156).

6. Thus Mitchell's (1927) research into the nature of business cycles was a way of revealing information about the economy that might prove useful to government and industry.

by comparing the proposed national planning board with the War Industries Board (WIB) of World War I. However, there was a problem in using the WIB as a metaphor to cope with overproduction in 1932 given its design to cope with underproduction of wartime necessities in 1918. In their insistence that their brand of planning would be compatible with American democracy, social management planners overlooked the fact that the WIB had curbed rather than broadened liberties and that such measures had been tolerated only because of the patriotic imperative of war. They maintained, however, an abiding faith in the unlimited potential of cooperation: If war had required teamwork, collaboration, and control from the center for mobilizing men and tanks, such factors could also be engaged for a successful peacetime economy. Although they were criticized for being vague on details, social management planners responded that planning was an evolutionary process that could be learned only by experimentation.

Technical-Industrial Planning

Economic democracy was an end to which technical-industrial planners aspired, but they differed from social managers in their emphasis on the industrial sector in their analysis of economic problems and solutions.[7] The ideas of Gardiner Means and Mordecai Ezekiel are exemplary. In 1937, as director of the Industrial Section of the Industrial Committee of the National Resources Committee (NRC), Means (1937a) advocated an economic research agenda on "the structure of industry." It would be "concerned primarily with the units through which industry is now carried on, the extent of concentration or dispersion of authority and of responsibility, of control and of interest. . . . It should result in recommendations as to the structure of planning

7. According to Gardiner Means (1940a, 16), "The system of policies consistent with [adjusting short-run price insensitivity] will add to government's other responsibilities a positive and continuing responsibility for insuring reasonably full employment." Mordecai Ezekiel (1939, 3) cited the travesty of "ten million wage earners and 25 million people . . . on the bare edge of existence" as justification for planning. Both were familiar with the work of social management planners Tugwell and Chase. As assistant secretary of agriculture (1933–36), Tugwell had worked with both Ezekiel and Means and suggested the latter for the Industrial Committee. Upon reading Chase's review of Means's *Modern Corporation and Private Property* (1932), Means (1933) was prompted to write, "You have said what [Adolph Berle and I] have been trying to say, but you have said it very much more lucidly so that I wish you had written the book yourself."

and acting for overall balance toward which this country should work." Means recognized that macropolicy was an important counterpart to his examination of microframeworks. He believed that investigations into achieving balance in the total economy would illuminate "effective solution[s]" to "more concrete problem[s]."[8] Consequently, as part of his research agenda, Means constructed disaggregated statistical models of the entire economy in order to analyze its resources (Qin 1993, 51–52).

In an NRC report based on research he conducted on the structure of the American economy, Means (1940a, 17) suggested, "It is possible that, in periods of deficient buying, the more important key industries could be induced to develop a combined program of expanded production which would both increase employment and supply the increased buying power capable of purchasing the additional goods produced." In the same publication, Ezekiel (1940, 41–45), an agricultural econometrician who served with Means on the Industrial Committee, drew out similar themes of industrial coordination, with oblique references to the "industrial expansion" program he had presented in *Jobs for All* (1939).[9] In the latter, Ezekiel suggested that "the . . . idea is to have each of the key basic industries prepare tentative programs for expanding its operations and pay roll in the year ahead, and then to check and revise those tentative programs against each other to be sure they fit together properly. Then each concern in these industries will be given advance orders for planned production, through contracts with a special government agency. These contracts will provide for the public purchase at a discount, of any portion of the programmed production which remains unsold" (3).[10] Ezekiel used the "ever-normal granary"

8. To this end, Means (1937a) advocated a "study of the way over-all operating policy now made by government . . . the way Federal Reserve policy, essential Treasury policy, international exchange policy, etc., actually come into being."

9. Ezekiel's subdued reference to his plan for expanding industrial output (first sketched in Ezekiel 1936) was a reflection of the noncontroversial advisory planning focus of NRC leaders like Charles E. Merriam and Frederic A. Delano. Although Means was willing to ask hard questions, he did not advocate enforcing answers. In his NRC report on production-consumption patterns, Means (1937b, Introduction, 5–6; emphasis added) stated, "The purpose of drafting such patterns is to *aid* in the making of government, corporate and private policy with the respect to the future."

10. Ezekiel (1939) envisaged "Industrial Authorities" as the administrative mechanisms for coordinating plans by industry; their work would in turn be integrated into the interindustry plan of a "Central Administrative Authority." Ezekiel proposed that prices should only fluctuate between a 10 percent maximum and minimum price range, with the minimum being

of the Agriculture Department (where he served as economic adviser)
—which stored excess crops from one year to the next—as the basis
for his "ever-normal warehouse." In popular expressions of technical-
industrial planning, however, the most pervasive metaphor was that of
scientific management, which had introduced science into the life of the
factory. Frederick Winslow Taylor's time and motion studies on the
plant floor had led to standardization of materials and processes, especially in multiplant firms, and apparent increases in production and
profitability. Significantly for technical-industrial planners, they had
shown that the planning of work could be separated from its execution.[11] Thus, in their accounts, technicians would take the lead in planning. Certainly Veblen's influence is palpable. It was, after all, Veblen
(1921, 141) who hoped for the overturning of "vested interests" by a
"Soviet of technicians."[12] Ezekiel (1936, 227) noted, "Our present confused economic system acts as a dam to hold back the flood of goods
and services our technicians and industries could produce, if we turned
them loose." Means's (1937b) proposed inquiry into the structure of
industry called for "the talents of political scientists, economists and
perhaps lawyers." In his opinion, "The coordination of operating policy
is fundamentally a technical job which should be handled within the
administration. This means that the membership of a coordinating
committee should be made up of technicians" (1938).

Business Economy Planning

Business economy planners, like technical-industrialists, considered
the experience of the multiplant firm the best metaphor for planning.
However, they saw that its success depended on management's ability
to coordinate the activities of each plant in accord with overall company goals. Greater stress, therefore, was placed on managers than on

---

the price at which government would buy unsold goods of the planned production. Those who
did not wish to comply with the "voluntary" contracts would be subject to a tax.

11. See, for example, the use of scientific management as the basis for technical-industrial
planning by H. S. Person (1932, 1934), director of the Taylor Society.

12. In Veblen's (1921, 133) view, the power of technicians rested on the fact that they controlled technology and information. Their expertise was the "indispensable factor in the
everyday work of carrying on the country's productive industry." The institutionalist character of Veblen's theories also influenced technical-industrial planners. Means (1940a, 16)
argued that inherited policies and the existing economic structure were not consistent.

technicians. Government was relegated to benevolent oversight: "Organized industry should take the lead, recognizing its responsibility to its employees, to the public, and to its stockholders—rather than that democratic society should act through its government. . . . If either the Individual States or the Federal Government act, the power of taxation has no economic restraints" (Frederick 1931, 22). Yet they, too, were motivated by the planning ideal, recognizing that "the responsibility for six millions of people out of work is too heavy to be borne without humility, shame and energetic thinking by the country's leading industrial leaders" (Frederick 1931, 14).

The aim of enlightened self-government through cartelization was expressed in the two dominant business economy proposals of the day: the 1931 Swope plan, authored by Gerard Swope, president of General Electric, and the U.S. Chamber of Commerce plan of 1931. Both advocated the reform of outmoded antitrust laws in order to achieve a vision of economic planning based on the metaphor of the trade association movement of the late nineteenth century. The Swope plan took a bottom-up approach, establishing trade associations with no overall coordinating body at the top other than a General Board of Administration made up of and appointed by employers and employees (along with public representatives) to oversee the plan's social insurance scheme. The Chamber of Commerce in contrast advocated a top-down strategy, with a National Economic Council as the foremost independent research body in the nation but with no formal industry groupings. Businesses would simply "enter into contracts for the purpose of equalizing production to consumption and so carrying on business on a sound basis." Contracts would be filed "with some governmental authority . . . [and remain] effective unless the governmental authority having supervision finds on its own initiative or on complaint that such agreements are not in the public interest, in which event such agreements would be abrogated" (quoted in Beard [1932] 1969, 204). At the heart of both plans was the idea of collective business action to outline trade practices, set standards in ethics and accounting procedure, share pertinent information, apportion market share, and set prices through production agreements. While business economy plans for cartelization and self-government were not surprising, they were original in their call for business-initiated comprehensive social insurance measures, including unemployment and disability insurance and pension programs.

Macroeconomic Planning

In the depression, macroeconomic planning came to be seen by advocates as the middle ground between the "standardized existence" of
social managers, the protected monopolies and "unsocial speculative
profit" of business "economists," and the microfocus of technical-
industrialists (Flanders 1932a, 96–97). Macroeconomic planning
meant countercyclical expenditure by government to bring the economy into equilibrium—to fill the gap between consumer spending
and the "level of income which could be reached were all factors
employed" (Barber 1996, 124)—in order to solve America's economic
problem, seen as the accumulation of savings (profits) faster than "productive" investment, which led to speculation and depression. Well
before John Maynard Keynes's *General Theory of Employment, Interest, and Money* (1936) appeared in the United States, many macroeconomic planners (who were not academic economists) were prepared to
challenge fiscal orthodoxy.

> The solution by way of taxation and public expenditure has other
> possibilities which must be explored. It is a shortsighted and sopho-
> moric prejudice which leads us to demand the balancing of govern-
> mental budgets within the fiscal year. Well-managed businesses are
> run on a long-time budgeting basis extending over the business cycle;
> and cities, counties, states, the Federal Government, and the finan-
> cial agencies with which they deal must be persuaded to follow suit.
> In the course of the business cycle there is a time to borrow and a
> time to retire indebtedness; there is a time to expand public works
> and a time to contract them; there is a time to tax and a time to
> relieve taxation; there is a time to expand the volume of money and
> a time to contract it. If these various actions are studied and con-
> trolled, they will act as effective balances on unemployment, on vari-
> ations in the price level, on the emergence of the sterile profits, and
> thus on the business cycle itself. (Flanders 1932b, 33–34)

An essential ingredient of "popular" macroeconomic plans in the 1930s
was a planning and research board (inside government but composed of
policy makers, business leaders, and technicians—especially economists) to gather and disseminate information about the aggregate levels of macrovariables such as employment and consumer spending that
would be useful to both public and private planning. These notions had

been gathering steam since the 1920s, when public works as a counter-cyclical tool were first advocated.[13]

Among academic and government economists in those years, Lauchlin Currie perhaps went the furthest in developing concepts of macroeconomic planning at the national level. Between 1922 and 1925, Currie was at the London School of Economics and discovered Keynes's early ideas about economic policy (Currie 1972, 139). Later, at the Treasury Department, Currie began to study the "net contribution of the federal government to national buying power." His work pointed out the ineffectiveness of increasing public works while simultaneously cutting government salaries and raising taxes (Sweezy 1972, 118). In the early days of the depression, Currie became increasingly disillusioned with the idea that expansionary monetary policy without requisite fiscal action would achieve economic recovery. In late 1934, he moved to the Federal Reserve, becoming the principal economic adviser to its chairman, Marriner Eccles, who shared his views on monetary and fiscal policy. In a 1935 memo, Currie (1972, 140) laid out the principles of the multiplier effect of government spending and called for a "relatively high monthly deficit of $400–$500 million," not to fall below $300 million until the recovery had gathered momentum. Circulation of the memo was restricted, Currie later recalled, because "one could not advocate publicly such magnitudes as $5 or $6 billion a year and remain respectable."

Others like Clark understood the possibilities of the multiplier but did not stress it in their writing (Sweezy 1972, 118; Salant 1986, 6). Clark may well have agreed with Tugwell and Means that counter-cyclical expenditure was just one part of the story of a balanced economy (Sternsher 1964, 108–9).

Synthesis of the Four Ideologies in the New Deal?

Franklin Roosevelt's arrival at the White House in 1933 inaugurated the New Deal; many hoped economic planning would be its central strategy. Roosevelt gave quasi support for planning but seemed torn between the progressive atomist tradition to which he was heir and the

13. Among these were the Kenyon bills of 1920 and 1921; the 1927 proposal by Senator George W. Pepper; and Senator Wesley L. Jones's and Maine governor Ralph Brewster's calls for advance public works planning in 1928.

new school of economic thought suggested by some of his closest advisers, including Tugwell, a key member of the "Brains Trust."[14] The tension between planning and fiscal orthodoxy evident in his presidential campaign was not resolved in the "First Hundred Days."[15] Tugwell noted that Roosevelt was a "symbol, agent, and vessel of our contradictions, our hopes, our external cynicism and our internal reaching for fellowship. . . . He was like the rest of us. . . . His New Deal would not have turned out to be like us or in tune with the times if he had been different" (quoted in Sternsher 1964, 110). As the president of all the people—with all their diversity of opinion about the problem of the depression, the modern economy, and planning—Roosevelt did not have a mandate for one of the four approaches. Consequently, New Deal programs became battlegrounds for economists of all persuasions, and programs were weakened by the very pluralism they represented. The National Recovery Administration (NRA) was but one example.

Roosevelt wanted to engage an "industrial plan" soon after he assumed office. Planners converged in Washington, but consensus was not forthcoming. Tugwell (1992, 351) recalled: "It came to loggerheads and we finally took it to F. D. R. Each side told a story and he too leaned toward shorter and quicker action but his mandate was to go away and agree." In fact, the National Recovery Act, passed by Congress in June 1933, contained something for everyone. Business economy planners got the suspension of antitrust laws by allowing businesses to enter into collusive price contracts. Social management planners got the promise of centralized industrial control, with government as the main partner in a collaborative union of economic actors. Technical-industrial planners got expert technicians in positions of authority; the act established a planning staff of economists and other professionals who would ostensibly chart and guide industrial development. Macroeconomic planners got Title II, the act's $3.3 billion public works provision.

But from the moment of passage, the act ran into difficulties. First,

14. For Roosevelt's digressions on planning and his use of the metaphor of city and regional planning in the 1910s and 1920s, see Roosevelt 1932. There he wrote, "I have been interested in not the mere planning of a city, but in the larger aspects of planning. It is the way of the future" (483). See also various campaign speeches reprinted in Beard [1932] 1969, 325–50.

15. At certain points, Roosevelt advocated public works, welfare, relief, and a progressive tax rate; at others, he called for tightening belts and balancing the budget (Sternsher 1964, 47; Barber 1996, 19–20).

there was the problem of using the WIB as a model (which reflected the influence of NRA administrator and WIB veteran Hugh Johnson). Whereas the WIB had encompassed comprehensive planning—central allocation of resources, price fixing, production—the peacetime NRA had no such latitude. Furthermore, the WIB had attempted to increase output and also set maximum prices, while the NRA attempted to set minimum prices and also control output. Because the NRA was the result of a tangle of designs and ideologies, it was not based on any clear planning idea or theory of recovery.

Not only was the experiment not working, but by 1934 the NRA appeared to be inhibiting recovery.[16] Social management planners soon found government's role marginalized in favor of business interests, and they were outraged by monopolistic abuses pursued behind the NRA's cover. Technical-industrial planners found business rather than technicians at the helm, without the benefit of a "real planning council" (Stuart 1933, 3). Macroeconomic planners were dismayed by the slow pace of public works spending, which defeated the intent and effectiveness of the Title II allocation.[17] When the act was declared unconstitutional by the Supreme Court in 1935, none mourned its passing, although there was never another program that contemplated planning on such a broad scale.

Elevation of the Macroeconomic Approach

The NRA did nothing to advance the cause of three of the planning ideologies, for despite the fact that it had not been a model for one approach, its failure cast a pall on social management planning with its comprehensive outlook (the NRA had attempted too much); dampened enthusiasm for technical-industrial planning (the NRA had not achieved industrial coordination); and discredited business economy planning (the NRA enforced monopoly at the expense of other economic interest groups).[18] However, economic events—namely, the

16. Although there was a slight rise in GNP from $56 billion in 1933 to $65 billion in 1934, this was hardly a stellar result, considering GNP of $103 billion in 1929 (*Historical Statistics* 1975, 224).

17. There was a difference in opinion between those who thought spending should be gradual and those like Johnson who felt funds should be spent rapidly. By the end of 1933, less than $1 billion had been spent (Graham 1976, 29–30).

18. Other New Deal programs also suffered from mixed economic notions. See Balisciano 1998.

recession of 1937–38 and the government's economic policy reaction—enhanced the stature of the fourth approach: macroeconomic planning.

The Federal Reserve's index of industrial production plunged 33 percent in the months between July 1937 and May 1938. A veteran's bonus paid out in 1936, which aided consumer spending and increased government expenditure, was not continued in 1937. Yet another deflationary action was the institution of payroll taxes under the new Social Security law; benefits payments were not begun to any degree until 1938.[19] The recession had shown that the multiplier effect of government spending (priming the pump) was not sufficient in itself, since the economy declined when the fiscal stimulus was withdrawn.

Roosevelt did not help matters with his desire to move toward a balanced budget. It no doubt made good 1936 reelection fodder that he could lay claim to relief, recovery, and orthodoxy, all at the same time. Roosevelt, true to his "class," never lost the feeling that unearned income weakened character; believing in the sanctity of balanced budgets, he only haltingly supported relief measures. Although cautioned by Federal Reserve chief Eccles, relief administrator Harry Hopkins, and others, the president did not heed the first warning signs of recession when they appeared in 1937. However, by April 1938 Roosevelt relented and asked Congress to resume large-scale spending. He had come, however grudgingly, to "understand" the power of fiscal unorthodoxy. This understanding was no doubt advanced by tutoring he received from Currie, who became the first economic adviser in the White House. Currie's influence was also tangible at the National Resources Planning Board (NRPB), which replaced the National Resources Committee in 1939, where he served on the Industrial Committee. The NRPB increasingly stressed themes related to macroeconomic planning in its publications (see Lee 1990). One of these, *After the War—Full Employment*, was written by Alvin Hansen (1941), whom Currie (1972, 141) described as his "most important recruit." In it Hansen (1941, 4) spelled out "the responsibility of Government to insure a sustained demand. . . . Private industry and Government together must act to maintain and increase output and income suffi-

19. Currie noted, "I think I always opposed the idea of a fund for social security on the ground of . . . the deflationary effect, and finally convinced Roosevelt on this point in early 1940" (quoted in Sweezy 1972, 118).

ciently to provide substantially full employment." Hansen had been skeptical about the tenets of macroeconomic planning throughout much of the 1930s, subscribing to the "crowding out" thesis of public works expenditure—government borrowing limited borrowing opportunities for private industry, which in turn delayed recovery (Barber 1987, 194). Among other factors, the 1937 recession confounded Hansen's business cycle theory, since a fresh collapse occurred when the economy was still operating substantially below capacity.[20] By 1938, with coaching from Currie (and a list of suggested words from Chase), Hansen was the "star" expositor of macroeconomic policy at the hearings of the Temporary National Economic Committee (Currie 1972, 141).

The rise of macroeconomic planning was also a function of the development of data on national income and expenditures and the dispersion of Keynesian ideas. Walter Salant (1986, 11) argued that the *General Theory* provided a *theoretical* foundation for popular conceptions of macroeconomic planning. Keynes's influence on *policy*, however, has been the subject of much debate.[21] Tugwell, who introduced Keynes to Roosevelt in 1934, recalled that after their first meeting the president told him, "Well, that damned Englishman is trying to tell us what we're doing already" (quoted in Frisch and Diamond 1966, 137). Rather, Tugwell stated, "in what later came to be called the Keynesian manner . . . he [Roosevelt] kept feeling for a balanced economy rather than a balanced budget" (quoted in Sternsher 1964, 136).

Wartime Planning

With the outbreak of war in Europe in 1939, the economy gained new momentum from Allied demand for American exports and defense production. As the possibility of American engagement heightened, government research units undertook studies of unrealized potential. Econ-

---

20. Barber (1987, 200) indicates that Hansen's intellectual transformation was influenced by Harvard's graduate fiscal policy seminar, which he joined in 1937. There he liaised with young economists, many of whom were struggling with fiscal questions from within New Deal posts, which helped redefine his own focus.

21. Leon Keyserling (1972, 135), Tugwell's student and second chair of the Council of Economic Advisers, asserted, "With all due respect to Keynes, I have been unable to discover much reasonable evidence that the New Deal would have been greatly different if he had never lived." Currie stated, "Although I considered myself a Keynesian from way back, I felt . . . we had little to learn for *policy purposes* from the *General Theory*" (1972, 141; emphasis in original).

omists like Robert Nathan at the Commerce Department pushed hard
for increases in defense spending without attendant decreases in public and private spending. They estimated that the economy was functioning at 80 percent of capacity and could support all-out defense
preparations while continuing New Deal programs.

In the piecemeal buildup to war, boards and agencies were created to
divvy up mobilization and management of the wartime economy. The
long-awaited successor to the WIB, the War Production Board (WPB),
was established in January 1942. The WPB did not, however, execute
war planning. One reason was its relinquishment to the military (the
Services of Supply) of final authority over assigning priorities and military contracts for most finished products needed for war. That left the
production board the realm of strategic raw materials and semifinished
goods. Greater coordination was further thwarted by a proliferation of
new agencies with overlapping functions.[22] A 1942 Bureau of the Budget report indicated, "Locomotive plants went into tank production
when locomotives were more necessary than tanks. . . . Merchant ships
took steel from the Navy. . . . The Navy took aluminum from aircraft.
. . . We built many new factories . . . we could not use and did not need.
Many of these . . . we could not supply with labor or . . . materials, or
if we had, we would not have been able to fly the planes or shoot the
ammunition that would come out of them" (quoted in Vatter 1985,
72–73). By the time mechanisms seemed to be worked out for more
centralized coordination, the war was drawing to a close, and controls
were dismantled with haste.

Victory came despite the lack of coordinated planning: Planning had
been complicated and perhaps chaotic, but the war was won. It fit a distinctly American mode of bargain and compromise; the resulting wartime blend of controls and market presaged the postwar mixed economy.
Although the war was not a triumphant moment for any one approach,
elements of the four could be seen in the fabric of wartime economic
planning. First, in accord with social managers, there had been moves
toward comprehensive planning and plans.[23] During the war, there had

22. An example of the competition for materials, personnel, and prestige was the creation
of the Economic Stabilization Board in October 1942 to "assist" the Office of Price Administration in stabilizing civilian price and demand (see Vatter 1985, 71–80). For a contemporary version of the evolution of administrative responsibility, see Stein, Magee, and Ronan
1943, 27–61.

23. For example, the WPB's distributive production requirements plan was heralded as "a

also been the establishment of public companies (e.g., the Rubber Reserve Company and the Metals Reserve Company), another central feature of their proposals. Second, in sync with technical-industrial planners, there had been attempts at industrial coordination, and technical expertise, especially from economists, was much in demand.[24] Third, in harmony with business economy planners, big business dominated war production.[25] Fourth, for macroeconomic planners, the war proved a successful test. It had indicated the willingness of government to spend as needed (albeit due to wartime necessity).[26] And in the face of inflationary expansion, it demonstrated government could apply fiscal brakes to keep the economy in balance.

The Promise of the Postwar Era

Before Pearl Harbor, some attention was given to the American economy after the "defense" period (National Resources Planning Board 1941). However, following America's entry into the war, postwar planning became a national pastime. At the federal, state, and local levels and across a wide spectrum of industries, universities, religious organizations, trade associations, and even breweries, postwar planning to win the peace became the order of the day.[27] Given such interest, it appeared that *planning* was at hand. It was not. The interwar economic, political, and intellectual milieu so hospitable to planning ideologies, with their "plural" economics, was not replicated after victory. A feared postwar recession never materialized. By 1948, the economy was operating at reasonably full employment, congressional foes equated planning with New Deal folly (in this camp were those who had helped to

great national budget of materials, a uniform accounting system, to balance supply against demand" (Gemmill and Blodgett 1942, 8).

24. A "Roster of Scientific and Specialized Personnel" begun in 1940 sought to match technical expertise with government and industry need. See Stein, Magee, and Ronan 1943, 52.

25. For a probusiness treatment of wartime production, see Walton 1956.

26. The federal deficit grew from approximately $1 billion in 1939 to $42 billion by 1945 (*Historical Statistics* 1975, 263).

27. *Postwar Planning in the United States* (Twentieth Century Fund 1943) listed nearly 150 entities in the United States focused on planning midway through the war. The brewery was the Pabst Brewing Company of Milwaukee, which sponsored a postwar planning contest that attracted thirty-five thousand entrants. In 1944, the winning plans were published in *The Winning Plans in the Pabst Postwar Employment Awards*. Herbert Stein won first prize, Keyserling came in second, and Ezekiel was among the top ten.

kill funding for the NRPB, leading to its demise in 1943), and ebullience for the socioeconomic experiments of the New Deal had been replaced by pragmatism.

Such attitudinal change contributed to a loss of credibility for social management planning. Although one might advocate extensive public ownership or a planning board to apportion production, as had proponents in the 1930s and during the war years, one was unlikely to find a publisher willing to print such plans by 1950. Increasingly, democratic collectivism was associated with authoritarian Soviet planning, a result of the escalating political tension between the United States and its former wartime ally. The dangers of autarkic planning were "exposed" by antisocialist economist Friedrich von Hayek. His antiplanning tract, *The Road to Serfdom* (1944), was even published in cartoon form in a bid to capture the attention of the public at large. Furthermore, if both depression and wartime emergency had not brought about comprehensive social planning, it was improbable that it would occur in the peace and relative prosperity of the late 1940s. Tugwell's fate is illustrative. Although his views were never popular with colleagues, he was at least allowed a place on an economics faculty in the 1930s (at Columbia); by 1950, he was consigned to a government department (at Chicago).

Out of favor as well in the postwar period were detailed examinations of microstructure, which had been one of the cornerstones of technical-industrial planning. Yet the importance of technical experts was obvious by the close of the war and therefore taken for granted in the years following (see Craufurd D. Goodwin's essay in this volume). Technical-industrial planners found themselves absorbed in other tasks. Means left the NRPB's Industrial Committee in 1940 when he found his approach to economic planning pushed aside (Means 1940b).[28] Later Means found work at the Committee for Economic Development (CED), a business policy and research organization that had a macroeconomic planning focus. His tenure at the CED is indicative of posts available to such economists after the war.[29] By 1947, Ezekiel was still at the Agriculture Department but no longer espousing innovative plans for industrial restructuring. In *Towards World Prosperity* (1947, 29), his only prognosis was that "stimulating and working out . . . long-range

28. For Means at the Bureau of the Budget, see Barber 1996, 138.

29. It is doubtful whether Means's tenure at the CED implied wholesale acceptance of the macroeconomic approach; Means (1937a) recognized it as one side of the scale in a balanced economy.

readjustments, and keeping all the many varied phases of agriculture and industry in proper dynamic balance . . . will be a long task."

Business economy planning was not revitalized after 1945. Many of the nation's largest companies had become even larger in the war. That fact, in combination with ready postwar markets, helped minimize business discontent and pursuit of economic modifications. Also, despite wartime relaxation of antitrust laws, traditional arguments against business collusion regained strength after the war. In this climate, government-sanctioned monopoly as national policy was improbable. Moreover, business moved toward acceptance of macroeconomics: Government's responsibility for building aggregate demand promised stable conditions without a great deal of regulation and control. In the longer term, the continuing success of the "military-industrial complex" provided new opportunities for business-government partnering.

Macroeconomic planning was aided by an "understanding of national income data and the sophistication in using the various estimates of multipliers and gaps which had developed in Washington during the war" (Jones 1972, 130). Availability of aggregate-level data and "understanding" of how to use it spurred econometricians like Simon Kuznets, Abba Lerner, and Wassily Leontief to continue their explorations into formalized models of the economy. The homegrown version of macroeconomic planning was "officially" melded with Keynesian theory following the war and was brought to generations of new scholars through economic textbooks like Paul Samuelson's classic *Economics: An Introductory Text* (1948).

Another measure of the shift toward a more consensual macroeconomic approach was the renaming of the National Economic and Social Planning Association as the National Planning Association (NPA). Although it was founded in 1934 by prominent social management and technical-industrial planners, new recruits after the war indicated that they would not join unless the words "Economic and Social" were removed from the name (Miller 1996). Gerhard Colm, who had been brought to the Bureau of the Budget by Currie, became the NPA's chief economist. With Colm's help and that of other economists like Thomas Blaisdell (Means's nemesis at the NRC), Kuznets, and Ezekiel, the NPA's *National Budgets for Full Employment* (1945) was published by the board of trustees, which declared, "We must prepare now for full and continuing employment under a peacetime economy. The basis of America's post-war economy should be private enterprise, with the

Government acting as impartial referee and effecting fiscal policies through taxation and expenditure programs, such as public works, that will mesh with private undertakings" (v).[30]

Conclusion

At midcentury, there was little room for plural approaches to economic planning. Instead, there was conformity around one ideology: macroeconomic planning. It did not necessitate major alterations to existing American institutions and appeared both economically attractive and politically feasible. Yet all four approaches are integral to the story of American economic planning and together contributed to the legacy of the planning ideal. In the immediate postwar era, the goal of economic democracy was universally accepted and became codified by the phrase "full employment." Roosevelt's 1944 Economic Bill of Rights set the target at sixty million jobs (see Hamby 1968).

Such notions were the impetus for the proposed Full Employment Act of 1945. The legislation stated one ideal explicitly: "All Americans able to work and seeking work have the right to useful remunerative, regular, and full-time employment." The word "right" (as an open-ended government responsibility), however, was considered objectionable (U.S. Senate 1945, 22) and was noticeably absent from the Employment Act of 1946, which stipulated that government would use "all practicable means" to foster "maximum employment, production and purchasing power." The watering down of the act was a disappointment to many planners, but the final version represented "a consensus that the government not only had the obligation to try to achieve the Act's objectives but . . . that it also had the power to do so" (Salant 1986, 17).[31] Furthermore, through the Council of Economic Advisers, the act crystallized another element common to plans of the period: a planning board to gather economic information and disseminate it to public and private enterprise.

When "planning" became a word "to curdle the milk of human kind-

30. Hansen was then a member of the board of trustees. Of the original founders, only one, labor leader Marion H. Hedges, remained.

31. Those who leaned toward social management planning regretted that the act did not require quantitative goals and coordinated, as opposed to ad hoc, action (see Keyserling 1972, 136). Some macroeconomic planners felt that the act did not clearly spell out fiscal policy as the key to achieving full employment (see Jones 1972, 131).

ness," it was retermed "policy" by some planning groups such as the NPA (Crane 1952). But as the cold war intensified, even macroeconomic planners were not immune from being branded "un-American," the code word for communist sympathizer.[32] Such developments indicated the passing of the heyday, though not the historical importance, of American economic planning.[33]

References

Atack, Jeremy, and Peter Passell. 1994. *A New Economic View of American History*. 2d ed. New York: Norton.

Balisciano, Márcia L. 1998. Economic Planning in America: Ideology and Implementation, 1930–1950. Ph.D. diss., London School of Economics.

Barber, William J. 1985. *From New Era to New Deal: Herbert Hoover, the Economists, and American Economic Policy, 1921–1933*. Cambridge: Cambridge University Press.

———. 1987. The Career of Alvin H. Hansen in the 1920s and 1930s: A Study in Intellectual Transformation. *HOPE* 19.2:191–205.

———. 1996. *Designs within Disorder: Franklin D. Roosevelt, the Economists, and the Shaping of American Economic Policy, 1933–1945*. Cambridge: Cambridge University Press.

Beard, Charles Austin. [1932] 1969. *America Faces the Future*. Freeport, N.Y.: Books for Libraries Press.

Chase, Stuart. 1931. *A Ten Year Plan for America: Planning for Stability*. Edited by J. G. Hodgson. New York: H. W. Wilson.

———. 1964. Chase to Fred Devine, 16 November. Box 11, Stuart Chase Papers, Library of Congress, Washington, D.C.

Clark, John Maurice. 1932. Long-Range Planning for the Regularization of Industry, Part 2. *New Republic* 69:3–23.

———. 1936. *Preface to Social Economics: Essays on Economic Theory and Social Problems*. New York: Farrar and Rinehart.

———. 1939. *Social Control of Business*. 2d ed. New York: McGraw-Hill.

Cowley, Malcolm. 1939. *Books That Changed Our Minds*. New York: Doubleday.

Crane, Burton. 1952. The Business Bookshelf. *New York Times*, 12 January.

32. In 1960, the Veritas Foundation published a pamphlet called *Keynes at Harvard*, a vitriolic attack against the supposedly leftist, anti-American economics of planners in the 1930s and 1940s. Chase (1964) was one of those accused. Although he was an advocate of social management planning in the 1930s, he favored macroeconomics by the 1940s. The change is evident in the series When the War Ends, which he undertook for the Twentieth Century Fund between 1941 and 1946.

33. See Goodwin 1976 for the importance of planning to debate over 1970s economic policy.

Crowell, B., and R. F. Wilson. 1921. *The Giant Hand: Our Mobilization and Control of Industry and Natural Resources, 1917–1918.* New Haven, Conn.: Yale University Press.

Currie, Lauchlin B. 1972. Keynesian Revolution: Discussion. *American Economic Review* 62:139–41.

Dewey, John. 1920. *Reconstruction in Philosophy.* New York: Henry Holt.

Director, Aaron. 1933. *The Economics of Technocracy.* Chicago: University of Chicago Press.

Ezekiel, Mordecai. 1936. *$2500 a Year: From Scarcity to Abundance.* New York: Harcourt Brace.

———. 1939. *Jobs for All.* New York: Alfred A. Knopf.

———. 1940. Economic Policy and the Structure of the American Economy. In *The Structure of the American Economy.* Part 2, *Toward Full Use of Resources.* Washington, D.C.: U.S. Government Printing Office.

———. 1947. *Towards World Prosperity.* New York: Harper and Brothers.

Flanders, Ralph E. 1932a. Economic Organization: Discussion. *American Economic Review* 22:95–97.

———. 1932b. Limitations and Possibilities of Economic Planning. *Annals of the American Academy of Political and Social Science* 162 (July): 27–35.

Foster, William Truffant. 1932. Planning in a Free Country: Managed Money and Unmanaged Men. *Annals of the American Academy of Political and Social Science* 162 (July): 49–57.

Frederick, J. G. 1931. *The Swope Plan: Details, Criticism, Analysis.* New York: Business Bourse.

Frisch, M. J., and M. Diamond. 1966. *The Thirties: A Reconsideration in the Light of the American Political Tradition.* De Kalb: Northern Illinois University Press.

Gemmill, Paul F., and Ralph H. Blodgett. 1942. *The American Economy in Wartime.* New York: Harper and Brothers.

Goodwin, Craufurd D. 1976. Changing Ideas of Planning in the United States. In *National Economic Planning.* Washington, D.C.: Chamber of Commerce of the United States.

Graham, Otis L., Jr. 1976. *Toward a Planned Society.* New York: Oxford University Press.

Gruchy, Allan G. 1939. The Concept of National Planning in Institutional Economics. *Southern Economic Journal* 6.2:121–44.

Haan, Hugo. 1931. *American Planning in the Words of Its Promoters.* Philadelphia: American Academy of Political and Social Science.

Hamby, Alonzo L. 1968. Sixty Million Jobs and the People's Revolution: The Liberals, the New Deal, and World War II. *Historian* 30.4:586–98.

Hansen, Alvin H. 1941. *After the War—Full Employment.* Washington, D.C.: U.S. Government Printing Office.

Hinrichs, A. Ford. 1934. Planning and the American Tradition. *Plan Age* 1.1A:8–11.

Historical Statistics of the United States. 1975. Part 1. Washington, D.C.: Bureau of the Census.

Jones, Byrd L. 1972. The Role of Keynesians in Wartime Policy and Postwar Planning, 1940–1946. *American Economic Review* 62:125–33.

Keyserling, Leon H. 1972. Keynesian Revolution: Discussion. *American Economic Review* 62:134–38.

Lee, Fred C. 1990. From Multi-Industry Planning to Keynesian Planning: Gardiner Means, the American Keynesians, and National Economic Planning at the National Resources Committee. *Journal of Policy History* 2:186–212.

Loucks, William. 1932. Public Works Planning and Economic Control: Federal, State, and Municipal. *Annals of the American Academy of Political Science* 162 (July): 114–20.

Means, Gardiner C. 1933. Means to Chase, 23 January. Box 1, Stuart Chase Papers, Library of Congress, Washington, D.C.

———. 1937a. Means to Charles E. Merriam, 23 January. Box 165, Record Group 187, 705.1, National Archives, Washington, D.C.

———. 1937b. Utilizing National Resources: Preamble and Introduction. Box 184, Folder 9, Charles E. Merriam Papers, University of Chicago Archives, Chicago.

———. 1938. Means to Frederic A. Delano, 3 June. Box 165, Record Group 187, 705.1, National Archives, Washington, D.C.

———. 1940a. The Controversy over the Problem of Full Employment. In *The Structure of the American Economy*. Part 2, *Toward Full Use of Resources*. Washington, D.C.: U.S. Government Printing Office.

———. 1940b. Means to National Resources Planning Board, 31 May. Box 217, Folder 13, Charles E. Merriam Papers, University of Chicago Archives, Chicago.

Miller, John. 1996. Interview by author, Sandy Spring, Maryland, April.

Mitchell, Wesley C. 1927. *Business Cycles: The Problem and Its Setting*. New York: National Bureau of Economic Research.

National Planning Association. 1945. *National Budgets for Full Employment*. Washington, D.C.: National Planning Association.

National Resources Planning Board. 1941. *After Defense—What?* Washington, D.C.: U.S. Government Printing Office.

Obolensky-Ossinsky, V. V. 1932. The Nature and Forms of Social Economic Planning. In *World Social Economic Planning*. New York: International Industrial Relations Institute.

Person, H. S. 1932. Scientific Management's Bigger Job. *Survey Graphic* 20.6:579–81, 642–44.

———. 1934. Nature and Technique of Planning. *Plan Age* 1.1A:4–7.

Qin, Duo. 1993. *The Formation of Econometrics*. Oxford: Clarendon.

Roosevelt, Franklin D. 1932. Growing up by Plan. *Survey Graphic* 20.5:483–507.

———. [1932] 1969. Agricultural Planning. In *America Faces the Future*. Edited by Charles A. Beard. Freeport, N.Y.: Books for Libraries Press.

Salant, Walter S. 1986. The Spread of Keynesian Doctrines and Practices in the United States. Unpublished manuscript.

Simons, Henry C. 1934. *A Positive Program for Laissez Faire*. Chicago: University of Chicago Press.

Soule, George. 1932. *A Planned Society*. New York: Macmillan.

Stein, Emanuel, James D. Magee, and William J. Ronan. 1943. *Our War Economy*. New York: Farrar and Rinehart.

Sternsher, Bernard. 1964. *Rexford Tugwell and the New Deal*. New Brunswick, N.J.: Rutgers University Press.

Stuart, Charles E. 1933. After NRA, What? An Engineer Looks to a Planned Economy. *New York Times*, 4 November.

Sweezy, Alan. 1972. The Keynesians and Government Policy, 1933–1939. *American Economic Review* 62:116–24.

Tippetts, Charles S. 1933. *Autarchy: National Self-Sufficiency*. Chicago: University of Chicago Press.

Tugwell, Rexford Guy. 1932. The Principle of Planning and the Institution of Laissez Faire. *American Economic Review* 22:75–92.

———. 1933. *The Industrial Discipline and the Governmental Arts*. New York: Columbia University Press.

———. 1982. *To the Lesser Heights of Morningside: A Memoir*. Philadelphia: University of Pennsylvania Press.

———. 1992. *The Diary of Rexford G. Tugwell*. Edited by Michael V. Namorato. New York: Greenwood.

Twentieth Century Fund. 1943. *Postwar Planning in the United States: An Organization Directory*. New York: Twentieth Century Fund.

U.S. Senate. 1945. *Summary of Federal Agency Reports on Full Employment Bill*. 79th Cong., 1st sess. Washington, D.C.: U.S. Government Printing Office.

Vatter, Harold G. 1985. *The U.S. Economy in World War II*. New York: Columbia University Press.

Veblen, Thorstein. 1921. *The Engineers and the Price System*. New York: Huebsch.

Walton, Francis. 1956. *Miracle of World War II: How American Industry Made Victory Possible*. New York: Macmillan.

Wolman, Leo. 1930. *Planning and Control of Public Works*. New York: National Bureau of Economic Research.

How American Economists Came to Love the Sherman Antitrust Act

Anne Mayhew

The puzzle is this: When federal antitrust policies began with the passage of the Sherman Antitrust Act in 1890, professional economists were unenthusiastic; in fact, they were frequently hostile to this new direction for public policy.[1] However, by the end of the 1930s, economists showed considerable enthusiasm for application of the act in the control of large firms and of the destabilizing effects their pricing policies were believed to have on the economy. The central problem of this essay is why the antitrust movement and the legislation of 1890, which was "characteristically and uniquely American," was not approved of by economists and why, even as "passionate public concern about the need for antitrust [had] waned . . . legal and economic professional opinion . . . [made] the antitrust laws important" (Hofstadter 1964, 116).

In this essay, I take issue with "Whiggish" explanations that describe a process whereby economists, from the early twentieth century, gradually learned to appreciate the importance of the Sherman Antitrust Act as they improved their theories of monopolistic and oligopolistic behavior. I argue that the approval of the act was a product of the 1930s and that it developed as a consequence of several issues that arose during that troubled decade. The relevance of my argument to the theme of this volume will be made explicit in the conclusion.

---

1. State antitrust policy antedates the federal statute but seems to have been little commented on by economists.

First, however, I should note that I am only tangentially concerned in this essay with the changing interpretation of the Sherman Antitrust Act by the courts and by the economists and lawyers who have argued in those courts. I will not deal with the enormous volume of literature that surrounds these changing interpretations. My concern is with how American economists have understood and presented the peculiarly American antitrust legislation in their basic texts and in their treatment of the American economy. That is, I am concerned with the changing thought about the Sherman Antitrust Act as part of larger changes in the intellectual tradition of American economics.

I should add that modern interpretations of the origins of the Sherman Antitrust Act are frequently based more on modern views of what the act should be about than on a careful reading of the history of the 1880s. The modern textbook story is that the act was passed to protect consumers from the rising prices and restricted output that resulted from the emergence of the trusts. This is an unlikely story; the act was passed when prices were falling sharply and output was growing rapidly, especially in industries that were the specific targets of the new legislation (Mayhew 1990; North 1966, chap. 2).[2] Just why public outcry over the emerging "trusts" led to the Sherman Antitrust Act is still contested. William Letwin (1965, 53), whose work on the origins of the act remains one of the best sources, rejects the proposition that the act was a reaffirmation of Congress's belief in laissez-faire and competition. He also dismisses the view that the act was "a fraud, contrived to soothe the public without injuring the trusts." His interpretation is that Congress had a muddled view that accurately reflected the muddled view of the public toward the trusts. For present purposes, it is suffi-

2. Belief that the Sherman Antitrust Act was a simple response to rising consumer prices persists. See, for example, the *Wall Street Journal* article on antitrust by Roger Lowenstein (1997), who wrote: "John Sherman was a prominent Republican senator from Ohio who had given no serious thought to antitrust until he lost the presidential nomination. . . . By then, both parties were keenly aware of the populist agitation on America's farms. Grain prices had been falling, but not the prices of consumer goods that farmers purchased." This last statement is simply untrue, though widely believed and repeated. The reality is that the wholesale price index fell from 135 in 1870 to 100 in 1880 to 82 in 1890. Prices of products of several of the industries where trusts were formed fell even more rapidly. For fuel and lighting, the index shows a decline from 134 in 1870 to 72 in 1890. See "Warren and Pearson Wholesale Price Index (Base Period 1910–1914)," in *Historical Statistics* 1975, 201. Prices continued to move downward during the 1890s and then, as Jenks (1900) shows, increased to approach the level of the early 1890s only in a number of commodities where effective trusts had been formed.

cient to say that the story of why Congress addressed complex public reaction by writing the antitrust bill is a story that has not been adequately told. My concern in this essay is not with why the act was passed but rather with the reaction of economists to it.

The Economists' Views, 1880s and 1890s

A survey of articles that appeared in the *Quarterly Journal of Economics* (*QJE*), *American Economic Review* (*AER*), and *Journal of Political Economy* (*JPE*) and of other works reveals that economists played almost no role in formulating the Sherman Antitrust Act and indeed were dismissive of it during the decades in which the act was formulated and enacted. In 1887, when the public discussion of the need for action toward the trusts had already become heated, Arthur T. Hadley (1887, 28) framed the issue: "There is nothing which the average citizen distrusts and fears so much as the power of great corporations. Nor is this distrust without foundation. Such corporations, in many instances, have a virtual monopoly in their own line of business, which is at variance with all our theories of industrial freedom. . . . The attempts to remedy this state of things by direct legislation are usually of little avail."

This was not a case of economists' natural suspicion of "direct legislation" as a cure for economic problems. In fact, Hadley and other respected economists of the time thought the trusts desirable, even if in need of some regulation. Hadley (1887, 39) found "hints" about the effective direction that control might take in recent changes in transportation law that derived from "coming to see that . . . regulated combination is better than irresponsible competition." Hadley, Henry Carter Adams (1887), and E. Benjamin Andrews (1889) all offered reasons why the newly emerging large firms were more beneficial than harmful. By introducing new technology that resulted in increasing rather than constant or decreasing returns, such firms benefited all.

Andrews (1889), in writing about a report of the Committee on Manufacturers of the U.S. House of Representatives, went even further in his defense of the new trusts. Andrews's analysis of the report's conclusions set professional opinion sharply apart from the more general public outrage over the new firms. He offered a quite explicit critique of competition as wasteful, as the cause of business stoppages, and ultimately as the cause of higher prices than would prevail given the new "understandings and associations" among businesspeople (136–37).[3]

Andrews went on to consider charges that the trusts had "secured extraordinary gains" that were not earned. He reached no clear conclusion. The same was true about the power of trusts to fix buying and selling prices arbitrarily. He considered the case of Standard Oil at some length and noted that prices of petroleum fell after the trust was formed, but he observed that prices of commodities in general, including those of crude oil, were declining over the same period, so little could be concluded. He showed that the margin between sharply reduced crude and refined oil prices remained about the same after the formation of the Standard Trust.

For Andrews, Hadley, and Adams, the new trusts, even though expressly recognized to have monopolistic power, were superior to more competitive arrangements, although their political power required new mechanisms of control. As Andrews (1889, 150) put it: "Our sources show that the witchery of the Standard Oil interest has penetrated even the political world. For some years it influenced, not to say dominated, in at least one great State, the legislature, executive, and courts. Its wiles in that field, described with large detail in the records of the Congressional committee, render very clear the political menace resident in these stupendous aggregations of wealth. Only the Nation's arm can cope with them."

Given the views of Hadley, Adams, and Andrews—which were dominant in the modern wing of the profession in the late 1880s and well into the 1890s—it is perhaps not surprising that there is almost no mention of the Sherman Antitrust Act itself and very little discussion of the industrial trusts in the *QJE*, the *JPE*, or publications of the American Economic Association (AEA) during the 1890s. This was clearly not because these journals were devoted to abstract theory at the expense of concern for current issues. Much was written about taxes, monetary policies, banks and banking reform, and so on. This range of topics should not be surprising: In the 1890s economic issues were associated with the depression, growing pressure for banking reform, the continued debates over gold and silver, and increased interest in an

---

3. It is worth noting that Andrews was an establishment figure in economics and in higher education who both wrote and spoke extensively as an economist and served as president of Brown University (Dorfman 1969, 179). His was a mainstream view among economists.

income tax. However, the trust issue continued to be of great public importance, and its absence from the journals is perhaps noteworthy in the same manner as Sherlock Holmes's nonbarking dog. Charles Bullock (1901, 168), writing just after the turn of the century, when economists were writing on the topic, suggested that the importance of the tariff and money questions during the 1890s drove articles about trusts out. However, this silence probably resulted as well from the difficulty of writing about the topic in a decade in which there was little agreement about what competition entailed and whether it was desirable (Morgan 1993; Henry 1995) and in which the opinion of economists was decidedly out of step with public views. There was no confidently held base on which to assert the superiority of professional opinion on the issues of trusts and monopolies.

It would be an error to cast the views of Hadley, Andrews, Adams, and the others who had spoken out during the 1880s, and whose views remained the professional standard during the 1890s, in anachronistic terms. It is tempting, for example, to think that they regarded government-organized planning, as advocated after World War I and into the 1930s, as the alternative to the Sherman Antitrust Act they dismissed. Although the regulatory powers given the Interstate Commerce Commission in 1887 were clearly seen as a reasonable approach, the economists who spoke out in the 1880s seem to have been modest in evaluating their own ability to suggest adequate solutions to the problems facing industrial firms and the nation. This was a time when competition was more often described as "cutthroat" and "destructive" than as beneficial. Monopoly, which economists had considered a consequence of government action, was now appearing for reasons that were hard to understand. Throughout the 1890s, tariffs (which were for other reasons also at the center of discussion) were often blamed for industrial concentration. A reduction in levels of protection, it was held, would diminish domestic market power. Discriminatory freight rates, which would, it was hoped, be addressed through appropriate regulation of the railroads, were also blamed.

Above all, my survey of the economic journals throughout the 1890s reveals uncertainty about what could and should be done by government to address the new, very large firms whose existence so alarmed much of the public. In his survey of the literature on the trusts in 1901, Bullock (1901, 216) concluded:

The moral and legal responsibility of our captains of industry must be made commensurate with the enormous powers that they wield; and the same moral restraints to which, in the last analysis, even believers in combination appeal, would prove a solvent of the very ills which monopoly is supposed to remedy. Then sound judgment can be fostered by the further development of industrial statistics; and, finally, the substitution of a moderate policy in the place of monopoly-hunger would be more helpful than all else. It may be found, in the long run, that a willingness to allow one's neighbors to live not only possesses more solid advantages than the "economies of combination," but is the only basis upon which private ownership and control of industry can continue.

How Economists Changed Their Minds:
The Whiggish View

George Stigler (1982, 1) observed that "for much too long a time, students of the history of the American antitrust policy have been at least mildly perplexed by the coolness with which American economists greeted the Sherman Act. Was not the nineteenth century the period in which the benevolent effects of competition were most widely extolled? Should not a profession praise a Congress which seeks to legislate its textbook assumptions into universal practice? And with even modest foresight, should not the economists have seen that the Sherman Act would put more into economists' purses than perhaps any other law ever passed?" But he went on to say that "a careful student of the history of economics would have searched long and hard, on July 1 of 1890, the day the Sherman Act was signed by President Harrison, for any economist who had ever recommended the policy of actively combating collusion or monopolization in the economy at large" (3).

In "The Economists and the Problem of Monopoly," Stigler (1982) argued that the economists' lack of enthusiasm may have stemmed from their belief that the new law would be ineffective in the face of industrial trends. Furthermore, he said, economists did not have very satisfactory theories of monopoly behavior on which to rest support for a procompetitive policy. As to why they changed their minds, Stigler suggested three possible answers: (1) With the passage of the Clayton Act in 1914, emphasis shifted away from combinations and toward collusion. This shift made it easier to see the prohibited activity as criminal and to see the law as a possibly effective remedy. (2) Recognition of the failure of "public regulation and ownership" (brought on by "the reputations of the NRA, incomes policies, and general price controls") created sympathy for antitrust (6). (3) Growing recognition that involvement in antitrust actions would be lucrative for many economists also created sympathy for antitrust. Stigler gave heaviest weight to the first explanation but confessed that he was not satisfied with the adequacy of any, or even all, of these explanations. He concluded, with some confidence, that it was only after further development of "technical price theory" that economists were able to lend strong support to "procompetitive policies." American economists did not have a strong body of monopoly theory from the European heritage to draw on, and it took them some time to develop such a theory, a process of slow accretion that began early in this century: "Competition is now much more vigorously supported than it was in 1890 primarily because we understand it much better today. In 1890, competition was a common sense notion in economics. . . . In no sense was the supremacy of competition challenged by the then small, emerging literature on monopoly" (9).[4]

Donald Dewey (1990, 35) offered an equally Whiggish analysis of why and how economists changed their minds about antitrust, but he gave more emphasis to experience with antitrust laws as the cause (rather than the consequence, as implied by Stigler) of advances in the theory that supported antitrust policy: "A strong case can be made that a great part of modern microeconomics is the creation of economists working in the United States; and that it has developed in response to our efforts to deal with issues forced on our attention by antitrust." Specifically, Dewey said that "somewhere between 1900 and 1920, majority opinion among American economists swung behind antitrust. The acceptance was rapid and total. If Marxists are excepted, not a single American-trained economist of any prominence questioned the desirability of antitrust in the interwar years, though many doubted its effectiveness" (25).

---

4. A different interpretation of the economists' opposition to the Sherman Antitrust Act, and one that I will not examine in this essay, was offered by Thomas J. DiLorenzo and Jack C. High (1988). They gave economists of the 1880s and 1890s high marks for foresight, arguing that opposition to the act was based on the same "new learning" that has caused some economists of recent times (Yale Brozen, Harold Demsetz, and others) to doubt the wisdom of applying the act to achieve their ideal of industrial competitiveness.

Dewey was quite wrong in his dating and in his assertion of unanimity among economists, but what is of interest here is how he accounted for the changing views. He did so by saying that economists were "persuaded by theoretical and empirical work . . . that the popular hostility to 'big business' had an economic justification" (1990, 25). He identified the precise turning point as occurring with the 1901 publication of Bullock's survey of the "trust literature." Bullock "found virtually no evidence that the wave of corporate mergers which was then sweeping the economy could be explained by the need to achieve economies of scale" (25). This reading of Bullock by Dewey means that no legitimate basis for the trusts had emerged. The turn to antitrust was then accentuated, said Dewey, by publication of John Moody's *Truth about the Trusts* (1903) and John Bates Clark and John Maurice Clark's *Control of Trusts* (1912).

Dewey (1990, 36–37) joined Stigler in emphasizing that it took some time for economists to understand the importance of antitrust because they had not attained our modern understanding:

We should remember that the Sherman Act is older than what is usually regarded as "big business." It is even older by a few months than Alfred Marshall's *Principles of Economics*, which is the classic treatment of markets populated by family firms producing specialty products. In 1890, more American economists knew their Adam Smith, David Ricardo, John Stuart Mill, and maybe Francis Amasa Walker. But their knowledge of economic theory did not extend very far beyond these writers, and one suspects that some of the Germanophiles among them did not even know this much. When it came to information about the economic system, American economists in 1890 knew little more than did American Congressmen and journalists.[5]

5. Dewey's (1990, 27–29) reminders about the relatively late development of a number of the standard tools of modern industrial organization analysis are worth mentioning: "Until 1928, no economist had published a marginal revenue curve, and until 1934, none had estimated profit rates for American manufacturing industries. The first statistical estimates of concentration trends at the industry level in the United States did not appear until the early 1950s. No estimate of the actual profitability of illegal collusion in the economy was published until 1976." I should add that Dewey was quite critical of a portion of the route followed to the current "new learning," for he regarded the emphasis that came to be placed on economies of scale and the motives for merger as blind alleys. In his view, whatever the motives and realities of scale economies, only the efficient can survive, and under these circumstances the antitrust policies that economists learned to love on their way to greater understanding of the nature of the firm and economy were regrettable necessities.

To the interpretations of Stigler and Dewey it is necessary to add only a few propositions to produce what is probably the majority view among economists who have wondered why economists changed their minds about antitrust. In the conventional wisdom, economists began to appreciate the importance of antitrust policy after the turn of the century. A major turning point (according to Dewey) came with recognition in the work of Bullock, Moody, and others that mergers were not inevitable consequences of industrial technology. The "trust-busting" activities of the Teddy Roosevelt era increased the conviction that the Sherman Antitrust Act could be effective. The passage of the Clayton and Federal Trade Commission (FTC) legislation promised enhanced effectiveness.

How Economists Changed Their Minds:
An Alternative Explanation

Indeed, a "multitude of writings dealing with the problem of trusts" appeared at the turn of the century, as Bullock noted in his survey in the *QJE* in 1901 (167). Bullock observed that there had been a flurry of work on the topic in the 1870s and the early 1880s, which was followed in the 1890s by silence and then by a great volume of work at the turn of the century. Bullock's article was important because it brought together, in a major journal, writing about the trusts that was appearing in a number of places and because it probably reflected views widely shared by economists. It was also important because it was part of the reentry of the issue of trusts into the economics journals after the silence of the 1890s.[6] By the end of the 1890s, perhaps, ever louder public opinion forced the issue of trusts into the pages of the economics journals even though the intellectual problem of how to treat the trusts had not been resolved. However, Bullock's article was not important in marking any fundamental change in the way economists viewed the trusts, although some new elements did become important.[7] A

6. Following passage of the Sherman Antitrust Act, combinations were no longer organized as trusts. Nevertheless, the word "trust" continued to be applied to large firms that grew both by merger and by vertical growth. This was true in both the popular and professional press, and I will continue to use the word here.

7. Carl P. Parrini and Martin J. Sklar (1983, 559) have argued that new thinking about the market that emerged between 1896 and 1904 "broke with both the classical model of the competitive market and its neoclassical variant." They concentrated on the work of Hadley, Jenks,

review of Bullock's survey and of some slightly earlier literature will illustrate this point.

The first major reappearance of the trusts in the journal literature came in 1899 when "The Chicago Trust Conference," written by Henry Rand Hatfield, was published in the *JPE*. This conference was organized by the Civic Confederation, a political action group that earlier had helped secure enactment of the Civil Service Act. According to Hatfield (1899, 4), "Professor John B. Clark presented the ablest economic discussion, captivating the audience alike by his impartiality and his scholarship." Hatfield said that Clark offered the only definition of trusts: "any combination so big as to be menacing" (5). In spite of this definition, Clark remained convinced that the trusts were largely beneficial, and the other economists involved in the conference shared this view. As Hatfield put it:

> The weight of evidence . . . supported the view that the modern system of large business establishments was the outgrowth of natural industrial evolution. This was necessarily the view of those who advocated trust methods, but it was also advanced by all save one of the professional economists, by the leading labor representatives, and even by some who were avowed anti-trust men. Professor H. C. Adams, the unique dissentient among economists, *distinguished between industries like railroads, which would naturally consolidate, and many manufacturing industries, whose recent trusting was caused by abnormal economic or juridical conditions.* (6; emphasis added)

Adams's view was to become one of the key ideas involved in the recasting of the trust problem. What did not change, as Hatfield made clear, was that he and others among the professional economists con-

---

and Charles A. Conant, "the prominent financial authority and journalist," and were interested primarily in the ways in which these three came to see business cycles and aggregate instability as consequences of oversaving and of industrial concentration. It is possible that their focus, which is different from the focus of this essay, does reveal a break in thought during the mid-1890s. From my perspective, there appears to be more continuity. It is also interesting to note that the explanations of cyclical instability that interested Parrini and Sklar are very much like the explanation offered by Veblen in *The Theory of Business Enterprise* (1904). Although I do not discuss Veblen in this essay because he did not write about the Sherman Antitrust Act, he was very much in the mainstream of turn-of-the-century economists who thought the nature of competitive interaction among firms had been permanently altered by the new industrial machinery.

tinued to be concerned about the political as opposed to the economic power exercised by those who controlled the trusts (7–8).

An additional point to be taken from Hatfield's report, one strongly reinforced by other articles that appeared in 1899–1901, is that the issue of the trusts was being formulated by economists as an issue of monopolies versus trusts. This contrasted with the earlier formulation of trusts as monopolies. Hatfield wrote: "The foregoing discussion has shown the importance of the theory of monopoly to the trust problem. It is true that not all the evils charged to trusts are dependent on monopoly. But, in general, trusts are criticized because they are held to destroy competition. The critics use trust and monopoly as synonyms; their corrective measures are aimed at the monopolistic features" (12).

This treatment of the problem was also apparent in an article by W. M. Coleman, "Trusts from an Economic Standpoint," published in the *JPE* in 1899. Coleman first argued that many of the public's concerns about trusts must be addressed by political scientists. All that the economist is concerned with is the question "Does the centralization of industry tend to augment or to reduce the compensation of the members of the society? When this question is correctly answered, economic science will have performed its duty" (19). Coleman went on to criticize economists for having "treated [the subject of industrial centralization] from a general as distinguished from a technical standpoint" (20). If economists would only "strip the problem of trusts of political complications"—that is, ignore the political complications—and then distance themselves from the "hysterical attack upon trusts" that Coleman suspected would be part of the upcoming political campaign, they could "apply to its solution the economic principles which have already been settled" (20). "In seeking for the correct answer to the question which we are considering, it is necessary, in order to avoid confusion, to consider first the economic effect of industrial centralization free from any feature of extortion due to monopoly; and, secondly, to consider the problem when complicated by the presence of that feature" (21). Coleman then argued that, correctly seen, the same economic principles involved in understanding the effects of the introduction and use of machinery apply to the trusts. With the introduction of both new machinery and the trusts, greater efficiency of production is achieved and labor and capital are released either for new uses or for expanded production in prior uses. Total output will be increased, and, absent monopoly, distributive shares will be fair. Coleman dismissed the probability that monopoly power would be a persistent problem on the grounds that excessive profits "breed instant and ferocious competition. No economist who has any respect whatever for the settled principles of the science can doubt that the law that prices move toward the cost of production expresses the operation of an irresistible natural force which cannot be withstood for any considerable period in a state of commercial freedom" (30).

In addition to laying out the problem in the style of economists, the rhetoric of Coleman's article placed the onus of showing that trusts might—in the absence of monopoly—be harmful on those who would doubt the "settled principles of the science." If there could be any doubt about his opposition to those who fought the trusts, Coleman cleared it up in this passage: "If skillfully presented to an audience and embellished by an appeal to the spirit of envy and class hatred, it [the picture of a great nation in thrall to a combination of capitalists] may be depended upon to catch many votes among the discontented; but it should not impose upon economists" (30).

Bullock (1901) classified the literature he surveyed into eight categories, two of which are of particular interest here.[8] These are (1) works, such as those of Coleman and Jeremiah Jenks (1900), that argue that the trust movement is inevitable and that its "causes, advantages, dangers and proper regulation" should be discussed (172) and (2) works that distinguish between the inevitable trusts and combinations (primarily manufacturing) that are the result of "special privileges and other abuses" (177). In this last category, Bullock listed Richard Ely's *Monopolies and Trusts* (1900) and P. de Rousiers's *Industries monopolisées aux Etats-Unis* (1898).

From roughly the turn of the century until 1914, an amalgamation of the earlier view that trusts were inevitable and the developing view that there were two kinds of trusts seems to have been effected, with important consequences for the direction of later debate. As illustration, I cite the work published by John Maurice Clark and his father, John Bates Clark, in 1912. This was a "modernized" version of *The Control of Trusts*, which J. B. Clark had published in 1901. Although J. B. Clark is said to have credited his son with the modernization (Dorfman 1971),

8. The others are official investigations and conference proceedings, work on finance and other special aspects of trustification, work on favors and abuses, writings of "panegyrists of the trust movement," suggestions for radical reform, and work on legal aspects.

both must have agreed with the change of tone, which was consistent with changes found in other work of the period. In his earlier work, Clark remained essentially protrust, stressing the inevitability and desirability of growth in the size of firms. The new giants would, he argued, be sufficiently controlled by *potential competition* (Clark 1901, 1904; Henry 1995). In 1912, much greater emphasis was placed on specific forms of government regulation to prevent "special privileges and corporate abuses": "In fact, the recommendations of the new version of *The Control of Trusts* . . . provided the most systematic exposition of the view on trusts, that was embodied in 1914 at President Wilson's urging in the Clayton Act and the Federal Trade Commission Act" (Dorfman 1971, 17). These recommendations included, of course, specific prohibitions on corporate behavior that might lead to anticompetitive effects. Although loopholes in the Clayton and FTC Acts that allowed corporations to argue that their behavior would not have anticompetitive effects were still very large, the acts did add substantially to the limited options for control under the Sherman Antitrust Act.

By 1914 two things appear to have happened. The first was that the antitrust movement, which had once been regarded by economists as a suspect, emotional, popular, and populist outcry, had become far more acceptable. This was probably a consequence of the muckraking literature and of court cases (Dorfman 1971).[9] Even though the Clarks and many other economists still regarded many of the trusts as consequences of a largely benevolent drive to make use of new technologies and to be more efficient, the evidence of considerable unseemly behavior was now substantial. Thus they supported some regulation of firms that sought to merge.

The second likely cause of support for the Clayton and FTC Acts was, however, continued dislike of the Sherman Antitrust Act itself. I again use the Clarks as evidence. In *The Control of Trusts* (1912, 3; emphasis in original), they wrote: "We know to-day that we *can* dissolve the trusts—that we can break up the big corporations into smaller ones—and this is distinctly more than we once knew." However, they expressed fear that dissolving the trusts "might do a balance of harm":

9. Dorfman (1971, 9) wrote of supportive correspondence between J. B. Clark and Ida Tarbell concerning her work on Standard Oil.

What will happen if we decide that the trusts are monopolies and proceed to break them up? Can anything happen, if that is done, but a repetition of the former experience—cut-throat competition, ruinous losses? . . . Moreover, if the government were relentless in its continued pursuit of combinations and were able to set up an inquisition that would detect and break up the secret agreements, would there then be any escape from a further price warfare that would spell ruin for many of those engaged? . . . In short, shall we have again the anarchic struggle of recent and unhappy memory— a thing which to many minds seems almost as bad as monopoly itself? (5)

Although in a later chapter the Clarks made explicit their belief that "the Sherman Act interpreted 'in the light of reason' calls for a policy that it is certainly possible to carry out" and one that "is in the general course indicated by economic principles" (73), the whole tenor of their argument makes it clear that their enthusiasm for the act, even if applied with large amounts of reason, remained tepid.

Although there is scant evidence for a radical increase in support among economists for the Sherman Antitrust Act in the first two decades of the twentieth century, some important changes had occurred in the process of passage of the Clayton and FTC Acts and in the debates leading up to them. One was that the range of inappropriate behavior by trusts with which economists concerned themselves had been narrowed in the manner recommended by Coleman a number of years earlier. The focus was now largely on price and on the relationships among firms. Concerns about political power had faded from the economic literature. The United States began the century with a strong spirit of sweeping reform, but by the time it entered into World War I, it had settled into pragmatic accommodation to an economy dominated by large firms (Dorfman 1969, chap. 14; Levy 1985).

An article by Myron Watkins that appeared in the *QJE* in 1928 illustrates a continued mixed and relatively pragmatic view of antitrust policy, but there are also subtle shifts in interpretation. In "The Sherman Act: Its Design and Its Effects," Watkins explained the purpose of the act in the modern way—to protect consumers against rising prices and restricted output. He then offered far more praise for the consequences of the act than economists had generally offered before. The explanation that Watkins offered for passage of the Sherman Act was that Congress, "for the first time exerted its paramount authority so as to make every species of business conducted in the national sphere subject to a common rule" (1928, 3). This was consistent, said Watkins, with the fact that "Congress had practically from the beginning exercised the full and complete power of regulation granted it by the same section of the Constitution which authorized federal regulation of interstate commerce" (2). What had changed was the "scope of economic intercourse from local and sectional markets to national markets," and it was this change that called forth the Sherman Antitrust Act.

The effectiveness of Congress in this act was to be judged, said Watkins, by three standards: the effect on consumers (the protection of whom was "undoubtedly the most important object"), the effect on actual producers, and the effect on potential producers ("maintenance of free enterprise"). On the first and third counts, Watkins found in favor of the Sherman Antitrust Act and antitrust. In the case of protection of producers, "only when the federal government assumes its social responsibility . . . and regulates by positive measures the adjustment of conflicting producer interests, may one reasonably anticipate . . . industrial peace, financial security, and business stability" (14). In short, additional regulation of competition among firms was needed.

Watkins did not see antitrust policy as an alternative to regulation. The Sherman Antitrust Act was an aspect of regulation, and the regulatory law was an evolving set of prohibitions and sanctions. Watkins's views are not unlike those expressed by the Clarks almost two decades earlier, and theirs were not unlike the views surveyed by Bullock. Large firms that exercised market power were accepted as inevitable. The goal of public policy was to devise regulatory tools that would prevent the use of that power in ways detrimental to consumers and other producers. In pursuit of this goal, the Sherman Antitrust Act itself was not a particularly important tool.

How Things Changed in the 1930s

If there is little evidence that economists underwent any drastic change of mind about the Sherman Antitrust Act in the first three decades of the twentieth century, there is a lot of evidence that the turmoil of the 1930s created an entirely new view of how public policy toward large firms could be built on the foundation of the act. Several issues and developments contributed to this change, among them the reaction to business plans for price maintenance; the failure of the National Recovery Administration (NRA); the growing conviction that administered prices contributed greatly to economic instability; and the appointment by President Franklin Roosevelt of the energetic Thurman Arnold to a division that was to carry on the fight against big business while the major economic initiatives of the New Deal shifted to aggregate stabilization efforts.

Reaction by economists to efforts by trade associations and other business organizations to monitor and manage prices within industries had actually begun during the 1920s. During the immediate post–World War I period, and from several different sources, enthusiasm had developed for an industrial policy that was a striking departure from the kind of pragmatic regulation of firms recommended by the Clarks and echoed by Watkins. Strong support for active cooperation among firms in the same industry became a major issue of public policy and legal hearings during the 1920s.

One source of support for cooperation among firms had long been building among engineers, who, in their professional associations, discussed the need for ways to combat the waste of competition and other business practices. In the heady days after the war, the president of the Federated American Engineering Societies (FAES), Herbert Hoover, said that engineers had the responsibility to "visualize the nation as a single organism and to examine its efficiency toward its only real objective—the maximum production" (quoted in Stabile 1986, 822). Under Hoover's guidance, the FAES launched a major study on waste in American industry that in some cases could be prevented by cooperation between firms. When Hoover became president of the United States, he took with him the engineers' technocratic ideals for the economy (Barber 1985; Himmelberg 1993).

Throughout the 1920s, strong advocacy for data collection and dissemination through trade associations had prompted some concern. For example, Watkins, in his 1928 article, said emphatically that even though giant corporations were perceived to be increasingly responsible, the Sherman Antitrust Act was needed. It was not, he said, "obstructive and obsolete," as "has been asserted by no less distinguished a body than the Committee on Revision of the Anti-Trust Laws, which was appointed by the American Bar Association in 1926" (5).

Although Hoover had abandoned much of his earlier support for the cooperation among firms that prompted both the organization of the

American Bar Association committee and Watkins's response, business leaders had not. In 1931, a sweeping variant of the earlier proposals for collecting and disseminating data through trade associations was put forward by Gerard Swope. The "Swope plan" "called for a program to coordinate production and consumption by requiring all industrial or commercial firms with fifty or more employees and engaging in inter-state commerce to join trade associations. These associations, in turn, would be empowered to gather and distribute information on business practices and conditions and—not least—to promote stabilization of prices" (Barber 1985, 121).

In 1932 a committee of economists chaired by Frank A. Fetter organized a response that stoutly defended the Sherman Antitrust Act against such proposals and against "the propaganda for the material modification or repeal of the Sherman Act that has been carried on for the past two years, apparently under the leadership of a Committee of the American Bar Association" (Fetter 1932, 465). Two of the "propositions and principles" urged for adoption as part of an antitrust plank in party platforms were

> rejection of the assertion made by those seeking to break down the Sherman Act, that it makes necessary the development of excessive capacity and wasteful over-production, and the equally false assertion that this was one of the causes of the present industrial depression . . . [and] recognition that the anti-trust law legislation has been frequently violated with impunity, and has been inadequately enforced throughout much of the period since its inception; this has resulted in the control of large areas of the industrial field by great combinations and by monopolistic practices having neither legal nor economic justification. (468)

The effect of the Swope plan on the one hand and of the statement of the Fetter committee on the other was to focus attention on the Sherman Antitrust Act as a bulwark against business collusion. The drama and intensity of the depression gave both the plan and the reaction to it a significance that made the Sherman Antitrust Act seem far more important than it had been for most economists in the preceding decades.

At the same time, another process lent support for the Sherman Antitrust Act as the basis of government policy toward business. The creation and then the collapse of the NRA helped discredit a strong voice among economists in the 1920s for regulated coordination of industrial policy among firms. From the same context that produced the engineering thought of Hoover and his colleagues, Thorstein Veblen very early in the century had pointed out the advantages for both producers and consumers of coordination among industrial firms.[10] Similar views continued to be expressed. In 1921, Rexford G. Tugwell published "The Economic Basis for Business Regulation" in the *AER*, in which he argued that "the Sherman Anti-trust act and the Clayton act cannot be said to have been highly successful as we review their results. The regulation of businesses affected with a public interest, a method of control becoming more and more important, is another attempt to make the necessary contact of politics with industry" (644). In 1930 in the *QJE*, Paul T. Homan surveyed books on industrial combination published between 1921 and 1929 and found evidence of a need for greater control and good reason to support new kinds of regulation to deal with the problem:

> There is at present no evidence whatever that considerations of either technical or commercial efficiency dictate the development of corporate monopolies. There is, however, abundant evidence that some considerable degree of concerted action within industries is preferable, in the interests of stability, to competition on the plane of mutual ignorance and powerlessness. . . . It seems probable that the sharp alternatives of monopoly and competition are about to retire as the categories wherewith to define public policy. In their place will be required, not merely definition of kinds of competition and degrees of monopoly, but the legal definition, as well, of specific types of control, combining competitive and monopolistic features, applicable to specifically designated situations, and administered under specific agencies of regulation yet to be devised. (375)

During the 1930s, in part because of policy debates within the Roosevelt administration, differences between the two views then held by economists of how to approach corporate power became more pronounced. One group was procompetitive, with emphasis on the use of the law to ensure competition; the other desired planning, with empha-

---

10. Of course, Veblen (1904) also wrote of the sabotage of industrial output by businesses. This sabotage was more likely to result, he thought, from rivalrous action among businesses than from coordination of plants brought under one management (chapter 3).

sis on the use of the law to regulate. William Barber (1996) has told the story of how, in the Roosevelt administration, ideas about regulation offered by Tugwell, ideas about the need for cooperative action within industries, and recognition of the importance of large corporations affected policy. Out of these ideas and a number of other ideas and goals, the NRA was developed.

For reasons that have often been discussed, the NRA did not last long. What is most important here, however, is that when the Supreme Court declared the NRA unconstitutional in 1935, the effect was to speed up the discrediting of the Tugwell proplanning view. The Roosevelt administration did not opt for the procompetitive view. Within the political arena, the choice was not between the two views of industrial policy held by economists. The demise of the NRA was instead a shift of focus away from a "structuralist" agenda and toward a macroeconomic agenda (Barber 1996, 53–68).

From the standpoint of economic thought, however, the effect was to place the proplanning view outside the mainstream. Although Tugwell probably did not represent the majority view when he proposed regulation of industry as an alternative to the application of the Sherman and Clayton Acts, he was not in a small minority. An unintended consequence of the demise of the NRA was to make these the views of an even smaller minority. (For a somewhat different, though not inconsistent, interpretation, see Márcia L. Balisciano's essay in this volume.)

Throughout the early days of the New Deal, Adolph A. Berle, Gardiner C. Means, and Tugwell had all been strong activists for regulation based on an acceptance of the inevitability of industrial concentration, but they also argued for the need to regulate concentrated firms in order to ensure the stability of the economy (Barber 1996, 6–8). However, by 1937 Tugwell and Berle were no longer part of the Roosevelt administration. As private citizens, they advocated newly developed and developing macroeconomic tools for stabilizing the economy.

When Arnold was appointed to head the Anti-Trust Division of the Justice Department in 1938, he "brought unprecedented vigor to his assignment . . . [and] initiated nearly half of the proceedings brought under the Sherman Act in the first 53 years of its history" (Barber 1996, 121). However, approval by economists of the vigorous application of a law about which they had long had doubts might not have been forthcoming save for three other things that occurred in the 1930s. The first had to do with intellectual developments in the discipline itself. The ideas that went into the formulation of the newly important competitive ideal had many sources. Some were very old, but many had developed during the interwar years in the United States. Dorfman (1969, 746) described the situation this way: "In the late 1920s a small number of workers (largely independent of each other) were developing the methods for constructing an extension of price theory to fit the area between 'perfect competition' and 'pure monopoly.' . . . Fortunately, by now an intricate set of tools, mainly diagrammatic, was at hand to describe what came to be known later as 'monopolistic competition' or 'imperfect competition.'"

Then, during the 1930s at the University of Chicago a number of bright young economists-in-training were experiencing a "religious conversion" (the description is Robert Bork's, quoted in Kitch 1983, 183) that included acceptance of Henry Simons's view of the role of antitrust. Simons's *Positive Program for Laissez Faire* was interpreted (Milton Friedman tells us) as strongly pro–free market in its orientation and as the basis for use of antitrust laws to achieve something like the theoretical state of perfect competition (in Kitch 1983, 178). To this heady mix was added the work of Edward Mason (1939), in which structure, conduct, and performance of firms were arrayed on a spectrum from highly competitive to monopolistic. The development of the theory associated with this approach, along with the contributions of the Chicago Law and Economics School (see Steven G. Medema's essay in this volume), created an intellectual arena in which both doctrinal and public policy contributions could mix.

Finally, the creation by Arnold of an antitrust bureaucracy satisfied the needs of the new patron, as identified by Craufurd D. Goodwin in his account of the development of modern economics in this volume. Remember that Stigler proposed that economists changed their minds about the Sherman Antitrust Act because they realized that it would be highly lucrative, but he was reluctant to accept that as an explanation. However, it does seem likely that the opportunity, in Goodwin's words, "to convince many in high places in government that their discipline could be useful" was appealing, even to those economists who had become convinced that there would be no need for an active government once competitive conditions were restored.

Conclusion

My argument in this essay is that both Stigler and Dewey were wrong to regard the economists' twentieth-century embrace of the Sherman Antitrust Act as a consequence of greater learning that began early in the century. Instead, I have argued that the changed view of the act came in the 1930s and for other reasons. Throughout the first three decades of the century, economists, along with the general public, came to see the regulation of the large firms that were here to stay as a necessary fact of modern life. The Sherman Antitrust Act was regarded as one element in a desirable mix of regulatory tools, but not by any means the most important.

During the 1930s, reaction to the Swope plan and rejection of the structural reforms that Tugwell, Berle, and Means proposed opened the door to a new approach. Ironically, Arnold, once a strong critic of antitrust laws, provided the opportunity for those who were eager to apply the tools of neoclassical analysis developed in the law and economics program at the University of Chicago and by Mason at Harvard. It is not necessary to accept Stigler's hypothesis that the opportunity for monetary gain promoted the enthusiasm of these economists for antitrust. It is sufficient to recognize that, because of the changes in policy making in the 1930s, a fertile field for antitrust theorizing was opened, and on that field the once scorned Sherman Antitrust Act became a very important piece of legislation.

Although Dewey (1990, 9), from his Whiggish vantage point, portrayed the respect given the Sherman Antitrust Act by modern economists as inevitable progress, he did, in passing, provide a paragraph that puts my argument well:

> No doubt, a number of chance circumstances played a part in the return of antitrust to favor. There was the flamboyant personality of Thurman Arnold. . . . There was the need felt by President Roosevelt and his advisors to be seen to be acting against "economic privilege" without unduly scaring businessmen. . . . But the basic "cause" of the revival was a meeting of minds between the hundreds of young economists and lawyers who entered federal service after 1933 and the populist Senators and Congressmen whose power rose with the Democratic majorities during the New Deal. It was, so to speak, a case of Frank Albert Fetter and Louis Brandeis meeting Wright Patman and finding out how much they had in common.

Ironically, that "meeting of minds" may well have served as a fount of microeconomic theory that extolled the virtues and relevance of atomistic competition even in an economy of trusts and created the orthodoxy that emerged at the end of the interwar era.

References

Adams, Henry Carter. 1887. The Relation of the State to Industrial Action. *Publications of the American Economic Association* 1.6:451–59.

Andrews, E. Benjamin. 1889. Trusts according to Official Investigations. *Quarterly Journal of Economics* 3:117–52.

Barber, William J. 1985. *From New Era to New Deal: Herbert Hoover, the Economists, and American Economic Policy, 1921–1933*. Cambridge: Cambridge University Press.

———. 1996. *Designs within Disorder: Franklin D. Roosevelt, the Economists, and the Shaping of American Economic Policy, 1933–1945*. Cambridge: Cambridge University Press.

Bullock, Charles. 1901. Trust Literature: A Survey and a Criticism. *Quarterly Journal of Economics* 15:167–217.

Clark, John Bates. 1901. *The Control of Trusts*. New York: Macmillan.

———. 1904. *The Problem of Monopoly*. New York: Macmillan.

Clark, John Bates, and John Maurice Clark. 1912. *The Control of Trusts*. New York: Macmillan.

Coleman, W. M. 1899. Trusts from an Economic Standpoint. *Journal of Political Economy* 8:19–33.

Dewey, Donald. 1990. *The Antitrust Experiment in America*. New York: Columbia University Press.

DiLorenzo, Thomas J., and Jack C. High. 1988. Antitrust and Competition, Historically Considered. *Economic Inquiry* 26:423–35.

Dorfman, Joseph. 1969. *The Economic Mind in American Civilization*. Vols. 4 and 5, *1918–1933*. New York: Augustus M. Kelley.

———. 1971. John Bates and John Maurice Clark on Monopoly and Competition. In John Bates Clark and John Maurice Clark, [1912] 1971, *The Control of Trusts*. 2d ed. New York: Augustus M. Kelley.

Fetter, Frank A. 1932. The Economists' Committee on Anti-Trust Law Policy. *American Economic Review* 22:465–69.

Hadley, Arthur T. 1887. Private Monopolies and Public Rights. *Quarterly Journal of Economics* 1:28–44.

Hatfield, Henry Rand. 1899. The Chicago Trust Conference. *Journal of Political Economy* 8.1:1–18.

Henry, John. 1995. *John Bates Clark*. New York: St. Martin's.

Himmelberg, Robert F. 1993. *The Origins of the National Recovery Administration*. New York: Fordham University Press.

Historical Statistics of the United States. 1975. Washington, D.C.: Bureau of the Census.

Hofstadter, Richard. 1964. What Happened to the Antitrust Movement? In *The Business Establishment.* Edited by Earl F. Cheit. New York: John Wiley.

Homan, Paul T. 1930. Industrial Combination as Surveyed in Recent Literature. *Quarterly Journal of Economics* 44:345–80.

Jenks, Jeremiah W. 1900. *The Trust Problem.* New York: McClure, Phillips.

Kitch, Edmund W., ed. 1983. The Fire of Truth: A Remembrance of Law and Economics at Chicago, 1932–1970. *Journal of Law and Economics* 26.1:163–234.

Letwin, William. 1965. *Law and Economic Policy in America: The Evolution of the Sherman Antitrust Act.* New York: Random House.

Levy, David W. 1985. *Herbert Croly of the "New Republic": The Life and Thought of an American Progressive.* Princeton, N.J.: Princeton University Press.

Lowenstein, Roger. 1997. Trust in Markets: Antitrust Forces Drop the Ideology, Focus on Economics. *Wall Street Journal,* 27 February.

Mason, Edward S. 1939. Price and Production Policies of Large-Scale Enterprise. *American Economic Review* 29:61–74.

Mayhew, Anne. 1990. The Sherman Act as Protective Reaction. *Journal of Economic Issues* 24.2:389–95.

Moody, John. 1903. *The Truth about the Trusts.* New York: Moody Publishing.

Morgan, Mary S. 1993. Competing Notions of "Competition" in Late Nineteenth-Century American Economics. *HOPE* 25.4:563–604.

North, Douglass. 1966. *Growth and Welfare in the American Past.* Englewood Cliffs, N.J.: Prentice-Hall.

Parinni, Carl P., and Martin J. Sklar. 1983. New Thinking about the Market, 1896–1904: Some American Economists on Investment and the Theory of Surplus Capital. *Journal of Economic History* 43.3:559–78.

Stabile, Donald. 1986. Veblen and the Political Economy of the Engineer: The Radical Leader and Engineering Leaders Come to Technocratic Ideas at the Same Time. *American Journal of Economics and Sociology* 45.1:41–52.

Stigler, George. 1982. The Economists and the Problem of Monopoly. *American Economic Review* 72:1–11.

Tugwell, Rexford G. 1921. The Economic Basis for Business Regulation. *American Economic Review* 11:643–58.

Veblen, Thorstein. 1904. *The Theory of Business Enterprise.* New York: Charles Scribner's Sons.

Watkins, Myron. 1928. The Sherman Act: Its Design and Its Effects. *Quarterly Journal of Economics* 43:1–43.

Wandering the Road from Pluralism to Posner: The Transformation of Law and Economics in the Twentieth Century

Steven G. Medema

One of the defining features of post–World War II economics is the application of neoclassical economic reasoning to areas traditionally considered noneconomic—political science, sociology, the law, and so on—the most successful of which is arguably the field of law and economics. If one spends much time examining the current literature in the field, including surveys of law and economics and its development, one comes away with the distinct impression that law and economics is a post-1960 phenomenon, dating roughly from the founding of the *Journal of Law and Economics* in the late 1950s and the publication of Ronald H. Coase's "Problem of Social Cost" in 1960.[1] In fact, of course, law and economics, conceived of as the study of the interrelations between legal and economic processes, is as old as economics itself, as evidenced, for example, in the ancient Greek discussions of the regulatory environment in the ideal state and the Scholastic discussions of usury and pricing (undertaken in light of Roman civil law). Moving a bit more in the direction of the present, Adam Smith, Karl Marx, Henry

This essay was prepared for the 1997 *HOPE* conference. I would like to thank the conference participants and, in particular, Malcolm Rutherford, Ross Emmett, Roger Backhouse, D. Wade Hands, Perry Mehrling, and Warren Samuels for their instructive comments on an earlier draft of this essay.

1. This literature also tends to convey the impression that law and economics is a rather homogeneous neoclassical enterprise, which is also somewhat misleading (Mercuro and Medema 1997).

Sidgwick, the German historical school, A. C. Pigou, and, inter alia, the early American institutionalists devoted significant attention to legal-economic relationships. Yet the existence of such work is noted only barely, if at all, in contemporary legal-economic scholarship, and, when noted, it is largely waved aside as something very different from (and irrelevant to) contemporary practice.

This much having been said, it is certainly not the case that law and economics was a prominent topic in legal and economic discourse prior to the twentieth century.[2] However, the first four decades of the twentieth century witnessed a surge of interest in both the legal and the economics communities in law and economics, most of which was of a form very different from contemporary law and economics, not just in the techniques brought to bear but in the general approach to and conception of the subject. Yet this type of analysis—indeed, law and economics generally—all but disappeared after World War II, only to reemerge in a vastly different form in the early 1960s. Since law and economics is an interdisciplinary subject, one might correctly expect that the underlying reasons for its transformation lie in the respective intellectual environments of economics and law during these periods. Although much has been written about the influence of the legal environment on these developments (e.g., Posner 1987; Duxbury 1995), what has been neglected, by and large, is the economics side of the issue: What forces within the *economics* community drove the transformation of law and economics, as practiced by economists?

This essay will attempt to probe this question, not with the goal of providing a singular, definitive answer but with the more modest goal of suggesting possible reasons for the transformation in the hope of providing a springboard for further work on this topic and perhaps some insights into the larger transformative processes within economics during the period in question. The transformation of law and economics as described herein will turn on the publication of Coase's "Problem of Social Cost" in 1960. While it is hardly novel to trace the rise of modern law and economics to this source, the point to be made here is rather different from the traditional view: "The Problem of Social Cost" is actually an essay written in the "old" law and econom-

2. This statement is false if one defines law and economics broadly to include the general interrelationships between government and economy. For present purposes, however, I define law and economics somewhat more narrowly.

ics tradition, but the reasons behind its writing and the form in which it was written raised an entirely new set of questions that were very much amenable to examination using modern microtheoretic analysis.

The next two sections briefly lay out the defining features of the "old" and the "new" law and economics.[3] Then the role of "The Problem of Social Cost" within this transformation process is discussed, and the underlying reasons for the decline of the old law and economics and the rise of the new are probed. Finally, some concluding comments are made on the recent developments in law and economics and their implications for the future of the field.

Old Law and Economics

In 1897, Oliver Wendell Holmes wrote that "for the rational study of law the black-letter man may be the man of the present, but the man of the future is the man of statistics and the master of economics" (469). It was not long before legal scholars attempted to bring this prediction to fruition, at least to some degree. The legal realists, largely forsaking the doctrinaire approach of traditional precedential jurisprudence, argued instead that law was a means to promote chosen ends and that those ends (and the best means of pursuing them) could be revealed by the study of, among other things, the economic impact of legal rules (Duxbury 1995; Mercuro and Medema 1997).

However, the push for greater interaction between law and economics was not confined to the legal community. Economists, sometimes hand in hand with the realists and sometimes apart from them, increasingly recognized the need for integrating legal and economic analysis. Calls for the integration of law and economics and the undertaking of studies toward this end were evidenced in American Economic Association (AEA) presidential addresses, sessions at the annual meetings of the AEA, and numerous books and journal articles (Samuels 1993). Many, but by no means all, of the economists involved in this scholarship were either tightly or loosely allied with institutional economics— Walton Hamilton (1932), Henry Carter Adams ([1887/1897] 1954),

3. For expositional convenience, I use the term "old" law and economics to refer to the law and economics associated with the interwar period and with the Chicago school prior to the early 1960s. Certain aspects of my discussion of old law and economics are based on Mercuro and Medema 1997. The "new" law and economics refers to the post-1960 law and economics associated with Posner and others.

Robert Lee Hale (1952), John R. Commons (1924, 1925), and Gardiner C. Means (Berle and Means 1932), for example. But regardless of school affiliation (and the lines between schools were very blurred during this era), the individuals urging this integration were not fringe players but ranked among the profession's most prominent members.

The defining feature of this analysis (as compared with contemporary law and economics) was that it saw the study of the legal process as an important facet of the study of the economic system. This view reflects the definition of "economics" as the study of the economic system rather than as an approach or a tool kit for the analysis of individual behavior. As such, the basic goal of the analysis was to do either or both of the following:

1. The analysis sought to explore the legal underpinnings of the economic system and how changes in legal rules impact the economic system, in particular, the allocation and distribution of resources and wealth in society. The perceived need for such analysis arose out of the belief that, because of the problem of scarcity, the economic system, including the operation of markets, is governed by the legal system, which, through rights creation, definition, and modification, channels power, opportunity, and so on—and thus allocation and distribution—in particular directions. This was evidenced in legal decisions as to the types of contracts that would be enforced; the valuation of property for pricing purposes (and the regulation thereof); and rules governing combination of firms and workers, hours of work, allowable levels of concentration, and so on.

2. The analysis examined the influence of the economic system on law. The interest in this vein of research was based on the recognition that economic forces are significant factors in the promotion of legal change, which, in turn, affects economic performance. In particular, economic forces exert pressures for and against legal change, both to promote new economic interests and to protect old ones. As such, law is seen as an instrument of control—a means by which certain ends can be achieved—and competing interests bring pressure to bear on government in the attempt to use law to promote their own ends.

These two facets of legal-economic scholarship were evidenced in the work of a variety of scholars writing from very different perspectives and paradigms (as exemplified in Samuels 1993), including individuals as diverse as John Bates Clark, Irving Fisher, Hale, and Commons.

Although Clark's marginal-productivity theory of distribution made him something of an apologist for the status quo (in contrast with, e.g., Adams, Hale, and Commons), he was nonetheless very interested in the relationship between the legal framework and the competitive market system. Clark (1894) believed that natural laws (such as the marginal-productivity theory) govern the competitive market system but that these laws are themselves subject to the influence of man-made law; the operation of natural law is channeled through the malleable legal institutions of society, and these legal institutions can facilitate or inhibit the development of the competitive market process. Although he believed that the outcomes dictated by natural law would ultimately triumph (and thus he believed in the primacy of economy over law), Clark felt that a study of legal-economic relations could reveal the legal measures that should be removed and the legal rules that should be employed to speed up the development of the competitive market system.

Fisher opens *The Nature of Capital and Income* ([1906] 1965) with a discussion of the concept of "wealth," followed by a chapter on the notion of "property." Noting that wealth implies ownership, which in turn involves rights over resources (18), Fisher argues that the study of wealth necessarily "brings economics into contact with the whole subject of legal and custom-sanctioned relations" (20), for "there can be no wealth without property rights applying to it, nor property rights without the wealth to which they apply" (22). As such, the presence or absence and the form (complete or partial) of rights influence wealth, the potential for creating wealth, the distribution of wealth, and the uses of wealth (36–40).

Two prominent figures identified with the study of law and economics during the interwar period were Hale and Commons. Hale's emphasis on the integration of economics and law was reflected both in his teaching—particularly his course Legal Factors in Economic Society—and in his writing, much of which dealt with the regulation of railroads and public utilities, fields in which an understanding of the interface between economics and law has always been fundamental.[4]

4. Extensive discussions of Hale can be found in Samuels 1973; Dorfman [1959] 1969; and Duxbury 1995.

Hale wrote extensively on the legal and economic theory of rate-base valuation, as well as on the regulation of rate structure and level, and his writings were instrumental in the adoption by the courts of the "prudent investment" doctrine of valuation for public utilities (Dorfman [1959] 1969, 161).

Consistent with the realism of the day, Hale's work was very much a challenge to and a critique of the dominant tradition of laissez-faire capitalism. Hale saw legal and economic processes as inseparable and described the economy as a structure of coercive power arrangements and relationships, which necessitated an understanding of the formation and structure of the underlying distribution of economic power. Moreover, he believed that the courts must undertake an intelligent balancing of the gains and losses resulting from the particular statutes brought before them, a process that required "a realistic understanding of the economic effect of the legislation" (quoted in Dorfman [1959] 1969, 163). Although Hale (1924, 1927) believed that ethical judgments ultimately must be the basis for the court's decisions, he felt that the judicial application of economic principles was necessary to ascertain the economic consequences—allocative and distributive—of the legislation whose constitutionality the court was asked to evaluate.

Commons optimistically believed that the primary economic institutions could be formed and reshaped (as needed) to conform to the social changes inherent in a society, a belief that led him to extensively probe the impact of institutions, such as the law, on economic structure and performance and to become actively involved in various reform activities. Commons ([1896] 1996, 225) believed that "no economic problem is more important than the just estimate of the part played by customary and statutory law in social evolution," and, perhaps not surprisingly, much of Commons's work involved an examination of the legal foundations of the capitalist economic system, particularly in his classic treatise, *Legal Foundations of Capitalism* (1924), which benefited from Commons's close contact with law through his involvement with the courts, government commissions, and the drafting of legislation. The emphasis of the book is on describing the role of law and the courts in determining the elements of an economic system. Commons undertook an analysis of a wide variety of cases, working rules, and statutes to probe their impact on the development of modern capitalism and thereby to illuminate the interrelations between legal and economic processes.

Commons's primary interest was to uncover the values underlying the working rules that govern social-economic relations, and he found them in the courts' use of the term "reasonable value." He discovered that legal history showed certain well-defined tendencies on the part of the courts to eliminate the destructive practices of capitalistic institutions, while at the same time ascertaining the "reasonable" policies that should be followed in a competitive system. Thus, "reasonable values" could be used to ground policies that would bring about compromises in arenas of economic conflict—namely, labor disputes, public utility–rate making, tax policy, pricing, and so forth (Bell 1967, 556–57). As the definition of the types of activities that were considered reasonable evolved over time, so too did the legal rules governing social-economic relations. For example, Commons examined the effects of law on the employment relation within the firm, on the market mechanism, and on the wage bargain, as well as, inter alia, the effects of the transformation of the legal definition of property and its impact on business relationships and practices. Through this analysis, Commons fleshed out the workings of the legal-economic nexus—the reciprocal interdependence of economy and law—and the implications thereof for the capitalist economic system.[5]

Although the realist-institutionalist interaction of the 1920s and 1930s did a great deal to bring law and economics together, a similar interaction, but with a distinctly different flavor, commenced in the 1930s at the University of Chicago. (For a more detailed discussion of the Chicago school during this period, see Ross B. Emmett's essay in this volume.) In 1934, Henry Simons, who had been a student of Frank Knight, published a pamphlet titled *A Positive Program for Laissez Faire*, in which he set down a blueprint for a legal/regulatory regime that would ensure the maintenance of competitive conditions in the face of increasing concentration in corporate America. Simons's proposals range from nationalization to placing legal limits on advertising to redefining the courts' criterion regarding the maximum firm size consistent with competition.

A debate over Simons's reappointment in the Economics Department was resolved by giving him a half-time appointment in the law school,

5. Through his work on proportional representation, Commons ([1907] 1974) made an early contribution to the economic analysis of political choices by exploring the manner in which rules influence the determination of whose preferences will count within the political process.

where he taught a course titled Economic Analysis of Public Policy, and his appointment there inaugurated the tradition that an economist would serve on the law school faculty. Although Simons was best known for his work in monetary theory, his price-theoretic perspective had a significant influence on, for example, Aaron Director, Milton Friedman, George Stigler, Gordon Tullock, and Warren Nutter. Moreover, his view that law should be structured so as to preserve competition reflected a perspective that has been one of the cornerstones of Chicago law and economics.

Simons helped ensure the continuity and growth of Chicago law and economics by bringing to the law school the individual most responsible for firmly establishing the Chicago law and economics tradition— Aaron Director. Director was a member of the economics faculty in the early 1930s, and his work had a distinct Chicago price-theoretic flavor. In 1946, he assumed the directorship of a university center affiliated with the law school that was dedicated to undertaking "a study of a suitable legal and institutional framework of an effective competitive system" (Coase 1993, 246), and upon Simons's death, he took over responsibility for teaching the course Economic Analysis of Public Policy.

Director was subsequently invited by Edward Levi to collaborate in teaching the antitrust course (an area of law particularly open to the influence of economic ideas), and through his teachings, he had a formidable influence on Chicago law students, including several individuals—for example, Robert Bork—who went on to become prominent scholars. Director formally established the nation's first law and economics program, founded the *Journal of Law and Economics*, and continued to trumpet the theme that regulation was the proper function of markets, not government, a message that often resulted in legal reasoning losing out to economic analysis.

The most substantial and enduring impact of early Chicago law and economics unquestionably has been in the field of antitrust law, the goal of which, within the Chicago tradition, is the promotion of efficiency.[6] Reflecting the Chicago emphasis on the efficacy of the competitive system, monopoly was viewed as occasional, unstable, and transitory—a potential outcome of the competitive process, but one that would soon be removed (in effect if not in reality) by competitive

6. A useful overview of antitrust from a Chicago perspective is contained in Posner 1976.

pressures. Thus rigorous antitrust enforcement was thought to be unnecessary, and even when monopolies were shown to generate long-term inefficiencies, the governmental cure was often thought to be worse than the disease because of the inefficiencies of government.

Although the events in the law school laid the foundation for the development of law and economics at Chicago, a full understanding of this development necessitates an appreciation of the scholarship generated by the faculty of the Economics Department, both before and after World War II.[7] Of the significant figures associated with the early Chicago school, Knight had the biggest impact on what has come to be known as Chicago law and economics. In simple terms, proponents of the early Chicago approach generally accepted the propositions that had been at the heart of economics since the writing of Adam Smith: In a liberal democracy, the rational pursuit of economic self-interest by economic actors was taken as given, competition was seen as inherent in and intrinsic to economic life, and market-generated outcomes were thought to be superior to those resulting from government interference with the market mechanism. Although during the 1930s these propositions (the latter two in particular) were increasingly called into question within the profession at large, their continuity within the Chicago school set the Chicago perspective apart from much of the rest of the economics profession.

The new generation of Chicago economists undertook to elaborate and extend these insights, demonstrating, in formal terms, the detailed nexus between competitive markets and efficient outcomes. Following the lead of Friedman and Stigler, postwar Chicago economists, buttressed by empirical research, argued for less government intervention, fewer wealth redistribution policies, reliance on voluntary exchange and on the common law for mediating conflicts, and an across-the-board promotion of more private enterprise, which, based on the evidence provided by their empirical research, would facilitate a more efficient allocation of resources.

A further early contribution to Chicago law and economics came through the work of Armen Alchian (1961) and Harold Demsetz (1964, 1967) on the economics of property rights.[8] The property rights

7. See, for example, Reder 1982 and the references cited therein.

8. For a concise overview of the early economics of property rights literature, see Furubotn and Pejovich 1972.

approach emerged as some economists began to (re)appreciate that legal-institutional arrangements that constrain the behavior of individuals and firms might have a crucial effect on the allocation of society's scarce resources. The main postulate of the economics of property rights is that the nature and form of property rights have a fundamental effect on the allocation of resources and the distribution of income in the economy, with the resulting implication that the study of alternative property right regimes could uncover insights into the performance of the economy. The argument consisted of two parts, one reflecting the influence of law on economy and the other the influence of economy on law. First, it was argued that the value of resources is tied directly to the bundles of rights associated with the resources; that is, the more complete and definite the specification of property rights (i.e., the less attenuated the rights structure), the more uncertainty is diminished, which, in turn, tends to promote a more efficient allocation of resources. Second, proponents of the property rights approach inquired whether the standard theory of production and exchange was capable of explaining the emergence of the institution of property rights over scarce resources. Their empirical research suggested an affirmative answer to this question: The emergence and development of new property rights can be explained as a consequence of value-seeking behavior brought on by new technologies and market opportunities.

New Law and Economics

The new law and economics has drawn its inspiration from several sources, most prominently Coase's "Problem of Social Cost" (1960) and Guido Calabresi's "Some Thoughts on Risk Distribution and the Law of Torts" (1961). Although the stimulation of economists' interest in this line of research came primarily from Coase (1960), both these articles showed, really for the first time, the wide applicability of the basic tools of neoclassical microeconomic theory and welfare economics to the evaluation of legal rules and their incentive effects. It was not long before economic analysis was being applied to assess the effects of all manner of legal rules: common-law rules of property, contract, and tort; statutes; criminal law; and constitutional law.

This scholarship represented one of the earliest applications of the tools of economic theory to the analysis of noneconomic phenomena and reflected a larger process in which economic analysis came to be viewed as an approach, method, or tool kit applicable to all areas of life in which choices are made rather than simply as the study of the economic system per se. The goal of this analysis was to elucidate how legal rules affect individual behavior within the legal arena through the adjustment of incentives.

1. In contrast to the standard legal view of individuals as reasonable agents behaving according to the norms and customs of society as reflected in legal rules, the economic approach posits agents as rational maximizers of their satisfactions.

2. Legal rules are viewed as prices that are taken as given by individuals and used by them in the process of calculating their utility/profit-maximizing response to these legal rules. Changes in legal rules thus function as changes in the constraints subject to which individuals maximize, with corresponding implications for individual behavior.

One of the implications of these first two points is that, whereas the traditional approach to law considers lawbreaking and lawbreakers unreasonable, the economics approach considers both lawbreakers and non-lawbreakers rational, their behavioral differences accounted for by the different constraints under which they maximize utility.

3. The assessment of legal rules proceeds on the basis of the efficiency of the outcomes generated by these rules, in contrast with the "justice" or "fairness" criterion underlying traditional legal reasoning (although Posner [1981] has argued strongly that efficiency comports with the dictates of justice).

A simple example will illustrate the economic approach at work and its contrast to the traditional approach to common-law questions. First, consider a factory, in an isolated location, that dumps chemical waste into a river. Suppose that land downstream is subsequently developed by farmers who use the water from the river to irrigate their crops. Finding that the chemicals in the river cause substantial damage to their crops ($1 million per year), the farmers file suit, asking that the factory be forced to compensate them for the crop damage. Under the traditional common-law rule of "coming to the nuisance," the factory would be allowed to continue its dumping in the river. However, suppose that the factory could install filtering devices that would eliminate the chemical pollution at a cost of $0.5 million per year. The economic approach would suggest that the factory should be forced to compensate the farmers for the damage, in which case the factory would choose to install the filters, since the cost of doing so would be less than the cost of paying the damages. In this case, the traditional common-law rule leads to an inefficient outcome, since it does not generate the least-cost response to the nuisance dispute.

What remains is to shed some light on what triggered the development of contemporary law and economics and why, along the way, the economic analysis of law was transformed from the study of broad questions of the relationship between law and economic activity into an exercise in applying microeconomic theory and welfare economics to the analysis and evaluation of legal rules.

The Transformation of Law and Economics:
Coase as "Accidental Tourist"

Perhaps the greatest irony of the transformation of law and economics is that the work on which this transformation turns, "The Problem of Social Cost," was an unintended result of law and economics of the *old* variety, originating in Coase's study of the broadcasting industry in the United States that was itself a continuation of his earlier study of the British broadcasting industry.[9]

In "The Federal Communications Commission" (1959), Coase took issue with the fiat-based mechanism by which broadcasting licenses were issued in the United States, arguing that since frequencies were scarce and valuable resources, greater attention should be paid to the efficiency of their allocation toward the end of enhancing the efficiency of the broadcasting industry. Noting that the market seemingly was never considered as a mechanism for allocating frequencies, Coase showed that a perfectly functioning market would cause frequencies to be allocated to those who valued them most highly and, more generally, that in any situation of well-defined rights and costless transacting, rights will be allocated efficiently, regardless of who initially receives them. But recognizing that markets always function at least somewhat imperfectly, Coase went on to consider the various impedi-

---

9. To understand the origins of "The Problem of Social Cost," one must examine the greater corpus of Coase's analysis of institutions. See Medema 1994 for discussions of these various works.

ments to achieving the allocation implied by a perfectly functioning market, considerations relevant to the issue of how a market in broadcast frequencies might actually work in practice. The culmination of his discussion was what might best be described as a plea to the policy makers for a comparative institutional analysis that took into consideration both the existence of alternative institutional structures for frequency allocation and the imperfections of each.

When Coase's conclusions regarding the efficacy of markets were challenged by a number of the leading figures of the Chicago school, Coase wrote "The Problem of Social Cost" in an attempt both to more fully develop and to generalize his earlier analysis. To illustrate his point about the efficiency of smoothly functioning markets in resolving disputes over rights, Coase invoked several British common-law cases to show, hypothetically, how rights would be rearranged among agents to end up in their highest-valued use, regardless of the legal rule in force. But recognizing that, in most cases, transaction costs would preclude such efficient voluntary reallocations, Coase went on to argue that the economic interests of society would be best served if externality policy were designed to promote the greatest possible value of output in society, which, given the inefficiencies associated with the operations of government, might involve using markets or Pigovian remedies or simply doing nothing at all about the externality problem. Most important for present purposes, Coase applied this perspective to the courts, arguing that judges should, at a minimum, take allocational considerations into account in making decisions about rights that impact economic performance.

But Coase (1960, 19) then went a step further, arguing that "it is clear from a cursory study [of the case record] that the courts have often recognized the economic implications of their decisions and are aware (as many economists are not) of the reciprocal nature of the [externality] problem." Moreover, he said, while "the courts do not always refer very clearly to the economic problems posed by the cases brought before them . . . it seems probable that in the interpretation of words and phrases like 'reasonable' or 'common or ordinary use' there is some recognition, perhaps largely unconscious and certainly not very explicit, of the economic aspects of the questions at issue" (22)—a sentiment also found in Commons 1924. Coase went on to illustrate these points with examples.

Viewed from the perspective of the present, "The Problem of Social

Cost" immediately calls to mind contemporary work in law and economics. Yet it was a work in the older mode,[10] aimed not at legal scholars and legal scholarship but rather at economists and the practice of economics. "What I wanted to do," said Coase (1993, 251), "was to improve our analysis of the working of the economic system. Law came into the article because, in a regime of positive transaction costs, the character of law becomes one of the main factors determining the performance of the economy." Coase consciously distanced himself from Posner, whose "main interest is in the legal system" (251), by noting that "I have no interest in lawyers or legal education" (quoted in Kitch 1983, 192) and acknowledging that "in the development of the economic analysis of the law [i.e., the new law and economics], . . . Posner has clearly played the major role" (Coase 1993, 251). In fact, Coase's work in the field subsequent to the publication of "The Problem of Social Cost" has consisted largely of further inquiries into the U.S. broadcasting industry and other regulatory institutions in an attempt to come to grips with what he has called "the institutional structure of production." This work is decidedly *not* along the Coase-theorem-related lines implied by what many took to be the message of "The Problem of Social Cost" (Medema 1994). Coase's rejection of the assumption of rational utility-maximizing consumers (see, e.g., Coase 1984) is instructive here, particularly considering subsequent developments in the field of law and economics.

The study of the relationship between law and economy came naturally for Coase, who had taken several courses in law and whose mentor, Arnold Plant (1974), had done pioneering work on the analysis of the economic implications of rules governing patents, copyrights, and intellectual property generally. Coase believed that important lessons could be learned by examining the relationship between law and economy—namely, by "examining cases, examining business practices, and showing that there was some sense to them, but it wasn't the sense that people had given to them before" (quoted in Kitch 1983, 193). This perspective, initially applied at Chicago in the area of antitrust, was expanded to various aspects of law, largely through the influence of Director and Coase as editors of the *Journal of Law and Economics*, "the aim of which," according to Coase (1993, 251), "was said to be

---

10. See Medema 1996 for a discussion of the commonalities between the law and economics of Coase and of the institutionalists.

the examination of public policy issues of interest to lawyers and economists."

Of course, Coase could not have anticipated the direction that law and economics would take subsequent to "The Problem of Social Cost." But his analysis (and Calabresi's) raised many issues for both economists and lawyers, including the choice-theoretic nature of the questions of legal analysis and the potential applicability of economic theory to the analysis of legal rules and legal decision making.

Explaining the Transformation of Law and Economics

The basic differences of approach between the old and the new law and economics can be described at two different levels of sophistication. At a basic level, the old law and economics was concerned with analyzing the interaction between the law and the economy (as an important or even necessary component of the economic theorizing process), whereas the new law and economics was concerned with applying economic theory to analyze agent behavior within the legal arena and had little or nothing to do with understanding the legal bases of the economic system. At a more sophisticated level, the old and the new law and economics represent distinctive versions of social theory. The old law and economics reflected a multifaceted, pluralistic (as regards the method of economic theorizing), interdisciplinary approach to the analysis of the institutional structure of society, one in which law and economy are mutually determined and determining. The new law and economics, in contrast, was part of a larger imperialist project within economics that, in effect, presented neoclassical microeconomic theory as social theory. Rational-choice analysis was presented as the key to understanding (and, in the hands of many, normatively prescribing) the behavior of agents in all manner of social contexts. That is, it was an overtly neoclassical enterprise that consciously reached beyond the boundaries of economics into other fields to influence the scholarship in those fields rather than to influence our understanding of the operation of the economic system.

What accounts for the demise of the old law and economics and its replacement by the new? One can see the evolution of law and economics from its "law and the economy" bent to the economic analysis of law in the pages of the *Journal of Law and Economics*, and by the early 1970s, the economic analysis of law had developed to such a point that Posner (1973) could write a substantial treatise on the subject.

Although the growth of law and economics stirred up much controversy within the legal community (such as academic turf wars, the issue of the applicability of the economic model of human behavior, and the "efficiency as justice" issue), no such qualms were evident within the economics community. Although there was some initial questioning of the appropriate boundaries for applying microtheoretic tools of analysis, many economists saw the application of economic tools to legal theory as a natural extension of the economic paradigm, a precedent for which already existed in public-choice analysis, which was well along the development path by this time.

The transformation of law and economics is in some ways a microcosm of the larger transformation within economics during this time, the major aspects of which I leave to other contributors to this volume. For present purposes, the key feature of these transformative processes was the expansion of the domain of economics but the narrowing of its scope and perspective in the postwar era.

The problem of pinpointing the causes for the decline of the old law and economics is compounded by the facts that the old law and economics was not homogeneous or monolithic and that the demise occurred in stages over time. The branch of law and economics rooted in the institutionalist-realist tradition was all but dead as an influential academic phenomenon by the mid-1950s. (For a discussion of the influence of the Social Gospel movement on the rise and fall of institutionalism and an attempt to assess the reasons for the "reproductive failure" of Wisconsin institutionalism, see Bradley W. Bateman's and Jeff Biddle's essays in this volume, respectively.) Meanwhile, old-style Chicago law and economics only really came into its own in the late 1950s, as evidenced by the establishment of the *Journal of Law and Economics* in 1958. This brand of law and economics held firm within the Chicago school well into the 1960s, before beginning a decline matched by the ascendance of the new law and economics.

That much having been said, we can trace the decline of the old law and economics to certain larger professional forces. First, the old law and economics, although by no means exclusively the property of the institutionalists, was, part and parcel, concerned with the study of institutions. As economics became increasingly defined around the neoclassical paradigm in the postwar era, however, it became progressively a-institutional. The questions addressed by economists, and thus the scope of economics itself, became increasingly defined by the Samuelsonian and Walrasian tools of analysis, which were singularly ill suited to tackle the analysis of institutions such as the legal-economic nexus.

Moreover, the spirit of complementarity and inclusion that characterized the interwar period diminished radically during the postwar period. The bounds of what passed for theory became increasingly narrowly defined, often, or even usually, being equated with the presence of formal mathematical models. The more intuitive approach characteristic of the old law and economics was no longer considered solid economic theory. This was particularly the case for institutional law and economics, as the institutionalists were increasingly denigrated as atheoretical or antitheoretical fact gatherers. This was true not just within the profession at large but also within the law and economics community, as witnessed by Stigler's comment that institutional economics "had nothing in it but a stance of hostility to the standard theoretical tradition. There was no positive agenda of research, there was no set of problems or new methods they wanted to invoke" (quoted in Kitch 1983, 170). Furthermore, lacking the "aesthetic appeal" of postwar theory, with its elegant systems of equations and high-powered empirical techniques, the more intuitive and nonquantitative empirical nature of the old law and economics was not nearly as attractive to budding scholars, nor was such research the road to professional rewards. (See Roger E. Backhouse's essay in this volume for evidence regarding the increasingly mathematical and quantitative nature of articles published in leading U.S. economics journals during this period.)

Another important factor at work was the increasing professional emphasis on the search for determinate, optimal solutions to the questions of economic theory and policy in the postwar era. Although the old law and economics did a great deal to elucidate the relationships between legal and economic processes, what it did not do (with the exception of certain aspects of early Chicago law and economics) or even attempt to do was set forth a framework for determining the optimal legal structure for the economic system. As such, this type of theorizing was bound to be discarded as having little to offer to a profession increasingly preoccupied with the search for such solutions.

While the search for determinate, optimal solutions to questions of economic theory and policy in part accounts for the decline of the old law and economics, it also plays an important role in accounting for the rise of the new approach. Most of the standard problems of public economics were quickly absorbed within this framework, but the Coase theorem and the illustrations Coase drew from the legal cases showed that the analysis of legal rules, too, could be placed squarely within the economist's world of determinate optimal solutions. Coase showed, as a means of setting up his analysis of how legal rules affect market outcomes in the real world of positive transaction costs, that within the standard neoclassical (zero transaction cost) framework the form of legal institutions has no impact on the working of markets. What economists seized on, however, was not Coase's intended message (the need for a change of approach to the questions of economic policy analysis) but rather the notion of modeling contests over rights in a neoclassical price-theoretic framework. Since any given assignment of rights expands the opportunity sets of some agents while restricting those of others, legal decision making could easily be converted into an exercise in optimal allocations, based upon which one could derive, in relatively straightforward fashion, the efficient legal rules to govern human behavior.

Thus, by a curious reconstructive twist, Coase's analysis of how legal institutions influence economic performance was twisted around to provide the supposed basis for the analysis of all manner of legal rules within the maximization-plus-equilibrium framework so much in vogue in postwar economics. And seeing a potentially fruitful extension of the economic paradigm into the legal arena, economists were quick to begin mining the new territory.

Moreover, Coase's suggestions regarding judges' applications of economic logic in their thinking stimulated a number of scholars— Posner in particular—to examine whether an efficiency logic might be underlying the development of legal rules across the common law. Doing so involved the rather straightforward application of individual decision-making calculus to agents faced with constraints imposed by common-law rules and the assessment of the resulting outcomes according to the dictates of Paretian welfare economics. And of course, where extant rules were found to be inefficient, the determination of rules that would induce optimal behavior was a natural extension.

A further reason for the openness among economists to the application of economic theory to legal reasoning (which perhaps led to a more positive reception to law and economics than to, e.g., economic sociology, at least early on) is that many of the legal questions the economists addressed had a substantial identifiable economic (i.e., dollar-valued) component, as illustrated in the previous example. Rights are valuable: Alternative assignments of rights generate alternative patterns and levels of benefits and costs among the affected parties. Moreover, legal rules, when established as precedents, provide incentives that channel individual decisions and actions in particular directions. From these points, it was just a short and natural leap to the conclusion that it is important to assess the degree to which legal rules promote the efficient allocation of resources, just as economists for decades had proposed efficiency-enhancing regulations through the political process. And it was just a further short leap to the analysis of *all* classes of legal rules (including those involving non-dollar-valued claims), given the assumption of a consistency of individual reasoning across the legal spectrum.

Coupled with this was the view (among economists) of economics as the queen of the social sciences, a perception flowing in part from its rigorous, testable theoretical models, which the other social sciences lacked. Although this factor helped fuel the imperialist tendencies of economists, it took on particular import for the success of the law and economics movement because law was at this time engaged in a search for moorings following the decline of legal realism (Posner, 1987). The idea of establishing a "scientific" basis for law through the application of economic theory created a degree of receptiveness within the legal community to economists' attempts at void filling that might well not have been present at another time, and economists were happy to attempt to fill this void.

Although the overriding concern of the present discussion is with positive law and economics, I would be remiss if I did not address the normative overtones that, at the very least, fueled the early development of the new law and economics within certain quarters. It goes without saying that the so-called interventionism of the institutionalists contrasts starkly with the Chicago approach to antitrust and the market-oriented nature of the Chicago approach generally. (For example, the institutionalists were prominently represented within the U.S. economic-planning bureaucracy described in Márcia L. Balisciano's essay in this volume. Anne Mayhew's essay in this book provides some insights into the normative features underlying the institutionalist and Chicago views of antitrust regulation.) But the post-1960 developments in law and economics provided a rather sturdy intellectual foundation for a market-oriented approach to legal decision making. The Coase theorem opened the door to the analysis of rights allocation within a traditional market framework and to the asking of a relatively simple question: If rights over scarce resources are allocated through the market for all manner of goods, why would the same not apply to rights over pollution, the ability to breach contracts, tortious harms, and so on? To a mind-set that finds market allocation most congenial, the Coase theorem opened up a vast new scope for the operation of markets. If market processes are allowed to work, legal outcomes will be exactly those dictated by the laws governing competitive markets. The implications of this insight were straightforward and quickly seized upon: (1) Let the market work in allocating rights; (2) facilitate the working of the market by removing legal impediments to its operation; and (3) when (1) and (2) are not possible, assign rights or design legal rules to mimic the outcome of a competitive market, the outcome that would have obtained in any event had there not been impediments to the market's operation.

This argument is amazingly powerful, since it implies that the law should simply be structured to let people do what they would naturally do if transaction costs did not preclude them from doing so. And in an era in which so-called activist judges were making decisions that often seemed to conflict with the ideology of the market, the implications of the economic analysis of law were welcome ammunition for those who favored the market. Thus it is not surprising that the new law and economics movement was launched from within the Chicago school, even given its important place within law and economics of the old variety. In addition, the willingness of certain conservative organizations to provide financial support for the law and economics movement (such as the John M. Olin Foundation, which provides substantial funding for a number of law and economics programs across the United States) helped facilitate both the program of research and the classroom dissemination of these ideas. (For a more general discussion of the influence of external funding on the direction of economic research over the course of the twentieth century, see Craufurd D. Goodwin's essay in this volume.)

It bears emphasizing that none of these normative conclusions is inherent in the examination of legal rules using the tools of neoclassical economic analysis, and it is both incorrect and irresponsible to equate the new law and economics with conservative ideology. Indeed, the scholars working in the field come from a wide variety of perspectives and draw many conclusions at odds with conservative ideology. However, it would be difficult to deny that law and economics has been used to promote certain normative agendas, not unlike, at times, institutionalist-realist law and economics. When combined with the goal of facilitating competitive market outcomes, the Pandora's box opened by "The Problem of Social Cost" gave ample opportunity for individuals so inclined to design legal rules that would comport with the dictates of competitive markets.

Conclusion

This essay has attempted to document, from the perspective of economics, the transformation in law and economics over the course of the twentieth century. Although the growth of the new law and economics was fueled by forces at work in both the legal and the economics communities, I have attempted to shed some light on the forces that attracted economists to the economic analysis of law and led them to neglect the issues raised by law and economics of the older variety.

The present essay takes us into the 1970s, when law and economics hit its stride, but much has changed since that time. In particular, the scope of law and economics—particularly in the methods employed and problems examined—has expanded greatly. For example, recent work on the foundations of behavior in the legal arena has challenged certain standard conclusions in the field (Medema 1997). More important for present purposes, there has been a substantial resurgence of interest in law and economics of the older variety, as evidenced in the work of Oliver Williamson, Douglass North, Yoram Barzel, Thráinn Eggertsson, Warren J. Samuels, and A. Allan Schmid, to name just a few.[11] Although certain aspects of this analysis have commonalities with the new law and economics examined above, what is important is that economists have begun to turn back to an examination of the institutional (including legal) underpinnings of the economic system—that is, to the roots of law and economics.

11. See Eggertsson 1990 and Mercuro and Medema 1997, chaps. 4–5, for surveys of this literature.

References

Adams, Henry C. [1887/1897] 1954. *Relation of the State to Industrial Action and Economics and Jurisprudence*. Edited by Joseph Dorfman. New York: Viking.

Alchian, Armen, A. 1961. *Some Economics of Property*. Santa Monica, Calif.: RAND Corporation.

Bell, John F. 1967. *A History of Economic Thought*. New York: Ronald Press.

Berle, Adolf A., and Gardiner C. Means. 1932. *The Modern Corporation and Private Property*. New York: Macmillan.

Calabresi, Guido. 1961. Some Thoughts on Risk Distribution and the Law of Torts. *Yale Law Journal* 70 (March): 499–553.

Clark, John Bates. 1894. The Modern Appeal to Legal Forces in Economic Life. *American Economic Association Publications* 9.

Coase, Ronald H. 1959. The Federal Communications Commission. *Journal of Law and Economics* 2 (October): 1–40.

———. 1960. The Problem of Social Cost. *Journal of Law and Economics* 3 (October): 1–44.

———. 1984. The New Institutional Economics. *Journal of Institutional and Theoretical Economics* 140 (March): 229–31.

———. 1993. Law and Economics at Chicago. *Journal of Law and Economics* 36 (April, part 2): 239–54.

Commons, John R. [1896] 1996. Political Economy and Law. *The Kingdom* 24 January. Reprinted in *John R. Commons: Selected Essays*. Edited by Malcolm Rutherford and Warren J. Samuels. London: Routledge.

——— [1907] 1974. *Proportional Representation*. 2d ed. Reprint, New York: Augustus M. Kelley.

———. 1924. *Legal Foundations of Capitalism*. New York: Macmillan.

———. 1925. Law and Economics. *Yale Law Journal* 34 (February): 371–82.

Demsetz, Harold. 1964. The Exchange and Enforcement of Property Rights. *Journal of Law and Economics* 7 (October): 11–26.

———. 1967. Toward a Theory of Property Rights. *American Economic Review* 57 (May): 347–59.

Dorfman, Joseph. [1959] 1969. *The Economic Mind in American Civilization*. Vols. 4 and 5, 1918–1933. Reprint, New York: Augustus M. Kelley.

Duxbury, Neil. 1995. *Patterns of American Jurisprudence*. Oxford: Oxford University Press.

Eggertsson, Thráinn. 1990. *Economic Behavior and Institutions*. Cambridge: Cambridge University Press.

Fisher, Irving. [1906] 1965. *The Nature of Capital and Income*. Reprint, New York: Augustus M. Kelley.

Furubotn, Eirik G., and Svetozar Pejovich. 1972. Property Rights and Economic Theory: A Survey of the Literature. *Journal of Economic Literature* 10 (December): 1137–62.

Hale, Robert Lee. 1924. Economic Theory and the Statesman. In *The Trend of Economics*. Edited by Rexford G. Tugwell. New York: Knopf.

————. 1927. Economics and the Law. In *The Social Sciences and Their Interrelations*. Edited by William F. Ogburn and Alexander A. Goldenweiser. Boston: Houghton Mifflin.

————. 1952. *Freedom through Law*. New York: Columbia University Press.

Hamilton, Walton H. 1932. Property according to Locke. *Yale Law Journal* 41 (April): 864–80.

Holmes, Oliver Wendell. 1897. The Path of Law. *Harvard Law Review* 10 (March): 457–78.

Kitch, Edmund W., ed. 1983. The Fire of Truth: A Remembrance of Law and Economics at Chicago, 1932–1970. *Journal of Law and Economics* 26 (April): 163–234.

Medema, Steven G. 1994. *Ronald H. Coase*. New York: St. Martin's.

————. 1996. Ronald Coase and American Institutionalism. *Research in the History of Economic Thought and Methodology* 14:51–92.

————. 1997. On the Trial of *Homo Economicus*: What Law and Economics Tells Us about the Development of Economic Imperialism. In *New Economics and Its Writing. HOPE* 27 supplement. Edited by John B. Davis. Durham, N.C.: Duke University Press.

Mercuro, Nicholas, and Steven G. Medema. 1997. *Economics and the Law: From Posner to Post Modernism*. Princeton, N.J.: Princeton University Press.

Plant, Sir Arnold. 1974. *Selected Economic Essays and Addresses*. London: Routledge and Kegan Paul.

Posner, Richard A. 1973. *Economic Analysis of Law*. 1st ed. Boston: Little, Brown.

————. 1976. *Antitrust Law: An Economic Perspective*. Chicago: University of Chicago Press.

————. 1981. *The Economics of Justice*. Cambridge, Mass.: Harvard University Press.

————. 1987. The Decline of Law as an Autonomous Discipline, 1962–1987. *Harvard Law Review* 100 (February): 761–80.

Reder, Melvin W. 1982. Chicago Economics: Permanence and Change. *Journal of Economic Literature* 20 (March): 1–38.

Samuels, Warren J. 1973. The Economy as a System of Power and Its Legal Bases: The Legal Economics of Robert Lee Hale. *University of Miami Law Review* 27 (spring/summer): 261–371.

————. 1993. Law and Economics: Some Early Journal Contributions. In *Economic Thought and Discourse in the Twentieth Century*. Edited by Warren J. Samuels, Jeff Biddle, and Thomas W. Patchak-Schuster. Aldershot, England: Edward Elgar.

Part 4

Mathematics, Formalism, and Style

From Rigor to Axiomatics: The Marginalization of Griffith C. Evans

E. Roy Weintraub

The theme of the conference of which this volume is the record contrasts a pluralistic interwar economics with a monolithic (neoclassical) postwar economics. Two conflicting metanarratives are in play in this idea. The first is the triumphalism of disciplinary progress, a morality play in which economics finally fulfills the Jevonian promise and becomes scientific through the use of mathematics. In this view, good science displaces bad thinking, loose thinking, and the inappropriately varied argumentation of economics. We may think of Paul Samuelson (1987) as an exemplar of this way of constructing the history of this period. The second is a construction of the interwar period as one in which the healthy variety of economic thought was forced onto the Procrustean bed of neoclassical theory. What emerged by the time of the neoclassical synthesis was an economics bereft of joy, intelligence, and humanity. We may think of modern institutionalists, neo-Austrians, and post-Keynesians as exemplars of this perspective. In either case, the usual question asked is "Why was pluralism replaced by neoclassicism?" The two metanarratives condition the meta-answers "So that Goodness would triumph" and "So that Evil would triumph," respectively. In both cases, however, it is apparently believed that mathematical theory "pushed out" nonmathematical theorizing in economics.

In this essay, I will not address the "why" question posed previously. Instead I will look closely at "what happened" in this period by reading Griffith Conrad Evans in conjunction with the mathematician Vito

Volterra, whose image of mathematics and mathematical life was rather different from that of the mathematical culture that emerged after World War II.[1] The work of Evans is particularly interesting, because his ideas were not ignored as being mathematically unsophisticated. Nor was he disconnected from the networks that validate acceptable contributions to the discipline (Morrey 1983; Rider 1989). Rather, it is my contention that the marginalization of Evans's ideas in the postwar period in economics is better understood as a result of a change in the conception of what mathematics itself could bring to a scientific field (see Philip Mirowski and D. Wade Hands's essay in this volume). An implication of this reading is that any narrative in the history of economics of the twentieth century that employs the idea of "increasing mathematization" should be read with skepticism.

Vito Volterra's World

In 1959, when Dover Press reprinted Volterra's *Theory of Functionals and of Integral and Integro-differential Equations*, Evans was asked to write the preface.[2] In a three-page note, he commented, "It was my good fortune to study under Professor Volterra from 1910 to 1912" (Evans 1959, 1). Evans was twenty-three during the period he mentions, and his 1910 Harvard Ph.D. had earned him a Sheldon Traveling Fellowship, which he used for postdoctoral study at the University of Rome. This was to be the signal event in his intellectual life, for beginning with his first published paper in 1909, "The Integral Equation of the Second Kind, of Volterra, with Singular Kernel," he was connected to the greatest Italian mathematician of the risorgimento, the intellectual leader of Italian science in the late nineteenth and early twentieth centuries. Indeed, by 1911 Evans published six papers on functional analysis and integral equations in Italian in Volterra's journal, *Rendiconto Accademia Lincei* (Proceedings of the Lincei Academy of Science, Physics, Mathematics, and Nature). The interests he developed in Volterra's Rome were to be the defining intellectual themes of his mathematical life, as his works continued to explore both potential theory from a perspective of classical mechanics and the theory of functionals.

---

1. This distinction between the body of mathematical knowledge and the image of mathematics is based on the work of Leo Corry (1989, 1996).

2. "Vito Volterra's World" is taken from the lovely article by Judith Goodstein (1984).

Along the way, Evans took time to write "The Physical Universe of Dante" in 1921 and to explain the Italian school of algebraic geometry to a large audience in "Enriques on Algebraic Geometry" in 1925. His last work, published in 1961 at age seventy-four, was "Funzioni armoniche polidrome ad infiniti valori nello spazio, con due curve di ramificazione di ordine uno." It is safe to say that his command of the Italian language and his early connection to the mathematical subjects created by Volterra linked Evans irrevocably to Volterra, who became his intellectual model. How else are we to read the following gracious and admiring passage?

> Volterra was close to the Risorgimento, close to its poets and their national ideals. In 1919 he was prevailed upon, in spite of a modest reluctance, to give a lecture on Carducci. I remember the occasion well because I had the pleasure of translating this, as well as his exposition of functions of composition, viva voce to an audience of students. He was also close to the Rinascento, with respect to his sensitivity to art and music and his unlimited scientific curiosity. His devotion to the history of science and his feeling for archeology were expressed respectively in the treasures of his personal library in Rome and in his collection of antiquities in his villa at Ariccia. He took a most prominent part in the international organizations of science and in extending the cultural relations of Italy. His career gives us confidence that the Renaissance ideal of a free and widely ranging knowledge will not vanish, however great the pressure of specialization. (Evans 1959, 3)

Volterra was the mathematician Evans wished to be; the mentoring of postdoctoral students is to this day frequently a process of professional modeling and career and interest shaping. In Evans's case, this was to be manifest in his lifelong connection to Italy and to Volterra himself.

We have the handwritten autobiographical notes that the aged and failing Evans tried to put together in 1967, fragments of an autobiography he could not complete. He said that command of the Italian language was not gained early or at home, for as a Harvard student of "Copy"—Charles Townsend Copeland—he frequently wrote literary themes in and "could read and enjoy French, German and Latin as well as English" (Evans 1967). At another place in these disorganized notes he recalls a series of images from the past and remarks that "towards the end of the war (Sept. 1918) I was up towards the front, on the Lido (if I remember correctly), to 'inspect' the Italian antiaircraft defenses. . . . Earlier somewhere near the mountains (Padova?) I remember however an open prairie, at the front way north of the Po (Battle of the Piave). Volterra and I were driven up in a big automobile to Padova and I was taken to the front." The point is clear. Even as memory and handwriting failed and his powers waned, Evans took great pride in the fact that his work and Volterra's were connected.

Since I will argue that Evans's interest in the mathematization of economics can be informed by Volterra's, we need to know more about Volterra.[3] Born in 1860, he and his mother were left destitute when his father died in 1862. They were taken in by relatives in Florence, where Volterra grew up and was educated. He was very precocious, and his teachers quickly recognized his remarkable abilities. One teacher, the physicist Antonio Roiti, intervened in family discussions about launching Volterra into a commercial career by making the high school boy his assistant in the physics laboratory at the University of Florence. There, Volterra won a competition to study mathematics and physics at the University of Pisa in 1880. After receiving his doctorate in 1882, with several publications in analysis in hand, he was appointed as assistant to the mathematician Enrico Betti and the following year won a post as professor of mechanics at Pisa. In 1900 he succeeded Eugenio Beltrami in the chair of mathematical physics at the University of Rome (E. Volterra 1976, 86).

In Rome, Volterra established his position as scientific leaderspokesperson of the new country. His research interests were wide ranging, and his position in Rome allowed him to stay at the center of activity:

Rome became the capital of the newly-created state of Italy in 1870. Under the leadership of Quintano Sella (1827–1884), a mathemati-

---

3. There is no full-length biography of Volterra. There are, however, several biographical essays, the first of which was an obituary notice of Volterra as a fellow of the Royal Society by Sir Edmund Whittaker in 1941. This essay, which contains a virtually complete bibliography for Volterra, was included in the Dover reprint of Volterra's book on the theory of functionals (Whittaker 1959) and was the basis of the Volterra entry in *The New Palgrave* (Gandolfo 1987). One other source of detail can be found in the excellent note by E. Volterra in the 1976 *Dictionary of Scientific Biography*; that piece has an exceptionally good guide to the secondary literature on Volterra and his role in Italian science and mathematics. Most of my own thinking about Volterra has been influenced by Giorgio Israel, who has written extensively on his life and work. Citations to Israel's work can be found in the references.

cian at the University of Turin who exchanged academic life for a ministerial post in the new government, Rome's scientific halls came to life again. With the help of the new Commissioner for Public Instruction, also a mathematician, Sella brought the cream of Italy's scientific faculty to Rome and transformed the capital's historic Accademia dei Lincei into a genuine National Academy of Science. Sella and his colleagues built the scientific world that Vito Volterra, then 40, inherited in 1900 when he took up his duties . . . in the nation's capital. [Volterra's] appointment as Senator of the Kingdom five years later reinforced the Risorgimento tradition of the scientist-statesman in the service of king and country. (Goodstein 1984, 607–8)

Volterra was concerned with all aspects of scientific understanding.[4] He was one of the leaders in making Albert Einstein's theory of relativity known, and he was a tireless worker for the public appreciation of scientific knowledge. In the present era of "science wars" and lost faith in the very notion of progress, it is difficult to recapture the optimistic world in which science, scientific knowledge, and technology or applied science were to lead to the new enlightenment. Volterra was the kind of new man to whom Henry Adams probably referred in "The Dynamo and the Virgin," an instantiation of the ideal of the scientific cum technical polymath. His interests in mathematics, for example, did not prevent his working at age fifty-five as a lieutenant in the Italian Corps of Engineers, during which period he also worked at the Aeronautics Institute in Rome, carried out aerial warfare experiments in Tuscany, and tested phonotelemetric devices on the Austrian front (Goodstein 1984, 610).

As a mathematician of the late nineteenth century, however, Volterra was from that generation so well represented by the fictitious character Victor Jakob in *Night Thoughts of a Classical Physicist* (McCormmach 1982). Volterra was a classical analyst whose mathematical work on functionals grew out of his generalization of differential equations to the more complex and rich theory of integro-differential equations: His mathematics articles in 1900–1913 include "Sur la stratification d'une masse fluide en équilibre" (1903), "Sur les équations différentielles du type parabolique" (1904), "Note on the Application of the Method of Images to Problems of Vibrations" (1904), and "Sulle equazioni integro-

---

4. See the very good compilation contained in the five volumes of Volterra's *Opere matematiche* (1957).

differenziali" (1909). These topics, however, were not well connected to the nascent Italian school of algebraic geometry launched by Cremona, developed by Eugenio Bertini, Corrado Segre, and Giuseppe Veronese, and brought to fruition by Castelnuovo, Enriques, and Severi. Volterra was thus more in the tradition of analysts like his mentor Betti and Ulisse Dini, for the former worked in the intersection of analysis and physics and the latter was concerned with the rigorous reformulation of mathematical analysis. Trained by both men, Volterra's

> own research was more closely linked to the applications. In Volterra's view it is the peculiar problems deriving from the experimental sciences that lead to the most fertile and useful theories, while general questions posited in abstract terms often lack any applications. This conception of the relationships between analysis and physics is directly linked to the French physico-mathematical tradition from Fourier to Poincaré. In fact the need for concreteness apparent in the fact of thinking of mathematical issues as linked to physical problems, together with the rigorous training received in Dini's school, helped to make Volterra particularly well-suited to tackling mathematical physics. (Israel and Nurzia 1989, 114)

The Victor Jakob of McCormmach's 1982 novel, though German, stands for the same kind of scientist found in many European countries at that time. Relativity was a great shock to the traditional vision, and quanta were difficult to domesticate. The crises of atomic theory and subatomic particles were on the horizon, and the issue of what kind of theory would promise the best explanation brought into question the idea of explanation itself. As Israel and Nurzia (1989, 115–16) put the matter:[5]

> The crisis in question stemmed from the discussion going on in the scientific world of the time concerning the advisability of maintaining the classical mechanic method of explaining natural phenomena based on the deterministic principle, as well as on the mathematical tool provided by differential equations. From the strictly mathematical standpoint this crisis lead to a split between "antiformalists," who favored a development of mathematics linked to experimental

5. Let me acknowledge my debt to Giorgio Israel, whose leadership role in interpreting the history of Italian mathematics has shaped my views here.

issues, and "formalists," who preferred development free from all constraints except formal rigor. The reactions to this crisis by the world of Italian mathematics varied enormously and a number of totally conflicting attitudes emerged. On the one hand there were those, like Volterra, who merely acknowledged the existence of a crisis and sought, if not a solution to the crisis, at least a solid foundation in their scientific practice and in the links between mathematics and topics of experimental design. . . . [It is for this reason that] Volterra supported and promoted scientific organizations whose main purpose was to provide a concrete means of bridging the gap between pure and applied science.

Although Volterra appears not to have left autobiographical notes or much material that directly expresses his views of the role of mathematics in applied sciences, we do have a document that, interpreted as a projection of his own views, may be helpful. This address at the inaugural festivities for Rice Institute (which later became Rice University) apparently has not been noticed by the few economists interested in Volterra. Delivered in French, the address was translated by Evans and was titled simply "Henri Poincaré" (V. Volterra 1915). Poincaré had just died, and Volterra's tribute to him was both a eulogy and an appreciation for a scientific and personal career, a tribute that well suited the foundation of a new institute dedicated to science in America. In attempting to place Poincaré in the history of mathematics and science, Volterra (1915, 146–47) spoke in some detail on the history of the study of differential equations and function theory in the latter part of the nineteenth century:

There are two kinds of mathematical physics. Through ancient habit we regard them as belonging to a single branch and generally teach them in the same courses, but their natures are quite different. In most cases the people who are greatly interested in one despise somewhat the other. The first kind consists in a difficult and subtle analysis connected with physical questions. Its scope is to solve in a complete and exact manner the problems which it presents to us. It endeavors also to demonstrate by rigorous methods statements which are fundamental for mathematical and logical points of view. I believe that I do not err when I say that many physicists look upon this mathematical flora as a collection of parasitic plants grown to the great tree of natural philosophy. . . . The other kind of mathematical physics has a less analytical character, but forms a subject inseparable from any consideration of phenomena. We could expect no progress in their study without the aid which this brings them. Could anybody imagine the electromagnetic theory of light, the experiments of Hertz and wireless telegraphy, without the mathematical analysis of Maxwell, which was responsible for their birth? Poincaré led in both kinds of mathematical physics. He was an extraordinary analyst, but he also had the mind of a physicist.

What we have here is Volterra's projection onto Poincaré of the kinds of values that he thinks mathematicians ought to exhibit in their work: not just a mathematical sophistication and power of analytical reasoning but a deep and thorough understanding of the scientific basis and connection of those mathematical ideas. Poincaré, mathematician and scientist, was Volterra's paradigmatic intellectual.

Volterra and Economic Theory

The distinction Volterra makes between grounding explanations on the physical characteristics of the problem and grounding explanations on mathematico-logico reasoning chains mirrors the distinction between nonformalist and formalist responses within the mathematics community to the crisis of the foundations of mathematics, the paradoxes of set theory, during the same period. In the case of both physics and set theory, mathematicians could, with the formalist response, ground the unknown on the known. For mathematics, the grounding was to be an axiomatization of the settled parts of mathematics, logic, set theory, and arithmetic, as a basis of both more advanced mathematical theory and the sciences built on the axiomatized mathematical structures so created. For Volterra, this formalist response was not rigorous: Scientific reasoning chains could not be based on the free play of ideas, axioms, or abstract structures. Instead, scientific models had to be based directly and specifically on the underlying physical reality, a reality directly apprehended through experimentation and observation and thus interpersonally confirmable.[6]

This point is important and bears repeating because the present-day

6. I thank Giorgio Israel for several conversations on this matter and for his insistence on this distinction. His article " 'Rigor' and 'Axiomatics' in Modern Mathematics" (1981) shapes this discussion.

identification of rigor with axiomatics obscures the way the terms were used at the turn of the century. Today we tend to identify the abstract reasoning chains of formal mathematical work with the notion of rigor and to set rigor off against informal reasoning chains. Being unrigorous signifies, today, intellectual informality. This is not the distinction that was alive in Volterra's world, however. For Volterra, to be rigorous in modeling a phenomenon was to base the modeling directly and unambiguously on the experimental substrate of concrete results. The opposite of "rigorous" was not "informal" but rather "unconstrained." To provide a nonrigorous explanation or model in biology, economics, physics, or chemistry was to provide a model unconstrained by experimental data or by interpersonally confirmable observations.

In Volterra's view, the strategy for approaching scientific explanation generally was to base reasoning on the most well-developed intellectual framework then extant, the framework of classical mathematical physics. His clearest statement of this position, of special interest to economists, was the 1901 article "Sui tentativi di applicazione della mathematiche alle scienze biologiche e sociale."[7] It is useful to examine one lengthy passage from this article, in which Volterra defines what, at the turn of the century, this position entailed for the field of economics:

> The notion of *homo oeconomicus* which had given rise to much debate and has created so many difficulties, and which some people are still loath to accept, appears so easy to our mechanical scientist that he is taken aback at other people's surprise at this ideal, schematic being. He sees the concept of *homo oeconomicus* as analogous to those which are so familiar to him as a result of long habitual use. He is accustomed to idealizing surfaces, considering them to be frictionless, accepting lines to be nonextendable and solid bodies to be nondeformable, and he is used to replacing natural fluids with perfect liquids and gases. Not only is this second nature to him: he also

---

7. This was Volterra's inaugural address at the University of Rome for a chair in mathematical physics. It was initially published in the *Annurio della Universita Roma* and reprinted in the *Giornale degli economisti* in 1901. It was translated into French in 1906 by Ludovic Zoretti as "Les mathématiques dans les sciences biologiques et sociales" (V. Volterra 1906b). For the reader's convenience, I will use the English translations of the relevant portions, by Giogio Israel in several of his works, although I will on occasion make use of an unpublished translation prepared by Caroline Benforado. Citations to Israel's translations are followed by citations to the original source in Volterra in Italian or French.

knows the advantages that derive from these concepts. If the mechanics scholar pursues this study he will see that both in his own science and in economics everything can be reduced to an interplay of trends and constraints—the latter restricting the former which react by generating tensions. It is from this interplay that equilibrium or movement stems, one static and one dynamic, in both these sciences. We have already referred to the vicissitudes of the idea of force in the history of mechanics: from the peaks of metaphysics we have descended to the sphere of measurable things. In economics, for example, we no longer speak as Jevons did about the mathematical expression of non-measurable quantities. Even Pareto seems to have given up his idea of *ophelimity*, which was the cornerstone of his original edifice, and is moving to purely quantitative concepts with indifference curves which so beautifully match the level curves and equipotential surfaces of mechanics. . . . Lastly our mechanical scientist sees in the logical process for obtaining the conditions for economic equilibrium the same reasoning he himself uses to establish the principle of virtual work, and when he comes across the economic differential equations he feels the urge to apply to them the integration methods which he knows work so well. (Israel 1988, 43 [V. Volterra 1906b, 9–10])

Volterra sought to mathematize economics and biology by replacing metaphysical mathematical analogies with rigorous mathematical models.[8] In economics, however, Volterra published only one official work, a review of Vilfredo Pareto: "L'economia matematica ed il nuovo manuale del Prof. Pareto" (1906a). Toward the end of that piece, Volterra cautioned:

By rigorously solving well-defined problems in a clearly delimited field, mathematical economics must offer us a secure foundation of positive data on which to base our judgment as to the procedures to be followed in various circumstances. But it always leaves open the discussion of the great moral and political questions to which such

8. Volterra himself, writing in 1901, when he was forty-one years old, could not have foreseen that from his mid-sixties until his death at age eighty he would be very concerned with modeling biological theories and with creating a field of biomathematics. A current search of the biology literature using the key word "Volterra" will produce hundreds of references to Volterra models, the most significant of which is the so-called predator-prey model of interspecies rivalry and population dynamics.

results should be applied. . . . But to ensure that one can fully justify the application of mathematics and to obtain the secure results one seeks, it is first of all necessary that the problems be formulated clearly and [be] based on definitions and postulates containing nothing vague. It is also essential that . . . the elements taken into consideration are treated as quantities that cannot elude measurement. (Ingrao and Israel 1990, 164 [V. Volterra 1957, 142, 144])

Ingrao and Israel (1990, 164) believe that Volterra, "despite his initial enthusiasm" for mathematical economics, "immediately came up against the difficulties inherent in the theory's fragile empirical foundations." Israel has returned to this view, with respect to Volterra and economics, on several occasions (Israel 1988, 1991a, 1991b; Israel and Nurzia 1989). His point is simple and clear: Volterra's view of science and scientific explanation, which entailed rigor in modeling in the sense of developing economic explanations from mechanical ones, came up against the nonempirical nature of economics and the impossibility of erecting mathematical economic theories on any empirical foundation whatsoever.

The larger issue, however, was that Volterra's perspective was increasingly unsatisfactory as a solution to the crisis in the natural sciences. Indeed the entire crisis, at least in physics, turned on the explanatory power of mechanical reductionism; far from being part of the solution, reductionist thinking such as Volterra's was itself the problem. The crisis, or rather the interlocked crises, of mathematics and physics was resolved by the formalist position on explanation, whereby mathematical analogy replaced mechanical analogy and mathematical models were cut loose from their physical underpinnings in mechanics. The result was that in the first decades of the twentieth century a rigorous argument was reconceptualized as a logically consistent argument instead of as an argument that connected the problematic phenomenon to a physical phenomenon by use of empirical data. Propositions were henceforth "true" within the system considered because they were consistent with the assumptions instead of being "true" because they could be grounded in "real phenomena." We can leave Volterra here and refocus on Evans, for a historian of economics can construct Evans out of these Volterra-emergent themes.

Evans: The Mathematician and His Interests

In 1912 Evans became one of the first two teachers at the Rice Institute in Houston. As the institute transformed itself into Rice University, Evans lent it his increasing renown and intellectual strength and his mathematical visibility. Today Rice recognizes his role in its program of Griffith C. Evans Instructorships in Mathematics, intended for promising young mathematicians. Evans's resignation from Rice in 1933 was sufficiently noteworthy that the *Houston Chronicle* wrote a story about it that recounted his career there. During his twenty-one years at Rice and in Houston, he had made his mark. After his promotion to full professor in 1916, he was married in 1917 to Isabel Mary John, daughter of state court judge Robert A. John of Houston, who was general counsel of the Texas Company for many years (*Houston Chronicle* 1973). Isabel John was a great-granddaughter of Sam Houston, and her niece married Price Daniel, who became a Texas governor. Evans, Boston Brahmin, was nothing if not well connected to the first families of Texas.

Newspaper clippings found in the Rice University Archives provide a glimpse of Evans's diverse tastes and interests. On 6 May 1915, the *Houston Chronicle* (1915a) reported on a lecture Evans gave on pragmatism that was the first of three lectures on "scientific aspects of philosophy." Evans began by addressing the gospel of Tolstoy and then suggested that "in regard to such basic [metaphysical] questions almost all thinkers have a basis of optimism. Their query is not 'are things right?' but 'how is it that all things are right?' and in their researches they seem to trust to what may be called the lucky star of humanity, injecting their personal interest in the outcome into the problem itself." Evans went on to discuss William James and his approach to settling or at least posing philosophical issues. He concluded that "we have no reason to suppose that all possible phenomena can be expressed by means of any finite system of terms. Instead of this, we may expect that, no matter how complete our system of conceptual terms may be, we shall find facts that require its continual extension. That is what we mean when we say that there will always be novelty in the world, and always new problems for the genius of man to attack and solve."

One week later, the *Houston Chronicle* (1915b) reported on Evans's talk on aesthetics, the second in the series of lectures. Evans began by suggesting that an important element in the discussion of art and aesthetics was the determination of how wide the aesthetic net should be cast. He suggested that knowledge of the aesthetic issues in mathematics could cast light on the general problem. The inability of mathematics to determine which geometry is "correct" leads to a position "that an arbitrary element enters into that most exact of sciences, mathematics. . . . The nature of mathematics is that it is entirely arbitrary, and its use is that in its growth, by the formation of arbitrary concepts, it limits itself more or less unconsciously to those who have mirrors in actual life. It is therefore a 'human interest' story." Beyond the technical skills required to be a mathematician, "other qualities of a far more subtle sort, chief among them . . . imagination, are necessary." He cites Benedetto Croce with approval and remarks that "art is expressed in intuition, that is, the synthesis of concrete imaginative elements. It is a spiritual, theoretical activity."

The third Evans lecture on the scientific aspects of philosophy was reported in the *Houston Chronicle* on 28 January 1916. He began this lecture on rationalism by noting that "each of the earlier two lectures ended with a problem which could not be solved in terms of the methods proper to the subject of the lecture itself." Evans framed the issues as fundamentally epistemological; paraphrasing Immanuel Kant, he asked, "How is metaphysics possible? How can we hope to know anything about metaphysical questions?" Kant further asked whether natural science is possible in the sense that natural laws are not laws of experience but creations of the human mind. Evans remarks that "the axioms of mathematics are merely the forms in which sensations must be presented to us in order to become mental representations, they are meshes through which our intuitions are formed, and derive their necessity from that fact. . . . Similarly the laws of the pure sciences of nature are merely the laws of the understanding. By means of them nature becomes intelligible. And they derive their certainty from that reason."

These three lectures, apparently never published, aid our understanding of Evans's perspective on the role of mathematics as a human activity and thus an activity connected to other human activities, like Alfred Marshall's "study of mankind in the ordinary business of life." Evans is an end-of-the-nineteenth-century rationalist, a Harvard pragmatist who believes in reason with a human face and a person's capacity to understand the world in which he or she lives. For many mathematicians and physicists, the earth had moved in the 1890s. Evans was writing on the eve of World War I, a time when civilization and its products would be shaken. There is no trace in Evans's own work, however, of the intellectual crisis that rocked turn-of-the-century physicists and mathematicians: Evans's scientific views remained intact.

Evans's war career was recorded in the Houston newspapers. The *Houston Post* (1918) noted his appointment as "scientific attaché" to the American embassy in Rome and observed that he was doing "research with the American Aviation Service. He was in Italy with the American and allied forces studying actual conditions. . . . He has been in war work in France, England, and Italy, . . . his ability as a linguist adding to his proficiency as a scientist in foreign countries." The paper followed this story with another in 1919 on Harvard's offer of a faculty post to Evans, which he turned down after his demobilization to return to Houston.

We can reconstruct Evans's career and interests after his return to Houston based on three articles he prepared for the *Rice Institute Pamphlet*. The first appeared in 1921 in a series of seven lectures observing the six hundredth anniversary of the death of Dante. Evans contributed a substantial article titled "The Physical Universe of Dante." This essay best portrays Evans as an unusual scholar, although he acknowledges the help of Volterra and other individuals in Rome, as well as his own father and a Professor Tyler of Boston. In the essay, Evans examines the context in which Dante wrote, situating him in a particular framework of knowledge about the physical universe. With a sharp command of the original source material, as well as wide-ranging knowledge of the secondary literature in the history of science, Evans discusses the issues of the calendar and astronomy to locate the sources of allusions and references in Dante's poetry and even delves into astrology as an interpretive system for comprehending the nature of Dante's physical universe. Evans continues his discussion of science with observations on biology and physics, together with some observations about the "discovery" of petroleum! He comments, for example, that "a striking error in Dante's notion of the civilized world is that of making the length of the Mediterranean extend for 90 degrees of longitude—perhaps an intentional remodeling of geography to fit allegorical interpretations" (103). This is connected to Evans's subsequent discussion of the geometrical properties of the earth's surface: "Witness the geodesy of the Third Tractate of the 'Convivio,' where the relative positions of poles, equator, and elliptic are discussed, and the relation of day to night. Here incidentally the radius of the earth is given as 3250 miles"

(103–4). Evans then continues with discussions of the relation of Dante's references to the heavenly motions to the then popular theories of the variable apparent motions of the heavens created "out of a system of uniform circular motions about centers themselves also moving uniformly" (107). Evans concludes by building a comprehensive model of the universe and the motion of the stars, the sun, the planets, and the moon from the medieval conceptions and those present in Dante's own discussion.

But in the final two paragraphs, Evans takes a delicious Whiggish turn, ending with the following:

> It is time perhaps for science to grow beyond the need of a mechanical interpretation. . . . Whenever there is one mechanical explanation, the transformation theory of dynamics tells us that there is more than one, and of these the simplest, as Einstein has shown us, is the most complicated. On the other hand, when we try to classify the phenomena that admit of mechanical explanation, and Professor G. D. Birkhoff tells us that any system of ordinary differential equations is nothing but a set of dynamical equations, and vice versa, it becomes evident that the future of science may soar farther from our own restricted mechanical point-of-view than ours has risen above the quaint interpretations of the Middle Ages. (117)

This essay followed a 1920 essay by Evans in the same pamphlet titled "Fundamental Points of Potential Theory." The essay was written to commemorate "three lectures delivered at the Rice Institute in the Autumn of 1919, by Senator Vito Volterra, Professor of Mathematical Physics and Celestial Mechanics, and Dean of the Faculty of Sciences of the University of Rome" (181).

Evans's essay is "a study of the Stieltjes integral in connection with potential theory" (252). He demonstrates the relation of the potential function thus defined to the integral form of Poisson's equation, which applies to any distribution of mass. Evans's object is the set of general forms of Green's theorem as applied to polarization vectors and solutions of Poisson's equation. The essay concludes with a study of the appropriate boundary value problems for harmonic functions and the general open region. The investigations represent "studies originated in 1907, when it first became apparent to me that the theory was unnecessarily complicated by the form of the Laplacian operator" (253).

The third article by Evans in the *Rice Institute Pamphlet* appeared in

1926. In this collection of five lectures observing the three hundredth anniversary of the death of Francis Bacon, Evans contributed "The Place of Francis Bacon in the History of Scientific Method." This essay captures Evans's own philosophical ambivalence. As a resident intellectual cum philosopher/historian of science, even though an amateur, Evans was obliged to contribute to this set of popular lectures on Bacon. Although as a mathematician Evans had no patience for Bacon, as a respectful scholar he knew he should take Bacon seriously because of the esteem in which Bacon was held by such figures as Gottfried Leibniz, John Locke, David Hume, and Kant. But he thought Bacon was not worth taking seriously; hence the essay's implicit dilemma.

Evans "solves" this problem by walking away from it. He begins by asking, "If there had been no Bacon, would the future of science have been essentially different, or would its development have been materially slower?" (73) He answers immediately, "I think we may give the negative answer to both these questions." He then examines a number of fields that could have claimed Bacon in a line of paternity, as it were. In none of them does Bacon play a role. Neither physics, nor astronomy, nor atomistic or relativistic theories, nor theories of electricity and magnetism, nor mechanics "pass[es] close to Bacon" for, "given Bacon's neglect of mathematics, it is not surprising that these mathematical methods go back on a line which Bacon does not grasp" (75–76). Certainly, too, in neither evolution, nor biology, nor chemical investigations did Bacon take much scientific part.

Evans states that it is not in science itself that Bacon deserves to be recalled. Instead, Evans locates him in a line with the great "skeptic Montaigne," for whom reason is "a dangerous tool, and he who uses it loses himself along with his dogmatic enemies" (84):

> Francis Bacon believes that he provides the way of putting in order the universe which Montaigne has left in such an unhappy state. He devises a method which he thinks will be easy to apply and will increase the domain of science enormously and rapidly. . . . Bacon tends to diminish the importance of the imagination in arriving at scientific truth. . . . What is to be the real method of turning natural history into science is the systematic use of the reason in the way in which Bacon explains . . . as an induction with the help of experiment. According to Bacon's idea it is possible to arrive at a scientific

theory by a process of exclusion, more or less as an argument by reductio ad absurdum is used in mathematics. . . . In other words, hypotheses are to be eliminated successively with reference to fact or experiment until only the hypothesis which must be true remains. (84–87)

Evans goes on with this discussion but returns to the point that clearly gnaws at him, that there is no place for the imagination. "Knowledge is to be advanced by the invention of new concepts. But what makes a concept significant?" (89) Evans here takes his stand with Leibniz and, in what is certainly his own voice, remarks, "It is brilliance of imagination which makes the glory of science" (90). One suspects that Evans believed Bacon had a deficient imagination.

Evans among the Econ

At a first pass, we can locate Evans's connection to economics in the sequence of articles that led up to his 1930 book. These five works all appeared in regular mathematics publications and essentially operated in the same fashion: They called the attention of mathematicians to interesting problems in an applied discipline.

The first article was titled "A Simple Theory of Competition" and appeared in the *American Mathematical Monthly* in 1922. In it, Evans postulated a rudimentary theory of competition in terms of specific functional forms. Basing his discussion on Augustin Cournot's volume and developing it in terms of the profits of several competitors, Evans examines a number of special cases. From a modern point of view, the interesting feature of Evans's discussion is that he works with quadratic cost functions and something akin to a linear demand function. His analysis operates entirely independently of a decision calculus for either producers or purchasers. With the three coefficients of the cost functions and the two coefficients of the demand function, a variety of special cases can emerge under different assumptions. Evans modifies his discussion by introducing more producers, different kinds of taxes, and other specifications of the cost curve. He ends by noting that the restriction to functions of a single variable is mathematically inessential. The deeper question is, "What is retained when we remember that what a producer is interested in is not to make his momentary profit a maximum, but his total profit over a period of time, of considerable extent, with reference to cost functions which are themselves changing as a whole with respect to time?" (379). Evans notes that this leads to problems in the calculus of variations and "can refer only to his lecture courses for a further treatment of this point-of-view. Nevertheless it seems the most fruitful way that a really theoretical economics may be developed" (380).

The next article appeared in 1924 in the *American Mathematical Monthly*. Called "The Dynamics of Monopoly," it picked up the theme developed in the 1922 paper of "change over time." Evans assumes, for a monopolist, an interest in making total profits as large as possible over a time interval. With an initial price and a final price, Evans sets up the problem of maximizing the appropriate integral. Following the statement of the problem, which refers back to Luigi Amoroso's 1921 discussion of economic dynamics, Evans states that "an editor of the *Monthly* —Professor Bennett—has said that one should be obliged to present a certificate of character before being initiated into the mysteries of the calculus of variations, to which study our present investigation belongs, since its fascination is so great that neophytes seek to introduce it into problems which would otherwise be perfectly simple" (78–79).

Evans then makes the matter of the dynamic behavior a sequence of discussions of special cases. He develops what he calls the Cournot monopoly price as one kind of solution associated with an appropriate end value. Most interesting to a modern reader, however, is his concluding section, which notes that "one purpose in writing the present paper, as well as the previous one, has been to show [that] the wide range of problems suggested are solvable by a moderate mathematical equipment, and to encourage others to read in a direction that cannot but be fruitful" (83). A footnote to this sentence reads, "For example, the works of Cournot, Jevons, Walras, Pareto, and Fisher. Those who can read Italian will find interesting the volume of Amoroso, already cited."

One begins to see in this discussion the applied mathematician Evans finding in the field of economics some problems to solve that had already been treated using what a mathematician would consider primitive mathematical techniques. For Evans, behavioral rules and theories do not appear, nor does a theory of price formation in markets. Rather, there emerges a discussion of output levels associated with different interrelationships among producers under a variety of cost curve assumptions.

Evans's first 1925 article, "Economics and the Calculus of Variations," appeared in the *Proceedings of the National Academy of Sciences* (1925a). It is a very different kind of article in that it presents a theory of the interconnection between economic modeling procedures and the calculus of variables as a mathematical structure. Evans operates in this work at a quite different level of generality from that in the essays on competition and monopoly, presenting a general systems vision, as it were. The paper begins:

> The writer is not the first to venture to state a general theory in mathematical terms of a subject which is not unfairly regarded as compounded somewhat indefinitely of psychology, ethics, and chance. Being more than a mere mixture, however, it is equally fair to say that a separate analysis may apply; indeed, in Economics we are interested in the body of laws or deductions which may be inferred from convenient or arbitrary economic hypotheses, however they may be founded—in fact, fiction, statistics, habits or morals—what we will. This process of inference, if it is worthy of the effort, may be made mathematical. (90–91)

Evans develops the notion of an abstract economy by dividing an economic system into a set of n compartments and letting dx_i/dt be "the rate at which the specific commodity or service i is produced in its compartment" (91). Defining a rate at which this commodity comes from the compartment and a rate at which it is present within the compartment and noting that there is a balance among these three rates and an input-output accounting identity at work, Evans defines a general system of economics as a set of M laws linking the behavior of the flow variables over time. Evans develops the flows and the balances over time in the framework of the calculus of variations, examining money and the equation of exchange in this context.

He concludes, "It may be remarked that the relation of economics to the calculus of variations is not accidental, nor the result of the generalization from previously found differential equations, since it is in the nature of an economics system that there should be a striving for a maximum of some sort" (94–95). In this article, Evans remarks in a footnote that "C. F. Roos, in an article not yet published, treats a . . . problem of a similar nature." Charles Roos was, of course, Evans's student at Rice and one of the founding members of the Econometrics Society.

This article on the calculus of variation and economics does not solve a particular problem but rather frames a conceptual one: how to model an economy or economic system. What Evans accomplishes here, although it stands outside usual schemes, is a dynamic input-output model of an economic system. Moreover, this dynamic model is mathematically coherent and rich enough to permit some inferences.

Evans's remarkable "Mathematical Theory of Economics" (1925b), which appeared in the *American Mathematical Monthly*, was originally read at the annual meeting of the American Mathematical Association in Washington, D.C., in 1924.

> One interest in research in the Mathematical Theory of Economics is that the necessary preparation for it either in mathematics or in economics is not so great as for theoretical research say in physics or chemistry, or even in biology. . . . It may well be that it is the lack of mathematical technique among economists which has prevented the theoretical side of the subject from developing as rapidly as the wealth of books and papers, devoted to it, would seem to indicate. On the other hand, if we turn to the trained mathematicians, we find them mainly engrossed in the more romantic fields of physics, chemistry, and engineering, except in the case of the extensive analysis of statistics, where contact is made with kinetic theory on the one hand, and social and biological data on the other. (104–5)

In the next several sections, Evans lays out Cournot's views on monopoly and competition and those of Irving Fisher, more or less restating the results of his earlier articles in the *American Mathematical Monthly*. In addition, he refers to the calculus of variations argument and notes Roos's (1925) article, which appears shortly thereafter in the *American Journal of Mathematics*.

Of interest, however, is the remarkable concluding section, "General Points of View." Here we begin to see why Evans was to be such an outlier among economists. He writes:

> There is no such measurable quantity as "value" or "utility" (with all due respect to Jevons, Walras, and others) and there is no evaluation of "the greatest happiness for the greatest number"; or more flatly, —there is no such thing. In a way, material happiness has to do with a maximum of production and a minimum of unpleasant labor; though again no such thing is realizable theoretically without an

arbitrary definition of a composite function which is to take on a maximum value; and in the composition of this function the labor and profit of various classes of people enter capriciously. One might define a ratio of weighted production divided by weighted amounts of labor, according to classes, and study what sort of lash, economic or otherwise, would serve to impel Society towards this limit; but the choice of weights would depend essentially on whether the chooser is born a Bolshevik or a member of the Grand Old Party! Compromises carry us into the field of ethics.

That does not mean that such study is unprofitable. Far from it. How otherwise are we to evaluate the schemes of reformers and prophets, major and minor? Moreover the groundwork of such studies must be made well in advance, before there is any direct occasion for them; otherwise they will fail us when we do need them. There is not only an opportunity for mathematics and economics, but even a duty; and on mathematicians in an unusual degree lies the responsibility for the economic welfare of the world. (110)

Thus, certainly by 1925, five years before his book on mathematics for economics, Evans has written himself outside the usual concerns of economists. He is dismissive, if not contemptuous, of the intellectual framework upon which neoclassical analysis had been founded: the subjective theory of value. For Evans, economists, even mathematical economists like William Stanley Jevons, Léon Walras, and most certainly Marshall, were on the wrong track and had little to contribute if they believed in the analysis of value or utility. Evans here takes on the crudest of materialist positions, choosing to operate his analysis strictly in terms of production and labor quantities because for him, as for Volterra, these ideas could be linked to measurable quantities. For an anti-Marxist patrician of an old Boston family, this position is interesting indeed.

Just in case economists did not get the point, Evans, writing in 1929 in the *Bulletin of the American Mathematical Society*, reviewed the 1927 edition of Cournot's book. Beginning his review by citing Marshall and John Stuart Mill on Cournot's genius, he proceeds to contrast Cournot's great understanding and insight with more recent treatments in mathematical economics. He does this by comparing a "Cournot [who] is almost alone in holding to a clear realization of the difference between measurable and nonmeasurable quantities" with more recent authors who do not (269). Evans writes that "one recent book on the mathematical principles of economics, typical of many others, builds its theory on the following basis: Write U(x, y, . . .) for an algebraic function of measurable quantities." This author's utility discussion is linked to changes in utility and therefore satisfaction. Evans notes, "Apparently this other author is unaware that he is begging the question. If loci of indifference are expressed by Pfaffian differential equations it does not follow that there is any function of which these are the level loci for such equations are not necessarily completely integrable. The question is not of names, but of existence. These supposedly general treatments are much more special than their authors imagined" (270). Evans's contempt for the misguided mathematical economist is quite open: He identifies the economist who said these things as "Bowley, *Mathematical Groundwork of Economics*, Oxford, 1924."

Thus, by the time Evans releases his book, *Mathematical Introduction to Economics*, into the world of economists in 1930, he is on record in print as believing that Jevons and his school, which of course means Marshall, and Walras and his school, which of course means Pareto, H. L. Moore, and virtually everyone else writing in mathematical terms, are entirely misguided for basing analysis on a nonquantifiable theory of value. Moreover, Evans has sneered in public at the mathematical competence of the author in England, A. L. Bowley, who had written the basic text in mathematics for economics.

Mathematical Introduction to Economics

It is, of course, primarily for his book *Mathematical Introduction to Economics* (1930) than Evans is remembered by economists. Written while he was still at Rice University, Evans's book represents an unusual conglomeration of topics and perspectives.

The first several chapters, on monopoly, units of measurement, price, cost and demand, and taxation, take up themes and specific examples Evans had introduced in his earlier publications on approaches of mathematics to economic problems. These chapters all have the Evans "hand" on them in their use of specific functional forms and in their deliberate avoidance of behavioral assumptions and statistical work. These analyses reflect an interest in specifying the market outcomes and developing relationships among variables to generate realistic or comprehensible special cases. Chapters 6–9, on tariffs, rent, rates of exchange, the theory of interest, and the equation of exchange and price level indices, operate at a slightly higher level of systematic abstraction, although for Evans, the treatment of these issues proceeds exactly the same as in the case of sales in a particular market.

It is, however, in chapters 10–12 that Evans makes his stand against the usual argumentation of economic theory. In chapter 10, for example, he states that "we must adopt a cautious attitude toward comprehensive theories." Arguing that although it is a temptation "to generalize a particular set of relations which has been found useful, by substituting variables for all the constants in the equation," he notes that "it may be questioned as to whether we have added to anything but our mathematical difficulties." It is not that he wishes to "abandon the search for general theories" but rather that "we shall gain much if we can formulate our propositions in such a way as to make evident the limitations of the theory itself." In a nutshell, "our endeavor then should be to make systematic discussions of several groups of economic situations, as theoretical investigations, and bring out the respective hypotheses which separate these groups" (110–11).

Evans uses this general discussion as a prelude to chapter 11's attack on economists' (Jevons's, Pareto's, Walras's) use of utility theory. He argues that those "authors with whom we are concerned . . . affirm that the use of mathematics need not be confined to [actual quantities of commodities and money] but may also be applied to the order relations among the subjective quantities" (116). Those subjective quantities involve pleasure, satisfactions, and vanities. Evans refocuses his attack on utility theory through the integrability problem—the impossibility of building indifferent surfaces from local optimization solutions.

Referring to what is probably the core set of intellectual principles that guided Evans in his thinking, he remarks that

> a mathematical critique similar to that just adopted is widely explicable, and is more penetrating than an analysis in terms of loose concepts where the words themselves, by their connotations, may apply theorems of existence which are untenable. . . . the concepts of beauty, truth and good are analogous to those which we have been discussing. In every situation, there is something not of the best— some ugliness, some falsity or some evil—and so the practical judgment which is to be a basis of action is not "what situation is absolutely correct?" but "which of several situations is best?" The problem

involved is the comparison of two or more groups of elements of esthetic character. By the possibility of making a judgment at all is implied the fact that between two such groups, which are not too widely separated or which are simple in the sense of containing few enough elements, one can assign greater value to the one than to the other. (121–22)

Evans takes the integrability argument to mean that "we can devise an approximate value function as a scale for small changes of the variables, but cannot extend it beyond a merely local field unless we are willing to make some transcendental hypothesis about the existence of such a function. . . . In experimental terms we are accordingly not permitted to use such terms as beauty, good and truth with any absolute significance; comparative adjectives would be better, or truer and these only as applied to situations which did not differ widely or differed only in one or two elements" (122).

The grand unifying theory of Birkhoff's aesthetic measure and the unification of value theory of Francis Ysidro Edgeworth's mathematical psychics are not for Evans. Evans the mathematician, interested in potential functions and integral equations, is rooted clearly and distinctly in the physical phenomena of measurable entities. If one can build a theory out of these bricks, well and good. But if the mathematics precludes the building, one must not rush ahead and assume the building is already there.

Evans Marginalized

The Griffith Conrad Evans Papers at the University of California, Berkeley's, Bancroft Library contain some materials related to Evans's view of his book and his attempts to manage its reception. The papers include, for example, an undated handwritten letter, probably to his editor H. J. Kelly at McGraw-Hill, about his desire to have Roos review the book for the *Bulletin of the American Mathematical Society*. He also suggests that Professor Snyder of Yale thinks the book can be used "in connection with their mathematical club. Professor Kellogg thinks he can use it in connection with tutorial work. In general the use as a text must come slowly, since such courses are just beginning in the universities—Cornell and Yale are the only ones (besides Rice, where I have four students)." He remarks that "I have not read Hotelling's review. It would probably irritate me, if he did not see what the book is for. . . . It is the only book in the subject with exercises which the student can practice on, and the only book in English which consistently keeps to a uniform level of mathematical preparation using mathematics correctly. . . . The level of training is that which the engineer possesses. . . . It seems to me that you rule out your most important clientele, namely the large number of engineers who usually buy your books."

The papers also contain two letters written by Henry Schultz at Chicago on 24 April 1931 and 8 May 1931, the first of which replies to a 20 April letter from Evans. It appears that the exchange developed out of Evans's learning that Schultz was to write a review and seems to be based on a draft of the review sent to Evans. It also appears that Schultz was concerned that Evans assumed too high a level of mathematical sophistication for most students of economics, although he does express admiration for Evans's treatment of a number of topics, in particular the dynamic problems approached through the calculus of variations. In a very interesting remark in his first letter, Schultz says, "Frankly, I am puzzled by your attitude. In my naivete, I assumed that Volterra and Pareto had reached an understanding on this question." After giving the reference to the 1906 exchange between Volterra and Pareto, Schultz asks, "Am I wrong? Are Pareto's revised views on utility and indifference curves—a revision which was necessitated by Volterra's criticism—still open to objection? If so, what is it? I should greatly appreciate further light on this question." He concludes the letter with, "I am awaiting your reply to my query regarding Pareto's mature views on utility."

Evans's reply is not to be found in the papers, but Schultz's letter of 8 May 1931 begins, "I am glad to get your letter of May 2 and to find that we are beginning to understand each other." Schultz refers to a story that Evans must have told in the 2 May letter about his "experience with a chemical firm." Schultz, in counterpoint, describes his own experience with data and fitting curves to data and concludes, "It appears that any attempt to get light on coefficients of production or business methods is at this stage likely to be unsuccessful."

It thus appears that Evans's views of utility involve issues of measures of utility or value. The nonquantifiable and the nonmeasurable were hardly fit subjects for mathematical investigations from Evans's point of view. To one trained in his manner in mathematics, a mathematical theory of value and utility would necessarily be nonrigorous. Rigor, as discussed previously, is associated with the connection of the conceptual categories to an underlying physical reality. Rigor most decidedly did not mean for Evans what it meant for later mathematicians, namely, something derivable from an axiomatization in a formal or formally consistent manner. The mathematician and mathematical economist Evans of 1930 is thus well connected to the Evans who studied with Volterra before World War I and to the Volterra who abandoned economics in its nonrigorous infancy just after the turn of the century.

Despite Evans's marginal position within the community of mathematical economists, it should be noted that the Evans Papers confirm his participation in the nascent subcommunity of mathematical economists. Roos, at Cornell in the 1930s, had been Evans's student at Rice. When Irving Fisher, Ragnar Frisch, and Roos wrote to solicit organizational support for the creation of the Econometrics Society, Evans replied almost immediately with his support and with suggestions of individuals outside the United States to write, including Ewald Schams, Jan Tinbergen, Wassily Leontief, and Paul Rosenstein-Rodan. He was reading the works of economists who used mathematics whether they wrote in French, Italian, or German, and his reading lists suggest a broad intellect interested in keeping his courses up to date and his students well informed.

Given Evans's views on the state of mathematical economics and the basis on which neoclassical theory had been constructed, the early reviews of the book were predictable. Writing in *Economica* in 1931, R. G. D. Allen concluded, "The book contains many instructive applications of mathematics to economic problems, but, as a whole, it is not a convenient introduction to mathematical economics either for the pure mathematician or for the economist. The latter will be deterred by the lengthy algebraic development and, in the later chapters, by the difficult mathematical analysis used; the former, after a general survey of the work of Cournot, Jevons, and Walras, will be well advised to proceed, at once, to the complete analysis of Pareto" (109). And the following year in the *Economic Journal*, another reviewer (Bowley 1932) noted:

> This book is interesting as showing a mathematician's approach to economics . . . but since there is no clear thread of economic theory

in the treatment and no attempt at a general theory of any wide region of economics, a mathematician without economic knowledge will not obtain any thorough grasp of that subject; while the trained economics student will find the mathematical treatment difficult and in many places of a quite advanced level, while he will be bothered by the unelucidated mathematical character of the solutions. In fact, the appendix to Marshall's *Principles of Economics* is far more useful to the student of economics, quite apart from more recent studies on mathematical economics. (93–94)

Considering that the reviewer was A. L. Bowley, how could Evans have expected a different reception?

Evans was not easily put off. In 1932 he published "The Role of Hypothesis in Economic Theory," one of the most interesting and prescient critiques of the foundation of neoclassical theory. This essay had previously been presented at a joint session of the Econometrics Society and the American Association for the Advancement of Science, on 1 January 1932.

The neutrality and generality of the title of Evans's article belie its subversive intent. He begins by making a distinction between a natural and a theoretical science, a difference that "lies essentially in the presence or absence of a free spirit of making hypotheses and definitions." In a theoretical science, as opposed to a natural one, definitions "become constructive rather than denotive and hypotheses are introduced and tried out, in order to see what sort of results may be deduced from them" (321). Evans then examines "the degree to which we may speak of a theoretical economics, and the extent to which we may call it mathematical."

Evans develops his argument by suggesting that "the main object of economic theory is to make hypotheses, to see what relations and deductions follow from such hypotheses, and finally, by testing the consequences in comparison with the facts of existing economic systems, to describe them in terms of those hypotheses" (322). His illustration is the concept of demand. He presents five separate demand functions, all of which embed specific assumptions or hypotheses. For example, one demand function might have quantity as a function of price alone, while a second might have quantity depending on both price and the rate of chance of price. In modern parlance, Evans is suggesting that we have a great deal of freedom in specifying the demand function.

The main line of argument follows quickly: "A simple concept in economics has been that of utility . . . but underneath such a definition there must lie assumptions, tacit or explicit. Even though we are not willing to assume that this psychic quantity is directly measurable, if we are to use it in equations we have nevertheless to be able to add small increments of it" (322).

He proceeds to suggest that in standard analysis "we leave out of account the question as to whether or not utility is itself measurable, but suppose that there is a quantity associated with it which is measurable and whose measure we may call an index of utility" (323). Evans continues by noting that a situation described by a vector x_1, y_1, z_1 is not compared directly with a second situation x_2, y_2, z_2 but, rather, that if I is the utility index of one state, we examine dI as decomposed into the x, y, and z changes as the equation $dI = Xdx + Ydy + Zdz$. Evans argues that this is the actual comparison problem. Consequently, one must recapture I from this equation: "In other words, we can build up an index function by means of the curves of indifference. But if the state of the system is given by three or more numbers, we also know that there does not exist in general such an index function. The expression of this fact in mathematical terms is the statement that an equation like $Xdx + Ydy + Zdz = 0$ is not completely integrable. If we wish to have a utility function, we must introduce some hypothesis on the coefficients x, y, z."

The problem is that, mathematically, such a process requires "that certain relations already hold between the variables x, y, z; and they are no longer independent. . . . Hence we must assume that all our situations relative to a utility function must not contain more than two independent variables, or else we must introduce directly a postulate of integrability. It seems an arbitrary limitation" (323–24).

Evans noted that economists have sometimes argued that within the system there are, in fact, sufficient relations among the variables to solve this problem. "Sufficient" in this case means that, for economists, there are as many equations as there are unknowns. On this point Evans remarks, "It is absolutely no check on the correctness of statement of the problem that the number of equations is the required number." He footnotes this remark with the comment, "This apparently is not a unanimous opinion among economists." His footnote goes on to state that Schultz, in reviewing Evans's book, smuggles integrability into the assumptions of the problem. In terms of comparing states,

Evans asks, referring to Schultz's argument, "How many individuals, for instance, can decide, without reference to process, which of the two situations he desires—peace, or justice, in China?" Evans concludes this discussion of utility by saying that if we are to "distinguish between cooperative and competitive elements in the system [we] . . . have already . . . grouped utility indices . . . and these have no transparent relation to the individual ones . . . and from this point-of-view the doctrine of laissez faire lacks mathematical foundation" (324).

The argument winds up with the question, "Would it not be better then to abandon the use of the utility function, and investigate situations more directly in terms of concrete concepts, like profit and money value of production, in order to take advantage of the fact that money is fundamental in most modern economies and to use the numbers which it assigns to objects? Concrete concepts suggest concrete hypotheses" (324).

Thus by 1932, after economists have had a chance to respond to the arguments of his book, Evans is unrepentant. Economists, especially mathematical economists of the neoclassical variety, have it wrong. Utility theory, as well as subjective value theory, founders on the integrability problem. One can only get out of the theory what one puts into it. This, of course, was Volterra's critique of Pareto more than a quarter of a century earlier. For Evans, in mathematical economics one should not be so concerned with the behavioral theories themselves. Economic theory, or at least mathematics as applied to economic theory, should trace the implications in logical systems of various hypotheses that themselves are grounded in quantifiable objects or concepts, and the implications are or should be developed to be themselves either testable empirically though data analysis or testable through common sense.

For Evans, as for Volterra, the issue was not formalist versus informalist or antiformalist mathematics but rigorous versus nonrigorous mathematics. Evans sought rigor in mathematical economics in the way that Volterra had: The mathematical models are not free but rather are tightly constrained by the natural phenomena they model.[9] Evans's

9. Let the record show, however, that Evans was in a position to affect the work of economists in the postwar period. In "American Mathematicians in World War I" and later work, Price (1988, 267) links Rothrock's (1919) information that "G. C. Evans of the Rice Institute was a captain of ordinance on special mission in France" to the comment that "since G. C. Evans was president of the [American Mathematical] Society in 1939 and 1940, he partici-

mathematics looked back, though Volterra, to the optimism of the turn-of-the-century solutions, which were to be abandoned by mathematicians later; to the great challenges faced by mathematics in dealing with set theory; and to that same mathematics in interpreting relativity and quantum phenomena. The move to axiomatics, well under way within the mathematics community by the 1930s and instantiated in economic argumentation by mathematical economists by the 1940s,[10] left no place in economic theory for Evans. It did, however, leave an alternative place for Evans.

As one of the founding members of the Econometrics Society in 1932, Evans subscribed to the call to "promote research in quantitative and mathematical economics . . . [in order] to educate and benefit its members and mankind, and to advance the scientific study and development . . . of economic theory in its relation to mathematics and statistics" (Christ 1952, 5, 11). The point is that Evans's views on mathematical modeling are the views of an econometrician or applied economist today or one who insists that the assumptions and conclusions of an economic model, a model constructed and developed mathematically, must be measurable or quantifiable. This distinction between "modelers" (or "applied economists") and "theorists" divides modern departments of economics even as both groups consider themselves to be neoclassical economists. That Evans's first important student was Roos, one of the early luminaries in econometrics and the founder of his own Econometric Institute in New York (Fox 1987), should allow us to reframe the idea of Evans's "marginalization": It was not that Evans abandoned canonical mathematical economics but that mathematical economics, increasingly connected to the new (very un-Volterra-like) ideas of mathematical rigor in both mathematics and applied mathematical science, moved away from Evans.[11] In a real

---

pated in the appointment of the War Preparedness Committee of AMS and MAA. We also have the knowledge that "the Aberdeen researchers included such key figures as [Oswald] Veblen, Griffith C. Evans, Marston Morris, Warren Weaver, Norbert Weiner, Hans F. Blickfelt, and G. A. Bliss, the first four of whom played significant roles in mobilizing the country's mathematical expertise during World War II" (Parshall 1994, 444). Thus, Evans was connected to the emergent cyborg sciences, economics among them, which developed from the collaborative work of economists and mathematicians during the war.

10. This is the subject of Weintraub and Mirowski 1994, a lengthy essay on Nicholas Bourbaki and Gerard Debreu.

11. There is thus a delicious irony in the fact that Debreu has his office at Berkeley in Evans Hall.

sense, the distinction between rigor as materialist-reductionist quantification and rigor as formal derivation, a distinction that was contested at the end of the nineteenth century but disappeared as formalism took hold in mathematics, reestablished itself in the distinction between econometrics and mathematical economics, between applied economics and economic theory. It is not unreasonable then to see Lawrence R. Klein as linked to Griffith C. Evans.[12] And I, as Klein's student, unravel the links.

References

Allen, R. D. G. 1931. Review of *Mathematical Introduction to Economics* by Evans. *Economica*, o.s., 11.31:108–9.

Bowley, A. L. 1932. Review of *Mathematical Introduction to Economics* by Griffith C. Evans. *Economic Journal* 42.165:93–94.

Christ, Carl. 1952. *Economic Theory and Measurement: A Twenty Year Research Report, 1932–1952*. Chicago: Cowles Commission.

Corry, Leo. 1989. Linearity and Reflexivity in the Growth of Mathematical Knowledge. *Science in Context* 3.2:409–40.

———. 1996. *Modern Algebra and the Rise of Mathematical Structures*. Science Networks—Historical Studies, vol. 17. Boston: Birkhäuser.

Evans, Griffith C. 1920. Fundamental Points of Potential Theory. *Rice Institute Pamphlet* 7.4:252–329.

———. 1921. The Physical Universe of Dante. *Rice Institute Pamphlet* 8.2:91–117.

———. 1922. A Simple Theory of Competition. *American Mathematical Monthly* 29:371–80.

———. 1924. The Dynamics of Monopoly. *American Mathematical Monthly* 31:77–83.

———. 1925a. Economics and the Calculus of Variations. *Proceedings of the National Academy of Sciences* 11.1:90–95.

———. 1925b. The Mathematical Theory of Economics. *American Mathematical Monthly* 32:104–10.

———. 1926. The Place of Francis Bacon in the History of Scientific Method. *Rice Institute Pamphlet* 13.1:73–92.

———. 1929. Cournot on Mathematical Economics. *Bulletin of the American Mathematical Society* 35 (March–April): 269–71.

12. "Evans did only a little work in nonequilibrium dynamics. . . . His principal influence upon the progress of economics came through the methodologies employed in his [1930] book, and through his students, among whom were Francis W. Dresch, Kenneth May, C. F. Roos and Ronald W. Shephard, and at one step removed, Lawrence Klein and Herbert A. Simon, who were colleagues or pupils of these students" (Simon 1987, 199).

———. 1932. The Role of Hypothesis in Economic Theory. *Science* 75. 1943:321–24.

———. 1959. Preface to the Dover Edition. In *Theory of Functionals and of Integral and Integro-differential Equations*. Edited by V. Volterra. New York: Dover.

———. 1967. Autobiographical Fragments. 74/178C, Box 6, Folder "Evans, G. C. Biography," Manuscript Collection, Bancroft Library, University of California, Berkeley.

Evans, Griffith Conrad, Papers, 74/178C, Box 6, Folder "Economics and Mathematics," Bancroft Library, University of California, Berkeley.

Fox, K. A. 1987. Roos, Charles Frederick. In *The New Palgrave: A Dictionary of Economics*. Vol. 4. Edited by J. Eatwell, M. Milgate, and P. Newman. New York: Stockton Press.

Gandolfo, Giancarlo. 1987. Volterra, Vito. In *The New Palgrave: A Dictionary of Economics*. Vol. 4. Edited by J. Eatwell, M. Milgate, and P. Newman. New York: Stockton Press.

Goodstein, Judith R. 1984. The Rise and Fall of Vito Volterra's World. *Journal of the History of Ideas* 45.4:607–17.

Houston Chronicle. 1915a. Scientific Aspects of Philosophy. 6 May.

———. 1915b. Scientific Aspects of Philosophy. 13 May.

———. 1916. Scientific Aspects of Philosophy. 28 January.

———. 1933. Dr. G. C. Evans Resigns from Rice Institute. 27 October.

———. 1973. Services Held for Dr. Griffith Evans. 10 December.

Houston Post. 1918. Rice Professor Attaché of Embassy at Rome. 30 December.

———. 1919. Dr. Evans at Washington after Service in France. 5 June.

Ingrao, Bruna, and Giorgio Israel. 1990. *The Invisible Hand: Economic Theory in the History of Science*. Cambridge, Mass.: MIT Press.

Israel, Giorgio. 1981. "Rigor" and "Axiomatics" in Modern Mathematics. *Fundamenta Scientiae* 2:205–19.

———. 1988. On the Contribution of Volterra and Lotka to the Development of Modern Biomathematics. *History and Philosophy of the Life Sciences* 10:37–49.

———. 1991a. Volterra's "Analytical Mechanics" of Biological Associations, First Part. *Archives internationales d'histoire des sciences* 41.126:57–104.

———. 1991b. Volterra's "Analytical Mechanics" of Biological Associations, Second Part. *Archives internationales d'histoire des sciences* 41.127:307–52.

Israel, Giorgio, and L. Nurzia. 1989. Fundamental Trends and Conflicts in Italian Mathematics between the Two World Wars. *Archives internationales d'histoire des sciences* 39.122:111–43.

McCormmach, Russell. 1982. *Night Thoughts of a Classical Physicist*. New York: Avon.

Morrey, Charles B., Jr. 1983. Griffith Conrad Evans. *Biographical Memoirs: U.S. National Academy of Sciences* 54:127–55.

Parshall, Karen H., and David E. Rowe. 1994. *The Emergence of the American Mathematical Research Community, 1876–1900*. Providence, R.I.: American Mathematical Society.

Price, G. Bayley. 1988. American Mathematicians in World War I. In *A Century of Mathematics in America*. Part 1. Edited by P. Duren. Providence, R.I.: American Mathematical Society.

Rider, Robin E. 1989. An Opportune Time: Griffith C. Evans and Mathematics at Berkeley. In *A Century of Mathematics in America*. Edited by P. Duren. Providence, R.I.: American Mathematical Society.

Roos, Charles F. 1925. A Mathematical Theory of Competition. *American Journal of Mathematics* 47 (July): 163–75.

Rothrock, D. A. 1919. American Mathematicians in War Service. *American Mathematical Monthly* 26:40–44.

Samuelson, P. A. 1987. Out of the Closet: A Program for the Whig History of Economic Science. *History of Economics Society Bulletin* 9.1:51–60.

Simon, Herbert A. 1987. Evans, Griffith Conrad. In *The New Palgrave: A Dictionary of Economics*. Vol. 2. Edited by J. Eatwell, M. Milgate, and P. Newman. New York: Stockton Press.

Volterra, E. 1976. Volterra, Vito. In *Dictionary of Scientific Biography*. Edited by C. C. Gillespie. New York: Charles Scribner's Sons.

Volterra, Vito. 1906a. L'economia matematica ed il nuovo manuale del Prof. Pareto. *Giornale degli economisti*, 2d ser., 32:296–301.

———. 1906b. Les mathématiques dans les sciences biologiques et sociales. Translated by Ludovic Zoretti. *La revue du mois*, 10 January, 1–20.

———. 1915. Henri Poincaré: A Lecture Delivered at the Inauguration of the Rice Institute. *Rice Institute Pamphlet* 1.2:133–62.

———. 1957. *Opere matematiche: Memorie e note*. 5 vols. Rome: Accademia Nazionale dei Lincei.

Weintraub, E. R., and P. Mirowski. 1994. The Pure and the Applied: Bourbakism Comes to Mathematical Economics. *Science in Context* 7.2:245–72.

Whittaker, E. T. 1959. Biography of Vito Volterra, 1860–1940. In *Theory of Functionals and of Integral and Integro-differential Equations*. Edited by V. Volterra. New York: Dover.

A Paradox of Budgets: The Postwar Stabilization of American Neoclassical Demand Theory

Philip Mirowski and D. Wade Hands

> I became an economist quite by chance, primarily because the analysis was so interesting and easy—indeed so easy that at first I thought there must be more to it than I was recognizing, else why were my older classmates making such heavy weather over supply and demand? (Samuelson 1992, 236)

Heavy Weather over Supply and Demand

It is now generally accepted that the neoclassical hegemony in the American economics profession dates from the period immediately following World War II. The standard story about the rise of this postwar orthodoxy is a relatively simple tale about the smooth transatlantic transmission of neoclassical ideas. It seems that Marshallian and Paretian economics simply crossed the Atlantic and took root in American soil with little or no transformation. For a variety of reasons, this simple story about the rise of the American orthodoxy—a kind of neoclassical creation myth, if you will—seems to have been accepted without any serious examination of the historical events that constituted the postwar parturition. Recently, the two of us have begun the

We would like to thank the many individuals who provided useful comments on this essay during the 1997 *HOPE* conference and to give particular thanks to Ross Emmett, Dan Hammond, Steve Medema, Perry Mehrling, and Mary Morgan for their remarks. This essay is an abridged version of the original conference paper; the longer version is available from the authors.

initial stages of a historical inquiry that will provide a more detailed account of the rise of the American orthodoxy, and this essay is one installment of this long-term project.

The first problem one encounters with this standard story is that the period preceding the establishment of the neoclassical orthodoxy is *not* a period dominated by a single price theory that might be progressively displaced. It is a period of extraordinary theoretical diversity, with not only a variety of non-neoclassical, particularly institutionalist-inspired, approaches but also a number of different neoclassicisms. For this and other reasons, we will argue that the secret to the stabilization of neoclassicism in America can be found in its persistent inability to enforce any monolithic orthodoxy in such a critical area as the formal treatment of demand theory. Although this undoubtedly owes something to broad cultural trends, we will temporarily resist such historiographic temptations and focus on one seemingly narrow analytical issue: the treatment of income constraint and income effects in standard "pure" neoclassical consumer theory.

To reduce the motley of prestabilization American economics to manageable proportions, we will focus on a particular subset of economists who shared some similar theoretical orientations. It seems that most of the few destined to become the progenitors of the postwar stabilization shared an initial fascination with the problem of the proper reconciliation of what was called the "law of demand" with the Walrasian-style maximization of individuals' utility with interdependent commodity prices. They each believed, to varying degrees, that the British Marshallian tradition had ceased to provide an adequate scientific foundation for the theory of demand and sought, each in their own way, to find a more appropriate but still broadly neoclassical basis for the "law." One of the reasons they deemed this particular aspect of price theory a significant obstacle to scientific progress was that they were each deeply influenced by two individuals who would turn out, in retrospect, to be the obligatory passage points for mathematical economics in America in the 1930s: Harold Hotelling and Henry Schultz. We have described this initial sequence of events in detail in an earlier article (Hands and Mirowski 1998), but we will recapitulate their problem situation. Our task here is to pick up the narrative thread where our previous article left off.

In short, we assert that in 1938–55 a number of economists innovated an array of solutions to the (multiple) problems of the relationship of the law of demand to neoclassical utility maximization and, more to the point, managed to institutionalize those solutions at three key centers of economic research: the postwar University of Chicago Economics Department, the Cowles Commission while it was located at the University of Chicago (1939–55), and Paul Samuelson's Massachusetts Institute of Technology (MIT). These innovations were noteworthy in that, however much the individual solutions were rooted in roughly the same broad intellectual tradition, they differed strikingly in a number of ways, most significantly in their treatment of the interdependent character of income constraints and income effects for the law of demand. Far from standing as a minor technical differentia or the quirks of expression that inevitably beset any communal intellectual project, this speciation within neoclassicism is significant and can be used to illuminate all sorts of other high-profile but seemingly unrelated controversies within the American orthodoxy. These divisions also help us understand the sheer resilience, strength, and vibrancy of the neoclassical school—to extend a biological analogy, it seems that an interlocking competitive ecosystem proved more hardy than the various patches of monoculture it replaced.

The Hotelling-Schultz Impasse

In depression-era America, very few economists thought that the solution to the appalling array of economic problems—crop failures, widespread unemployment, falling prices, the concentration of power in large trusts, calls for national economic planning, and so on—would come from a rigorous reexamination of the foundations of the utility maximization–based theory of demand. In fact, a large contingent believed precisely the opposite: that recent experience had effectively repudiated any economic theory based on such abstract principles. Nevertheless, this is the very project that Hotelling initiated in his 1932 article on the Edgeworth taxation paradox and prosecuted with singular intensity in tandem with Schultz from 1932 until Schultz's death in November 1938.

As we argued in Hands and Mirowski 1998, Hotelling and Schultz discovered in each other the perfect complement to their independently chosen research programs in economics. Schultz's interest in the empirical estimation of demand functions began under his mentor Henry Ludwell Moore at Columbia University, but later at the University of

Chicago, he came to the position (opposed by Moore) that such functions had to be based on the mathematical approach of Léon Walras and Vilfredo Pareto (Mirowski 1990). Schultz was searching for a tractable mathematical economics that would acknowledge pervasive interdependence at the market level but also that could actually be used to diagnose the real problems of agricultural production in the 1930s. Schultz founded a statistical laboratory to conduct the empirical research but also worked fervently to ground the derived empirical relationships in the type of individual maximizing behavior he felt would guarantee that there were underlying and dependable "laws" behind the estimated functions.

Hotelling first became involved in estimating agricultural demand functions during his work at Stanford's Food Research Institute in the late 1920s. His initial interest was in Fisherian hypothesis testing (an enthusiasm shared with Schultz), but he also developed an appreciation for the mathematical neoclassical theory that buttressed this effort. As a member of the Columbia Economics Department in the early 1930s, he not only became involved in the effort to produce a mathematical theory that would underwrite demand functions but also argued that such foundations would be relevant to practical issues like the evaluation of welfare and diagnosing the causes of the Great Depression. Nowhere was this dual commitment more evident than in his 1932 article on the Edgeworth taxation paradox. Edgeworth's demonstration that the imposition of a tax on a particular good could actually lower both its price and the price of a related good seemed to offer a serious challenge to the theory of demand, and Hotelling's article was an attempt to propose an alternative neoclassical model that would provide better foundations and avoid these (and other) problems.

Schultz was the *Journal of Political Economy* (*JPE*) editor of Hotelling's article, and this contact initiated an intensive correspondence about the statistical consequences of his demand theory. As we described in detail in Hands and Mirowski 1998, Hotelling proposed two novel ways to "derive" a demand curve: one (subsequently ignored) from a cumulative normal density function and the other from an unconstrained optimization of the quantity $U-\Sigma px$. The latter, which Hotelling called his "price potential" model, in direct analogy with the treatment of the motion of a particle in classical mechanics, would guarantee downward-sloping demand functions and straightforward welfare indices even in a world of pervasive interdependence. Although it possessed a number of other virtues, the Hotelling model had the drawback that the "income" or "budget" term was not treated as a fixed entity independently of the equilibrium outcome. This bothered Schultz, but he nonetheless chose to collaborate with Hotelling to explore various justifications for the novel treatment of the budget in the utility maximization problem.[1] Schultz, after all, was searching for a theory of interdependent demand curves, and this seemed a viable formal candidate, even though it was not to be found in Walras or Pareto. The novel treatment also gave rise to some additional symmetry (or "integrability") restrictions that Schultz immediately tested and found to be violated in the agricultural demand functions he estimated. Hotelling and Schultz then discussed the various auxiliary hypotheses one might use to explain the failure, with Hotelling focusing on pure theory, while Schultz tended to be concerned with statistical and data problems. During this period Schultz and Hotelling became aware of the now-standard Slutsky symmetry conditions. Hotelling acknowledged the Slutsky equation but viewed it as just another, more "Walrasian," way to underwrite observed demand curves. Although the Slutsky approach of maximizing an individual's utility function subject to a fixed income constraint had a certain appeal, Hotelling found it unsatisfactory because it (unlike his own theory) had only a limited ability to provide welfare theorems and did not guarantee that demand curves sloped downward. When Schultz decided to test the Slutsky and Hotelling symmetry conditions as rival hypotheses, he found (much to his dismay) that both conditions appeared to be contradicted by the data.

Here the saga of Hotelling and Schultz essentially draws to a close with a denouement satisfying to neither of them. Schultz wrote up the results of his decade-long search for the Walrasian principles underlying demand curves in his 1938 *Theory and Measurement of Demand*. It is seldom recognized that the book is essentially a swan song for empirical Walrasian economics: Schultz bravely reported the empirical debacle in detail and then produced a litany of excuses why things had not

1. Here we must signal that this was not simply an appeal to the special case of the Marshallian constant marginal utility of money, nor was it straightforwardly a special case to be rigidly restricted to some separate sphere of production. These issues are discussed in detail in Hands and Mirowski 1998. For the present, it suffices to insist that Hotelling and Schultz were engaged in a process of negotiation over the meaning and significance of the budget term, which would imply revision of a whole array of other theoretical terms in tandem, including but not restricted to the measurability of utility, the treatment of money, the significance of complementarity, the nature of interdependence, and so on.

worked out as hoped. The book ended with a promissory note that was never redeemed, since Schultz died in a car accident in November 1938, just as the book appeared in print.

The reaction of Hotelling to the empirical disappointments and the loss of Schultz was no less unexpected and presents more of an explanatory challenge to the historian. Initially, Hotelling showed every sign of wishing to continue to pursue his initial price potential program.[2] He continued to teach a graduate course in mathematical economics at Columbia, but the war and its own demands intervened. On 15 April 1943 he was formally appointed consultant to the Applied Mathematics Panel of the National Defense Research Council in recognition of his work in putting together the Statistical Research Group (SRG) at Columbia. Until it was dissolved in 1946, the SRG worked on the testing of bombsights, the statistical effectiveness of various bombing strategies, gun equilibration on ships, compressed flow through nozzles, the use of ordinary least squares (OLS) in antiaircraft fire control, aerodynamic pursuit curves for overhead attacks, and numerous other projects. This group included Allen Wallis, Milton Friedman, George Stigler, Leonard Savage, and Abraham Wald.

The evidence suggests that Hotelling had essentially stopped reading economics by 1940. Requests that Hotelling comment on subsequent developments were met with reiterations of points he had made in the 1930s. In a letter of recommendation for Tjalling Koopmans's move to Yale University in 1955, he managed to avoid citing or discussing any of his work in economics (Hotelling 1954). His class notes also suggest that he restricted his lectures almost exclusively to problems tackled in his 1930s works. It might be thought that with the loss of Schultz, his

2. Indeed, it seems that for Hotelling, the price potential model had become equated with the very idea of rational action *tout court*. Evidence for this comes from Hotelling's undated, unpublished note titled "On the Nature of Demand and Supply Functions": " 'Rational Actions' may be taken to mean a system of demand functions such that a 'potential' U exists with $p_i = \partial U/\partial q_i$. Such demand & supply functions may well be taken as central, all others being treated as more or less casual deviations, often of only temporary importance. But U may be a function not only of the q's but of their time—or space—derivatives. . . . Also, each person's U may depend upon the consumption of others (emulation; competitive display; but also less wasteful types of activity, as when in intellectual cooperation a particular subject occupying the focus of attention of a group may, advantageously to society, be pushed). The statistical determination of $\partial p_i/\partial q_j$, which equals $\partial p_j/\partial q_i$ for 'rational action,' involves a least-squares solution & ideas of correlation which generalize ordinary calculus of correlation by replacing individual variables by matrices. These matrices will, moreover, by [*sic*] symmetric, giving rise to interesting theory."

prime collaborator and interlocutor, he "had no one to talk to"—a characterization that often crops up in the retrospective memoirs of others—but it seems unlikely given the vast array of young talent he influenced and had access to.

There is another possible explanation: Hotelling never entirely repudiated his 1932 price potential model. He taught it well into his career and late in life conceived an interest in experimental work to directly measure individual utility functions—an eventuality more in tune with the 1932 model than with the behaviorism so rife during that period. All signs point to a belief in a relatively more tangible and recoverable version of utilitarianism, one more congruent with his own conceptions of straightforward welfare indices and less bothered by "proper" treatments of the budget constraint, which he regarded as an auxiliary consideration. But after the war, there was simply nobody left who shared this particular vision of a scientifically legitimate neoclassical price theory.

Hotelling was of course aware of the Slutsky decomposition from at least 1935, and his repeated postwar references to "measuring welfare" seem ambiguous unless they are juxtaposed to his 1932 convictions about the necessary character of the integrability conditions (1932b, 452). We can now see the postwar neoclassical consensus—that to be a mathematical economist, one must start with Walras and Slutsky and nowhere else—as a localized (and American) cultural prejudice highly correlated with prior exposure to the Hotelling-Schultz dialogue of the 1930s. Once the community focused its attention definitively on the Slutsky equation, to the exclusion of all other versions of demand theory, the only issues that could be addressed were ones that could be refracted through the prism of substitution and income effects. The issues that had captivated Schultz and Hotelling—issues like what was the proper role of empiricism in demand theory? what could be said in the way of legitimate political statements about the welfare consequences of the market? to what extent did this indicate a break with the formalism of the potential field?—could now only be discussed in this idiom, if at all.

Chicago: They Do Things They Won't Do on Broadway

The first economist off the mark to respond to the Hotelling-Schultz impasse was Paul Samuelson in 1938, but an understanding of the personalities of all three schools requires a narrative less concerned with temporal precedence than with capturing local traditions. It thus behooves us to begin with the University of Chicago Economics Department, the site of most of the early activity in the American revision of demand theory. Chicago not only contained Schultz's statistical laboratory but also was the home of the Cowles Commission from 1939 to 1955.

Those looking for the roots of the Chicago school often think they can discern them in the 1930s, but in fact the department was quite diverse during that period. Schultz himself was a conservative in politics but an advocate of the Walrasian brand of mathematical economics combined with faith in the Fisherian theories of statistical inference. There was Paul Douglas, a less technically inclined empiricist favoring a mild form of technological determinism but a high-profile liberal in political beliefs. There was Jacob Viner, who upheld an older style of Marshallian economics, and there were some representatives from the period of institutionalist strength. And finally there was the group revolving around Frank Knight, including Aaron Director, Henry Simons, and Lloyd Mints. Because it was predominantly Knight's students and supporters, including Friedman, Stigler, and Wallis, who subsequently constituted the core of the postwar Chicago school, greater continuity is often imputed to the school than actually existed. Nevertheless, some direct affiliations can be drawn from Knight to Friedman and Stigler, especially with regard to the issues that surround the Hotelling-Schultz impasse.

One thing that helps us understand the postwar stabilization is an appreciation of the changes that took place in the Chicago Economics Department just prior to and during World War II. Knight's group had been treating Schultz with open contempt by the late 1930s, when Schultz's death in 1938 removed him from the scene. The election of Douglas to the position of Chicago alderman in 1939 heralded the beginnings of his political career and his absence from departmental activities, neutralizing another Knight opponent. The retirement of H. A. Millis in 1940 and the departure of Simeon Leland for Northwestern University in 1946 (Reder 1982, 10) greatly attenuated the institutionalist wing of the department. And Viner's departure for Princeton University in 1946 removed another competing brand of theory.

The pivotal figure in this wartime regime was Oskar Lange. Joining the department in 1938, he quickly found himself the senior advocate of

the Walrasian approach to price theory and the sole local partisan of
"econometrics." It is not irrelevant to our story that by 1938 he was the
prime defender of planning in the socialist calculation debate, an early
interpreter of Keynesianism, and a Marxist. His initial impact on the
Chicago scene was to polarize conceptions of formal economics in even
starker terms than one might find elsewhere. In the minds of many at
Chicago, Walrasian mathematical theory became conflated with socialism, crude numerical empiricism, and politically naive welfare economics. Knight assumed proprietary rights over graduate price theory
during the latter part of the war, but it was Lange who taught John
Hicks's *Value and Capital*. As Patinkin (1995, 372) notes, "it was the
socialist Oskar Lange who extolled the beauties of the Paretian optimum achieved by a perfectly competitive market—and Frank Knight
who in effect taught us that the deeper welfare implications of the optimum were indeed quite limited."

The situation was further disturbed by the unanticipated arrival of
the Cowles Commission in September 1939. The move was arranged
largely by Alfred Cowles and Robert Hutchins, then president of the
University of Chicago; the Economics Department had little say in the
matter. Theodore Yntema of the School of Business was named director of research, and the only members of the Economics Department to
be named to the Cowles staff were distinctly junior: Lange, Gregg
Lewis, and Jacob Mosak. In retrospect, it is clear that Cowles was relatively weak just after the move. Some Cowles staff members declined
the move to Chicago, like Wald, who went to Columbia. Yntema was
largely an absentee research director from 1939 to 1942, and by 1942,
half the staff members were involved in war research (Christ 1952, 23).
The situation might have been tailor made for Lange to enter the void
and recast the Chicago department in his own image, but it never came
to pass; he was a visitor at Columbia in 1942–43, and by 1945 he
resigned from both the commission and the university to become Pol-
ish ambassador to the United States.

Despite Stigler's (1988, 148) claim that in 1947 "there was no
Chicago School of Economics" (see also Bronfenbrenner 1962), it is
clear that Knight and his group were successful in advancing their
agenda during the war, and by 1944 they were engaged in open intellectual warfare with the Cowles Commission (Reder 1982, 10; Hammond 1993, 231). Friedman's role as self-appointed tormentor of Cowles
and acknowledged leader of the Economics Department was para-

mount, beginning with his return to Chicago in 1946; thereafter the Chicago school was consolidated with Wallis's appointment as dean of the Business School in 1955 and Stigler's appointment to the Walgreen professorship in 1958. Although none of these figures can be regarded as carbon copies of Knight, the relationship of Chicago to the stabilization of neoclassicism can be triangulated as a moving equilibrium between Knight and Schultz, Knight and Friedman, Friedman and Schultz, Friedman and Hotelling, and Friedman and Cowles.

Although there are, of course, many differences between Knight and Friedman, one cannot make much headway in comprehending Chicago price theory without beginning with Knight. Knight's seductive appeal for the stellar parade of graduate students in the 1930s and 1940s cannot be underestimated, despite his rather Delphic style of lectures and cynicism about the future of social science. Thus it is of profound import that Knight chose the period of maximum disarray of his opponents to launch his attack on newer developments in demand theory. In the signal *JPE* article of 1944, Knight explicitly criticized the "new" school of Hicks, Eugen Slutsky, and Schultz and thereby implicitly criticized their local surrogates, such as Lange and Jacob Marschak. The general thrust of the article was that all the folderol concerning anomalous demand curves was a monumental red herring for economic theory. "It is a fairly simple matter to explain the general shape—the descending slope—of the demand curve" (300). Although primarily philosophical, the attack was fairly subtle and foreshadowed much of the later Chicago tradition in price theory.

Knight's critique of the Slutsky approach was carried on simultaneously at different levels. At the most foundational level, Knight ridiculed the idea that imitation of classical mechanics would serve to reveal any hidden "laws" behind the law of demand: "Motives are not analogous to forces" (310). His next level of attack concerned the whole ordinalist self-denial of psychological commitments and the associated cognitive agnosticism. According to Knight, all sorts of psychological precepts were required for economic analysis, and his pragmatism conflicted with the nascent orthodox line about the cognitive impenetrability of other minds. Knight's third level of attack was both empirical and theoretical. On the empirical side, he credited his own theory with having the "great advantage of eliminating the spurious 'Giffen paradox'" (300), and on the theoretical side, he made an argument that echoed Hotelling's own defense of his 1932 model: It had the benefit of "making the theory of consumption logically parallel with the theory of production" (300).

Finally, Knight made explicit reference to the Chicago tenet that separate income effects are politically dangerous:

> The general point of view and habit of mind reflected in the Hicks-Slutzky [*sic*] analysis has wide ramifications in the recent literature and has led to utter confusion in the whole body of economic thought. We refer, of course, to the huge corpus of discussion beginning with Keynes' *General Theory* and following the lead of that work. J. R. Hicks's book, *Value and Capital*, is especially interesting as a general treatise which combines the theory of Keynes's treatment of unemployment and money with the Slutzky analysis of demand and theory of utility. (300, n. 10)

Knight believed that the idea that one could analytically decompose movements along a microeconomic demand curve into income and substitution effects would lead to the conviction that one could actually factor out variations in macroeconomic incomes from price-theoretic considerations and thus open the door to (insidious) Keynesianism.

Knight rarely made any argument elegantly or systematically, and the 1944 *JPE* article was no exception. His philosophical objections were sprinkled throughout an article that was ostensibly a technical critique of the Hicks-Slutsky approach to demand theory. Although the fine points of the offensive were muddled, the overall thrust of the technical critique was that the "Slutsky school" had not adequately considered the implications of posting the invariance of income or the budget constraint. By holding the prices of all other goods and money income fixed when deriving the demand curve, Knight insisted, the Slutsky approach had failed to recognize that real incomes continuously change. Because he believed monetary theory had to be built into the foundations of price theory, Knight argued for an alternative derivation of demand that only expressed the effects of changes in relative prices through the device of holding the value of money constant by compensating changes in the prices of other goods. Knight's disdain for mathematics essentially prevented him from specifying how this could actually be accomplished.

Knight's article clearly exhibits the rough-hewn building blocks of the Chicago orthodoxy that would ultimately be sculpted by Friedman, Stigler, Gary Becker, and others. The approach began with an ontological commitment: "The demand curve . . . [is] undoubtedly the most solidly real of all the functional relations dealt with in economic theory" (310). It followed that no "more fundamental" laws would be discovered to buttress demand curves and that no additional legitimation was needed. All applicable predictions and usable economic statements would start and end with the theory of supply and demand—period. Interestingly enough, this did not proscribe such exercises as the derivation of the demand curve from constrained utility optimization, and (slightly diverging from Knight) one might even entertain the Slutsky decomposition into income and substitution effects. But the ambition of testing the Slutsky symmetry restrictions was a dangerous delusion resting on a serious misunderstanding of the very nature of price theory. One should not believe for a minute that there was some "real" invariant out there, like income, psychological motive, or technology; nothing is really invariant in a dynamic economy. For Knight, the "compensating variations" that would successfully isolate income effects most likely could never be carried out in actual practice, much less inferred from an observed sequence of actual exchanges; an income effect was a virtual (and rather dangerous) notion. That is why Knight and his group had become convinced that Schultz had been barking up the wrong tree and why Friedman could not countenance the Cowles Commission's quest for the Holy Grail of "structure."

The most influential statement of Chicago demand theory, Friedman's 1949 article, "The Marshallian Demand Curve," proudly displays its intellectual heritage by insisting that its conclusion is "identical with that reached by Frank Knight in a recent article" (135), namely, the 1944 article. Phalanxes of scholars have combed Friedman's "methodology" article for philosophical precursors that render its theses more comprehensible, just as smaller platoons have plundered and scoured Alfred Marshall to explicate Friedman's "Marshallian Demand Curve."[3] Although these are interesting exercises, we would like to sug-

---

3. The most painstaking and perceptive case that Friedman's demand curve cannot be found in Marshall is Aldrich 1996. We can do no better than suggest that the reader interested in the fine technical points of the argument begin there. We also view our argument as consistent with that found in Hirsch and De Marchi 1990: "Looking to Marshall to help is just as likely to confuse" (36); "it is only with the help of Knight, we suggest, that one can derive a coherent political economy from Friedman's writings" (285). What we add to their theses is the historical context that can explain the genesis of the doctrine and the position it occupied versus other constructions of orthodox neoclassical price theory.

gest another way to understand these texts. One need not search for Friedman's demand curve in Marshall, any more than one needs to find his philosophy in Karl Popper or John Dewey. Friedman's demand curve grows out of Knight, via Schultz and Hotelling. It was the culmination of a whole sequence of reviews and articles, most notably Friedman 1941, Friedman and Wallis 1942, and Friedman 1946, seeking a way out of the impasse bequeathed him by Schultz's palpable failure. These articles are the traces of a mighty struggle with the meaning and significance of income for neoclassical price theory, and it is no coincidence that the work for which Friedman is most famous, such as the "permanent income hypothesis" and the mantra that "money matters," derives directly from his empirical work on the measurement of professional incomes and the estimation of relevant demand functions in the late 1930s (Friedman and Kuznets 1945).

What are the main precepts of Friedman's theory of demand, which became the foundations of the Chicago approach? First and foremost, he agrees with Knight that the demand function is the primary entity in price theory. Early on, he adopted the position that to "go behind" the demand curve to its foundations in laws of utility or "indifference" is largely a waste of time. It could not further the quest "to obtain exact knowledge of the quantitative relation of consumer expenditures to prices and incomes for the purpose of predicting the effect of changes in economic conditions on the consumption of various commodities" (Friedman and Wallis 1942, 188). Of course, the analyst should not repudiate something like utility altogether, since it "may be a useful expository device," but one should not "mistake the scaffolding set up to facilitate the logical analysis for the skeletal structure of the problem." By the time of his *Price Theory* (1966), he identifies utility as a convenient fiction: "We shall suppose that the individual in making these decisions acts *as if* he were pursuing and attempting to maximize a single end" (37; emphasis in original). The divergence from Knight comes in relinquishing all rights to criticize utility as a scientific concept and instead linking its legitimacy to the uses it serves, namely, as a language to motivate and discuss observable demand curves. Friedman the statistician here inverts Knight the "ideal type" philosopher: Good empirical demand curves underwrite dubious quasi psychology rather than vice versa.

The upshot of all these considerations for Friedman was emphatically not the conclusion that demand theory was in a sorry state but rather the endorsement of maximum freedom with regard to the treatment of income and income effects. What he came to call "Marshallian price theory" was perfectly fine as far as it went; the confusion over income effects was taken as a symptom of what was still missing from a truly comprehensive neoclassical theory (as in Knight), and that was *monetary theory*: "The important point is that the existing theory of relative prices does not really help to narrow appreciably the range of admissible hypotheses about the *dynamic* forces at work. Monetary theory, interpreted broadly, has somewhat more to offer" (Friedman 1951, 113; emphasis in original).

To those in other neoclassical camps, it seemed that Chicago was losing all interest in "rigorous theory." For example, Friedman's *Price Theory* simply ignored those like Martin Bailey (1954) who criticized his method of aggregation, even though Bailey was on the faculty at Chicago from 1955 to 1965. The first edition of Stigler's *Theory of Price* did not even see fit to mention the Slutsky equation, while the second edition relegated it to a single footnote (1952, 303). Stigler (1965, 151) did notice the Slutsky equation in his history of demand theory, but only to try to summarily bury it: "Economists tacitly agreed that it is better to have a poor, useful theory than a rich, useless one." He asked, "Can one say more about the demand functions if they are derived from the utility functions?" (147). This process culminated in Becker's (1962, 4) assertion that "the fundamental theorem of traditional theory—that demand curves are negatively inclined—largely results from a change in the opportunities set alone and is largely independent of the decision rule." In other words, in exploiting maximum freedom to make "income" whatever we wish it to be, we need not be held to any explicit conception of underlying intentional psychology or functional interdependence at all in order to get a downward-sloping demand curve. The moral of the story is to go forth and deploy demand (and supply) functions wherever markets might potentially exist, and income effects be damned (Reder 1982).

Curiously enough, in retrospect one can still discern how this all began with Hotelling. What was needed were simple stories with clean empirical implications that could be retailed in concise phrases to clients of the economics profession. This, said Friedman, was the sine qua non of a useful model. Hotelling's price potential model would have provided that as well, except that too many economists found the non-conservation of income difficult to swallow. Consequently, they imposed fixity of income, only to discover that one must not take it too seriously, at least in Chicago. The next step might have been to double back to the Hotelling model to reevaluate its attractions and drawbacks, but that did not happen, primarily because the approach to demand theory now became confused with tangential issues: prostatist versus antistatist politics; the intrinsic attractions of mathematical formalism; the extent of commitment to utilitarian psychology; the correct format for statistical inference; the resonance or dissonance with Keynesian macroeconomics; the significance of imperfect competition for price theory; and much more. But through all the blooming, buzzing confusion, Chicago never lost sight of its most immediate rival in demand theory: the Cowles Commission.

Out of the Cowles and into the Fire

Before the Cowles Commission came to Chicago, it was not the standard-bearer for general-equilibrium theory that it would become in the 1940s. Charles Roos and Harold Thayer Davis, the first two research directors, were avid supporters of mathematical economics and econometrics, but neither was enamored of Walras or Pareto. Before Chicago, the commission's entire funding derived from Alfred Cowles and his family, and the benefactor's inclinations tended toward practical studies of financial assets and government policy. Yntema's directorship from 1939 to 1942 had very little impact on the commission's research. The pivotal change came with Lange, who recruited Leonid Hurwicz in 1942 and Marschak as research director in 1943.

The extent to which Marschak's priorities came to dominate the Cowles Commission in the 1940s is still not sufficiently appreciated. Marschak was a Russian mechanical engineer and former Menshevik who had studied economics at Berlin and Heidelberg, and his earliest theoretical contributions, like those of Lange, were in the socialist calculation debate. In the 1930s, he was regarded as one of the few experts on the statistical estimation of demand functions, and he had participated in some widely noted controversies over pitfalls in demand estimation with such major figures as Wassily Leontief and Ragnar Frisch (Hendry and Morgan 1995). Thus he was viewed in Chicago as an heir-apparent to the program of Schultz. In his 1939 review of *Theory and Measurement of Demand*, Marschak (1939b, 487) seems to take up the torch dropped by the fallen comrade. Although he credits Schultz with "reviving and applying economic theorems of Pareto and Slutsky," he hints that Schultz may have been guilty of certain "errors or ambiguities," which were now set straight. Nevertheless, he makes it clear that he intends to come up with multiple auxiliary hypotheses to append to Schultz's procedures, without once acknowledging the downbeat prognosis that Schultz's text tendered and that his own proposed hypotheses were intended to explain away. Marschak never once openly entertained the idea that the Walrasian neoclassical program might be at fault. For him, the Walrasian program was always unreflectively equated with science, and he surrounded himself with like-minded souls. Marschak's irrepressible—some would add premature—confidence that thorny conceptual issues were on the cusp of being resolved by some new mathematical formalism helped create a hothouse environment for the cultivation of mathematical neoclassical economics at the commission.

Marschak's work during the decade from roughly 1938 to 1948 was primarily bent to this purpose. As he put it in the Schultz festschrift, "To test theories describing the interdependence of economic variables, empirical equations of the Schultz type are not a useful tool" (quoted in Lange, McIntire, and Yntema 1942, 150). But Marschak's inventiveness outran his stalwart purpose, since in this period he came up with too many reasons why Schultz had to be revised, thus raising the disturbing possibility that no particular empirical phenomenon could be ruled out even by the most sophisticated techniques for statistical demand estimation. Some auxilliary hypotheses proposed by Marschak in this period, all strictly confined within the framework of the Slutsky equation, included the following:

1. Changes in the distribution of income were not taken into account in the equations (1939a, 1943).
2. The income constraint could be treated as something in between Hotelling's endogenous specification and a purely exogenous invariant by portraying it as a random variable.
3. Income invariance could be loosened by the imposition of lags or some deterministic dynamics.
4. Systematic shifts in supply and demand functions must be empirically identified for purposes of analytical separation (1939a).
5. The analytical need to make a comprehensive accounting of all other relevant factors in an interdependent system could be obviated by means of previously overlooked statistical criteria (Hendry and Morgan 1995).

6. Another auxiliary hypothesis based on Mosak 1938, which Marschak would promote into conventional textbook wisdom, was that the Hotelling price potential model was in fact a theory of production factor demands and not consumer demand and therefore had to be combined with the Slutsky model at one remove rather than treated as a rival model.

The story that Marschak directed research along the path bequeathed by Schultz and Hotelling is not part of the existing histories of the Cowles Commission. Perhaps this is because most authors have focused on the creation of an independent abstract discipline called "econometrics" as the predominant telos of the postwar commission (Christ, 1952, 1994; Epstein 1987; Hildreth 1986; Morgan 1990). Indeed the Cowles Commission is usually identified with the probability approach to econometrics, the identification problem, the correction of estimation bias, and the genesis of Keynesian macroeconometrics rather than with the theory of demand. We are suggesting an alternative reading that shifts the center of gravity by looking at the whole record of the commission during the 1940s. After Marschak, Cowles was perceived as first and foremost the uncompromising partisan of Walrasian general-equilibrium theory, including staunch adherence to the Slutsky equation, and the commission's other formidable accomplishments were often seen as subordinate to this larger purpose.

It seems that when Marschak moved to Chicago, he took advantage of the disarray to recast the commission in his own image. He swept the stables clean of any alternative methodological approaches to price theory, most notably George Katona's anthropological and psychological approach to research on price controls. He revived the moribund Cowles Papers series and instituted a series of Cowles seminars at Chicago. He replaced the previous Advisory Council with an Advisory Committee more to his liking (Christ 1952, 26). He had brought a Rockefeller grant to study demand analysis with him from New York and now sought to parlay this into long-term institutional funding for the commission. Once at the commission, Marschak apparently had settled on questions of statistical estimation as the primary source of "protective belt" hypotheses surrounding prior attempts at demand estimation, but at Rockefeller he ran into a brick wall, which he attributed to the machinations of institutionalists at the National Bureau of Economic Research (NBER). Hence, the strife between Cowles and the

NBER that culminated in the infamous 1947 "measurement without theory" controversy between Koopmans and Rutledge Vining was in fact initiated by Marschak and seemed to be as much about access to funding and legitimacy as it was about fine points of statistical analysis (Mirowski 1989a).

These attempts to capture outside funding had repercussions back in Chicago. Rockefeller Foundation officer Joseph Willits complained to University of Chicago dean of social sciences Robert Redfield that Marschak's proposal was confusing and ill motivated. Marschak (1944) responded with a revealing letter to Redfield that justified his ambitious plans and sought to differentiate Cowles' research program from the work of Schultz. He indicated that problems in price theory had originally justified "the adaptation of statistical method to the (not yet sufficiently recognized) peculiarities of economic data." Although Marschak did manage to obtain $7,500 from Rockefeller, which he used to hire Koopmans, this was nothing like the long-term institutional support he desired.

During these struggles, the commission had essentially arrived at its position on the correct way to go about estimating a structural system of demand equations, best represented by the famous Cowles Commission Monographs 10 (Koopmans 1950) and 14 (Hood and Koopmans 1953). Although these works are often portrayed as definitive statements about proper econometric technique (Christ 1994; Hildreth 1986), they met with opposition from many contemporaries. The problem was that although "structure," "system," and "interdependence" were rallying cries at the commission, it did not take long to discover how intractable true generality could be once researchers began to spell out the implications of these themes. Those who had passed the Walrasian litmus test did not give a second thought to utility or preferences as *vera causae*, but the problem became salient in that pesky variable, income. Koopmans (1950, 394) posed the obvious question: "When is a system complete?"

> The causal principle . . . regards as exogenous those variables which influence the (remaining) endogenous variables but are not influenced thereby. The causal principle is often used also if it applies only approximately. . . . [An] example is found in the formation of quantity and price of a consumers' good that attracts only a small fraction of consumers' expenditure. In such cases, consumer income

is often taken as an exogenous variable, operating at the demand side, although of course consumers' income itself depends on the demand for *all* commodities. . . . There is no sharp line of demarcation between the application of the approximate causal principle and what deserves mention as a third principle of consideration: the purpose of exposition.

The significance of this admission is that it signals just how imprecise the phenomenon of the invariance of the budget constraint could be from the viewpoint of the empirical economist; systems have arbitrary boundaries that are conditional on the uses to which they are put. In pervasively interdependent systems, closure is a relative concept. Conservation principles require closed systems, but closure had been practically ruled out of bounds by the rejection of any experimental protocol (Mirowski 1989b). A charitable reading might suggest that the morals of this passage are not very different from those extracted from Friedman in the previous section; but in fact, the Cowles approach is quite different. Marschak and Koopmans repeatedly insisted on phrasing such questions as technical problems: problems of "causal identification," "statistical definitions of exogeneity," vigilance against "observational equivalence," "corrections for simultaneous equations bias," and so on. All this tough-minded technocratic language tended to suggest that the data would ultimately settle these issues, which did resonate with the logical positivism coming to be embraced in America. But experience with the actual regressions and getting one's hands dirty in the data tend to undermine this dream.

The number of logical elisions, leaps of faith, and undermotivated compromises at the commission began to look daunting by the late 1940s. Suppose, for instance, that you proved willing to arbitrarily truncate the full Walrasian system in order to arrive at a small system of tractable demand equations, which then by some technical trick were rendered causally identified. The first problem that must be confronted is that Walrasian theory is thoroughly deterministic, but the data appear stochastic. After flirting with the idea that randomness should enter through measurement error, the commission members rapidly backpedaled to the position that the appropriate specification was "errors in equations" (Hildreth 1986, 31). Gaussian distributions were assumed with very little justification. This could not straightforwardly be chalked up to convenience or simplicity; it was the specification that least deranged the mathematical structure of the Walrasian system by keeping stochastic considerations fully quarantined from the definition of equilibrium (Mirowski 1989c), but it also became the stock excuse for the exclusion of any other potentially relevant causal variables. Thus, development of the very class of statistical model was rapidly being shaped by a priori images of the appropriate theory underlying the phenomena.

But the story gets worse. Marschak, Trygve Haavelmo, Meyer Girschick, and Lawrence Klein wanted to put the new techniques to work verifying neoclassicism, but when they attempted to do so, the results were uniformly disappointing. To estimate a demand system, one had to confront the problems of aggregation, time trends, historical change of structure, index numbers, and so on—in other words, all those uneasy choices first tackled by Schultz. Any specification of the relevant subset of commodities was bound to appear arbitrary to a dyed-in-the-wool Walrasian, as would the choice of exogenous identifying variables. Finally, if one plowed ahead anyway, what one discovered was that some parameter signs were wrong, and many standard errors were orders of magnitude larger than for old-fashioned single-equation OLS models. Indeed, it was effectively impossible to point to anything especially novel that was learned about demand functions from the new estimates in this period; mostly they did not differ substantially from the parameters extracted by simpler means.

Two generalizations can be made about the Cowles program of the 1940s relative to the Hotelling-Schultz impasse of the 1930s. First, the commission members grew so fascinated by their shiny new statistical tools that most of their writings were absorbed with endless discussions of the baroque complexities of identification, exogeneity, limited information–maximum likelihood estimation, and all the rest; the estimation techniques seemed to become the point of the whole exercise. The result was that they generally lost sight of the whole program of testing price theory; repeated ritual invocations of Neyman-Pearson language could not repress the fact that pervasive freedom in model selection and immunizing stratagems could never be adequately encompassed by the framework of Type I/Type II errors. Henceforth, Schultz's concerns simply faded away. The integrability conditions so central to the validity of the neoclassical program in the 1930s slowly became downgraded to the status of a mathematical curiosum in the 1950s at Cowles, not because they passed any stringent tests but rather because the proliferating tests passed them by.

The second issue involves Keynesian macroeconomics; it is important to understand why the commission's structural economics became much more closely associated with Keynesian macroeconomics than with neoclassical price theory. As we have seen, Walrasian biases may have shaped the format of simultaneous equations econometrics, but it did not follow through to actually provide a plausible framework for empirical practice. In this regard, two- and three-equation Keynesian models were much more amenable to structural estimation than full-blown Walrasian systems. They sported natural closure conditions; the Keynesian synthesis interpretation rendered them modular, in that one could always contemplate adding another sector; the definitions of the variables were thought to better approximate the entities contemplated by the theory; and policy variables seemed to capture exogenous intervention much better than the vexed income variables in demand estimation. Sometime between the first flush of enthusiasm in 1944 and 1947, structural econometrics at the commission stopped being about price theory and switched allegiance to Keynesianism.

The forging of the unholy alliance between Slutsky and Keynes at Cowles was of course Knight's worst nightmare, and it was Friedman who took it upon himself to carry the war back home to the commission. Friedman felt that the entire Cowles program of structural estimation was a vast waste of time. Time and time again, he told Marschak and Koopmans to their faces that their intricate statistical procedures failed to solve any real scientific problems. Friedman admitted later: "I was a major critic of the kind of thing they were doing in Chicago. I introduced the idea of testing their work against naive models, naive hypotheses, and so on. So I was very unsympathetic to Koopmans from the beginning" (Hammond 1993, 231).

Although examination of the later reincarnations of the Cowles Commission would take us beyond our allotted time frame, one development does have profound implications for the stabilization of neoclassical price theory in America. In brief, given the failure of the Schultz program via Marschak, retention of the basic program would require that the scientific credentials of neoclassical economics be validated by some other authority. The redirection of the Cowles Commission is poignantly captured by the revision of its motto in 1952 from its previous "Science Is Measurement" to "Theory and Measurement." Actually, "Theory and Rigor and More Theory" would have been more accurate, since the commission wholeheartedly embraced the Bourbakist program of axiomatization and formalization in order to bolster the flagging fortunes of the Walrasian program (Weintraub and Mirowski 1994). In caricature, if a concerted program of statistical testing could not place demand theory on firm footing, then perhaps a comprehensive axiomatization of Walrasian general-equilibrium theory could effectively do the job.

An exploration of the various twists and turns that led neoclassical highbrow theory to circumvent the Hotelling-Schultz impasse at the commission after 1950 would lead us too far afield. It would begin with Koopmans's search for a totally neutral and institution-free theory in activity analysis; it would continue with the impact of John von Neumann's game theory on modern mathematical economics (Leonard 1995; Mirowski forthcoming a); it would marvel at the way in which statisticians like Hurwicz, Koopmans, and Marschak abruptly turned their efforts away from any constructive empiricism and toward a theoretical portrayal of the economic agent as a miniature econometrician; it would track the increasing influence of the RAND Corporation and the military on the commission's research interests (Leonard 1991; Mirowski forthcoming b); it would take into account the changing meaning of "dynamics" within the Walrasian program (Weintraub 1991); and much more. Yet no such list, however augmented and extended, would be complete without a culmination in the infamous Sonnenschein-Mantel-Debreu results of the 1970s, which settled the issue of the relationship of Walrasian general equilibrium to the theory of demand in a sternly negative way: In general, Walrasian theory placed no restrictions on excess demand functions except for homogeneity of degree zero and Walras's law (Sonnenschein 1972).[4] But all that lay in the future; let us now turn to the third version of postwar neoclassical price theory.

4. Here we must register out disagreement with the very interesting history of our period by Ingrao and Israel (1990, esp. 284–88). Those authors present the history of price theory as a single unified thread, with a single break in the 1930s–40s, when mathematically sophisticated authors renounced physical metaphor for the rigors of mathematical formalization. They conclude that the Sonnenschein-Mantel-Debreu (S-M-D) results are the fruits of that reorientation in that axiomatization has now definitively revealed the empirical emptiness and conceptual limitations of the Walrasian program. This essay demonstrates that we would challenge their theses on a number of counts: (1) Neoclassical theory, even within a single nation, is not monolithic in its core doctrines but fractured and fragmented. (2) Many of the main American protagonists in the 1930s and after persisted in taking their cues from physics, though it tended to be from vintages contemporary with their experience. (3) The S-M-D results would impact different versions of neoclassicism with differing degrees of damage, depending on their variant attitudes toward the treatment of the income constraint, the Slut-

The Revealing Story of Paul Samuelson

Samuelson's revealed preference approach to consumer choice theory represents the third facet of our demanding triad. Entering the University of Chicago the same year that Hotelling's paper appeared in the *JPE* and just five years before the arrival of the Cowles Commission, Samuelson found himself in the thick of the fray of the 1930s dispute over the theory of demand. As he put it, "The year 1932 was a good time to come to the study of economics" (Samuelson 1983, 4).

Although the Chicago and Cowles approaches involve (perhaps shifting) epistemological visions of the legitimate foundations for economic science, it is Samuelson's approach that is most explicit about its cognitive preferences. That economic concepts are scientifically legitimate only when they are operationally meaningful became Samuelson's epistemic battle cry quite early in his career. Scientific concepts are meaningful or significant only if they are defined by a set of intersubjectively observable procedures or operations, and the goal of scientific theory is to redescribe, not to explain, that which is observed in the empirical domain (Cohen 1995; Samuelson 1965; Wong 1978).

Although "empirical" is the watchword for Samuelson's vision of economic science, Schultz's *Theory and Measurement of Demand* was not the way to achieve it from his perspective. It is fair to say that Samuelson has been as consistently critical of the efforts of Schultz and others to empirically test the theory of demand as he has been of the antipositivist approach of Knight's "Swiss guards" (Samuelson 1983, 7). "Some of the skepticisms of Knight and Jacob Viner concerning the empirical statistical studies that their colleagues Paul Douglas and Henry Schultz were attempting, I readily admit, were well taken" (Samuelson 1992, 241). In fact, Samuelson's criticism has not been restricted to efforts to empirically test the theory of demand; increas-

---

sky equation, and the centrality of the law of demand vis-à-vis Walrasian theory. (4) Most denizens of the Cowles Commission did not find S-M-D very distressing, since they had already renounced the laws of supply and demand.

Once these lessons are absorbed, it becomes clear that Ingrao and Israel's narrative is just an inversion of the more conventional Whig account, written from the constricted vantage point of one subset of one school of American neoclassicism. To find these confusions in such otherwise discerning authors reveals why a comprehensive history of demand theory in the twentieth century is still desperately needed.

ingly over the last few decades, he has been critical of econometric testing in general.

> Let me make a confession. Back when I was 20 I could perceive the great progress that was being made in econometric methods. Even without foreseeing the onset of the computer age, with its cheapening of calculations, I expected that the new econometrics would enable us to narrow down the uncertainties of our economic theories. We would be able to reject false theories. We would be able to infer new good theories. My confession is that this expectation has not worked out. (Samuelson 1992, 243)

This puts the champion of positivist economics in a rather peculiar position. The person who is often viewed as one of the staunchest advocates of the empirical science of economics does not do, nor does he have much faith in, the type of econometric work that dominates the empirical practice of the contemporary mainstream he helped create. This paradox has implications for Samuelson's entire career, but we will focus on his version of demand theory.

The problem for Samuelson was to find a way of formulating the theory of demand that would be consistent with his positivist-operationalist methodology while simultaneously avoiding the type of econometric testing associated with Schultz. How could this possibly be done? How could one steer the ship of economic science between the Scylla of apriorism and the Charybdis of Schultz's economic estimates while honoring the law of demand and accepting only neoclassical givens? His answer, published in 1938, was to ground demand theory on what later came to be called the theory of revealed preference. In essence his answer was to change the place where the empiricism lived in the neoclassical theory of demand. Instead of having empiricism enter at the back end—by testing the empirical implications deduced from the theory—the revealed preference approach would place empiricism right up front at the beginning of the exercise. If the epistemologically dubious notion of subjective utility could be replaced with a strictly behaviorist—thus objective, observational, operational, and meaningful—concept of consumer action, demand theory could be reconstituted on what Samuelson considered legitimate scientific foundations. A demand theory based on a behaviorist-inspired notion of human action (i.e., response) would already be empirical at the start, thus eliminating the need for after-the-fact econometric testing like that of Schultz, while also being free of any residual subjectivism or apriorism. Samuelson could kill two Chicago birds with one well-placed stone.

In the original 1938 presentation, Samuelson argued forcefully that his goal was "to develop the theory of consumer's behavior freed from any vestigial traces of the utility concept" (71). He required three postulates for this result. The first two postulates had been standard in the Slutsky approach: He assumed first the existence of a single-valued demand function $x_i = x_i(p,l) = x_i(p_1, \ldots p_n, l)$ for each good satisfying the budget constraint $\Sigma px = l$ and, second, that demand functions are homogeneous of degree zero in prices and money income. The third postulate is the assumption that ultimately came to be called the revealed preference condition:

$$\Sigma x'p \le \Sigma xp \text{ implies that } \Sigma xp' > \Sigma x'p' \tag{RP}$$

In this postulate, x is the bundle of goods at price vector p, and x' is the bundle of goods purchased at the price vector p'. If bundle x' was affordable at p but was not selected, then x must have been more expensive at p', since it was not selected. In the language of the later literature, since x' was affordable at p but was not chosen, the bundle x was "revealed preferred" to x'; thus if x' was chosen at p', it must be because x is more expensive at these prices.

Samuelson was careful in the original article to avoid the word "preference" or any other term that might imply subjective evaluation or intentionality. The 1938 article strictly maintains the behaviorist idiom of "selection" throughout; the theory was, after all, meant to replace the intentional theory of subjective utility, preference, and choice. From these three postulates, Samuelson was able to derive what he considered the main result of the utility-based theory of demand: a generalized version of the law of demand. According to Samuelson, he started with the operational-observable condition RP and ended up with an observable generalized law of demand; not only could economics do without the nineteenth-century notion of cardinal utility, but also now it could do without the concept of ordinal utility or well-ordered preference. The shroud of utility metaphysics was cast away, and economics was now indeed "part of the advancing army of science" (Samuelson 1983, 10).

The substantive result of ordinal utility theory that did not follow from RP was the Slutsky symmetry condition, known at the time to be equivalent to the integrability of the demand functions:

$$\frac{\partial x_i}{\partial p_j} + x_j \frac{\partial x_i}{\partial l} = \frac{\partial x_j}{\partial p_i} + x_i \frac{\partial x_j}{\partial l} \tag{S}$$

Although Samuelson admitted that RP did not generate the Slutsky condition, he did not find the omission problematic, since he did not find integrability very interesting (in 1938):

> The only possible interest that integrability can have (except to those who have an historical attachment to the utility concept) would be in providing us with the additional knowledge concerning a certain reciprocal relation [S]. . . . But it is this very implication which makes it doubtful and subject to refutation under ideal observational conditions, although I have little faith in any attempts to verify this statistically. (Samuelson, 1938, 68)

In Hands and Mirowski 1998, we suggested a number of reasons why Samuelson's interests—his vision of welfare economics, his reading of the lesson from physics, and so on—might lead him to be uninterested in integrability. There is no reason to repeat this discussion here, but there is reason to point out at least two immediate ironies in Samuelson's 1938 attitude toward integrability. First, as we will see below, by 1950 he had become quite interested in integrability and its relationship to RP. In fact, by the publication of his Nobel lecture in 1972, he used the (stronger) integrability conditions from Hotelling's 1932 model as his single "illustrative economic example" of the power of mathematics in economic analysis. It seems ironic that what was dismissed as an anachronism in 1938 was thought to be the best example of successful economic science for the Nobel audience. Second, there is the ongoing irony of the outspoken positivist-empiricist who has little faith in statistical verification; worse yet is the apparent inconsistency of a person who equates "empirical with "meaningful," claiming that integrability is not empirically true while simultaneously denying that it should be tested. It seems the old Chicago demon still resisted exorcism.

Samuelson ([1948] 1968) continued the argument and introduced the term "revealed preference" in his next major article on demand theory, although his focus seemed to change substantially during the intervening decade. The condition RP remains in the 1948 article, but it is now a way of *constructing* a consumer's indifference map; it is now a way of *revealing* the consumer's preferences. RP moves from a way of eliminating preference from the theory of demand to a way of uncovering preferences for the theory of demand. The behaviorist idiom disappears, and the (now) standard mentalist language of preference, choice, and ordinal utility returns with a vengeance.

A more significant change occurs in Samuelson's 1950 article, in which he attempts to provide an intuitive explanation of the integrability condition. Hendrik Houthakker had argued earlier in 1950 that what was needed was an RP-based condition that would be both necessary and sufficient for *all* the implications of ordinal utility theory—including integrability—and introduced the so-called Strong Axiom of Revealed Preference to do the job. Samuelson admits in the 1950 article that the problem of integrability "could not yield to this [Samuelson's] weak axiom alone" (370) and that Houthakker's stronger condition would indeed be needed to achieve the desired results. His general tone is ebulliently consummatory: "We are now in a position to complete the programme begun a dozen years ago of arriving *at the full empirical implications for demand behavior* of the most general ordinal utility analysis" (369; emphasis in original).

Despite the positive spin Samuelson puts on integrability, it seems a bit strange that he would be so pleased that an RP-based theory has been shown to be observationally equivalent to ordinal utility theory. As Stanley Wong (1978, 121) points out, "It is puzzling how Samuelson can consider revealed preference theory to be the logical equivalent to ordinal utility theory and at the same time argue that the former theory is observational while the latter is not." For a positivist, if two theories are logically and observationally equivalent, they are the same theory. It appears that revealed preference no longer frees demand theory "from any vestigial traces of the utility concept," but rather it simply provides an alternative way to theoretically describe the observational domain of utility theory—an observational domain that Samuelson earlier seemed to think was an empty set. As Houthakker (1983, 63) put it: "The stone the builder rejected in 1938 seemed to have become a cornerstone in 1950."

It is also useful to point out that the issues raised by the Hotelling-Schultz impasse continue to set the general problematic for Samuelson's demand theory. By 1950, Hotelling's 1932 work had been downgraded to a model of a competitive firm, but the issues raised and problems created by the work of Schultz and Hotelling remained clearly in Samuelson's mind.

As a partial digression, I should mention the 1932 work of Hotelling on the related problem of profit-maximization by a firm *not* subject to a budgetary constraint. Integrability conditions arise there which are related to, but distinct from, those that arise in the case of a consumer under budgetary constraint. In this connection, the reader can be referred to Henry Schultz' 1937 book which gives an extensive discussion of the integrability question: while not itself an entirely satisfactory resolution of the problem, Schultz' pages give a very good summary of the uncertainties that pervade the literature. (Samuelson 1950, 357; emphasis in original)

Although Samuelson's theory of revealed preference is proudly displayed in the demand theory chapter of every microeconomics textbook, a number of recent commentators have concluded that the overall project has been a dismal failure. As Shira Lewin (1996, 1316) put it in a recent survey of economics and psychology: "In spite of Paul Samuelson's (1938) high hopes, the revealed preference approach had proved empirically useless. Like the indifference theory it was meant to replace, it too would become an artificial theoretical construct of little, if any, explanatory value."

Of course, as damning or as interesting as such criticisms might be, they do not detract from our thesis that Samuelson's revealed preference approach to the theory of demand represents a third effort to extricate demand theory from the Hotelling-Schultz impasse.

How We Stopped Worrying and Learned to Love Walras

Since our little chronicle has gone on for quite a while and has taken a number of twists and turns, it is perhaps useful to review the central story line. We have four main themes, or perhaps three main themes and a point of departure. The point of departure is the existence of diversity in 1930s demand theory. In the 1930s, there were many theories of demand, differing primarily but not exclusively with respect to what each viewed as the relevant foundational invariant; these include Henry Moore's "just a statistical relationship" view; the Cournot-Cassel "start with demand functions" view; Hicks and Allen's "marginal rates of substitution" approach; Hotelling's 1932 work; revealed preference; Slutsky; and other less influential approaches. The American scene was one of hearty diversity and thus a far cry from its common image as the passive repository for smooth transatlantic transmission of Marshallian or Paretian ideas. Even when one narrows the field to authors who were self-consciously "neoclassical"—those who started from individual preference or utility, used mathematical optimization, and so on—profound diversity remains. Although this point of departure is not standard in the historical literature, we do not think it very controversial, and we have provided here very little documentation to support its existence (Hands and Mirowski 1998 does better, but even it is not complete).

The first of the three themes this article does document is that although the multiple branches were pruned during the period of neoclassical stabilization, they did not get pruned back to a single stem. A better analogy than pruning off branches from a single trunk is to think of many small threads being twisted together into a much tighter bundle or skein but never forming a single homogeneous strand. The second point is that the Chicago school, the Cowles approach, and Samuelson's revealed preference theory constitute the three major distinct strands of the postwar skein. These three programs vary with respect to stated purposes; the importance of empirical testing; the underlying vision of scientific method; ideological sensitivities; aggregation; and, most relevant to our third theme, the role of income and income effects. This third lesson, building on our earlier work, is that the Hotelling-Schultz impasse was the obligatory passage point for all three of these versions of demand theory; each was a response to the problems encountered by Schultz and Hotelling in the early 1930s, and each is distinctively defined by the way in which it tried to circumvent these difficulties.

Even those persuaded by our narrative may still ask, So what? Even if there are three strands of neoclassical demand theory—the Chicago, Cowles, and revealed preference approaches—and even if they are in fact three different responses to the Hotelling-Schultz impasse, so what? Although we generally feel that interpretations are the responsibility of readers and not authors, we are willing to close with two brief comments regarding the overall direction and significance of our project. The first is that it is a big project, and this is just one small part of a much larger story that is yet to be told and that even in the earliest stages seems to be a far different story than that available, explicitly or implicitly, in any extant historical literature. Second, we believe that our story helps us understand the strength of neoclassicism in a novel way. Rather than saying it simply chased out the competition—which it did, if by "competition" one means the institutionalists, Marxists, and Austrians—and replaced diversity with a single monolithic homogeneous neoclassical strain, we say it transformed itself into a more robust ensemble. Neoclassical demand theory gained hegemony by going from patches of monoculture in the interwar period to an interlocking competitive ecosystem after World War II. Rather than presenting itself as a single, brittle, theoretical strand, neoclassicism offered a more flexible, and thus resilient skein of three strands. Each subprogram had the capacity to absorb certain forms of criticism and thus deflect those criticisms away from the vulnerable areas in other subprograms, where they might do the most damage. Attack general-equilibrium theory for its lack of empirical relevance, and one is quickly directed toward Becker, Stigler, and the grand Chicago tradition of applied microeconomics. Go after Chicago for its loose use of subjective utility and a priori categories, and one is quickly told how the relevant preferences are operationally defined and could be revealed by direct observations of consumers' choices. Finally, go after revealed preference theory for emptiness as a tautological definition of consistency in choice, and one is immediately shown the way through the equivalence results and right into the heart of the complete Walrasian general-equilibrium model. Pace Harry Truman, the buck stops nowhere. We think this insight goes a lot further toward explaining the postwar success of neoclassical economics than any of the arguments presented in the standard internalist or externalist histories.

References

Aldrich, John. 1996. The Course of Marshall's Theorizing about Demand. *HOPE* 28:171–217.

Bailey, Martin. 1954. The Marshallian Demand Curve. *Journal of Political Economy* 62:255–61.

Becker, Gary. 1962. Irrational Behavior and Economic Theory. *Journal of Political Economy* 70:1–13.

Bronfenbrenner, Martin. 1962. Observations on the Chicago School(s). *Journal of Political Economy* 70:72–75.

Christ, Carl. 1952. History of the Cowles Commission. 1932–52. In *Economic Theory and Measurement: A Twenty Year Research Report, 1932–1952.* Chicago: Cowles Commission.

———. 1994. The Cowles Commission's Contributions to Econometrics at Chicago, 1939–1955. *Journal of Economic Literature* 32:30–59.

Cohen, Joshua. 1995. Samuelson's Operationalist-Descriptivist Thesis. *Journal of Economic Methodology* 2:53–78.

Epstein, Roy. 1987. *A History of Econometrics*. Amsterdam: North-Holland.

Friedman, Milton. 1941. Review of *Monopolistic Competition and General Equilibrium Theory*, by R. Triffin. *Journal of Farm Economics* 23:389–90.

———. 1946. Lange on Price Flexibility and Employment. *American Economic Review* 36:613–31.

———. 1949. The Marshallian Demand Curve. *Journal of Political Economy* 57:463–95.

———. 1951. Comment on Christ. In *NBER Conference on Business Cycles*. New York: NBER.

———. 1966. *Price Theory: A Provisional Text*. Rev. ed. Chicago: Aldine.

Friedman, Milton and Simon Kuznets. 1945. *Income from Independent Professional Practice*. New York: National Bureau for Economic Research.

Friedman, Milton, and W. A. Wallis. 1942. The Empirical Derivation of Indifference Functions. In Lange, McIntire, and Yntema 1942.

Hammond, J. Daniel. 1993. An Interview with Milton Friedman. In *Philosophy and Methodology of Economics*. Vol. 1. Edited by B. J. Caldwell. Aldershot: Edward Elgar.

Hands, D. Wade, and Philip Mirowski. 1998. Harold Hotelling and the Neoclassical Dream. In *Economics and Methodology: Crossing Boundaries*. Edited by R. Backhouse, D. Hausman, U. Mäki, and A. Salanti. London: Macmillan.

Hendry, David, and Mary Morgan, eds. 1995. *The Foundations of Econometric Analysis*. Cambridge: Cambridge University Press.

Hicks, John. 1939. *Value and Capital*. Oxford: Oxford University Press.

Hildreth, Clifford. 1986. *The Cowles Commission in Chicago*. Berlin: Springer-Verlag.

Hirsch, Abraham, and Neil De Marchi. 1990. *Milton Friedman*. Ann Arbor: University of Michigan Press.

Hood, W., and T. Koopmans, eds. 1953. *Studies in Econometric Method*. Cowles Commission Monograph 14. New Haven, Conn.: Yale University Press.

Hotelling, Harold. 1932a. Edgeworth's Taxation Paradox and the Nature of Demand and Supply Functions. *Journal of Political Economy* 40:577–616.

———. 1932b. Review of Ragnar Frisch's *New Methods of Measuring Marginal Utility*. *Journal of the American Statistical Association* 27:451–52.

———. 1935. Demand Functions with Limited Budgets. *Econometrica* 3:66–78.

———. 1954. Hotelling to Lloyd Reynolds, 24 September. Box 5, Miscellaneous Correspondence "R," Harold Hotelling Papers, Columbia University, New York.

———. N.d. On the Nature of Demand and Supply Functions. Box 26, File "Mathematical Economics," Harold Hotelling Papers, Columbia University, New York.

Houthakker, Hendrik. 1950. Revealed Preference and the Utility Function. *Economica* 17:159–74.

———. 1983. On Consumption Theory. In *Paul Samuelson and Modern Economic Theory*. Edited by E. C. Brown and R. M. Solow. New York: McGraw-Hill.

Ingrao, Bruna, and Giorgio Israel. 1990. *The Invisible Hand: Economic Theory in the History of Science*. Cambridge, Mass.: MIT Press.

Knight, Frank. 1944. Realism and Relevance in the Theory of Demand. *Journal of Political Economy* 52:289–318.

Koopmans, Tjalling, ed. 1950. *Statistical Inference in Dynamic Economic Models*. Cowles Commission Monograph 10. New York: Wiley.

Lange, Oskar, Francis McIntire, and Theodore Yntema, eds. 1942. *Studies in Mathematical Economics and Econometrics*. Chicago: University of Chicago Press.

Leonard, Robert. 1991. War as a Simple Economic Problem. In *Economics and National Security*. Edited by C. Goodwin. Durham, N.C.: Duke University Press.

———. 1995. From Parlor Games to Social Science: Von Neumann, Morgenstern, and the Creation of Game Theory, 1928–1944. *Journal of Economic Literature* 33:730–61.

Lewin, Shira. 1996. Economics and Psychology. *Journal of Economic Literature* 34:1293–1323.

Marschak, Jacob. 1939a. Personal and Collective Budget Functions. *Review of Economics and Statistics* 21:161–70.

———. 1939b. Review of Henry Schultz's *Theory and Measurement of Demand*. *Economic Journal* 49:486–89.

———. 1943. Demand Elasticities Reviewed. *Econometrica* 11:25–34.

———. 1944. Marschak to Robert Redfield, 15 February. Rockefeller Foundation Archives, Sleepy Hollow, N.Y.

Mirowski, Philip. 1989a. The Measurement without Theory Controversy. *Economies et sociétés* 11:65–87.

———. 1989b. *More Heat than Light*. New York: Cambridge University Press.

———. 1989c. The Probabilistic Counter-revolution. *Oxford Economic Papers* 41:217–35.

———. 1990. Problems in the Paternity of Econometrics: Henry Ludwell Moore. *HOPE* 22:587–609.

———. Forthcoming a. *Machine Dreams*. Cambridge: Harvard University Press.

———. Forthcoming b. RAND/OR. *Social Studies of Science*.

Morgan, Mary. 1990. *The History of Econometric Ideas*. Cambridge: Cambridge University Press.

Mosak, Jacob. 1938. Interrelations of Production, Price, and Derived Demand. *Journal of Political Economy* 46:761–84.

Patinkin, Donald. 1995. The Training of an Economist. *Banca Nazionale del Lavoro Quarterly Review* 48:359–95.

Reder, Melvin. 1982. Chicago Economics: Permanence and Change. *Journal of Economic Literature* 20:1–38.

Samuelson, Paul. 1938. A Note on the Pure Theory of Consumer's Behaviour. *Economica* 5:61–71.

———. [1948] 1968. Consumption Theory in Terms of Revealed Preference. *Economica* 15:243–53. Reprinted in *Utility Theory: A Book of Readings*. Edited by A. N. Page. New York: Wiley.

————. 1950. The Problem of Integrability in Utility Theory. *Economica* 17:355–85.

————. 1965. Professor Samuelson on Theory and Realism: Reply. *American Economic Review* 55:1164–72.

————. 1972. Maximum Principles in Analytical Economics. *American Economic Review* 62:249–62.

————. 1983. Economics in a Golden Age: A Personal Memoir. In *Paul Samuelson and Modern Economic Theory*. Edited by E. C. Brown and R. M. Solow. New York: McGraw-Hill.

————. 1992. My Life Philosophy: Policy Credos and Working Ways. In *Eminent Economists: Their Life Philosophies*. Edited by M. Szenberg. New York: Cambridge University Press.

Schultz, Henry. 1938. *The Theory and Measurement of Demand*. Chicago: University of Chicago Press.

Sonnenschein, Hugo. 1972. Market Excess Demand Functions. *Econometrica* 40:549–63.

Stigler, George. 1952. *The Theory of Price*. Rev. ed. New York: Macmillan.

————. 1965. *Essays in the History of Economics*. Chicago: University of Chicago Press.

————. 1988. *Memoirs of an Unregulated Economist*. New York: Basic Books.

Weintraub, E. Roy. 1991. *Stabilizing Dynamics: Constructing Economic Knowledge*. New York: Cambridge University Press.

Weintraub, E. Roy, and Philip Mirowski. 1994. The Pure and the Applied: Bourbakism Comes to Mathematical Economics. *Science in Context* 7:245–72.

Wong, Stanley. 1978. *The Foundations of Paul Samuelson's Revealed Preference Theory*. Boston: Routledge and Kegan Paul.

The Money Muddle: The Transformation of American Monetary Thought, 1920–1970

Perry Mehrling

The history of twentieth-century American monetary economics is, in one possible reading, a story of discontinuity. The field was quite active during the 1920s, more or less disappeared in the depression and war years, reemerged only slowly during the 1950s, and developed during the 1960s along the two competing lines that came to be known as "monetarism" and "Keynesianism." Not surprisingly, given the gap of the 1930s and 1940s, postwar monetary economics differed significantly from the monetary economics of the 1920s. The dormant decades saw a sea change not only in monetary institutions (the Glass-Steagall Act) but also in the social function of economic analysis (the rise of big government) and in styles of economic thinking (the Keynesian revolution). As a consequence, postwar monetary thinkers typically proceeded as though theirs was a field sui generis and simply ignored earlier writings, which seemed to come from another world as well as from another time.

In building their field anew, postwar authors could not easily proceed inductively from the operational details of individual banks and their interaction in the banking system as prewar authors had done. The most recent monetary experience of depression and wartime provided scant empirical basis for spinning theories about peacetime prosperity. Instead, postwar authors typically proceeded deductively from the neo-

The original version of this essay was prepared for the 1997 *HOPE* conference.

classical theory of value, although not because of any particular commitment to the deductive method or to individualism as such. Rather,
the theory of value, despite all its problems (e.g., imperfect competition), seemed to them the most solid core of ideas economics had to
offer. When building anew, one is wise to start with solid foundations.
For better or for worse, postwar monetary theory therefore came to be
structured around the ideas of money supply, money demand, and equilibrium. Postwar monetary debate was conducted in a language that
may be called "monetary Walrasianism"—Walrasian in the sense that
the economy was conceived as a set of simultaneous equations in which
prices move to equate supply and demand for each good, and monetary
in the sense that one set of equations was conceived as equating money
demand and money supply. The work of Patinkin (1956), Modigliani
(1963), Tobin (1969), and others became the canonical texts of postwar
monetary Walrasianism.

Discontinuity is clearly a major part of the story, but from a longer
and broader perspective, elements of continuity come into focus that
provide an essential context for the full story of the transformation of
monetary economics. In the history of monetary thought, there have
always been two basic approaches to the study of money and banking,
depending on whether money or banking is taken as the starting point
of analysis. The locus classicus of the two approaches is the debate in
England between the currency school and the banking school over the
1844 Peel Act (see Mehrling 1996c). To understand American monetary debate, it is essential to appreciate how the debate between these
two theoretical approaches has played out against the backdrop of
political debate about the role of banks in American democracy. In the
late nineteenth century, the quantity theory of money (currency school)
became associated with populist agitation for monetary inflation
because of William Jennings Bryan and the Free Silver movement
(Rockoff 1990), while the alternative credit theory of money (banking
school) became associated with the eastern banking interests that
opposed Bryan. This interplay of theoretical debate with monetary politics continued throughout the twentieth century.

In the story of continuity, the key figures are Milton Friedman and
Edward Stone Shaw. In their intellectual formation, both must be
understood as pre-World War II economists, although both did their
mature work in the rather different postwar context. As such, they provide a crucial link between the 1920s and the 1960s that helps us see

the similarities as well as the differences between the two periods. Furthermore, because they began their inquiries on the subject of money in radically different places, the comparison between Friedman and Shaw helps reveal the shifting fault lines in American monetary debate. Friedman began with money, whereas Shaw began with banking. Friedman was, as everyone knows, the origin of postwar monetarism, and Shaw (with his student and collaborator John Gurley) was, as is often forgotten, the origin of the Keynesian strain of monetary thought more usually associated with James Tobin.

Both monetarism and Keynesianism evolved in directions that led away from their Friedman-Shaw origins, but the Friedman-Shaw link with prewar traditions nevertheless provides a useful lens through which subsequent developments can be viewed. That lens brings into focus a number of issues that have long puzzled observers, the most significant of which is the vexed question of what exactly separates the monetarist view from the Keynesian view. The heat of the postwar debate is hard for outsiders to understand, in part because it was framed as a dispute about the slopes of certain Hicksian curves, the size and number of lags, and other technical issues. As many have commented, on the surface the monetarist Friedman and the Keynesian Tobin appeared to be reasoning on the basis of more or less the same model, a substantial agreement that made the evident deep disagreement hard to fathom. The energy on both sides can be understood better once one appreciates that the monetarist-Keynesian debate was only the latest chapter in a dispute that runs throughout the history of American monetary economics. That dispute has always been about much more than mere monetary theory, embracing also the more fundamental question of the proper role of money within the American social and political structure.

The heat of the postwar monetarist-Keynesian debate provides evidence that, although the neoclassical language might have become hegemonic, what economists wanted to say with that language remained as pluralist as in the interwar years. The problem was that the language itself constrained what could be said or at least constrained what could be expressed with sufficient clarity that it could be broadly understood. Because the theory of value abstracts from monetary phenomena in an effort to explain exchange ratios, ultimately the project of developing monetary theory on value-theoretic foundations is deeply incoherent. More particularly, Walrasian general equilibrium (in its Arrow-Debreu formulation) ultimately has no place for money (Hahn 1965). Monetary Walrasianism thus turned out to be an oxymoron at best and at worst a Procrustean bed onto which neither the currency school approach nor the banking school approach could easily fit. The apparent virtue of the language—that it transforms highly charged theoretical and political issues into narrowly technical questions resolvable on empirical grounds —turned out in the end to be a will-o'-the-wisp, always dancing just out of reach. The wandering monetary debate never quite got around to a forthright assault on the deep problems that structure the field, and one reason was that the deep problems were hard to formulate in the new language of monetary Walrasianism.

The Interwar Years

Monetary thinkers of the interwar period inherited their conception of the subject from the pre–World War I debates between the titans Irving Fisher and Laurence Laughlin, in particular their confrontations at the 1904 and 1911 meetings of the American Economic Association. The two men stood at opposite poles in their approaches to monetary theory: Laughlin promoted his own version of the banking school view, whereas Fisher promoted a version of the quantity theory of money cleansed, he claimed, of the taint of Bryan. The heat of their encounters, however, was clearly kindled from the more flammable fuel of their diametrically opposed policy conclusions. Whereas Laughlin was a staunch defender of laissez-faire and the automatic mechanism of the gold standard, Fisher advocated scientific management of the currency directed toward stabilization of prices and thus also, he claimed, business cycles. In the ensuing drama, Laughlin played the battle-weary veteran still nursing scars from his earlier bouts with the populist supporters of Bryan. Fisher played the fresh challenger, the crusader in possession of the one and true faith that was all the more compelling for its presumably scientific basis. It was a battle of abstract ideas, but one fraught with far-reaching consequences, situated as it was within the larger political debate about the creation of a central bank.

The establishment of the Federal Reserve System in 1913 meant that, after the immediate distraction of war, American monetary debate tended to organize around criticism of the Federal Reserve's operations (Dorfman 1959, chaps. 11–12; Barber 1985). Nevertheless, that debate retained its pre–World War I public character. When Fisher wished to influence monetary policy in the 1920s, he did not simply address himself to the central bankers but also built a popular price stabilization movement to pressure Congress to enact his favorite policy into legislation (Fisher 1934). Similarly, those who wished to defend the Federal Reserve also had to address themselves to the public (Burgess 1927). What was new in the 1920s and is often overlooked amid the Sturm und Drang of the public debate was the increased space available for intellectual debate to proceed separately from political debate. Precisely because the normative political debate focused on the Federal Reserve, there was more room within the economics profession for consideration of the positive intellectual questions. Exemplary in this regard was the work of Allyn Young.

Young grew up during the battle between Laughlin and Fisher, but when he came to teach the subject in the 1920s, he turned instead to the British economist Ralph Hawtrey, whose work represents the crowning achievement of Britain's long experience with central banking. In *Currency and Credit*, Hawtrey (1930, 35) offered his theory as a version of the quantity theory, but he rejected explicitly any simple causal link between the quantity of money and the price level. Instead, he was interested in understanding how an expansion of business and expansion of credit support each other in a process of *mutual* causation. He traced changes in prices to changes in spending ("consumers' outlay"), and he linked the quantity of money ("unspent margin") to the price level only through that spending (59–60). Insisting always on the fundamental involvement of the monetary system (through banks) in financing production and trade, Hawtrey emphasized that monetary interventions inevitably have consequences ranging far beyond their effect on prices. Treating currency as subordinate to credit, his primary focus was on the interest rate, not on the quantity of money, as a tool for intervention. All these views allow us to place Hawtrey in the banking/active management category in figure 1 and to understand Young's (1920) promotion of Hawtrey as an attempt to separate the dispute about approaches to monetary theory from the political dispute about social control of banking.

In Young's engagement with Hawtrey's work, one can see him finding his own intellectual balance between the competing traditions of American monetary thought (Mehrling 1996b). Like Laughlin and the banking interests, Young supported the gold standard. Like Fisher and the populist interests, Young supported monetary intervention to stabi-

Pre–World War II

School	Active Management	Passive Accommodation
Currency school	Irving Fisher Lauchlin Currie	
Banking school	Ralph Hawtrey Allyn Young	J. Laurence Laughlin Benjamin Anderson

Post–World War II

School	Active Discretion	Passive Rules
Currency school		Milton Friedman
Banking school	James Tobin	Alvin Hansen Edward S. Shaw

Figure 1   Typology of Monetary Theories

lize business cycles. In retrospect, it is clear that Young's ability to carve out an intermediate position in the highly charged monetary debates of the 1920s was helped by the continuing balance of political forces, a balance in which the Federal Reserve stood as a fulcrum, with populist forces on one side weighing against banking interests on the other. The monetary disaster of the 1930s upset that political balance and thus eliminated the intellectual space in which Young had done his work.

In the crisis of the 1930s, old patterns reasserted themselves, and debate reverted to the Fisher-Laughlin axis. The dispute between Lauchlin Currie (a student of Young) and Benjamin Anderson provides evidence of such a reversion. After Currie wrote his book *The Supply and Control of Money in the United States* (1934), Anderson (1935) attacked Currie as "the uncompromising advocate of an extremely tight and inflexible version of the quantity theory." Currie (1935, 703) responded by attacking Anderson's "crude statement" of "the nineteenth century Banking Principle," a characterization that Anderson rejected. It is clear from their exchange that neither Currie nor Anderson was able to absorb the intellectual contribution of the other and that the energy driving their dispute was more about the desirability of active intervention than about which view of money should guide policy choice.

Outside academe, political fault lines were even more in evidence (see Barber 1996). The failure of the Federal Reserve to stem the deepening depression of 1929–33 ultimately proved a stronger argument for the activism preferred by populist forces than any of their previous political agitation had been. Franklin Roosevelt's victory was understood by all as a victory of the common folk and a defeat for Wall Street, and as part of that victory, the balance of monetary debate swung toward the quantity-theory activists. However, in the ensuing years, activism—including devaluation in 1934 and domestic expansion thereafter—failed to yield very convincing results, and renewed depression in 1937 ultimately meant defeat for the activists as well. As a consequence, the vigorous debate of the 1920s, having already narrowed in the early 1930s, ultimately disappeared after 1937, not because either side conquered the other but because real-world events defeated both contenders.

The rout of traditional social forces and the evident bankruptcy of the traditional poles of monetary debate left an intellectual vacuum. In this context, the new ideas coming from across the ocean in John Maynard Keynes's *General Theory* rose rapidly to prominence, as much because of the proved demerits of the alternatives as because of their own unproved merits. In the debate about money, the main effect of the Keynesian influence was to widen the range of possible stabilization policies to include fiscal as well as monetary measures, with the consequence that one could thenceforth advocate restraint in one dimension combined with activism in the other. In the American context, this extra fiscal dimension provided a wedge for splitting apart the traditional populist bundling of activism with the quantity theory of money.

The Postwar Years

Alvin Hansen showed the way by opposing the use of monetary policy for stabilization, preferring instead a policy of "low and stable" interest rates in order to accommodate fiscal expansion during peacetime as well as war. Influenced by the anti-quantity-theory views of French economist Albert Aftalion, Hansen embraced fiscal policy and Keynes as the more effective outlet for his activist impulses. In Hansen's (1949,

1953) view, both Keynes and Aftalion were successors to Thomas Tooke, the great British banking school theorist. Thus, in terms of the traditional categories of American monetary debate, Hansen was staking claim to the banking/passive rules position in figure 1. It is important to emphasize, however, that he did so not because he favored restraint more generally (as did Laughlin) but rather in spite of (and even because of) the fact that he favored activism generally. Also note that, by the time of Hansen's works, the prewar distinction between active management and passive accommodation had modulated into the postwar distinction between discretion and rules (see Simons 1936), both essentially forms of active intervention. Depression and war had effectively eliminated the strong laissez-faire position. Hansen's rule—fixed low-interest rates—was among the first to be proposed, but it would not be the last.

As will become clear, Hansen's example established the structure of the post–World War II monetarist-Keynesian debate as a replay of the pre–World War I Fisher-Laughlin debate, but with the political sides switched. Aside from that leadership role, however, Hansen did not contribute much to postwar monetary debate, since as an activist he preferred to focus his attention on the more effective levers of economic policy and as an economic scientist he was never much interested in banking. From his research on business cycles, Hansen had concluded that money was more an effect than a cause, and he was content to promulgate that conclusion without much further analysis of the precise mechanisms within the banking system that led to it in practice. Elaboration of a new Keynesian monetary economics was therefore left to others, as well as elaboration of a new counter-Keynesian position. The former task began with the Gurley-Shaw project at the Brookings Institution during the 1950s, and the latter was undertaken by Friedman and Anna J. Schwartz at the National Bureau of Economic Research (NBER).

It has already been noted that Shaw and Friedman were prewar economists in their intellectual formation. More specifically, they were both pre-Keynesians, and, even more important, both were offsprings of the American institutionalist tradition, albeit hailing from different branches of that tradition. Shaw came from the Richard Ely–Young branch, and Friedman came from the Thorstein Veblen–Wesley Clair Mitchell branch (Mehrling 1997; Hirsch and De Marchi 1990; Backhouse 1995, chap. 11; Hammond 1996). In methodology, both were pragmatists in the mold of John Dewey, committed to scientific inquiry as an inductive process that abstracts general patterns from the data of experience. Both began with the data—Shaw with the balance sheets of financial intermediaries, and Friedman with time series of monetary liabilities. Both aimed ultimately to abstract a general theory from that data—Shaw by using the methods of accounting he had learned from his Stanford professor J. B. Canning, and Friedman by using the business cycle methods invented by his teacher Mitchell.

Bringing their prewar sensibilities into the postwar period, both Shaw and Friedman located themselves outside the monetary Walrasianism that became orthodoxy, and they did so for much the same reasons. Although both accepted the basic apparatus of Marshallian microeconomics, both rejected Keynesian macroeconomics as a framework for monetary analysis on the grounds that static equilibrium had little to offer for understanding the dynamic disequilibrium processes that were the essence of monetary phenomena. Both were also convinced, against the grain of orthodoxy, that monetary phenomena were important in their own right, not just reflections of more important real phenomena. As a consequence, at a time when most other economists sought incremental progress within a common intellectual framework, both Shaw and Friedman were forced to develop their own frameworks.

Despite their common intellectual formation, from the beginning Shaw and Friedman approached money from opposite directions. Shaw always placed banks at the center of his analysis, starting with his 1936 dissertation and continuing through his 1950 text *Money, Income, and Monetary Policy*. The Brookings project began in 1954 as a study of trends in commercial banking, and one of the most lasting contributions of *Money in a Theory of Finance* (Gurley and Shaw 1960) was an appreciation of banks as financial intermediaries and consequently an appreciation of the extent to which money is an "inside" asset. The same lesson was the basis of the debt intermediation view promoted by Shaw in his final book, *Financial Deepening in Economic Development* (1973). Shaw began with banks because he viewed banking institutions as the essential infrastructure of a decentralized market economy. Indeed, the function of banking was so important to him that he was unwilling to subordinate it to the goals of mere macroeconomic stabilization. It follows that Shaw fits into the banking/passive rules category in figure 1, along with Hansen, although he rejected Hansen's suggested rule and advocated instead stable growth of the reserve base to provide for growth of the financial infrastructure in line with economic growth (Shaw 1958).

Friedman, by contrast, always began with money. Indeed, in his 1948 "Monetary and Fiscal Framework for Economic Stability," which was the starting point of the NBER project "Monetary Factors in the Business Cycle," he urged elimination of banking by raising required reserves to 100 percent (Hammond 1996, chap. 3). Thenceforth, for Friedman, money was always first and foremost the liability of the government, not of banks. Even more, given his background in consumer theory, Friedman was inclined to treat money as a form of wealth, an "outside" capital asset with the peculiar property that its production was costless. In his view, the theory of money demand, or "velocity," linked changes in money supply to changes in nominal income through the quantity equation: $MV \rightarrow PY$. In principle, monetary policy could be used for macroeconomic stabilization, but the length and variability of lags made such use impracticable. Friedman's (1960) well-known recommendation for a constant money-growth rule as the guarantor of long-run price stability places him in the currency/ passive rules category in figure 1.

Not surprisingly, given the similarity of their projects, there was considerable rivalry between Shaw and Friedman. Early drafts of the Gurley-Shaw book were targeted explicitly at the quantity theory of money, as well as at the Keynesian theory of liquidity preference. Similarly, Friedman's 1960 advocacy of a constant money-growth rule can be seen as responding to Shaw's (1958) similar advocacy by providing very different grounds for the policy. What is surprising is that these initial jabs were also the final ones, not the prelude to a full-fledged debate. What happened? For both men, monetary Walrasianism presented itself as the more compelling intellectual opponent in the years after the publication of Patinkin's *Money, Interest, and Prices* (1956).

The story of why monetary Walrasianism became dominant must be told elsewhere. Suffice it to say that the rise of big government, which brought with it a rise in the demand for clear technical answers to detailed technical questions, had a lot to do with it on the demand side, and the influx of European émigré economists, many of them from engineering backgrounds, had a lot to do with it on the supply side (see Craufurd D. Goodwin's essay in this volume). The full story is no doubt more complicated; certainly it is by no means clear that the government was demanding what the economic engineers were prepared to supply. For present purposes, however, it is more important to trace the consequences than to examine the causes of the dominance of monetary Walrasianism.

The first consequence was a change in the language of monetary debate. Thus, the first two chapters of Gurley and Shaw 1960 argue within the framework of Patinkin 1956, and the appendix by Alain Enthoven (a student of Shaw and a recent Massachusetts Institute of Technology Ph.D. at the time) places the Gurley-Shaw theory within the framework of neoclassical growth theory. Similarly, Friedman's "Theoretical Framework for Monetary Analysis" ([1970] 1974, 32, 48) explicitly presents the quantity theory as a set of money demand and supply equations grafted onto a Walrasian system of commodity demand and supply equations (see also Friedman 1969, 3). For both Shaw and Friedman, these "formal" statements of their views subsequently became the standard references, not the more literary statements such as Shaw 1958 and Friedman 1960.

The second consequence was a shift in the subject of monetary debate toward stabilization. The monetary Walrasian language was designed to aid discussion of short-run stabilization, and the choice to speak that language necessarily also involved a choice of subject matter. Thus, the Gurley-Shaw theory was assimilated within the orthodox IS/LM framework as an argument about the ineffectiveness of countercyclical monetary policy on account of the prevalence of money substitutes (Tobin and Brainard 1963). And Friedman was assimilated as an argument about the relative effectiveness of monetary policy on account of the interest inelasticity of money demand. Thus, the contribution of these two institutionalists, neither of whom cared much for monetary Walrasianism or stabilization policy, was transformed (or reduced) into an empirical dispute over the slope of the LM curve.

The advent of monetary Walrasianism transformed the style and subject of traditional monetary debate, but it must be emphasized that influence operated in the other direction as well. Whereas the contributions of Shaw and Friedman were arguably diluted (and distorted) by their adoption of monetary Walrasian ground rules, monetary Walrasianism itself was enriched and reshaped by their interventions. From Shaw and Friedman, monetary Walrasianism gained a vital connection to the traditional concerns of American monetary debate. Most significant, Tobin, the leading monetary Walrasian, in his literary voice revealed himself as a proponent of the banking school approach, although he preferred to call it the "New View" (Tobin, 1963). Thus the monetarist Friedman and the Keynesian Tobin reiterated the pre–World War I Fisher-Laughlin debate, with the difference that now the currency school approach was associated with conservative policy views and the banking school approach was associated with more activist views.

In historical context, what the heat of the monetarist-Keynesian debate was all about becomes clear. Like the Fisher-Laughlin debate, it was about not only the fundamental nature of money but also its appropriate role in American society. Unfortunately, and also as in the Fisher-Laughlin debate, the titans largely talked past each other, despite their agreement to conduct the debate on the common ground of monetary Walrasianism. The language of Walrasianism allowed postwar debate to avoid the inflammatory rhetoric of populists versus bankers that had stymied communication during the Fisher-Laughlin era, but the new language turned out to pose obstacles of its own.

The problem was simply that the logic of Walrasianism left no place for money. As early as 1911, Young pointed out that the Walrasian model was already implicitly a monetary model because it posited a uniform price system that was inconceivable without the arbitrage operations of a monetary system. Postwar monetary Walrasianism, however, brought in money, not as the critical infrastructure of a decentralized market economy but rather as a separate sector of the economy sitting alongside the "real" sector. It was a way to talk about money if you already had another way to think about money, as both Friedman and Tobin did. It was, however, a deeply problematic way of thinking about money if you were starting from scratch, as the next generation of students inevitably was. In this sense, it could be argued that the elements of discontinuity ultimately proved stronger than the elements of continuity, at least for the history of postwar macroeconomics (see Mehrling 1996a). Monetary Walrasianism was a new language that, like any language, made it easier to talk about some things but harder to talk about others. Money, unfortunately, turned out to be one of the hard topics.

References

Anderson, Benjamin M. 1935. Money and Credit in Boom, Crisis, and Depression. *New York Times Annalist*, 3 May.

Backhouse, Roger E. 1995. *Interpreting Macroeconomics: Explorations in the History of Macroeconomic Thought*. London: Routledge.

Barber, William J. 1985. *From New Era to New Deal: Herbert Hoover, the Economists, and American Economic Policy, 1921–1933*. Cambridge: Cambridge University Press.

———. 1996. *Designs within Disorder: Franklin D. Roosevelt, the Economists, and the Shaping of American Economic Policy, 1933–1945*. Cambridge: Cambridge University Press.

Burgess, W. Randolph. 1927. *The Reserve Banks and the Money Market*. New York: Harper and Bros.

Currie, Lauchlin. 1934. *The Supply and Control of Money in the United States*. Cambridge, Mass.: Harvard University Press.

———. 1935. A Reply to Dr. B. M. Anderson, Jr. *Quarterly Journal of Economics* 49.4:694–704.

Dorfman, Joseph. 1959. *The Economic Mind in American Civilization*. New York: Viking.

Fisher, Irving (with Hans R. L. Cohrsson). 1934. *Stable Money: A History of the Movement*. New York: Adelphi.

Friedman, Milton. 1948. A Monetary and Fiscal Framework for Economic Stability. *American Economic Review* 38 (June): 245–64.

———. 1960. *A Program for Monetary Stability*. New York: Fordham University Press.

———. 1969. *The Optimum Quantity of Money and Other Essays*. Chicago: Aldine.

———. [1970] 1974. A Theoretical Framework for Monetary Analysis. *Journal of Political Economy* 78.2:193–238. Reprinted in *Milton Friedman's Monetary Framework: A Debate with His Critics*. Edited by Robert J. Gordon. Chicago: University of Chicago Press.

Gurley, John, and Edward S. Shaw. 1960. *Money in a Theory of Finance*. Washington, D.C.: Brookings Institution.

Hahn, F. H. 1965. On Some Problems of Proving the Existence of Equilibrium in a Monetary Economy. In *The Theory of Interest Rates*. Edited by F. H. Hahn and F. P. R. Brechling. London: Macmillan.

Hammond, J. Daniel. 1996. *Theory and Measurement: Causality Issues in Milton Friedman's Monetary Economics*. Cambridge: Cambridge University Press.

Hansen, Alvin. 1949. *Monetary Theory and Fiscal Policy*. New York: McGraw-Hill.

———. 1953. *A Guide to Keynes*. New York: McGraw-Hill.

Hawtrey, Ralph G. 1930. *Currency and Credit*. 3d ed. London: Longmans, Green.

Hirsch, Abraham, and Neil De Marchi. 1990. *Milton Friedman: Economics in Theory and Practice*. Ann Arbor: University of Michigan Press.

Mehrling, Perry. 1996a. The Evolution of Macroeconomics: The Origins of Post Walrasian Macroeconomics. In *Beyond Microfoundations: Post Walrasian Macroeconomics*. Edited by David Colander. Cambridge: Cambridge University Press.

———. 1996b. The Monetary Thought of Allyn Abbott Young. *HOPE* 28.4:607–32.

———. 1996c. The Relevance to Modern Economics of the Banking School View. In *Money in Motion: The Circulation and Post Keynesian Approaches*. Edited by Ghislain Deleplace and Edward J. Nell. London: Macmillan.

———. 1997. *The Money Interest and the Public Interest: The Development of American Monetary Thought, 1920–1970*. Cambridge, Mass.: Harvard University Press.

Modigliani, Franco. 1963. The Monetary Mechanism and Its Interaction with Real Phenomena. *Review of Economics and Statistics* 45.1:79–107.

Patinkin, Donald. 1956. *Money, Interest, and Prices*. Evanston, Ill.: Row, Peterson.

Rockoff, Hugh. 1990. The "Wizard of Oz" as a Monetary Allegory. *Journal of Political Economy* 98.4:739–60.

Shaw, Edward S. 1950. *Money, Income, and Monetary Policy*. Chicago: Irwin.

———. 1958. Money Supply and Stable Economic Growth. In *United States Monetary Policy: Its Contribution to Prosperity without Inflation*. New York: American Assembly.

———. 1973. *Financial Deepening in Economic Development*. New York: Oxford University Press.

Simons, Henry C. 1936. Rules versus Authorities in Monetary Policy. *Journal of Political Economy* 44.1:1–30.

Tobin, James. 1963. Commercial Banks as Creators of "Money." In *Banking and Monetary Studies*. Edited by Deane Carson. Homewood, Ill.: Richard D. Irwin.

———. 1969. A General Equilibrium Approach to Monetary Theory. *Journal of Money, Credit, and Banking* 1.1:15–29.

Tobin, James, and William C. Brainard. 1963. Financial Intermediaries and the Effectiveness of Monetary Controls. *American Economic Review* 53.2:383–400.

Young, Allyn. 1911. Some Limitations of the Value Concept. *Quarterly Journal of Economics* 25.3:409–28.

———. 1920. Review of *Currency and Credit*, by Ralph Hawtrey, and *Stabilizing the Dollar*, by Irving Fisher. *Quarterly Journal of Economics* 34.2:520–32.

Contributors

Roger E. Backhouse is professor of the history and philosophy of economics at the University of Birmingham. His most recent books are *Truth and Progress in Economic Knowledge* (1997) and *Explorations in Economic Methodology* (1998).

Márcia L. Balisciano is completing a doctorate in economic history at the London School of Economics. Her thesis is titled "U.S. Ideologies of Economic Planning, 1930–1950: Economic Visions for a Better America." She has most recently collaborated on a paper, "Positive Science, Normative Man: Lionel Robbins and the Political Economy of Art," with Steven G. Medema for the 1998 *HOPE* conference, "Economists and Art, Historically Considered."

Bradley W. Bateman teaches writing and economics at Grinnell College. He is the author, most recently, of *Keynes's Uncertain Revolution* (1996).

Jeff Biddle is professor of economics at Michigan State University. His research in labor economics and the history of economic thought has appeared in such journals as the *American Economic Review*, the *Journal of Political Economy*, the *Journal of Labor Economics*, and *History of Political Economy*. His current research concerns the development of the economics profession in the United States during the twentieth century.

Ross B. Emmett is John P. Tandberg Chair of Economics at Augustana University College. The focus of his research has been the work of Frank H. Knight. In recent work, he has begun to broaden his focus through work on the history of the University of Chicago Economics Department.

Craufurd D. Goodwin is James B. Duke Professor of Economics at Duke University. His book *Art and the Market: Roger Fry on Commerce in Art—Selected Writings, Collected and with an Interpretation* is forthcoming from University of Michigan Press in 1998.

D. Wade Hands is professor of economics at the University of Puget Sound. He is one of the editors (with John Davis and Uskali Mäki) of *The Handbook of Economic Methodology* (forthcoming) and is currently working on *Reflection without Rules: Economic Methodology and Contemporary Science Theory*.

Anne Mayhew is professor of history and associate dean of arts and sciences at the University of Tennessee. Among her current projects are a book on Clarence E. Ayres and his contributions to U.S. institutional economics.

Steven G. Medema is associate professor of economics at the University of Colorado at Denver. His research interests include law and economics and the economic role of government in the history of economic thought. His latest book (with Nicholas Mercuro) is *Economics and the Law: From Posner to Post Modernism* (1997).

Perry Mehrling is associate professor of economics at Barnard College of Columbia University. His most recent book is *The Money Interest and the Public Interest: The Development of American Monetary Thought, 1920–1970* (1997).

Philip Mirowski is Carl Koch Professor of Economics and the History and Philosophy of Science at the University of Notre Dame. He is the author of *More Heat than Light* (1989) and the editor of *Natural Images in Economics* (1994). He is finishing a book, titled *Machine Dreams*, on the impact of the "cyborg sciences" on late-twentieth-century economics, a multivolume *Collected Economics Works of William Thomas Thornton*, and a survey of the economics of scientific inquiry.

Mary S. Morgan is professor of the history and philosophy of economics at the University of Amsterdam and reader in the history of economics at the London School of Economics. She is currently working on the history and role of model building in economics.

Malcolm Rutherford is professor of economics and chair of the Department of Economics at the University of Victoria. He has published extensively on the history of American institutional economics and is the author of *Institutions in Economics: The Old and the New Institutionalism* (1994).

E. Roy Weintraub is professor of economics and director of the Center for Social and Historical Studies of Science at Duke University. His recent books concern the modern history of the interconnection between mathematics and economics.

Index

Adams, Henry Carter, 231
  legal-economic relationships, 204
  Sherman Antitrust Act, view of,
    181–83, 188
Addams, Jane, 44
Adler, Mortimer, 140–41, 145
administered-pricing, 19
AEA. *See* American Economic Association (AEA)
AER. See American Economic Review (AER)
Aftalion, Albert, 299–300
After the War—Full Employment (Hansen), 168
Alchian, Armen, 210–11
Aldrich, Morton A., 55
algebra, use of in theory articles, 91
Allen, R. G. D., 252
American Communist Party, 57
American Economic Association (AEA)
  directories, 88, 120, 126
  journal of, 86–87
  officers of, 4
  presidential addresses, 204
  resignations, 55
American Economic Review (AER), 86–86
  age of authors, 97n

classification of authors by type of affiliation, 95
institutional affiliation of authors, 101, 102–4
mathematics, use of, 92
nationality and affiliation of authors, 95–96
regression analysis, 94
Sherman Antitrust Act, views of, 181–82
American Institute of Christian Sociology, 34–36
American Journal of Mathematics, 245
American Mathematical Monthly, 243–44, 246
American monetary economics, 1920–1970, 293–306
  interwar years, 296–99
  monetary theories, typology, 298
  postwar years, 299–300
American Socialist Party, 39
Amoroso, Luigi, 244
Anderson, Benjamin, 298–99
Andrews, E. Benjamin, 181–83
Annals of the American Academy, 87
antitrust, 215
  Chicago approach, 220
  See also Sherman Antitrust Act

Arnold, Thurman, 194, 197–98
  personality of, 199
Arrow, Kenneth, 29, 100
Ayres, Clarence
  firing of, 56, 57
  New Republic, 60

Bach, George Leland, 73, 78
Backhouse, Roger E.
  changes after 1945, 17, 20
  journal articles, 1920–1960,
    85–107
  popularity of methods, 6
Bacon, Francis, 242–43
Bailey, Martin, 273
Balisciano, Márcia L.
  New Deal, planning, 23
  planning approach of, 5, 46,
    153–78, 220
Bateman, Bradley W., 29–52
  American Economic Association
    (AEA), 4
  market solution, 10
  Social Creed movement, 5
  Social Gospel movement, 14
Becker, Gary, 170
Bellamy, Edward, 54
Bemis, Edward W., 55
Benforado, Caroline, 235n
Benton, William
  business leadership, 69
  CED, officer of, 70
Berkeley, University of California,
    101, 105
Betti, Enrico, 230
Biddle, Jeff, 22, 108–33
Birkhoff, G. D., 241, 250
Blaisdell, Thomas, 173
Bork, Robert, 209
Bowen, Howard, 58
Bowley, A. L., 248, 253
Brady, Dorothy, 16
Brains Trust, 62, 69, 166
Brewster, Ralph, 165n

Brookings, Robert, 68–69
Brookings Graduate School, 22
Brookings Institution
  creation of, 68–69
  grants to, 75
  Gurley-Shaw project, 300–301,
    303
  International Studies Group, 76–77
Browder, Earl, 57
Bryan, William, 294
Buckley, William F., Jr.
  *God and Man at Yale: The Supersti-
    tions of "Academic Freedom,"*
    58–60
*Bulletin of the American Mathemati-
    cal Society*, 247, 250
Bullock, Charles
  Sherman Antitrust Act, view of,
    183, 187–88, 190
Bureau of Agricultural Economics,
    13
Burns, Arthur, 71, 146–48
Bush, Vannevar
  Science, the Endless Frontier, 65
business, as patron of economics,
    67–74
business economy planning, 162–63
business education, 71–74. *See also
    specific university*

Calabresi, Guido, 211, 216
California, University of
  Evans, papers of, 250
Calkins, Robert, 78
careers of economists, 1920–1946,
    118–29
  early-career job types, 124
  graduate programs, characteristics
    of, 120
  late-career job types, 125
Carey, Henry, 54
Carnegie Corporation, 68
Carnegie Endowment for Inter-
    national Peace, 74

Carnegie-Mellon University
    Graduate School of Industrial
        Administration, 73
CEA. *See* Council of Economic
    Advisers (CEA)
CED. *See* Committee for Economic
    Development (CED)
Chamberlain, Neil, 78
Chamberlin, Edward, 85
Chase, Stuart
    defenses against, 70
    planning, 156n
    social management planning,
        159–60
    technical-industrial planning, 160n
    Veritas Foundation pamphlet, 175n
Chicago, University of, 198, 199
    authors of journal articles, 1920–
        1960, 100–101
    Committee on Social Thought
        (CST), 142
    debate over general education,
        139–42
    disciplinary competence, 142–48
    economics curriculum, changes in,
        7, 23, 134–50
    firing of radical economists, 55
    legal-economic relationships,
        Chicago school and, 208–11,
        215, 217–18
    post–World War II economics, 262,
        266–74
    progressive-pragmatist education,
        136–39
"The Chicago Trust Conference"
    (Hatfield), 188
Christian Progressives, 44
Christian Socialism, 36
Civil Rights Movement, 42
Clark, John Bates
    Carnegie Endowment for Interna-
        tional Peace, appointment to, 74
    Control of Trusts, 186, 190–93
    legal-economic relationships, 206

marginalism, 3, 37, 46, 48
    Sherman Antitrust Act, view of,
        188
Clark, John Maurice, 85
    articles by, 45–46
    Control of Trusts, 186, 190–93
    institutional and neoclassical
        theory, 4
    macroeconomic planning, 165
    orthodox theory, 2, 3
    social management planning, 157,
        159
Clayton Act, 191–92, 197
Coal industry proposals, 22
Coase, Ronald H.
    "Federal Communications Com-
        mission," 213
    judges' application of logic, 219
    operation of markets, theorem and,
        221
    "Problem of Social Cost," 202–4,
        211, 213–16, 222
cold war
    academic effects, 16
    economic ideologies, 14, 20
    post–World War II, fears of com-
        munism, 56–58
Coleman, W. M., 189–90
Colm, Gerhard, 173
Columbia University
    authors of journal articles, 1920–
        1960, 100–101, 105
    Statistical Research Group (SRG),
        265
Committee for Economic Develop-
    ment (CED), 70–71, 172
Committee on Social Thought (CST),
    142
Commons, John R., 85
    controversies, 22
    data collection, 45
    documentary histories, 2
    Herron, George D., reaction to, 36
    institutionalism, 109

Commons, John R. (*continued*)
  leadership of, 41
  legal-economic relationships,
    205–7
  Legal Foundations of Capitalism,
    207
  return from private sector, 37
  Stable Money League, 3–4
consumer theory, 20
Control of Trusts (Clark and Clark),
  186, 190–93
Cooper, William W., 73
Copeland, Charles Townsend, 229
Copeland, M. A., 2, 6
Copeland, Morris, 119n
Cornell University
  authors of journal articles, 1920–
    1960, 100
Council of Economic Advisers (CEA),
  62–63, 174
Cournot, Augustin, 243, 244, 246,
  247
Cowles, Alfred, 268, 274
  NBER and, 276–77
Cowles Commission, 267
  arrival of, 268, 282
  early years of, 12
  Keynes-Slutsky alliance, 280
  Marschak, domination by, 274–76
  measurement without theory
    debate, 10
  post–World War II economics,
    262
  seminars, 147
creativity, changes, 43–46
Croce, Benedetto, 239
Croly, Herbert, 44
CST. *See* Committee on Social
  Thought (CST)
Currency and Credit (Hawtry), 297
Currie, Lauchlin
  American monetary economics,
    298–99
  Bureau of the Budget, 173

  macroeconomic planning, 165,
    168–68
  *The Supply and Control of Money
    in the United States*, 298

Daily Maroon, 141
Daniel, Price, 238
Dante, writings on, 229, 240–41
Davenport, H. J., 3
Davis, Harold Thayer, 274
debate over general education
  Chicago, University of, 139–42
Debs, Eugene, 39
defense, nuclear war, 64
Delano, Frederic A., 161n
Demsetz, Harold
  property rights, economics of,
    210–11
Dewey, John, 44, 272
  social management planning, 157,
    159
Director, Aaron, 267
  Journal of Law and Economics,
    209, 215
  responsibilities at Chicago, 209
Douglas, Paul, 70, 267, 282

early-career job types, 124
Eccles, Marriner, 165, 168
Econometrica, 87
  age of authors, 98n
Econometric Institute, 256
econometrics
  1920–1960, journal articles, 94
Econometrics Society, 245, 252, 256
Economica, 252
Economic Bill of Rights, 174
Economic Journal, 252
Economics: An Introductory Text
  (Samuelson), 173
*The Economics of Defense in the
  Nuclear Age* (Hitch and
  McKean), 64
Economic Stabilization Board, 170n

Edgeworth, Francis Ysidro, 250, 262
efficiency, 44–45
Efroymson, Clarence, 96
1890s, 32–37, 54. *See also* Sherman
    Antitrust Act
Einstein, Albert, 231
Eisner, Robert, 16, 58
Ely, Richard T., 44
    American Institute of Christian
        Sociology, 36
    data collection, 45
    Monopolies and Trusts, 190
    Outlines of Economics, 37–38
    persecution of, 55
    *Property and Contract in Their
        Relations to the Distribution of
        Wealth*, 41
    reform efforts, 41
    Social Gospel movement, 34–35
Emmett, Ross B.
    University of Chicago economics
        curriculum, changes in, 7, 23,
        134–50
empirical articles, defined, 89
empirical techniques
    1920–1960, journal articles, 93–95
employment
    Employment Act of 1946, 62, 77
    Full Employment Act of 1945,
        174
    interwar period, 168. *See also* New
        Deal
Employment Act of 1946, 62, 77, 174
Enke, Stephen, 64
Evans, Griffith C., 19, 227–59
    Bacon, Francis, writings on,
        242–43
    California, Griffith Conrad Evans
        papers, 250
    Dante, writings on, 229, 240–41
    economics, connection to, 243–48
    *Mathematical Introduction to Eco-
        nomics* (Evans), 248–50
    mathematician, as, 238

mathematization of economics, 230
    "The Role of Hypothesis in Eco-
        nomic Theory," 253
Ezekiel, Mordecai, 171n, 173
    New Deal, planning, 12
    technical-industrial planning,
        160–61
    Towards World Prosperity, 172–73

FAES. *See* Federated American Engi-
    neering Societies (FAES)
"Federal Communications Commis-
    sion" (Coase), 213
Federal Council of Churches, 41
Federal Reserve System
    establishment of, 296–97
    Great Depression and, 299
    macroeconomic planning, 165, 168
    World War II, 96
Federal Trade Commission Act,
    191–92
Federated American Engineering
    Societies (FAES), 194
Fetter, Frank A., 3
    resignation from AEA, 55
    Sherman Anti Trust Act, defense
        of, 195
*Financial Deepening in Economic
    Development* (Shaw), 301
Fisher, Irving, 85, 252, 304
    American monetary economics,
        296–98
    marginalism, 46
    The Nature of Capital and Income,
        206
    Stable Money League, 3–4
Flexner, Abraham, 71
    grants, comments on, 75–76
Ford, Henry and Edsel, 77
Ford Foundation
    business education reform, 72
    generosity of, 77–78
foundations, as patrons of economics,
    74–78

Foundations for Economic Education, 58

The Foundations of Economic Analysis (Samuelson), 29, 85

Free Silver movement, 294

Friedman, Milton
American monetary economics, 294–95, 300, 302–3
"The Marshallian Demand Curve," 271–73
"Monetary and Fiscal Framework for Economic Stability," 302
money and banking seminar, 147
Price Theory, 272–73
Simons, Henry, debate over reappointment of, 209
Statistical Research Group, 265

Frisch, Ragnar, 252, 274

Full Employment Act of 1945, 174

"Fundamental Points of Potential Theory" (Volterro), 241

Furniss, Edgar S., 60

Gaither, Rowan, 78

Galbraith, John Kenneth
Buckley, William, and, 60–61
institutional affiliation, 100
persecution of, 58

Gates, George A., 32–37

General Theory of Employment, Interest, and Money (Keynes), 100n, 164, 170, 299

George, Henry, 54

German émigrés, 88n

Gideonese, Harry, 140–42

Girschick, Meyer, 279

Gladden, Washington, 32–33
Social Gospel movement, 34

God and Man at Yale: The Superstitions of "Academic Freedom" (Buckley), 58–60

Goodwin, Craufurd D., 53–81, 198
cold war, 14
institutionalism, decline of, 21

post–World War II, 13
World War II, government departments, 9; 12–13

government, as patron of economics, 62–67

graduate economics education. *See specific university*

Graduate School of Industrial Administration, 73

Great Depression
call for economic action, 5, 11–12
Federal Reserve and, 299
institutionalism and, 46–47
planning and, 154
religion, influence on, 43

Greenberg, Clement, 135

Gurley, John, 295, 300–301, 303

Haavelmo, Trygve, 279

Hadley, Arthur T.
institutions, studies of, 3
post–World War II economics, 13
Sherman Antitrust Act, view of, 181–83

Hagen, Everett F., 58

Hale, Robert Lee, 205–8

Hamilton, Earl, 145

Hamilton, Walton H.
articles by, 45–46
Brookings, Robert, correspondence, 68
case studies, 2
coal industry proposals, attacks for, 22
legal-economic relationships, 204

Hands, D. Wade, 260–92
consumer theory, 20

Hansen, Alvin
After the War—Full Employment, 168
American monetary economics, 299–300
defenses against, 70
macroeconomic planning, 168–69

persecution of radical economists, 57–58
stagnationist version of Keynesian economics, 69
Harding, President Warren, 45
Harrod, Roy, 48
Harvard Corporation, 58
Harvard University
authors of journal articles, 1920–1960, 100–101, 105
business education, 73
Keynes at Harvard (Veritas Foundation), 175n
Parsons report, 66–67
Hatfield, Henry Rand
"The Chicago Trust Conference," 188
Hauge, Gabriel, 71
Hawtry, Ralph
Currency and Credit, 297
Hayek, Friedrich von, 142
The Road to Serfdom, 172
Haymarket Riots (1886), 34
Hedges, Marion H., 174n
Herron, George D., 32–37, 44
scandal, 39–40
heterodox approaches, 85
Hicks, John R., 48
Value and Capital, 170
Hicks-Slutsky approach, 170
higher education, as patron of economics, 54–62
business education, 71–74
persecution of radical economists, 55–61
Hillquit, Morris, 39
Hitch, Charles J.
The Economics of Defense in the Nuclear Age, 64
Hitler, Adolph, 96
Hoffman, Paul
business leadership, 69
CED, officer of, 70
Ford Foundation and, 78

Homan, Paul T.
Sherman Antitrust Act, view of, 196
homo oeconomicus, 235
Hoover, President Herbert
Federated American Engineering Societies (FAES), 194
planning idea and, 156n
Sherman Antitrust Act, 194–96
Hopkins, Harry, 168
Hotchkiss, Dean, 71–72
Hotelling, Harold
Cowles program and, 279
Friedman's demand curve, 272, 273–74
institutional affiliation, 100
legitimacy of economics, 65
post–World War II economics, 261–66
review of Evans' book, 250–51
Samuelson, Paul, and, 286, 287
Hotelling-Schultz impasse. *See* Hotelling, Harold; Schultz, Henry
Houston, Sam, 238
Houston Chronicle, 238–39
Houston Post, 240
Houthakker, Hendrik, 286
Hull House, 44
Hume, David, 242
Hurwicz, Leonid, 16, 274, 281
Hutchins, Robert, 136, 268
Gideonese's campaign against, 142
reform proposals, 140–41, 145

Illinois, University of
authors of journal articles, 1920–1960, 100
persecution of radical economists, 58
Industries monopolisés aux Etats-Unis (Rousier), 190
Innis, Harold, 145
institutional affiliation of authors, 1920–1960, 100–104

institutionalism
　decline in, University of Wisconsin,
　　22, 108–33
　1920s, 46
　orthodox theory, 2–4
　scientific investigation, 6–7
　setbacks, 48–49
　waning of, 21–23
institutions
　1920–1960, journal articles,
　　100–104
Interstate Commerce Commission, 183
interwar period (World War I and II)
　American monetary economics,
　　296–99
　legal-economic relationships,
　　206–8
　planning, 153–69
　pluralism, 1–4
　social management planning,
　　157–60
　standards, changing, 5–11
Iowa College, 32, 34
Israel, Giorgio, 230n
Ives, Charles, 44

Jacoby, Neil, 70
Jakob, Victor
　Night Thoughts of a Classical
　　Physicist, 231
James, William, 238
Jenks, Jeremiah, 190
Jevons, William Stanley, 247
John, Isabel Mary, 238
John, Robert A., 238
Johnson, Hugh, 167
Jones, Wesley L., 165n
Jordan, David Starr, 55
journal articles, 1920–1960. See
　　1920–1960, journal articles
Journal of Law and Economics, 216
　editors, 215
　founding of, 202, 209
　significance of, 217

Journal of Political Economy (JPE),
　　86–87
　age of authors, 97–98n
　Hotelling and Schultz articles, 263
　institutional affiliation of authors,
　　101
　mathematics, use of, 92
　Sherman Antitrust Act, views of,
　　181–82, 189–90
JPE. See Journal of Political Economy
　　(JPE)
Justice Department
　Anti-Trust Division, 197

Kansas State University
　firing of radical economists, 55
Kant, Immanuel, 242
Katona, George, 276
Kelly, H. J., 250
Keniston study, 120
Kenyon bills, 165n
Kerwith, Jerome, 140
Keynes, John Maynard
　General Theory of Employment,
　　Interest, and Money, 100n, 164,
　　170, 299
　persecution of, 57–58
　Roosevelt, introduction to, 169
　Slutsky, alliance with, 280
　See also Keynesian economics
Keynes at Harvard (Veritas Founda-
　　tion), 175n
Keynesian economics
　"commercial," 71
　heresy, as, 58
　market economics and, 16–17
　Marxism and, 15
　revolution, 99n
　stagnationist version of, 69
　success of, 14
　supplanting by, 47–49
Keyserling, Leon, 63, 171n
King, Martin Luther, Jr., 42
King, William Lyon Mackenzie, 74

The Kingdom, 32
Kingdom movement, 32–37
  decline of, 43
  growth of, 39
Klein, Lawrence R., 257, 279
Knight, Frank, 3, 69, 85, 267
  example, as, 146
  general education, debate over,
    140–42
  influence of, 144, 145
  institutional affiliation, 100
  legal-economic relationships, 210
  marginalism, 46
  Marshall, Alfred, article on, 271
  natural science method, on, 6
  realism and, 44
  "The Ricardian Theory of Produc-
    tion and Distribution," 144
  Slichter, attack on, 47
  Slutsky approach and, 269–71
Koopmans, Tjalling, 277–78, 281
  confrontation, 47
  Yale University, move to, 265
Kuznets, Simon, 173

Lange, Oskar, 145, 269
  influence of, 144
  recruiting by, 274
  Walrasian approach, 267–68
late-career job types, 125
Laughlin, Lawrence, 296–98
  American monetary economics,
    304
Lazarsfeld, Paul
  survey on threats to academic free-
    dom, 61–62
legal-economic relationships, 202–24
  definition of economics, 205
  interwar period (World War I and
    II), 206–8
  new law, 211–13
  old law, 204–11
  transformation of law and econom-
    ics, 213–22

Legal Foundations of Capitalism
    (Commons), 207
Leibniz, Gottfried, 242, 243
Leontief, Wassily, 173, 274
Lerner, Abba, 173
Levi, Edward
  antitrust course at Chicago, 209
Lewis, H. Gregg, 268
  disciplinary competence and,
    146–47
List, Friedrich, 54
Locke, John, 242

macroeconomic planning, 164–65,
    167–69
Macy, Jesse, 34
Malinowski, Bronislaw, 140
marginalism, 3, 37, 46, 48
market solution, 10
Marschak, Jacob, 269
  Cowles Commission, domination
    of, 274–76
  Hotelling-Schultz impasse and,
    276–81
  neoclassicism, verification, 278–79
  *Theory and Measurement of
    Demand*, review of, 274–75
Marshall, Alfred, 239, 247
  Friedman's article on, 271–73
Marshall, Leon C.
  Chicago, University of, 137–39,
    143
"The Marshallian Demand Curve"
    (Friedman), 271–73
Marx, Karl
  legal-economic relationships, 202
Marxism
  Keynesian economics and, 15
Mason, Edward, 198
Massachusetts Institute of Technology
    (MIT)
  institutional affiliation of authors,
    101, 105
  post–World War II economics, 262

Masters, Edgar Lee, 44
*Mathematical Groundwork of Eco-
    nomics* (Bowley), 248
*Mathematical Introduction to Eco-
    nomics* (Evans), 248–50
mathematics
    move to, 16, 48–49
    1920–1960, journal articles, 92
    role in economics, 19–20
Mayhew, Anne, 220
    market solution, 10
    New Deal, planning, 23
    Sherman Antitrust Act, 179–201
McCarthyism
    impact on economics, 15, 17
McKean, Roland N.
    *The Economics of Defense in the
        Nuclear Age*, 64
Means, Gardiner C.
    administered-pricing, 19
    Committee for Economic Develop-
        ment, 172
    legal-economic relationships, 205
    macroeconomic planning, 165
    New Deal, planning, 23
    technical-industrial planning,
        160–62
Medema, Steven G.
    legal-economic relationships,
        202–24
    primacy of economic efficiency, 10
    Wisconsin school of institutional-
        ism, 22
Mehrling, Perry
    American monetary economics,
        1920– 1970, 293–306
    continuity of ideas, 21
    new style of economics, 18
Merriam, Charles E., 161n
Michigan, University of
    careers of economists, 1920– 1946,
        118–29
Millikan, Robert, 76
minimum wage, 41n

Minnesota, University of
    careers of economists, 1920–1946,
        118–29
Mints, Lloyd, 145, 267
Mirowski, Philip, 20, 260–92
MIT. *See* Massachusetts Institute of
    Technology (MIT)
Mitchell, Wesley Clair, 85
    business cycle, 67
    National Bureau of Economic
        Research (NBER) and, 45,
        147–48
    national security, economics and,
        65
    objective methods, 9
    quantitative methods, 2, 4, 6
    separation between science and
        policy advocacy, 22
    social management planning, 159
Modigliani, Franco, 16, 58
"Monetary and Fiscal Framework for
    Economic Stability" (Friedman),
    302
monetary economics, 1920–1970,
    293–306
monetary Walrasianism, 294–96,
    302–4
Money, Income, and Monetary Policy
    (Shaw), 301
Monopolies and Trusts (Ely), 190
Moody, John
    Truth About the Trusts, 186
Moore, Henry Ludwell, 248, 262–63
Morgenstern, Oskar, 64
Mosak, Jacob, 268
Moulton, Harold, 76–77
muckrakers, 44

Nathan, Robert, 170
National Bureau of Economic
    Research (NBER), 22
    beginnings of, 45
    Cowles, strife between, 276–77
    grants to, 74

model developed by Mitchell, 147–48
new economics, 300, 302
National Defense Research Council, 265
National Economic Council, 163
National Industrial Recovery Act, 46–47
National Planning Association (NPA), 173
National Recovery Administration (NRA), 12, 62, 69, 166
  failure of, 194, 197
  WIB as model, 167
National Resources Committee (NRC)
  Industrial Committee, 160–61
National Resources Planning Board (NRPB), 62, 168
  Hansen, proposal by, 69
  Industrial Committee, 172
National Science Foundation (NSF), 65, 67
  creation of, 77
natural science method, 6–7
The Nature of Capital and Income (Fisher), 206
NBER. *See* National Bureau of Economic Research (NBER)
Nearing, Scott, 55
Nef, John
  debate over general education, 140, 142
  disciplinary competence and, 145
neoclassical economics, interwar context, 3–4
Neumann, John von, 281
New Deal, 56
  backing of, 49n
  economic policies of, 5, 11, 23
  planning approaches, influences of, 155–69
  Wisconsin institutionalism and, 114
New Republic, 44, 60
new style of economics, 18–21

Neyman-Pearson language, 279
Niebuhr, R., 43–44
Night Thoughts of a Classical Physicist (Jakob), 231
1920–1946, careers of economists, 118–29
  early-career job types, 124
  graduate programs, characteristics of, 120
  late-career job types, 125
1920–1960, journal articles, 85–107
  age of authors, 97–99
  authors, 95–99
  classification of authors by type of affiliation, 95
  contents of articles, 88–85
  database analysis, 86–88
  econometrics, 94
  empirical techniques, 93–95
  institutional affiliation of authors, 100–104
  mathematics, use of, 92
  nationality and affiliation of authors, 95–96
  regression analysis, 94
  theoretical and applied economics, 88–91
1920–1970, American monetary economics, 294–306
1920s, 46–48
1930s
  Sherman Antitrust Act, 193–98
Northwestern Congregationalist, 32
Northwestern University
  careers of economists, 1920–1946, 118–29
NRA. *See* National Recovery Administration (NRA)
NRC. *See* National Resources Committee (NRC)
NRPB. *See* National Resources Planning Board (NRPB)
NSF. *See* National Science Foundation (NSF)

nuclear war, defense, 64
Nutter, Warren, 209

objective methods, 9–10
oligopoly demand curve, 96
John M.Olin Foundation, 221
Opie, Redvers, 76–77
orthodox economics, interwar
    context, 3
*Our Country: Its Possible Future
    and Its Present Crisis* (Strong),
    32
Outlines of Economics (Ely), 37–38

Pabst Brewing Company, 171n
Paley Commission, 77
Pareto, Vilfredo, 236, 251
    criticisms of, 255
    Moore influenced by, 263
Parsons, Talcott
    Social Science Research Council,
        report to, 66–67
Patinkin, Don, 16
Peel Act (1844), 294
Pennsylvania, University of
    firing of radical economists, 55
Pepper, George W., 165n
Perlman, Selig, 109
persecution of radical economists,
    55–61
Ph.D. programs
    careers of economists, 1920–1946,
        118–29
    characteristics of programs, 120
    characteristics of programs employ-
        ing graduates, 128
Pigou, A. C., 202–3
planning, 5, 23, 46, 153–78
    business economy planning,
        162–63
    ideologies, 158
    macroeconomic planning, 164–65,
        167–69
    post–World War II era, 171–74

social management planning,
    157–60
technical-industrial planning,
    160–62
World War II, 169–71
Plant, Arnold, 215
pluralism, 2–5
    interwar pluralism, 1–2
Poincaré, Henri, 233, 234
Point Four Program, 58
Popper, Karl, 272
A Positive Program for Laissez Faire
    (Simons), 208
Posner, Richard A.
    legal-economic relationships, 215,
        217, 219
post–World War II economics, 13, 30,
    260–92
    American monetary economics,
        299–300
    higher education, attacks on acade-
        mic economists, 55–61
    planning, 171–74
    supply and demand, 260–62
pragmatist education
    Chicago, University of, 136–39
    New Plan for the College, 136
Pratt, John, 76
Price Theory (Friedman), 272–73
Princeton
    authors of journal articles, 1920–
        1960, 101
"Problem of Social Cost" (Coase),
    202–4, 211, 213–16, 222
Progressives, 5, 44
    Chicago, University of, 136–39,
        145
    New Deal, backing of, 49n
    reform vs. Progressivism, 39n
    Wisconsin institutionalism and, 114
*Property and Contract in Their Rela-
    tions to the Distribution of
    Wealth* (Ely), 41
property rights, economics of, 210–11

Protestantism, 30–31, 39, 41, 49
religious depression, 43n

QJE. See Quarterly Journal of Economics (QJE)
Quarterly Journal of Economics (QJE), 86–87
age of authors, 97–98n
institutional affiliation of authors, 101
mathematics, use of, 92
Sherman Antitrust Act, views of, 181–82, 187–88, 192–93, 196

Rand, Carrie, 39–40
RAND Corporation, 64
Rauschenbusch, Walter
Kingdom Movement, 33
rise of, 40
war, feelings on, 42–43
Redfield, Robert, 277
regression analysis
1920–1960, journal articles, 94
Reid, Margaret, 16
Rendiconto Accademia Lencei (Volterra), 228
Review of Economics and Statistics, 87
Review of Economic Studies, 87
age of authors, 98n
Reynolds, Lloyd, 78
"The Ricardian Theory of Production and Distribution" (Knight), 144
Rice Institute, 233, 238–41
Rice Institute Pamphlet, 240–42
Rice University, 248
Riis, Jacob, 40
The Road to Serfdom (Hayek), 172
Rockefeller, John D.
Laura Spelman Rockefeller Memorial Foundation, 75, 79
Rockefeller Foundation, 277
establishment of, 74
Laura Spelman Rockefeller Memorial Foundation, 75

Roiti, Antonio, 230
"The Role of Hypothesis in Economic Theory" (Evans), 253
Rome, University of, 235n
Roos, Charles
articles by, 246
Econometric Institute, 256
Econometrics Society, 245, 252
mathematical economics, 274
NRA and, 12
review of Evans' book, 250
Roosevelt, President Franklin D.
Arnold, Thurman, appointment of, 194
Brains Trust, 62, 69, 166
Economic Bill of Rights, 174
Keynes, introduction by Tugwell, 169
planning ideologies and, 165–66, 168
Sherman Antitrust Act and, 196–97
victory, reasons for, 299
See also New Deal
Ross, Edward A., 55
Rousier, P. de
Industries monopolisés aux Etats-Unis, 190
Ruml, Beardsley
business leadership, 69
Laura Spelman Rockefeller Memorial Foundation, 75–76, 79
Russell Sage Foundation, 74
Russian planning, interwar period, 156

Salant, Walter, 169
Samuels, Warren, 4
Samuelson, Paul, 48, 282–87
age of authors, on, 97
Economics: An Introductory Text, 173
The Foundations of Economic Analysis, 29, 85

Samuelson, Paul (*continued*)
  Hotelling-Schultz impasse, 266–67,
    286, 287
  institutional affiliation, 100
  Keynesian revolution, 99n
  persecution of, 58
  post–World War II economics, 13,
    262
Savage, Leonard, 265
Schultz, Henry
  Cowles program and, 279
  death of, 267
  empirical techniques, 93
  Friedman's demand curve, 272
  post–World War II economics,
    261–66
  review of Evans' book, 250–51, 254
  Samuelson, Paul, and, 282–83,
    286, 287
  *Theory and Measurement of
    Demand*, 264, 282
Schultz, Theodore, 70
Schwartz, Anna J., 300
Science, the Endless Frontier (Bush),
    65
scientific investigation, 6–7
scientific jury system, 76
Seligman, E. R. A., 38
Seligman, Edwin, 3
Sella, Quintano, 230–31
Shaw, Edward Stone
  American monetary economics,
    294–95, 300–303
  *Financial Deepening in Economic
    Development*, 301
  *Money, Income, and Monetary
    Policy*, 301
Sherman, John, 180n
Sherman Antitrust Act, 179–201
  alternative explanation, 187–93
  economists' views, 181–93
  1930s, 193–98
  Whiggish view towards, 184–87
Shubik, Martin, 64

Sidgwick, Henry, 202–3
Simon, Herbert, 73–74
Simons, Henry Calvert, 70, 267
  general education, debate over, 141
  influence of, 145
  legal-economic relationships, 208
  *A Positive Program for Laissez
    Faire*, 208
  reappointment of, debate, 208–9
  social management planning and,
    157
Sinclair, Upton, 44
Slichter, Sumner
  articles by, 45–46
  Knight, attack by, 47
Sloan, Alfred P., 76–77
Sloan Foundation, 74
Slutsky, Eugen, 269
  Keynes, alliance with, 280
  See also Slutsky equation
Slutsky equation, 264, 266, 269–71,
    273, 275, 283
Small, Albion, 35
Smith, Adam, 202, 210
Social Creed movement, 5
  acceptance of, 14, 15
  agenda of, 31
  influence of, 42
  principles of, 40–41
Social Gospel movement, 30–32
  collapse of, 5
  decline of, 41, 48
  influence of, 42–43
  language of, 14–15
  leadership of, 34
  message of, 38–39
  scandal and, 39–40
Social Science Research Council,
    66–67
  grants to, 75
Solow, Robert, 29
Soule, George, 159–60
Laura Spelman Rockefeller Memorial
    Foundation, 75, 79

Stable Money League, 4
stagnationist version of Keynesian
    economics, 69
Stalin, Joseph, 156
standards, changing
    interwar period (World War I and
        II), 5–11
Standford, Mrs. Leland, 55
Stanford University
    firing of radical economists, 55
    Food Research Institute, 263
    institutional affiliation of authors,
        101, 105
state obligation to support sciences,
    debate over, 64–65
Stein, Herbert, 171n
Steiner. Edward O., 42–43
Stigler, George
    institutional economics, comment
        on, 218, 268
    Simons, Henry, debate over reap-
        pointment of, 209
    Statistical Research Group, 265
    Theory of Price, 273
    Walgreen professorship, 269
Stowe, Harriet Beecher
    Uncle Tom's Cabin, 32
Strong, Josiah, 32–37
Sumner, William G., 11
The Supply and Control of Money
    in the United States (Currie),
    298
supply and demand
    post–World War II economics,
        260–62
Swope, Gerard
    business economy planning, 163
    "Swope plan," 195, 199

Taussig, Frank, 3, 85, 100
Taylor, Frederick W.
    Progressivism and, 44
    technical-industrial planning, 162
technical-industrial planning, 160–62

Temporary National Economic
    Committee, 77
Terbough, George, 70
Texas, University of
    firing of radical economists, 56, 57
theoretical and applied economics
    1920–1960, journal articles, 88–91
    theory and empirical articles, 91
Theory and Measurement of Demand
    (Schultz), 264, 274–75, 282
theory articles
    algebra, use of, 91
    defined, 89
theory-empirical articles, defined, 89
The Theory of Business Enterprise
    (Veblen), 188n
Theory of Functionals and of Integral
    and Integro-differential Equa-
    tions (Volterro), 228
Theory of Price (Stigler), 273
Thielens, Wagner, Jr., 61–62
Tobin, James, 295
Towards World Prosperity (Ezekiel),
    172–73
transformation
    character of, 1–26
    contexts of, 29–81
    1920–1960, 85–107
The Trend of Economics (Tugwell),
    138
Truman, Harry, 63
    Bush, Vannevar, report of, 65
    Point Four Program, 58
Truth About the Trusts (Moody), 186
Tugwell, Rexford, 2
    academic career, 172
    articles by, 45–46
    experimental economics, 6
    Keynes, introduction to Roosevelt,
        169
    macroeconomic planning, 165
    National Recovery Administration
        (NRA), 197
    New Deal, planning, 12, 23, 46, 166

Tugwell, Rexford (*continued*)
  persecution of, 57
  Sherman Anti Trust Act and, 196
  social management planning, 157,
    159
  technical-industrial planning,
    160n
  The Trend of Economics, 138
Tullock, Gordon, 209
Type P trainers and economists,
  117

Uncle Tom's Cabin (Stowe), 32

Value and Capital (Hicks), 170
Veblen, Thorstein, 2
  engineers, importance of, 45
  Sherman Anti Trust Act and,
    196
  social management planning,
    159
  technical-industrial planning,
    162
  The Theory of Business Enterprise,
    188n
Veritas Foundation, 58, 175n
Viner, Jacob, 3, 267
  influence of, 144, 145
  marginalism, 46
  Princeton, departure for, 267
  skepticism, 282
Volterra, Vito, 227–37
  economic theory and, 234–37
  "Fundamental Points of Potential
    Theory," 241
  Pareto, Vilfredo, critique of, 255
  Rendiconto Accademia Lencei
    (Volterra), 228
  *Theory of Functionals and of Inte-
    gral and Integro-differential
    Equations*, 227

Wald, Abraham, 265
Walgreen professorship, 269

Wallis, Allen, 265
  dean, appointment as, 269
Walras, Léon, 247, 263
Walrasian mathematical theory,
  267–68, 281
War Industries Board (WIB), 160,
  167
War Production Board (WPB), 96,
  170
Watkins, Myron, 192–95
Weber, Max, 140
Weintraub, E. Roy
  changing nature of mathematics,
    31
  Evans, Griffith C., marginalization
    of, 227–59
  science and mathematics, relation-
    ship between, 19, 20
WIB. *See* War Industries Board
  (WIB)
Willits, Joseph, 277
Wilson, President Woodrow
  Clayton Act, 191
  ethics and, 45
  Federal Trade Commission Act,
    191
  Progressive Era and, 137
  Social Gospel movement, 42
Wirth, Louis, 140
Wisconsin, University of, 22
  authors of journal articles, 1920–
    1960, 100–101, 105
  careers of economists, 1920–1946,
    118–29
  institutionalism, decline of,
    108–33
Witte, Edwin, 109
Working, Holbrook, 93
World Social Economic Congress, 156
World War I
  Progressive Era and, 137–38
  reactions to, 42
  War Industries Board (WIB), 160,
    167

World War II
nationality and affiliation of
authors, 95–96
planning, 169–71
War Production Board (WPB), 170
See also Interwar period (World
War I and II); post–World War II
economics
WPB. *See* War Production Board
(WPB)
Wright, Frank Lloyd, 44

Yale University, 265
careers of economists, 1920–1946,
118–29
Yntema, Theodore, 268
CED, officer of, 70
Young, Allyn
American monetary economics,
297–98
realism, 3

Zoretti, Ludovic, 235n